HARLOW

The Lively Arts

HARLOW

AN INTIMATE BIOGRAPHY

IRVING SHULMAN

Mercury House, Incorporated
San Francisco

First published in 1964 by Bernard Geis Associates, New York. This
trade paperback edition published in 1989.

Copyright © 1964 by Irving Shulman and Arthur Landau

Published in the United States by
Mercury House
San Francisco, California

Distributed to the trade by
Consortium Book Sales & Distribution, Inc.
St. Paul, Minnesota

Mercury House and colophon are registered trademarks of
Mercury House, Incorporated

Manufactured in the United States of America

Library of Congress Cataloging-in-Publication Data

Shulman, Irving.
    Harlow : an intimate biography / Irving Shulman.
        p.   cm. — (The Lively arts)
    Reprint. Originally published: New York : B. Geis Associates,
1964.
    ISBN 0–916515–61–3 : $15.95
    1. Harlow, Jean, 1911–1937.   2. Motion picture actors and
actresses—United States—Biography.   I. Title.   II. Series.
PN2287.H24S48   1989
791.43′028′092—dc20
    [B]   89–32142
                                                                  CIP

FOR

*Jean Harlow fans who will endure
the worst television commercials to see once again
their Blonde Bombshell.*

ACKNOWLEDGMENTS

My indebtedness to Arthur Landau, without whom this story obviously could never have been told, is expressed in an introductory note. I should also like to acknowledge the many contributions of Saul David and of Beatrice Landau. Lillian Schwartz, a librarian for the Academy of Motion Picture Arts and Sciences, was most helpful in making available to me all the material the Academy library has on Jean Harlow. Kay Mulvey, Ruth Hamp and the late Frank Whitbeck were also unsparing of their time, and the librarians of the Los Angeles Public Library were most cooperative in making available to us their newspaper files of the Thirties. And last, to all of the people—from studio executives to clerks—who supplied material only on the condition that their contributions remain anonymous (Hollywood is still a funny town), we give our thanks.

A NOTE ON HOW THIS BOOK CAME TO BE

How could it be possible for the writer to know so many things that went on behind so many closed doors? Only one person could have been aware of all these facts—and she died at the age of 26.

The answer is that there was one man who knew every detail of Jean Harlow's life—Arthur Landau, Jean's discoverer and agent. Landau was much closer to Jean than any member of her family. He *was* her family. And he knows everything there is to know about her—simply because she told him everything.

Arthur Landau, now in his seventies, had determined years before never to reveal the true story of Jean Harlow. In fact, when I first met him in 1956 and committed the unpardonable *gaffe* of asking what Paul Bern's strange suicide note really meant, Landau stared at me in disappointment, shook his head sadly and walked off. I called an apology after him, but he did not stop. We crossed paths several times after that, but I was too embarrassed to mention Harlow.

Years later, in the spring of 1961, I received a telephone call from Saul David, formerly editor-in-chief of Bantam Books and now a motion picture producer. Saul asked me to meet with Landau at the latter's house.

At the meeting, Arthur told me that he felt the time had come to tell the story of Jean Harlow—the whole truth, as only he knew it. He showed me a packing crate filled with papers, and when I had spent almost a week examining them—letters, notes, telegrams, newspaper clippings, business records, personal memoranda and a large collection of diaries in which he had recorded almost daily conversations with Jean during the hectic years of their relationship—I knew this was a book I wanted to write.

Like most people who remembered Harlow, I had, at first, been drawn by the sensational aspects of her life, by a desire to know what had *really* happened in one of the most publicized scandals of modern times. But as the doors were opened and the secrets and sorrows were revealed, I realized that Arthur Landau had told me a truly classic story, the tragedy of a woman and her time.

IRVING SHULMAN

⭐
Chapter One

IT was almost three in the morning when the telephone rang. Arthur Landau lifted the receiver from its hook as his wife asked who was it now, for God's sake, and didn't people in Hollywood let agents sleep anymore? With his left hand Arthur signaled Beatrice to fall asleep again, but he knew she would not. The radium-coated minute hand of the alarm clock moved forward, and Arthur blinked to clear his focus of the last of whatever it was he had been dreaming about.

Arthur waved to reassure his wife that there was nothing to worry about; the ring had come from the telephone installed for Jean Harlow's convenience so she could speak to her agent at any time of the day or night. Later, at breakfast, Beatrice Landau would tell Arthur what she had told him many times before: he was too good to his clients, and if he didn't talk turkey to them about respecting his private life, she would. Arthur knew he would nod, promise to scold Jean or whoever had telephoned him at an unreasonable hour, and do nothing, because the best clients called their agents rather than someone else. And that an actress as important as Harlow was still willing to consult her agent, still had such confidence in her official representative that she would call him at three in the morning, was heartening to Arthur. Actors and actresses were mimes, walking conceits with enormous egos inflated to smother deeply rooted acid doubts of their ability, and in an atmosphere where ego had to be constantly pampered to forestall the pirates ever ready to raid an agency list, all calls were taken, no matter

3

the hour or circumstances. In the Landau home there were other telephones with identifying rings for the major clients; the phones were distributed through most of the rooms of the house, even the bathrooms, although Beatrice daily protested their intrusion.

Carefully modulating his voice, speaking directly into the mouthpiece, then listening intently, Arthur Landau heard Jean laugh and call him Pops.

"Get you outta bed?" she cooed.

He heard music behind Jean and wondered where she was. "I was doing some reading," he lied. "Where are you?"

"At home," she said. "And I want you to come right over. Beatrice too."

"She's asleep," he lied again. "I'm in my den."

"So you come over," she replied, and he heard her draw a deep breath. "Right now. Because I want you to meet the man I'm gonna marry." Then she hung up. And Arthur sat up.

Knowing something of women, Arthur told Beatrice why he had to leave the house; but he would wait if she would dress in a hurry.

Beatrice Landau shook her head. "Just phone me," she said. "I'm not meeting the man she's going to marry without doing my hair. Who did you say he was?"

"I didn't," Arthur said.

"You didn't ask?"

"She hung up," he explained patiently as he stepped into his trousers. "I guess she wants it to be a real surprise."

Beatrice sighed and turned from the light to search for sleep again. Without success.

"You're sure she didn't say?" she called to Arthur as he shaved in the bathroom.

Arthur wiped his razor. "She didn't."

From Arthur's rented home at 304 South McCarty Drive in Beverly Hills to the house Jean rented at 1535 Club View

Drive in West Los Angeles was a distance of less than ten minutes through silent streets free of traffic. Driving with care, Arthur mentally catalogued some of the screen stars and personalities with whom Jean had been friendly. In recent months she had gone dinner-dancing at the Cocoanut Grove with Clark Gable, had been escorted to a costume party by MGM publicity chief Howard Strickling, had gone sailing with Carey Wilson. As always Jean and each of these men had been strikingly photographed, and one shot of Jean was becoming famous: it had been snapped as she had golfed in a thin sweater and bell-bottom slacks, and the full swing with the driver had almost pushed her breasts and nipples through the light yarn. And there were movie columnists and reporters who had attempted to make a flaming engagement of Jean having two dates with the same man. But Arthur had seen Jean once a day in the past week and had spoken to her at least ten times each day—and she had been flippant or casual about her dates.

There were many lights in the windows but no noise, and there was only one car parked before Jean's two-story pseudo-Spanish house. As Landau parked his car the front door of the house was flung wide to cast a rectangle of light as a welcoming carpet down the path. Then Jean appeared in a dressing gown and fluffy boa. Champagne glass of welcome in her right hand, she called for him to hurry.

"Pops." She kissed his cheek and nuzzled his forehead. "You took so long to get here. It isn't every day a girl gets engaged."

"I had to dress."

"You should've come in your nightie and booties," she insisted, handing him the glass.

Her babying tone was a private joke, partly a tease about Arthur's diminutive height and partly her way of showing affection for the man who had guided her career—and who had at last freed her of entangling and restrictive contracts. Although Jean received all the attentions and deferences due a

5

star, her salary was not commensurate with her importance at the box office. At MGM Jean now earned twelve hundred and fifty dollars a week, fifty thousand a year more than paid to her in 1930 when she was under contract to Howard Hughes. Still, sixty thousand a year was an economic injustice for a star of her magnitude, and Arthur was doing what he could to increase her salary more rapidly than called for by her current studio contract. And Jean was satisfied with his efforts, although her stepfather, Marino Bello, believed he could do better if Arthur would permit him to lay the law down to the money people at Metro. How quickly, Arthur thought, a loudmouthed phony could forget it had cost MGM sixty thousand dollars to buy Jean's contract from Howard Hughes, and that the most important thing then had been to keep Jean on the screen and the hell with her salary, which would be adjusted later.

Arthur kissed Mama Jean's cheek and included her in his toast.

"You look great," he said. "Just like a bride-to-be yourself. Marino," he greeted Jean's stepfather, "this is an occasion all right." Then Arthur noticed Paul Bern sitting in a deep chair. Bern was one of Irving Thalberg's assistants, and that he was present at so important an occasion could only mean he had been tapped for greater authority. "Paul, some news."

Bern, a quiet little man with thinning hair and wispy mustache, nodded slightly and permitted Marino to refill his empty champagne glass. About to make his toast, Arthur looked around to include the prospective groom.

"It's Paul!" Jean squealed as she took Arthur's hand again. "Couldn't you guess?"

Not in a million years, he was tempted to say. Instead, he smiled. "I wanted to hear you say it." He winked broadly, then raised the glass to honor the occasion and drank slowly to give himself time to recover. Paul Bern was the last man he would have associated with Jean.

Why? There were good reasons, more than enough of

them. For one thing, Paul Bern was short, barely as tall as Jean in his built-up shoes. For another, Paul was in his early forties, only a year younger than Arthur, and Jean was twenty-one. Still, he was well-spoken and well-behaved, and these qualities had given him a reputation for good behavior and intelligence. This reputation earned him invitations to the better parties, where he occasionally escorted beautiful actresses. He was also a fairly good writer, editor, stage manager and director, who had worked with some of the top studios in Hollywood. He had joined MGM in 1930 as administrative assistant to Irving Thalberg, the studio's (and the industry's) acknowledged *Wunderkind*. In his own way, for a proper satellite reflects the star, Paul Bern moved in an orbit of talent —and what was more important for success, in a young, hyper-thyroid industry, he had not made any dedicated enemies or offended any of the giants.

Well, Arthur thought, in as mercurial an environment as Hollywood the steady, sober man certainly made the best husband and public image. The film capital, not fully recovered from the dope, sex and murder scandals of the Twenties, was now coping with *real* bootleggers, speakeasies and gambling joints, and with plush whorehouses where important actors and actresses were clients and performers. The paradox of immoral-moral personalities which the public demanded of their favorites had not yet been solved and might never be, for if the actors and actresses on the silver screen were to portray sexual voluptuaries, how could they be convincing, yet lead conventional private lives?

If they were made for adults, films without sex played to empty rows of seats; but to present sex tastefully, in dress to suit the increasing boards of censors setting up office throughout the United States, was a ticklish business of wardrobe, and at MGM studios the problem was being met by Thalberg's implementation of Mayer's intelligent projection: anything that is historical or looks rich must be moral. Paul Bern was a Thal-

7

berg disciple commissioned to preach that doctrine, and Arthur remembered that certain people whose opinions he valued had spoken of Paul as a man who might be promoted to a baronial desk complete with yes-men. He grasped Paul's hand in a new grip of congratulation, then stood on tiptoe to peck at Jean's cheek.

"I'm really proud of you, Jean," Arthur said to her. "Choosing a man like Paul proves you've got mature judgment."

"Thanks, Arthur," Paul said. "We're really pleased that you are."

"Very much." Arthur's head bobbed. "A hundred per cent."

It was past four, but Jean insisted she was wide awake and Paul, nodding happily, agreed that if Marino would lend him a razor he would leave for the office about nine and sleep at the conference table. For there was plenty to talk about.

"I want the pleasure of hearing Jean make plans without camera, lights and some director's eye on her." He pulled her to the arm of his chair and kissed her palm. "I want to hear Jean make plans for our love."

"Then there's lots of work to do," Arthur said. "Who else's been told?"

"I called Louella," Mother Jean said and clasped her hands as if in prayer. Mrs. Bello, an attractive but matronly woman with good complexion and blonde hair, was slightly taller than Jean. Most people considered Mama Jean simple rather than stupid and smiled at her romantic stories of great station and ancestry and her claims that the Harlows, the Carpentiers—the great family of her first husband—and the Bellos were entitled to display some of the noblest coats of arms approved by the most respected heraldic colleges. "She was so excited! And she even wanted to talk to Jean."

"Very nice." Arthur made a mental note to call Louella later that morning to tell the ranking columnist how, long ago, he had told Jean that if and when she decided to remarry, she was to tell Louella first. "She'll try to have it in the morning papers, at least in the later editions."

"And I called Howard Strickling." Paul smiled at the memory of waking him. "He's probably called Louella too."

That the first prothalamion announcement to the queen of the Hearst chain had been made by Jean, the second by the studio's official spokesman, pleased Landau. Louella Parsons would do everything possible to scoop the rest of movieland's reporters, and if she failed, something would have to be done to assure her the decision to marry had occurred only minutes before she was informed, to convince her that the impulse to marry was as much an act of God as an earthquake or tornado. After all, these too didn't always coincide with edition deadlines.

"Fine," Arthur said, still grinning. But one pressing matter had to be discussed immediately with Paul Bern. The agent took Bern's arm and quietly steered him into the little den cluttered with large maps on which little flags marked the locations of buried treasure and lost mines known only to Marino Bello but revealed to anyone who might have money to invest.

"Just a little private talk about my rights as an agent," Arthur jested after he shut the door. Then he moved a chair and sat where anyone opening the door would have to bump him. "After all, Paul, now you're both my clients, really. And if there's a little one, ten per cent of the baby belongs to me."

Bern smiled.

Arthur pretended to drink and marveled at Bern's calmness at becoming one of the most envied men in the world. Within hours the engagement would be public news, jokesmiths would be inspired, and Jean and Paul would become the subjects of the newest crop of dirty stories. The last one Arthur had heard at the Brown Derby had not amused him: Jean was walking down Hollywood Boulevard, and as she passed two pansies one of them sighed and said that for the first time in his life he wished he was a Lesbian.

He might have to speak to Howard Strickling about doing something to keep the jokes about Paul and Jean at a minimum. Right now there was the immediate problem to be settled.

"You're getting a fine girl," Arthur began. "So I hope you don't mind, Paul, if I speak frankly?" Encouraged by Paul's nod, Arthur smiled an apology, then continued. "You'll set up housekeeping? Where?"

"At my home, naturally," Paul replied. "Jean's seen the house and likes it."

"Isn't it a little . . . lonesome?"

Paul shrugged. "I think of it as secluded and private. A place to play my records loud without disturbing anyone but the birds."

"I see," Arthur said, and didn't.

"I asked Jean where she wanted to live and she didn't mind that I suggested the house," Paul continued. "You've never been to my home?"

"I haven't," Arthur said.

"It's an oversight for which I'm sorry. Really, Arthur, it's quite comfortable and much more impressive than . . ." Paul waved his hand in a polite gesture that dismissed Jean's house.

"Of course Jean can do it over," Paul added. "Seeing it's been a bachelor's hall. So she can decorate it as she likes."

"Good," Arthur said. "Now what about your other establishment?" He was pleased that he had been able to ask this question without coughing.

Paul recrossed his legs and stared thoughtfully at the polished toe of his shoe. "A happily married man in this country doesn't keep a mistress. At least not the first year."

"Now, Paul—"

"A weak joke," Paul interrupted. "I'll have to end the arrangement you're trying not to blush about."

"If you want me to talk to her—" Arthur offered.

"No need." The faintest smile of worldliness raised the corners of Paul's thin mouth. "She'll understand."

"I'd pay the rent through the first of the year," Arthur suggested, to prove he was also acquainted with kindness and chivalry. "But it has to be a clean break, Paul. Absolutely. Of course, it'd be best if she got out of the city."

Paul nodded emphatically, then shook his head. "She likes acting even if she can't."

"Which shouldn't stand in the way of my trying to get her a little contract," Arthur replied. "That's if she doesn't bother Jean or you."

"You're very kind."

"I'd like to think of myself as practical and straight-thinking," Arthur said. He looked at the door to the living room. "So I think Jean ought to know. Not that there's anything to confess," he assured Paul. "But someone stupid—some good friend anxious to see how deep he can put a knife into your back"—he faltered—"and if Jean found out from someone else . . ."

"Not that many people know." Paul smiled easily and stood to pat Arthur's shoulder. He opened the door and caught Jean in his arms. "Jean's one of the few people who does," he said, holding her. "I told her before I proposed."

Jean snuggled deeper in Paul's arms while Arthur, sleepy but relieved, embraced them both to prove his happiness. Only the men closest to Paul, at most no more than half a dozen, had known of the pretty girl and the little white house kept in a quiet West Hollywood street. Arthur Landau had met Paul's mistress several times, but never with Paul; and no one could say that he had ever seen Paul and his mistress together in public. The man was definitely discreet.

"Very serious, you two." Jean stepped back, gathered the fluffy boa to fit as a ruff beneath her chin, and stared from Paul to Arthur. "Paul's told me, Pops," she said to Landau. "And he hasn't seen her since we started going together a month ago. And I like Paul better this way," she continued so rapidly her speech slurred. "No one's ever said he made passes at extras, which is more than I can say for a lot of so-called important people."

Arthur rubbed his hands briskly, a signal that it was time to talk of other things. But the entrance of Marino Bello compelled them to include him in, and Marino immediately took over the chairmanship. The subject was the wedding. "It's got to be in a big church, and if the Christian Scientists don't have one that's big enough I might get someone to speak to the bishop about lending us a cathedral."

"You don't have to do anything like that," Jean said. "And don't speak to anyone."

"I won't have to. In a couple of hours people will be calling me and your mother. Still, it has to be a big church and lots of class because you're going to be married"—he tapped his forehead and grinned broadly—"to more'n a million men at the same time!" Mama Jean, who had followed him in, clung to his arm and nodded happy agreement.

Paul quietly overruled them: it would be in bad taste to have a lavish, expensive wedding in the middle of the depression. Jean Harlow was no Marie Antoinette, to flaunt her extravagance before a hungry populace.

"Jean's been taken to America's heart." Paul mouthed the banality without embarrassment. "So we shouldn't do anything to have her place taken away."

"All the country loves my little girl," Mama Jean protested, and nudged Marino to come to her assistance. "She has to have a big church wedding. People expect it of her."

"Stop it!" Jean shouted. Arthur moved to calm her, then paused because Paul had taken her hand. "Whatever Paul wants is what I want." She was calmer now but her jaw line was still fixed. "Paul and me—we talked it over and right off agreed on a quiet wedding. So let's have a round for everyone,"

Jean suggested, and her tone made it clear that her mind was made up. Marino shrugged his shoulders and left the room for more glasses.

Jean displayed the cigar band she wore until Paul could get to a jeweler's for an appropriate ring, then the happy group opened the front door to welcome the fresh June morning, and Marino Bello, very drunk now and orating in Italian to Paul, insisted on standing in the middle of the neat lawn, glass high, to toast the happy couple. Obviously he was getting a little graphic about their happiness. Even Jean understood the gestures, if not the language, and she held Paul's hand tighter as they stood in the center hall and waited for Mother Jean to come into the house.

"Tell me," Jean asked her mother, who stood at the door and mewed at Bello to stop making a fool of himself, "isn't there some way we can keep him from coming to the wedding? I'd pay to send him to Europe until my hair turns old and gray."

☆

Chapter Two

Darling Mrs. Landau and Pops,

Today I came home from the theater and found these goblets and sherberts.

What precious friends you are to remember me in such a beautiful way. My Lord, Pops and Mrs. Landau, how can I write to you and express what is in my mind and heart. All I can say is that I love your expression of friendship for me and— yours was my *first* wedding gift.

My love and heartfelt appreciation,

"Your Blonde Child"

That morning's newspaper announcement was, of course, a complete surprise, even to the studio, although publicity chief Howard Strickling spoke wisely of having been in on the secret for some time. Now Strickling marshalled his staff to get busy on the romance, and within minutes a release was ready.

FROM: Publicity Department
        MGM Studios
        Culver City, California

DOT BIOGRAPHY OF JEAN HARLOW

JEAN HARLOW . . . Beautiful, blonde, ivory-skinned daughter of American pioneers was born in Kansas City . . . good old U.S.A. . . . and is Hollywood's triple threat woman . . . That is to say . . . when she can't boot the old ball . . . she forward passes and that sort of thing . . . If movie roles should ever become scarce . . . hardly likely for this platinum doll! . . . she could pack her duds and sign up for world tours of movie stages . . . and be held over so much she'd never come home . . . That's why we're happy to see she's getting married to Paul Bern and will make her home in Sunny Cal . . . Can she sing! . . . Can she dance! . . . Can she flip a quip with an agile hip! . . . But don't sell our gal short . . . She got her education in private schools . . . Ferry Hall no less which is the Buckingham Palace of all girls' schools . . . She came out here for a vacation and the movies snapped her up because Sunny Cal shares its treasures with the world . . . She made a bet she could crash the movies but the doors were wide open . . . She charlestoned through "The Saturday Night Kid" . . . wowed them in "Hell's Angels," thrilled them in "Public Enemy," "The Secret Six," "The Iron Man," and "Goldie" . . . Then came "PLATINUM BLONDE" . . . But she's also her studio's darling as "Red Headed Woman" . . . Other stars turned green-eyed with envy over this MGM part . . . but it was a natural for Miss Harlow . . . for in it she has many love scenes with Chester Morris . . . and she doesn't turn her damper down! . . . And now . . . why not . . . marriage bells! . . . Thanks for your good wishes . . . world!

It is an interesting literary irony that the studio harpist assigned to pluck out the above biography neglected to describe or identify Jean's groom. The student of events can only conclude that the name of Bern was meaningless and that the writer, if he knew the man, knew nothing about him, and to play safe decided to leave the conventional details of biography to less inspired *minnesingers,* who used facts and dates and other specific trivia to conceal the poverty of their tuneless songs.

Because one story does not an edition make, other studio flacks created their share of rhetorical hyperbole which was distributed with purple flourishes to the swarming reporters. Photographs of the bride-to-be were in great supply, but romantic biographical data and photographs of Paul Bern were not to be had; the man didn't own a limousine, polo pony, or skiff, not even a gold money clip. But studios are geared for emergencies and the impossibilities of true life, and within an hour after the thin, almost empty folder on Bern was pulled from the file, "Thalberg's strongest right arm" was being photographed by the studio. The orders had come from Mayer himself, who wanted his romantic executive to appear even more romantic.

But there were several problems to overcome before Paul Bern could be presented to the curious public. Bern was forty-two and Jean Harlow was twenty-one, a sober difference of years that could have been forgiven a soldier of fortune or a pirate, or a man who looked like either of these—but not a slight, balding man who resembled a frightened waiter too timid to leave the cover of a potted palm. Max Lief, a Broadway wit recently arrived in Hollywood, observed that a man was as old as the girl he feels—but even that didn't seem to help much. The man was a nonentity, for chrissakes, and the public would certainly wonder how that kind of a nothing could get himself a number like Harlow. The writers of popular history did their utmost to explain. They failed.

On December 3, 1889, Paul was born to Henrietta Hirsch and Julius Levy in Wannsback, Germany. Several years after Paul's birth the family emigrated to the United States and settled in a New York City neighborhood that was not yet a slum, but would be. After some half-hearted attendance at the city schools and an unsuccessful attempt to pick a trade or profession, he enrolled at the American Academy of Dramatic Arts. Although he was an average student without distinguishing feature or ability, Paul was determined to make his way in the American rather than the Yiddish theater, and he began by changing his last name to Bern. His slight physique and slighter talent limited his roles, so he devoted himself to other facets of the theater, and between 1911 and 1915 he was employed as a stage manager and assistant director.

When he came to Hollywood, Paul was quickly identified as another of the men of small stature and average appearance gifted with the knack of not screwing things up. At the MGM Culver City studio he worked as a supervisor, and at last he was rewarded by promotion to Irving Thalberg's staff. The rising graph-line of success would be evident to even the dullest reader, but the knottiest question had not been answered: how to explain this man as Jean's choice for love, marriage and—most incredible of all—bed.

Too much explanation could injure a man who now had to be liked by everyone, so one bright publicity man dubbed Paul "an adviser to the stars." The edge was taken off because the studio was unable to find a luminary gracious enough to come forward and admit being advised in some great crisis by Bern. One enthusiastic reporter noted for fatuous simile and comparison attributed to Bern the personality and gentleness of a St. Francis. On June 22, 1932, the day after Jean Harlow and Bern filed notice at the marriage license bureau in Los Angeles of their intention to wed, another imaginative turner of phrases noted that:

> Miss Jean Harlow has captured the "little father confessor" of Hollywood for a husband and we have lost our most famous bachelor.

Nobody in Hollywood can efficiently weep over
their troubles except on Paul Bern's coat lapel.
He has brought sympathy and helpfulness to
more sorrowing souls than any other person I
have ever known. He must sleep like a fireman
with his boots by his bedside.

Summing up all that was written, every Hollywood pundit
predicted the finest union of body and spirit. The Los Angeles
Record used its front page for a good photo of Jean Harlow,
which showed her beauty to wholesome advantage; Paul Bern
was with her and nothing had been done to retouch his re-
ceding hairline or eliminate a long shadow down his right
cheek. The photo's caption was "Yes—Even Jean Fell." Below
the lovers' portraits was the lyrical information that "Even
Hollywood's flaming platinum blonde can't help getting hit
when Cupid goes hunting."

The photo did not please L.B. Mayer, and he called a
conference to debate whether the *Record* should be barred
from the Culver City lot. Timorous attempts were made to
reason with the rajah until he pounded the desk and shouted
that suppose *he*, for example, were to decide that he was going
to shed Mrs. Mayer—of course, it would never happen, but
just suppose—and suppose *he* were about to marry some beautiful actress: would they, his executives—*some* executives!—sit
by and do *nothing* if a thirty-dollar-a-week newspaper photographer without talent enough to shine shoes took a picture
of him and reproduced it so that he looked like a nothing?

"Would you let that happen?" Mayer demanded of the
silent, solemn men in his office. "You're no better than blood-
sucking traitors!"

He stalked from the conference table, and slowly the
executives rose and dispersed to their separate offices for Bromo
Seltzers, booze and tears.

Other stories from day to day became increasingly rhapsodic, but no more informative. It was soon reported that "film circles, having known of a friendship between Mr. Bern and Miss Harlow the past three years, nevertheless were surprised to find it developing into a romance." Which was the understatement of the year.

Later, weeks later, Jean told Arthur of her first introduction to Paul, how he had telephoned her and asked, so hesitantly, if she would have lunch with him. She had accepted, and to her surprise Paul had really appeared interested in what she had to say and hadn't once looked at her knockers. Lunch led to dinners, and she found she enjoyed Paul's conversation about books and music and places abroad. She first appeared in public with Paul when they attended the opening of *Grand Hotel* at the Chinese Theater and she wore her red wig. Then, with amusement, she accepted his invitation to Sunday night supper at his home—alone—and had expected the customary persuasions and passes. But nothing had happened, which had chagrined and puzzled her.

The next step had been so unexpected. She had asked Paul to have Sunday dinner at her house, and when Mother Jean and Bello had left the table for something or other, he had touched her fingers with his, raised his wine glass and asked if she minded his drinking to a beautiful, understanding woman who was, he hoped, going to be his wife after he got rid of his mistress? Jean's eyes filled with tears; she gulped and pressed her cheek against his hand. That was it.

On June 23 the Los Angeles *Record* began a multipart story of "Platinum Venus" by Relman Morin, the "cinematters" editor of that paper.

The first installment, written in high Ciceronian style, invited the reader "to look at Venus," and compared her to the goddess born from the waves. Speaking of Jean, the author noted that "she, too, came out of nowhere, a sudden burst of exquisite loveliness. She, too, has created the waves and reached the shore. It's a different sort of shore, and the waves are those of public acclaim. Her name is Jean Harlow."

To compete with the biographical prose-gumbo of the *Record,* on June 24 the *Examiner* scored a scoop by captioning a photo of Paul Bern's timbered Bavarian cottage, with swimming pool "beyond tree in lower right-hand corner," as *HIS Home to be HERS!*

His house will be her house.

A week from now it will be their home.

Paul Bern, motion picture producer whose engagement to Jean Harlow, stage and screen player, was announced several days ago, will present his bride-to-be with a deed to a $60,000 house.

The house will come as a complete surprise to Miss Harlow, who as yet has no intimation of it.

If the gift was a surprise to Jean Harlow, it was a greater surprise to Paul Bern, who immediately told Landau that he had no intention of giving anyone his house.

"I told you she could decorate the house," he said. "But give her *my* house? Even my attorney called and wants to know if I've had my head examined."

"So what're you doing to do?" Arthur asked. "I'm sure Jean doesn't expect your house, and giving it to her is really meaningless—it's community property if you do and community property if you don't."

Paul thought about this for several moments. "Because someone makes a good suggestion is no reason to ignore it," he said decisively. "I'm giving Jean the house. I'll call my lawyer now."

Later newspapers on that day of largesse announced that the marriage would take place on July 2 at the home of the bride and that the ceremony would be performed at eight in the evening by Superior Judge Leon R. Yankwich, a jurist well known for his studies in motion picture contracts and property rights. John Gilbert was to be best man for Bern, but bridesmaids were dispensed with so that no feuds and jealousies would blossom from the happy occasion. The guest list was modest but distinguished: it included Mr. and Mrs. Louis B. Mayer, Irving Thalberg and his wife, Norma Shearer, and Mr. and Mrs. David Selznick.

Most papers did not mention Arthur Landau, although he supervised most of the arrangements, and Arthur read with amusement the latest, gaudiest stories about Jean and the nobility of her background, the old ancestral manor house, the acres of boxwood and the retinue of faithful, devoted servants. He read how she had become an actress as a madcap lark to win a bet or a dare; how, to attract attention, she had arrived at the studios in a rented Rolls Royce driven by Marino Bello in a chauffeur's uniform.

Baloney and all, Arthur managed to get Jean through two arduous weeks of three-a-day appearances at the Los Angeles Loew's State, where her latest picture, *Red Headed Woman,* was being shown, and where Jean appeared on stage in the wig she had worn in the picture. Arthur also did what he could to assure Jean that she was good enough for Bern, and to convince her that people who wrote her dirty letters and sent her disgusting pictures were sick. The wisest thing she could do at this time was to avoid reading any mail.

"You don't want advice," Arthur scolded as Jean tore a dirty photograph received that morning. "You want me to agree with you. So tell me"—he pointed to the scraps of several letters in her wastebasket—"how can I advise you to read stuff like that?"

Jean did not answer but continued to tear the photo into confetti-sized bits of paper. But she would read other dirty letters, look at other dirty pictures mailed to her, and suffer.

The wedding, scheduled for the evening of July 2, was less than a week away, and the arrangements for the ceremony were simple. The reception was scheduled for the Sunday afternoon of July 3 in the garden of the home Paul had given Jean. Invitations had been sent out to more than a hundred guests, and Marino Bello had made the sensible observation that at least two hundred uninvited guests would crash the party—it would be wise to have ample food and potables to take care of the overflow crowd. To clinch his argument, Bello revealed that he had invited many people on his own, how many he could not exactly say, but as a Latin and descendent of noble Latins, centuries of hospitality motivated him in everything, and especially in matters of generosity and important celebration. They had to allow for people they really didn't know and would never see again, people who would return to Iowa and Idaho and have something to talk about for the rest of their lives—and to placate such people and keep them from taking the house, there had to be food and drink for them. More of everything was ordered, and on the morning of his wedding day Paul Bern instructed his house couple, caterers' help, and hired police to be firm, forceful but polite, and pointed out where the infiltrators most likely would attempt their incursions of his home and grounds. All items of real and average value were locked into an upstairs bedroom to which Paul alone had the key.

Saturday morning, July 2, 1932, was a bright hot day, and on a last-minute impulse Jean decided to honor her fans and appeared at the Loew's State. A studio limousine delivered Jean to the theater, where she was mobbed by fans who had come on a tip from a radio newscaster. At last she appeared on stage and threw kisses to the excited audience, whose hysterical adulation delayed the feature by almost a full hour until the exhausted star almost fainted and had to be helped from the stage. She was delivered at home a few minutes after five to prepare herself for the ceremonial ritual. Mama Jean scolded her daughter for taxing her strength, but Jean replied that she had at least shown herself to some of her million fans unable to attend the wedding.

There were white roses from Paul, yellow and pink roses from other stars and industry greats, from Howard Hughes and even from financial administrators who never left their offices in New York and sneered openly at the vulgarity of the business—but none of the massed flowers were moved into the beamed living room where the ceremonies would take place.

The wedding had been planned for informality, and although the women were beautifully gowned, the men wore a variety of business suits. The wedding photograph reveals only one man of elegance, one man who truly knew how to dress for the wedding of one of America's most important women—Marino Bello. Except for John Gilbert, who managed to look impeccable in a tweed suit with patch pockets, Bello was the handsomest man in the wedding party.

Close examination of the group wedding photograph proves it to be surprisingly sad, for the living room is small, with overstuffed, nondescript and dowdy appointments and limp, drab draperies at the windows. And the smiles of the guests around the newly wedded pair are forced—except, again, for Marino Bello, who appeared to be enjoying every moment. Jean wore a full-length white silk dress with a shawl collar suitable for the evening and silk strap sandals with low heels, in a vain attempt to appear shorter than Paul. And the groom, in his double breasted blue suit, white shirt with its too large collar and carnival bright tie, could only manage the smallest smile of pleasure as he posed for photos with Jean.

After the ceremony Marino attempted to capture John Gilbert to tell him about his noble Italian ancestors who had driven the Saracens from Sicily, but Gilbert wrenched himself free to escape to the side of Irving Thalberg. Gilbert's career was in sad decline, and he had only agreed to be best man because he hoped his studio might care enough to devise a sound gadget that would give him a hypermasculine voice.

The maids and hired butlers served small sandwiches, caviar of first quality, champagne and coffee. Eyes bright and cheeks flushed with champagne, Marino insisted upon reading the congratulatory telegrams, which included wires from the governor, both California senators and the representatives in the House. There were wires from foreign stars, studios and people Jean and Paul did not even know by name. Marino continued to read, although his stepdaughter's suffering was obvious, but at last he concluded with a grandiloquent boast that tomorrow everyone would be entertained royally because he was royalty.

Actors and actresses, called upon by the nature of their craft to register emotions that may be in direct opposition to their own feeling at a particular moment, learn to express the moods and emotions called for by an arrangement of features, movements, and voice. Then, in real life, when they feel the emotions of love, hate, sorrow, joy or whatever, it is difficult for the observer to believe that the actor or actress is not rehearsing a role; the audience sees only a skillful mime unable to distinguish between the sincerity of the occasion and the urge to continue a performance.

Several guests doubted that Jean was really angry with Marino, for in many movie takes Jean had fastened the same steely concentration of gaze on the subject of her dislike, then had lunched happily with the person who had offended her in make-believe. Other guests believed Jean was annoyed with Marino and were amused that she could not stare him into silence. She finally relaxed when Paul, her husband of several hours, whispered that every wedding had to have someone to play the buffoon and that she wasn't to worry about Marino because soon, soon they would be going to their new home—now in Jean's name—and Paul would make certain, from Monday on, that Bello understood his welcome and status in the Easton Drive house would depend upon his behavior.

"I can't help crying." Jean touched her eyes. "I'm happy for us, for me, for knowing that we're married and that I'm going home with you. But I've got to leave Mama with him."

"It'll be all right." Paul patted his wife's hand and smiled at Virginia Bruce as she wished them well and said good night. "Everything will be all right. Now wipe your eyes, Jean. People're beginning to leave."

Judge Yankwich left at eleven, then other guests followed his example. John Gilbert shook Paul's hand again, repeated that he was the luckiest man in the country, then kissed Jean's forehead and told her that he knew she would live happily ever after, as all fairy princesses did. While he was wishing Jean well, the Mayers and Thalbergs left.

Shortly after midnight Arthur and his wife blessed the newlyweds again and left for their own home. It had been a long, hot, irksome day, but the evening had cooled nicely and Arthur looked forward to a good night's rest before the reception the next day. He planned to sleep late, then be at the Easton Drive house by noon to supervise the placement of the tables and tip all the help in advance. He would also have to meet the Carmichaels, the couple who worked for Bern as butler and cook, and coach them in getting along with Jean.

At home in bed, the memory of the day's excitement kept Arthur awake. Unable to sleep, he went into the living room to rest in an easy chair drawn to an open window. Seated in his robe and smoking what he had sworn would be the last cigarette, Arthur wondered about Jean: what her new political position at the studio could be. Mayer had been quite merry at the wedding and had spoken pleasantly to the newlyweds. Jean would never rival Norma Shearer as first lady of the Culver City dream factory, but power and prestige were not Jean's ambitions. Her hopes were simpler.

To be an actress—truly considered as an actress—was Jean's wish, and married to Paul Bern this was not impossible. Paul could coach her, and his judgment would be respected; or, if he decided, as a sensible man would, to have objective professionals train Jean, the coaches chosen for his wife would be the best.

An insistent ringing jarred Arthur from his reverie in the overstuffed chair. He started for the phone of another client, then realized the ringing phone was Jean's.

Shaking himself fully awake, Arthur wondered what last-minute detail could have been important enough to interrupt this honeymoon that was being vicariously savored throughout the world, wherever there were men.

It was almost four in the morning. Beatrice had awakened to ask what was the matter now, for heaven's sake? But Arthur couldn't answer his wife, because Jean was sobbing hysterically into the phone.

"Come get me!" she wept huskily. "I'll be waiting outside the house. Come get me and don't ask questions! He's liable to wake up!"

Chapter Three

As if to make his automobile less visible, Arthur used only his parking lights as he drove up Benedict Canyon. Dawn diluted the darkness and washed the hillside in rose and gold, but the canyon was narrow, and sycamores and oaks along the road held night in their branches. He drove as if he were a conspirator; once he almost ran into a ditch because it was impossible to concentrate on his driving. Agitation made the steering wheel tremble in his grasp.

Marriages in Hollywood ended quickly. But no matter how he searched his memory for precedent, Arthur could not remember a marriage that had ended hours after the ceremony and even before the reception. What would the studio say? A luncheon for the newlyweds had been planned on their return to the studio. Arthur groaned. Newspapers would have a field day. . . .

Could he persuade Jean to remain married a reasonable length of time—a year, six months, at least a week? There must be something wrong with Jean; or was God personally interested in the girl's unhappiness? Her first marriage had ended *after* the first night. This one *during* the first night. Some record for America's foremost sex symbol.

There was more light now, and as Arthur drove up Easton Drive he saw Jean step from the shelter of a linden tree. He swung the car into a U-turn and reached across the seat to open the door.

"Hurry!" Jean slid into the seat and moaned. "Get me out of here. You've got a handkerchief?"

Arthur gave Jean a monogrammed silk square from the breast pocket of his robe and Jean pressed it to her eyes. He saw how she bit down on the silk which she had stuffed into her mouth. "For God's sake, Jean! You all right?"

She nodded jerkily and brushed back the loose strands of hair that fell across her face. Her eyes were red and swollen.

At last she removed the handkerchief from her mouth, used it to make a little covering for her hair and knotted the silk corners under her chin. Arthur noticed that she wore a heavy carpet-patterned bathrobe that belonged to Paul Bern. The white silk hem of her nightgown hung below the robe.

"I'm cold, Pops." She shivered and tried to sit on her bare feet. "Awfully cold."

"Sit back. Then you'll be able to tuck in your feet."

"I can't," she groaned.

"What's the matter?"

"Pops . . ." She began to cry steadily and slumped until Arthur felt the weight of her head against his thigh. "I need a real father, Pops. Besides an agent, your blonde child needs real parents to help her."

"Don't cry," Arthur said. "Or cry but don't talk. Not until we get home."

"I've got no home, Pops. I want to come live with your family, with Beatrice and Richard and you. You think they'll let me?" Richard was Arthur's thirteen-year-old son.

He was stern. "They would but I wouldn't. Stop talking. Stay put and let me drive. And when I pull into my garage you do just like you're told until we get you into the house." Arthur quickly reviewed which neighbors on McCarty Drive arose early on Sunday mornings. It was too early for church, no one was a dedicated fisherman, even the golf nuts didn't leave before eight. Still, some cat or dog in an adjacent house might have to be let out, so he had to be careful. He touched

Jean's back in a gesture of sympathy and heard her startled cry of pain. "We're almost home," he said.

Lights bright, he stepped on the gas as he swung into the driveway of his home, shifted into neutral, then cut the engine to coast silently into the garage. Gently helping Jean to sit up, he put his slippers on her cold bare feet and helped her walk the length of the dark, narrow garage. Beatrice, who had been waiting for them, opened the service porch door while Arthur hurried Jean across the twenty feet of open space. For a moment he hesitated, remembering that Richard's room was at the back of the house and the boy might for some reason—anything was possible *now*—be awake and working with his stamps. But he remembered that Richard was spending the week-end with a friend and wouldn't be home until about eight that night.

"I was sick with worry," Beatrice said as she helped Jean into the kitchen. "What is it?"

"The little bastard!" Jean groaned, raised both arms and groaned again. "Help me out of his filthy robe."

"But what's wrong?" Beatrice asked as she untied the sash.

Jean whimpered as she slipped free of the robe. The night-gown was Empire and the shirring held Jean's breasts high so that their rounded fullness fell over the lace eyelet border of the neckline. "Beatrice, don't be bashful in front of Arthur. Just take it easy and pull down the straps. Please!" Her voice became shrill. "Do you wanna help me or not?"

Jean's eyes were glazed with pain as Beatrice screamed and Arthur gripped the edge of the sink. There—they could see that she was not being an actress. Now Jean stood with her right shoulder forward in an attempt to see her back, striped by five long angry welts between the hips and shoulder blades. The welts were turning harsh blue and the fourth welt above the kidneys was beaded with little blood blisters. Pain dilated her eyes, and she chewed on the knot of Arthur's silk handkerchief as the Landaus stared in numb disbelief, until

Beatrice, recovering first, ordered Arthur to get some aspirin, cotton, and baby oil from the bathroom and a pillow for Jean to sit on, because she could see several broad bruises on Jean's buttocks.

"And bring one of my bedjackets so she can cover herself," she called after Arthur.

"Don't bother," Jean said. "How bad's my back?"

"I wish we could call a doctor," Beatrice replied. "I think we should. What got into him?"

"The little bastard's a maniac! A dirty rotten Goddamned sex fiend!" Jean tensed as a quick spasm of pain drained her lips of color. "We can't call a doctor but we oughta call the insane asylum. Tell me, did Arthur ever hit you?"

"Of course not. And he'd better never!"

"The wop's hit my mother." Jean continued to shiver as twinges of pain doubled her forward. "Hit her plenty," she gasped. "Once I tried to clout him with a bottle but missed. But sometimes my mother's impossible." She bit her lips and began to cry. "I don't want to call her."

"You don't have to now. There's nothing she could do. Arthur," Beatrice called as he re-entered the kitchen, "what's taking so long?"

"Finding the cotton," he snapped. "It was on your closet shelf, not in the bathroom."

Eyes closed as if this could blind her to the images and destroy the memories of recent hours, Jean began to speak. Slowly, at first, still stopping to gasp from time to time, Jean wept that Paul had been very drunk when he struck with his cane.

"Be thankful for small favors—if he wasn't so drunk he would've caught me across the head, because that's where he aimed," Jean continued. She paused to tell Beatrice that the oil felt good against her back. "Will I be able to stand seeing myself in a mirror?"

"You'll need one to get dressed," Beatrice said. "But don't

look at your back. If you're not bashful I'll help you bathe and dress."

"Dress for what?" Jean asked.

Beatrice squinted. "The wedding reception."

"Reception! How can I go to that?" Her lips were drawn in hate. "Or maybe I should, because then I could kill him. Pops, what's the most I could get for murdering him?"

"I never want to hear you talk like that," Arthur said, glad for some reason to draw his eyes from Jean's full, firm breasts, whose enlarged nipples were almost the size of thimbles. "Beatrice," he said, "do you think she *can* go to the reception?"

"There's nothing to think," Beatrice said shortly; hers was the hard practicality of a housewife who knows that disaster must never interfere with routine and obligation. "She has to be at his—her house by twelve the latest."

"I don't ever want to see that house again," Jean said. "I won't even go back there to get my clothes."

"Jean's right!" Arthur shouted. "How can she go back there after this?" Jean's flayed back glistened with oil. She was breathing more regularly, and her bared breasts rose and fell in rhythmical movement. "How can we think of anything except breaking Bern's Goddamned neck?"

"Exactly how a man thinks." Beatrice turned to Jean and took her hands. "You've got to go through with the reception," she said. "Later we'll talk about what you have to do. But if you don't go this won't be just an ordinary scandal, and you haven't been in the business long enough for that. And what's worse, people won't believe it wasn't your fault—"

"I'll show them my back!"

"You'll do nothing of the sort. The aspirins help you?"

"I don't feel worse."

After Jean managed to control a new freshet of tears, Beatrice raised the nightgown straps and helped her to the kitchen table for coffee.

"Maybe Arthur shouldn't be here," Beatrice suggested before she spoke to her husband. "Isn't there something you should be doing? You look tired. Why don't you rest for a couple of hours?"

Arthur scraped his chair closer to the table. "Remember me? I'm her agent," he said to Beatrice. "And if anyone should be making herself scarce it might be you."

"Cut it out. Stop sounding like Mama Jean and Bello." Jean pushed the cup aside and pressed her fingertips to both eyes. "He's crazy," Jean said at last. "Some kind of sex nut. Worse than anything I've ever heard of. Worse than any pictures I've ever seen."

Whatever illusions Jean had had about pure, lyrical romance had been destroyed long ago by her mother's brashness in the bedroom, by the mail she received, the peepholes made in her dressing room so that the walls looked like sides of Swiss cheese, by the panting attention she got wherever she went. Almost four years of picture-making had taught her that chaste romance on the screen was reserved for the relationship of a man for his horse, a boy for his dog, a farmer for his land, and old people sufficiently gray for rockers. But love between young men and women was sex, out-and-out sex, and as much of it as the censors would permit.

Harlow also knew what she was, what women thought she was and what most men hoped she was. She knew that her public admired her for being so aptly suited to portray the slut next door, but what most of the world did not know was that she had not been to bed with a man—or woman—since her abortive first marriage to Chuck McGrew, with whom she had only known the initial, disappointing experience of inexperience.

When she had been divorced from McGrew in 1929, Arthur had explained to reporters and the curious world at large that Jean's marriage at sixteen had been too much flaming youth very quickly put on ice—and he hoped that two such nice kids as Jean and Chuck wouldn't be misquoted or treated harshly by the press. Both had lived apart, without scandal, two kids doing the best they honestly could to overcome a mistake, with neither of them making a slip since that runaway marriage.

In Arthur's presence people agreed with his explanation, but once he left the room, Arthur knew people laughed at his naiveté and went on to discuss Jean as they wanted her to be. They searched through their lists of lovers, seducers and satyrs in the hope of recognizing or discovering who had really been in the hay with Harlow. Good business practice demanded that he smile pleasantly at the dirtiest inquiry about her. If the interrogator was a someone of importance, he had to wink or shrug or laugh off a blunt demand to tell them what he thought of Jean as a piece, and to move with controlled equanimity from nasty situation to nastier situation until, as Jean Harlow's agent, his days and nights were increasingly devoted to diplomacy, self-control and the protection of his platinum blonde.

And as an agent with other clients, all of them jealous of each other, weighing and evaluating his services, even computing in minutes the time he spent with them, counting the number of times he telephoned and how long he talked, comparing the attentions they received with his well known devotion to Jean, he had become a skilled improviser of fictions to convince them that regardless of importance, the Arthur Landau Agency was dedicated to all its people. There were actors and actresses whose weekly salaries were more than Harlow earned in a month, and they insisted on balancing salary earned and commission paid with attention received. Other clients, for the most part men, might play with their fountain pens and suggest casually, as if it really didn't matter, that they would be delighted to sign again with the Landau office if some little out-of-season present, for instance Jean,

33

would be given to them for one night; see, they weren't greedy. And Arthur had lost an important actress, blessed with the countenance and demeanor of a saint, because he had exploded when she stated frankly and graphically, her long red nails tapping the edge of his desk, that she wanted to remain a client, one of the family—but only if Jean would think of her bed as her home away from home.

Of all the secrets he knew, of all the secrets he had ever discovered by accident or design, the one Arthur and Beatrice now shared with Jean was the most awful and dangerous, for it involved not only the actress, but all the wedding guests, and Judge Yankwich, who had performed the ceremony. In an environment where people had been broken by rumors and innuendo, the hurt that could be done by this beating was enough to scourge the entire industry. Now, people would ask, hadn't Judge Yankwich known he was marrying Jean Harlow to a cruel, insane, sex pervert? What sort of agent was Arthur Landau not to have protected his client against the five broad welts across her back? And what sort of studio was MGM to employ a man like Bern in a top executive position? The newspapers had called him "advisor to the stars," "little father confessor," "the man with the gentle eyes," and all of these had been based on stories supplied by the studio. Howard Strickling would suffer. Irving Thalberg would suffer. At a time when his romantic career hung in the balance because his voice recorded as a juvenile squeak, John Gilbert would suffer. Howard Hughes was big enough, unconcerned with public opinion and publicity not to care what was written about him. But Louis B. Mayer . . . the thought of all the men and women stopped in mid-career and barred from the screen because they had offended LB, or LB thought they had offended him, made Arthur shudder. Francis X. Bushman's career had ended after his fine performance in MGM's *Ben Hur* because Mayer believed the actor had refused to meet Mayer's family in his theater dressing room. The social slight was the indiscretion of Bushman's new valet, unacquainted with the exclusive producer, but Mayer refused to forgive and forget until all studio gates were barred against Bushman. The boss of MGM made no distinction between real affronts and those he conjured in fancy; the punishments he meted out were the same.

So it didn't matter that Mama Jean and Marino would be at the reception, that Judge Yankwich might be there, that John Gilbert and Thalberg and Norma Shearer and Clark Gable and Chester Morris and Spencer Tracy and Virginia Bruce would be there, that Cagney had definitely accepted an invitation. What did matter was that Louis B. had accepted. He would be there with Mrs. Mayer and the Selznicks, and if Jean failed to make an appearance at her own wedding reception, her absence would be construed as a snub, because to date Mayer had vetoed every suggestion to renegotiate Jean's salary. It would be interpreted as a personal rebuff, and no one—not even a star—could insult the head of the greatest studio before all the world. Arthur shuddered again.

"Jean, how do you feel?" he asked.

"Awful," she said. "But I don't hurt so much. You think my back'll be scarred?"

"I'm going to call Doctor Herman Sugarman," he said. "Someone who knows something has to look at you."

"Who's he?" Jean asked. "One thing for sure, my mother and Marino mustn't know."

"He's an old friend who practices downtown," Arthur explained as he returned with his address book, "but he doesn't live far from here. I'm going to tell him what's what and have him come over. None of us *wants* to be at the reception, Jean, but all of us are going to go. So I'm calling the doctor."

Dr. Sugarman, an internist who was also on the medical faculty of the University of Southern California, administered to Jean's back and gave the actress a massive dose of aspirin.

Jean had to attend the reception, and more efficacious pain-killers would have put her to sleep for half a day. He also suggested that the actress do what she could to keep people from embracing her. Later she could take the stronger sedative and try to fall asleep on her stomach.

"Nothing's broken," he assured Jean, "and I am hopeful that he didn't hurt you internally. But you should have X-rays. Where're you going for your honeymoon, Mrs. Bern?"

Jean touched the collar of the pink bedjacket as Beatrice Landau tied the throat ribbons. "The name's Harlow, and we weren't going anywhere. I'm appearing at Loew's State."

Sugarman slowly closed his medical bag. "In any other case I'd prescribe rest. But you should have those X-rays."

"I'll bring her to your office," Arthur said. "Just name the time, Doctor."

"Before her first stage appearance," Sugarman said. "I'll be there and you can drive your car into the alley behind the Pacific Mutual Building and bring Miss Harlow up in the freight elevator. I'll arrange it. Then I'll take the pictures and look at your back at the same time."

Jean placed a hand over her kidney. "It hurts most here."

"For the record we'll do a urine analysis," Sugarman said. "But I'm sure we'll find nothing. You're a healthy woman, Miss Harlow. Young, healthy and famous." He smiled reassuringly. "What time do you do your first show?"

"At two on Monday," she said.

"Be at my office at twelve-thirty," he said. "It'll be the Fourth of July, so I won't have to cancel any appointments and we'll have all the privacy we need. If I have to see you again we'll make other arrangements."

"Will the black and blue marks show through Jean's dress?" Beatrice asked.

Sugarman raised a shoulder. "She could wear two slips. Dark pink or peach. Too bad she can't wear black. Or she could wear a flowered dress and keep out of the sun. Keep in the shadows, Miss Harlow."

"I wish you'd come to the reception, Doctor," Jean said. "I'd feel better if you were there. Bring your wife."

"She'll be delighted." Sugarman inclined his head in a little bow. "It isn't necessary, but she'd never forgive me if she found out we were invited and didn't go. But I won't stay near you," he warned.

Jean offered him her hand. "As long as you're not too far away. And I want you to look at the Goddamn dirty little bastard I married, Doctor. Because he's a lot sicker than I am. And right now I feel like dying."

Shielded by one of Beatrice's broad-brimmed hats, Jean hurried into the car, where she rested on her stomach on the back seat while the short ten-minute drive to the Bern house was accomplished without incident. A clock chimed eight as Arthur eased Jean to a sofa in the living room, whispered she was to sit there, not to be frightened, and he would look for Bern.

The bridegroom of some eleven hours was not in the master bedroom, where the bed was in proper disarray, nor in the master bathroom; he lay sprawled, nude and drunk, on the rug of his den. Head against the Chippendale claw and ball of a desk leg, thin pale buttocks against a chair, Paul Bern snored with his mouth open, twitching his characterless mustache.

Silently hating the man at his feet, Arthur wanted to kick the slight, pasty body of "the little father confessor." Instead he rolled the unconscious man to his back to discover what had never been suspected by anyone in the industry: Paul Bern had the sack and penis of an infant boy. Potbellied, hairless except for fine, dainty patches under the arms and around the genitals, Paul had hips that were finely rounded and propor-

tioned for a woman. Now he stirred slightly, mumbled un-
intelligibly, and raised a hand to wipe at his face, then rolled
over to push his mouth and nose into the patterned rug and
weep for several moments.

Kneeling over Paul, undecided about what to do, Arthur
saw again how flat Paul's buttocks were, how delicately fine
was the contour of his back. The white pasty skin tempted
Arthur to remove his belt and whip Bern into sobriety, but for
this, too, Mayer might hold him responsible. And if he forgot
himself and killed this man, who deserved it, the scandal would
be doubled, trebled, and Jean—Beatrice too—would suffer more
than any woman deserved. There were less than four hours
until noon, and he had to think of the reception; nothing else
mattered.

"Paul." Arthur shook the nude man. "Paul, try and get
up."

Bern brushed weakly at Arthur's hand, then covered his
eyes with a pale forearm.

"Paul, try—you've got to. I'm going to help you. Do you
understand me?"

"I—who are you?"

"Open your eyes."

"Where's Jean? What're you doing here?"

"On your feet. Is there any help in the house?"

Bern rolled over to collapse on his face. "I gave them the
night off, because people on their honeymoon—" Sobs completed
his thought more graphically than the most dramatic dialogue.

Grateful that Paul wasn't more of a man in size and weight,
Arthur half dragged, half carried him to a bathroom at the end
of the hall, seated him on the lidded commode, soaked a hand
towel and patted his cheeks. Once or twice he slapped Bern
with the towel, and at last the nude man moaned that he was
awake and where—oh God help him!—where was Jean?

"We'll talk later." Arthur found it difficult to look at Paul, because the secret he had discovered was something one man should never know about another. "Now you need a shower."

"I can't stand. What're you doing here, Arthur?"

"Helping you. I think a bath'll be just as good."

"I don't want your help."

"Don't think for a second I want to give it."

After the water was in the tub, Arthur hurried to the den, stripped to his underwear, then returned on the run to help Bern into the tub. Now he ran colder water and squeezed a sponge over Paul's head. As water trickled down the back of Paul's neck and between his shoulder blades, he rocked in despair and clasped and unclasped his hands as little cries of terror escaped his tight lips. Squeezing sponge after sponge over Bern, Arthur found he could only pity the man.

Bern had thrown off enough of his torpor to understand questions and reply coherently, and he wiped feebly at his face and mumbled disconnected words that built into apologetic phrases—he was sorry he had become drunk, but there seemed nothing else to do . . . nothing else to do . . . Then, just at the moment when Arthur sensed that Paul was about ready to be helped from the tub, Jean burst into the bathroom and momentarily leaned on the sink to bear the pain of her exertion.

"Sonofabitching little fairy!" She screamed and flailed at Paul with both hands. "You've got no right to be alive!"

Arthur pushed Paul against the tile wall that backed the tub and spread his other arm to keep Jean off. "Make some coffee," he ordered.

"Coffee!" she shouted. "I'll give him poison!"

"I wish you would," Paul mumbled.

"Let me at him, Arthur!" She tried to pass her agent. "I'm warning you—let me by! I'll fire you, Pops! So help me God I'm gonna fire you if you don't let me get at him!"

Arthur slapped Jean hard across the face. "Maybe I'll fire

you," he told the stunned actress as she rubbed her cheek. "Right now. And I'll take Paul with me and leave you here to face Louis Mayer and your other guests."

"What kind of traitor are you?" she demanded, but she made no further attempt to reach Paul as he slid down the wall into the tub. "Look at him!" She pointed at her husband, on his hands and knees in the water. "The gentlest man in Hollywood. The cinema cavalier!" She rubbed a spot above her left hip. "You stinking bastard, you did something to my kidney!"

"When the doctor examined you it was the other kidney," Arthur said wearily. "Please, please make some coffee."

"All right," she said. "But listen, you!" She pointed at Paul, whose forehead was pressed against the tile, "I oughta kill you. If I told Marino, I bet he'd tear you apart. Then the whole world could see what a fake you are. Good, kind, selfless, courteous! Such good manners and intellectual conversation. You're just a rotten awful fag with a dangle half the size of my pinkie! Oh, shut up, Pops!" she snapped at her agent. "I'm gonna fix the coffee. And you better not give him none of it."

Arthur supported the back of Paul's head and wiped at his own forehead with the damp sponge. "Jean," he pleaded, "forget the coffee and go take a nap. That'll do us all some good."

Jean flung a tube of toothpaste at Paul and struck him in the chest. "Sleep!" Her voice began to rise as she dropped the borrowed robe and tore down the front of her sheer nightgown to reveal the full breasts, the rounded mound of her belly and the pubic curls trimmed short, truly blonde but not as light as the hair on her head. Several of the curls were matted with blood from a half-moon bite several inches below the navel. "Look at what my so-called husband's done to me! Look at my legs. I was ashamed to show them to you or the doctor because Beatrice was there. Look at the way he chewed me! Go ahead, Pops, look! See what I'm gonna show the doctor!"

Arthur waved aside the nude woman, then turned away not to see her body and the blue, black and mauve bruises left by Paul's teeth across her inner thighs.

"He's a cannibal!" She continued to scream as Arthur pushed her into the corridor and slammed the door. "A God-damn cannibal!"

It was a comedy of horror, a pure slapstick of misery as Arthur attempted to lift Paul out and keep himself from falling into the tub. Despite his own revulsion, he had to get Paul Bern into the kitchen, get some coffee into his stomach, then see that he was dressed and sober enough to play the host. Paul's body was wet and he could not stand, yet he began to fight assistance. As he managed to step from the tub, he slipped from Arthur's grasp, crawled across the tile floor and vomited into the commode. The sounds of retching were a welcome relief.

Soaked, so that his underwear clung to his body, Arthur stood at the side of this disgraced man and encouraged him to continue retching. It would empty his stomach and make him feel better. But his temptation was to make the man feel worse. Much worse.

Jean sat at the dining room table and cursed at everyone, everything, every twinge of pain that kept alive the memory of her abuse. Arthur prepared the coffee, fed it to Paul and helped the exhausted man to his den. The blinds were drawn, the little room was cool and restful, but Arthur sweated and wondered what to do next. The reception was hours away, and soon Paul's servants, the Carmichaels, would return to the house to supervise the temporary help. All the cast would begin to assemble, but would Jean and Paul be able to play out their roles as principals?

Arthur tiptoed into the living room. Jean was resting her blonde head against the table. He returned to the den. Paul slept in the deep leather chair. And as Arthur waited for

Beatrice to bring him fresh underwear and aspirin, he continued to hear again and again Paul Bern's sobbing voice and what he had said.

"Every man . . . every man I know gets an . . . erection . . ." Bern had wiped at his eyes until his breathing became more regular. "Just by talking about her, other men get them." He had reached for the agent's hand, "Arthur, didn't I have the right to think Jean could help me at least that much?"

Chapter Four

By birth, background and circumstance it appeared that Harlean, daughter of Dr. Montclair Carpentier and Jean Harlow Carpentier, would have all the middle-class advantages. Dr. Carpentier had an average dental practice, and his wife's family, also of average circumstances, were willing to share their assets with their only daughter and grandchild. The Harlows were known and rated in Kansas City as sound, respectable people.

Harlean was blonde, attractive and normally doted upon by her parents and the Harlows; in an interview she gave years later, Jean (who by that time had adopted her mother's maiden name) said it wasn't until she went to school that she learned her name was Harlean, a feminization of her mother's family name, and not The Baby.

Kansas City, Kansas, was not too large a city, and despite its weather, the city's site at the juncture of the Kansas and Missouri Rivers was pleasant and picturesque. Samuel D. Harlow was a real estate broker with some reputation for unusual dogmatism about politics, foreigners, suffrage for women, and dogs, even if they were kept on leashes. If Sam Harlow felt that Kansas should and no longer did belong to the people who had made the territory into a great state, his xenophobia can be explained by his arrival in the territory in 1860 as a one-year-old in the prairie schooner his parents had used to make the overland trip from Tennessee.

Ella Harlow was a pleasant, retiring woman who complemented her husband's place in the company by the dress, appearance and good works proper for unimaginative ladies. Their daughter Jean was a Kansas blonde with a slight tendency to weight, innocuously mannered, and with some vague ambitions for working as a secretary in an office, unfulfilled because she slept late and could not learn to type well.

Jean's marriage to Dr. Carpentier was noted in the social columns of the local papers, and, after an interval satisfactory to the most purse-mouthed finger counter, Harlean was born on March 3, 1911 in the modest home of her grandparents.

By June 24, 1932, as Relman Morin turned in his second chapter of "Platinum Venus" for the Los Angeles *Record*, the house on Olive Street had grown to proportions sufficiently noble for the birth of Jean Harlow:

> March 3, 1911.—From the street through a network of trees, you could see the great, grey house. An old house, but sturdy, its granite towers had hurled themselves against the sky for a quarter of a century.

> There was an oaken door, so heavy that the Harlows never deigned to front it with the customary "storm door." The winters are severe in Kansas City, but no icy wind or driving sleet had ever penetrated the chinks of that thick portal.

> Inside, a long hall, flanked on either side by high-ceilinged rooms, led to a marble staircase.

> Two men were pacing its length. One was tall, massive, heavy-shouldered, thick-limbed, staunch as the old house he had built. Jean Harlow's grandfather.

The other was slight of build, nattily dressed. He wore rimless spectacles, and had the air of his profession. He was a doctor. Jean's father.

Suddenly the white-capped head of a nurse appeared over the iron railing on the second floor. "You may come up now," she called.

"It's a girl."

At the age of eight Harlean was enrolled in the Barstow School for Girls, over the objections of her father but at the insistence of Mr. Harlow, who believed in classes of people and in proving one's superiority through one's ability and willingness to pay for schooling.

When Harlean was nine her parents separated without recrimination, quietly terminating a marriage that had been a dull mistake, endured so long only for the sake of Harlean. The only excitement in their marriage had been the presence, and the rages, of Mr. Harlow, but after that dour man was persuaded to go home the relationship between the younger people proved a tepid tea. Montclair found his wife so vapid that her dullness could not be acceptably glossed over as good manners, and the wife found her husband less romantic than one of his rote lectures on oral hygiene. Still, there were no recriminations; the Carpentiers understood they owed their community and Harlean the best of a bad situation, and they behaved with propriety before and after the divorce. In Kansas City and its adjacent communities for several years thereafter neither parent was seen in the company of the opposite sex.

Mrs. Jean Harlow Carpentier returned to her parents' home, occupied her old bedroom, and humbly accepted her role as a marriage failure. Meekly, with only an occasional tearful protest of short duration, she acquiesced to her father's dictum about Harlean: she was to be raised by him alone; he had not interfered with his wife in her raising of Jean, and look at how badly both of them had failed. Ella Harlow, although she sided with her daughter in a whisper, capitulated quickly to her husband's louder voice and left Harlean to the supervision of her husband.

In his firm, consistent and prideful ignorance, Sam Harlow was determined to succeed with his granddaughter where he had failed with her mother; thus The Baby's education consisted of being photographed often in pretty dresses and costumes, and having her temperature taken at a sneeze, which led Mr. Harlow to discourage visits from The Baby's playmates. Although Mrs. Harlow regretted that little girls did not visit Harlean, she was too preoccupied with a secret problem of greater importance: why had Mary Baker Eddy, whom she had begun to read in secret, been required to wear spectacles in her later years? Was this a victory of matter over Mind?

The Baby's mother used tears to protest her father's determination to replace her as natural mother. But Sam Harlow ignored his daughter and her arguments, and in despair Jean Carpentier went to Chicago to get a drink, visit some casual kissing cousins and really look for a job.

The unhappy woman soon realized she was unsuited for any skilled employment. Because quarters were cramped with her distant relatives, she moved to a hotel to rest and cry alone. One evening she screwed up sufficient courage to have dinner alone at the College Inn and was surprised when a drink was sent to her table. The waiter pointed out Marino Bello, also dining alone, and Jean smiled when Marino raised his wine glass. Because Jean had begun her dinner and Marino had not, he moved to Jean's table and introduced himself. He was a man unaccustomed to picking up women who were ladies, he said, but Mrs. Carpentier had looked so sad, and he had noticed that she did not wear a wedding ring. Her beautiful blondeness had taken him so that he just had to ignore his scruples and send the drink as a gesture of sincere admiration.

"I hope I didn't offend?" Marino asked.

Jean shook her head. "I can't remember because I'm so glad you did." His foreign accent was too romantic.

Dark, cosmopolitan, well-groomed and certain of himself as he ordered and discussed the sauces with the head waiter, Marino Bello sensed that the attractive divorcee from Kansas City was willing to behave as if she lived in Chicago. Mama Jean's visits to Chicago became more frequent, and when she took to telephoning him between visits from Kansas City telephone booths, Marino believed it was time to propose marriage to this handsome, well-groomed and presumably well-off woman. And she, of course, was willing, as she had been willing to have him in her bed—because she loved him with a passion that had startled her more than anything she could remember. After her first climax she had wept so much that Marino had been frightened—until she explained that she had heard of such happiness but never known it.

In love with Marino and passion, she still believed there was too great a barrier of religion and background between them to make marriage possible. But Marino insisted he was ready to die for love if he could not live by it, and Jean, fearing that Marino would carry out his threat, rushed to Chicago. In the hotel room, Marino kissed the swooning woman's arms from wrist to shoulder before he bit her gently above the collarbone. Then, with a skillful change of pace, he left Mama Jean nude on the bed and stood dramatically at the hotel window, where he declaimed his descent from a line of crusaders and rulers of Trieste and Sicily. His forbears had held vast estates, and he was certainly superior by lineage, blood, intellect and the positive influences of an Old World culture to any of Mrs. Carpentier's most impressive ancestors, *sgarbato*, who had covered themselves with untreated skins when his house wore velvet. Jean turned her face to the wall until she heard Marino open the window and threaten to throw himself to the pavement. Then, to forestall this tragedy, the former Mrs. Carpentier rushed into her lover's arms and begged him to remain alive. They would marry as soon as he wished.

The marriage ceremony was a civil one, and only after the judge suggested that Marino kiss his bride did Jean feel fear. Marino had placed a simple gold band on her finger and suggested that she return alone to Kansas City to break the good news to her family while he wound up his affairs in Chicago. Recently resigned from his job as a salesman of imported Italian foods and olives, Marino was looking for something in the field of finance, to put to fullest use his knowledge of world affairs. Fearing the reaction of acquaintances and friends, and especially of her former husband and her father, the new Mrs. Bello had suggested they ought to remain in Chicago. But Marino vetoed this; he was fed up with a Chicago that believed everyone with an Italian name was related to Johnny Torrio—what good was that if Torrio wouldn't give him a break? Marino believed it was time to move to a smaller city where a man with ambition, vision, drive and a few connections or dollars to back him could make the American dream of success come true.

In the morning, as married lovers, they parted at the railroad station. That night Mama Jean telephoned her second husband and hiccupped wetly into the mouthpiece that her father threatened an immediate annulment of the marriage. But her father had been oratory and threats, nothing more, and had settled the matter to his satisfaction by forbidding his home and city to his new son-in-law. If Jean wanted to return to her Italian gangster in Chicago she was free, white, twenty-one and stupid.

"Come back," Marino had told her. "But be sure to tell him that the motto of my house is 'honor survives,' something your father knows nothing about." Marino was very touchy about his descent from a line of Sicilian crusaders, possibly because it was fictitious.

"But he won't let me take Harlean!" Jean wept.

"Who is Harlean?" Marino asked.

"My daughter. She's only eleven and she needs me!"

She heard Marino sigh deeply. "I didn't know you had a daughter, Jean. You never told me. Listen," he added, "you're upset. Do you want me to come there for you? I'd like to tell your father a couple of things."

"Don't. But I want to tell you about Harlean."

"You'll tell me when I see you," Marino said.

"But he won't let me take her with me!"

"Until we set up housekeeping maybe it's better to leave your daughter—what's her name, Jean?"

"Harlean. She's eleven and just beautiful. People say she looks just like me and I know you'll love each other."

"Where does Harlean's father live?" Marino asked. "And what did Harlean say when you told her you were married again?"

"My father wouldn't let her out of her room and her father's a dentist here. I told you about him, Marino."

"That's the only part you told me!" Marino shouted. "Now come back to Chicago and leave your daughter where she is until I figure out what to do!"

In Chicago, Jean Bello only remembered Harlean when she had to write begging letters to Mrs. Harlow for little loans to tide them over until Marino found a position commensurate with his talents. Marino was willing to work at anything, even as a waiter—but if he took a job at one of the big hotels or better restaurants he ran the risk of serving men with whom he was now engaged in the most delicate financial negotiations. Right now Marino was negotiating the financing of a Canadian

49

gold mine with two members of the Hungarian nobility and a Spanish grandee related to the Patiños of the Bolivian tin mines.

For four years, between 1922 and 1925, Marino and Jean Bello lived in Chicago. They moved from one second-rate hotel and apartment to another, and Marino supported them by working as a waiter and wholesale food salesman, and by selling unlisted five-and-dime stocks in a variety of ventures in Canada, Mexico and New Zealand. And in all that time Mother Jean was permitted by her father to return to Kansas City only for the Christmas Day of 1924 and 1925.

During her mother's enforced exile in Chicago, Harlean continued at the Barstow School, and there are retired teachers in Kansas City who remember Harlean Carpentier as an average student in their classes, different only because she seldom invited children to visit her at home. Children who braved such visits were willing to be spanked rather than return to the house on Olive Street.

At the age of eleven Harlean gave promise of being an attractive teen-ager and beautiful woman, and somehow she managed to resist the unnatural interference of her grandfather in her schoolwork and friendships, in the books she read and the gum she chewed. Dr. Carpentier appeared to be helpless in all discussions and arguments with her grandfather, and after Jean's second marriage, Mr. Harlow openly accused his former son-in-law of having deliberately plotted a divorce. The insulting charge so astonished the mild-mannered dentist, he refused to visit the Harlow house and insisted that Harlean come to his office for their weekly meetings.

The divorce was the first major crisis in the Harlow household, daughter Jean's marriage to Marino Bello was the second, and the third was the day that a screaming, frightened Harlean hid herself in a closet. Ella Harlow, by a short note filled with hesitant dashes, informed Mr. Harlow of what had happened. Huddled in a dark corner of the closet behind her dresses, doubled with cramps and with shame and fear of the unknown, Harlean recited random Christian Science precepts that came to mind until, as if in answer, she heard her grandfather bellowing from the center hall landing. When, when would his responsibility end, he demanded? It was really too much for any one man to be burdened with so much responsibility! And why was his wife standing around and twiddling her thumbs when she should be on the phone speaking to a doctor—not some Christian Science Reader—and arranging for the doctor to send over a good sensible nurse—not too young—who would explain to The Baby what was happening, why, how to cope with this new responsibility, and why it was more important now than ever before to stay out of trouble with boys.

The nurse arrived and comforted Harlean. Mr. Harlow declared it was his bounden duty now to keep both eyes on Harlean, because Goddamned if she was going to go out with boys before she was eighteen—and then he would pick the boys.

Because Harlean's development was more rapid and fuller than usual for her age, the girls in her school became catty and quarrelsome. And at home Harlean's grandfather took to speaking to her as if she were not in the room, addressing her with his eyes hidden behind the widespread newspaper or fixed on the overhead light fixtures. And many nights Harlean heard Grandfather Harlow lecture Grandmother Harlow on what she had to do: keep evil away from *his* granddaughter. And she was to warn their daughter—coming home for Christmas—that if she even suggested any attempt to take Harlean to Chicago she would be ordered from the house and never permitted to return.

For the second Christmas, Mother Jean arrived in Kansas City with gifts for her parents and Harlean. Among the packages were several gifts from Marino for Harlean, and Harlean had purchased a pair of cufflinks for the stepfather she had never seen. Although Mama Jean was overjoyed at being really home, the cold she had caught on the train kept her from kissing her daughter. By nightfall Mrs. Bello's lungs were congested, and Mr. Harlow overruled his daughter and wife and sent for a doctor, who diagnosed the cold as an aggravated bronchitis that could easily have developed into pneumonia.

Two nurses helped tend Mrs. Bello, and Christmas in the Harlow house was a season of long faces and hushed voices. Mrs. Bello fretted and wept until her father agreed to telephone Marino in Chicago. Marino demanded the right to see his wife and told Mr. Harlow he was taking the next train. He arrived two days later because he had required the added time to wind up his many affairs in Chicago. Now he was prepared to concentrate, without distraction, on getting his Jean well.

"You can sleep in the room at the end of the hall," Mr. Harlow said.

"I'd prefer to sleep in the same room with my wife," Marino suggested. "I think it'll be good for both of us."

"I don't know about that."

"Let's ask the doctor when he gets here," Marino said. He had studied the substantial home and decided that Jean's convalescence would certainly last until late spring and possibly through the summer.

"But right now, Mr. Harlow," Marino said solemnly, "I'd like to be alone for a while. Alone while I pray for our Jean."

Chapter Five

In later years, after Harlean took her mother's name for the screen, the truths of her mother's illness became a myth. As Mrs. Bello told and retold of the dramatic siege with grim death, it became more wonderful and miraculous—and most wonderful of all was the switch in the victim's identity. In their preparations of screen treatments of the life of Jean Harlow, later writers used the miraculous illness as the head-waters for a sea of tears. For, as the story was now told by Mother Jean, it was The Baby who had become ill, sometime between the ages of thirteen and sixteen. Whether Harlean's illness was infantile paralysis, spinal meningitis, scarlet fever or diphtheria was never definitively established, but all the mysterious illnesses had the same result: the future movie star's legs became paralyzed and wasted. After months of pain-ful agony it was decided to tell Harlean—she was not yet Jean, so only a single violin would throb rather than an entire string section—that she would never walk again. A physician and therapist came to fit Jean with leg braces and crutches. Now, depending upon the writer and his emotional interpretation, the story takes divergent courses, but all lead to the tearful sea.

Some writers say that Jean, pale but beautiful and spunky, refused to wear the ugly appliances of leather and iron, and by gritty determination and ability to endure unusual pain, taught herself such remarkable exercises—unfortunately their descriptions are lost to medical science—that full strength returned to her legs and she walked again.

Other writers, favoring older, oftimes neglected folk who find difficulty in qualifying as heroes and heroines, insist it was Jean's grandmother, that silent woman—but is there ever a need for mountains to speak?—who banished the doctor and his ugly braces from the house, and then, by long hours of determined prayers, restored The Baby to full health. However, all the writers agree that after Jean's first hesitant steps she whirled and danced before she fell. They further agree that Jean recovered quickly, and mother and daughter wept together in joy. And if the Harlow biography had been made, mother and daughter, wet cheek to wet cheek, would have heard a heavenly tiomkin of voices raised in hosannah.

However, back in the real world of Kansas City, in March, 1926, whatever the truth of myth-to-be, Harlean's grandfather realized that his daughter, through the unfair manipulations of illness and sentimental convalescence, had re-established herself in a favored position with her child. And Marino Bello had made it quite evident that not only did his wife and he intend to live with the Harlows, but he expected to be introduced in Kansas City as a son-in-law Mr. Harlow was pleased to have in his home. Confronted by a city sharper capable of haughty belligerence in more than one language, Mr. Harlow capitulated.

The house was large enough for Marino and his wife to occupy a large pleasant room at the far end of the second floor corridor, and this room became a place of much joy as Mama Jean found herself recovered and once again capable of moaning with ecstasy. After a week of tight-eyed, cheek-mottled anger, Mr. Harlow invited Marino to lunch.

"Are you beating my daughter?" he asked.

Marino placed his knife and fork carefully on either side of his plate. "Excuse me," he said. "Did I hear you right?"

"You did." Harlow's forehead perspired freely. "Mrs. Harlow and I—we go to bed—and from your room—and I know The Baby must also be hearing the way her mother moans." Confusion made the old man's hands tremble. "I'd rather think you were beating her than she was making those sounds because . . ."

"I'll speak to Jean." Marino offered a large, monogrammed handkerchief to Sam Harlow. "I'll tell her to try and sound as if she's snoring." He looked around at the prosperous businessmen who had nodded their greetings to Harlow. "But right now I'd like to talk to you about my getting into something."

"There's no hurry," Harlow said.

Marino shrugged casually and brushed a crumb from the table. "A good guest never pushes his host," he said.

Marino bided his time and occupied himself with daily correspondence and reading the biographies of giants of finance and industry. He also fussed in the kitchen, drew on a fund of stories to amuse The Baby, and, with the approval of her mother and the unspoken disapproval of the elder Harlows, taught Harlean the tango, led her through the continental waltz and even instructed his stepdaughter in how to use lipstick.

At last, grudgingly and with some fear, Sam Harlow invited Marino to lunch again with him in public. Whatever misgivings the old man had about the reception of this dark-skinned foreigner with his slight accent were soon dissipated, for Marino was sharp, witty and charming. But he was unable to interest anyone in financing an expedition to explore a newly discovered treasure galleon off the Panama coast.

Dr. Carpentier, however, had bumped into Marino at the post office, had accepted him with polite, professional interest and had even thanked him for doing something to inhibit Sam Harlow's domination of Harlean.

"I do what I can," Marino said modestly. "A girl that age needs a father, not a grandfather."

"I'd say she needs both." Carpentier matched modesty

with politeness. "But the best thing for Harlean would be to get her out of that house. The old man's a twister and you've got to be in a storm cellar to feel really safe when he's around."

Marino winked as if he had trained lions. "Oh, he can be handled. Any time you want to visit Harlean you don't have to stand on ceremony or wait for visiting days. A man has a right to see his daughter any time he wants to. She's a very pretty girl, Doctor Carpentier."

The dentist nodded. "She has a pretty mother. And Jean looks lots younger since you married her."

"Being sick sometimes does that to a person."

"No, Mr. Bello, it's something more. Some people can do things for other people."

Marino raised his hand in a small gesture of deprecation. "It's maturity, Doctor. Some people don't grow up until they actually leave their home. Jean never did with you. But in Chicago we had our own lives."

"And here?"

"I stand up to Sam Harlow," Marino said. "Doctor, we're both men of the world?"

"Sometimes I like to think I am."

"Then we can talk about Jean, because we both know her"—Marino paused as if choosing a word in a thesaurus—"intimately. But with you she was a little girl, because her mother and father were here. Whatever she did with you she must've thought was wrong." He smiled as Carpentier's forehead beaded in fresh perspiration. "In Chicago she didn't have to worry about her mother and father calling on us just before or right after or even while—you understand?" Marino winked again at Carpentier, who rubbed his sweatband harder and harder, as if to erase it from his hat. "And don't think that for a minute I don't have my troubles with Jean now that we're living in the same house with the old folks at home."

"But she looks so good!"

"Because it's a contest," Marino explained. "Who's going to have his way, me or her father. And I never liked goats. When I was a boy on one of my family's estates the goats were afraid of me, because as soon as I saw one I hit him over the head with a stick. Some day I must tell you about our estates in Europe."

"I'd like to hear about them," Carpentier said. "I've wanted to say if you need some dental work or just want your teeth cleaned and checked, come in. I do the teeth of all the family, and I'd like to include you."

"Thank you." Marino offered the taller man his hand. "I appreciate that. And because you're family I want to see you socially more than professionally. And I want you to visit me and Jean and Harlean more often. I try to be a father to Harlean, but I don't want to take your place. She's very pretty, Doctor. Boys look at her, and she gives them a lot to look at."

"I didn't know."

"You should talk to her." Marino smiled to acknowledge the curious stare of a woman who was storing up details of the meeting of husbands past and present to tell to her friends. "Jean is embarrassed and her grandmother—Mrs. Harlow— I'm pretty sure she also believes in storks."

The men shook hands again, and later that day Dr. Carpentier telephoned Harlean and asked her to meet him for dinner. Sam Harlow permitted his granddaughter to go with her father but said he would sit on the porch until she returned. Marino and Jean insisted that he looked lonesome and joined him out of doors. Marino sat with Jean on the creaking porch glider and pressed her palm with his manicured nails to feel her tightened grip as she shivered.

But now two headlights speared the darkness. The car moved slowly until it stopped at the house and Montclair Carpentier got out to open the door on Harlean's side. But his daughter was across the sidewalk and part way up the path to the house by the time Dr. Carpentier reached the sidewalk. Choked by sobs, she entered the house and ran up the stairs without replying to anyone's questions.

"What'd you do?" Sam demanded of his former son-in-law.

"I took my daughter to dinner and had a talk with her about growing up," Montclair explained as he fanned himself with his straw hat.

"You don't have to do neither," the old man snapped. "She gets all the bringing up she needs around here."

"Daddy, please." Jean touched her father's sleeve. "Let's go inside."

"Not him, he doesn't." Sam Harlow moved to block the front door. "I've got a good mind—"

"—you've got a bad mind," Carpentier said firmly. "And there's nothing I want to say to you tonight that I won't regret tomorrow. Jean, Marino, good night."

"Good night," Marino called after the dentist. "Me'n my teeth'll be in your office tomorrow."

Montclair waved and slammed the car door behind him.

Sam Harlow raved, Mama Jean and Mrs. Harlow wept, Harlean refused to open the door of her room. The bad news had been broken: The Baby was being sent away to grow into Harlean.

In later years, when much was made by the studios of Jean Harlow's superior education, there was some dispute as to whose idea it had been to enroll the fifteen-year-old girl at a private boarding school. Ferry Hall, a school of impeccable reputation, was located in Lake Forest, Illinois, on twelve acres of gracious lawns and trees. To be admitted to Ferry Hall was a social achievement; to graduate from the school was a scholastic accomplishment. Ferry Hall girls were schooled in the arts, sciences and social graces under the supervision of teachers capable of dealing with education, the facts of life and goatish boys.

When the studios decided to sell their Platinum Bombshell as the reverse of Cinderella, Jean Harlow was presented as a finished product of that most exclusive of all finishing schools, and Mama Jean and Marino took credit for their daughter's enrollment. However, Sam Harlow and his wife would confide to their closest friends that they had chosen Ferry Hall in order to give The Baby the best schooling possible for a young lady and, just as important, to get her away from the presence and influence of Marino Bello. But in truth, Harlean's father had telephoned the school, arranged for Harlean's admission, and then told the Harlows and Marino. He might have been divorced from his wife, but not from his daughter, he told them with quiet determination, and she was going to boarding school even if he had to go into court to enforce his decision.

"Harlean cried the night I brought her home because I'd told her what I had in mind," her father explained. "Still, she's going."

"She's so young." Ella Harlow looked to her husband for approval of this observation. "And it's a slap at the schools here. Why, we have much better people in Kansas than they have in Illinois."

Dr. Carpentier looked at his pocket watch. "I've an appointment," he said. "Harlean goes to Ferry Hall and that's final." He removed a booklet from his inner coat pocket and offered it to Marino. "That's the required school wardrobe and the other things Harlean'll need. I think her mother"—he continued to speak to Marino as if Mama Jean weren't present—"should do the shopping and send me the bill."

Harlean entered Ferry Hall in September, 1926, and was there for less than a year. She had her full height of five feet two inches and weighed about a hundred and eighteen pounds. A creamy type of blonde with expressive blue eyes and a kewpie mouth that made boys wet their lips, Harlean did well at school dances, but was only an average student who might have done better if she had been less self-conscious about the

59

full maturity of her bosom and less homesick. The school regimen was too disciplined, too sudden a transition from the hothouse anarchy she had known in Kansas City.

Girls at school were required to write home at least once a week, but Harlean wrote at least every other day and sometimes twice a day. She was happy at school, she wrote, but when could she come home and go to school again in Kansas City, where all the kids she knew were having the greatest times, seeing boys as schoolmates and not as visitors from Mars? Still, there were too many too-friendly boys with Roman hands, so she was glad the school was strict—which made it all into a bigger mess. She only knew one thing for certain—she wanted to come home.

Sam Harlow and his wife longed for their granddaughter, but they writhed in shame because Mama Jean paraded around in black negligees, too enraptured with her very own Latin lover to give thought to her homesick daughter. Harlean's letters complained that her father wrote only briefly, on a dental pad, and that her mother used such little notepaper that ten words filled a side.

Not that she wasn't popular with boys, Harlean wrote. There was one Chicago boy in particular who wrote her every day, and she enjoyed his gooey letters, even though they had cost her the friendship of a girl she didn't care about at all. Charles McGrew, whose family was in the stock market, had been this girl's date at a Saturday afternoon dance, but he had filled in some of Miss Carpentier's card. He had confided that he thought the Saturday dances really stupid, especially for someone who was twenty-one, and that he only attended because his aunt knew the mothers of some of the girls at Ferry and he had to go to the dances if he expected to keep getting one of the family cars. The homesick girl wrote that Chuck was fun, *really* twenty-one and a smoothy. Although she liked him more than any boy she'd ever met, she was still willing to give up Chuck if only her mother would do something about taking her home.

The letters failed, a long distance call failed, but Mama Jean promised her daughter she would be visiting her soon and they would discuss the matter in person.

On January 19, 1927, Mama Jean and Marino arrived in Chicago, because Mrs. Bello had begun to have doubts about Marino's interest in her, and had insisted they go through another marriage ceremony, to be followed by another inspirational honeymoon. Marino thought the demand nonsense, but he agreed, and the married couple were married again.

The next day Marino kept several appointments with old cronies. Mrs. Bello visited Harlean at school, and Harlean controlled her tears to listen patiently as Mama Jean exclaimed over and over again how pretty her daughter was becoming, that she should be proud because her hair was so blonde, and that it was wrong for Harlean to make such a to-do about wearing a brassiere.

"They make me self-conscious," Harlean said as she sat with her mother on a secluded sofa.

"But all girls of a certain age or size have to wear them," her mother said.

"Not in ancient Rome or Greece I bet. Chuck said that Etruscan women—they were older than the ancient Romans—they wore dresses that showed their boobies."

"A nice boy doesn't tell girls such things!"

"Chuck's nice, honest. And not real fresh. And bras make me feel like my breath's being cut off."

"It's a state of mind," Mama Jean said. "I felt the same way when I first started to wear a brassiere. Later on you'll have to wear a corselet."

"I won't."

"You will," her mother said. "Girls who don't wear the

right foundations—well, boys think they're cheap and willing to do cheap things."

"Chuck's never said so or looked at me that way. So it's a lotta bushwah."

"Harlean! They don't teach you that here. This Chuck sounds to me like a bad influence."

"Oh, I've learned plenty they don't teach anywhere," Harlean continued meaningfully. Staring thoughtfully at her mother, she bit on her fleshy lower lip. "There's things I'd like to ask you."

"I'm really not qualified," Mrs. Bello stammered. "And there're certain things you should get from teachers instead of your mother."

Harlean laughed and leaned back against the flowered upholstery of the sofa. "Can you just see me or any of us here asking a teacher about muzzling and what to do when a boy won't stop playing handsy? Or why you feel sort of hot in the tummy when he touches you in certain places? It hasn't happened to me," Harlean said quickly as Mama Jean's eyes widened, "but one of the girls here said it made her feel good and that it was supposed to happen to anyone who was modern. Now do you still want me to be in school away from home?"

"Are you a good girl? Harlean, tell me!"

Harlean shrugged. And Mrs. Bello, frightened that something awful might happen to The Baby, promised Harlean she would tell Dr. Carpentier that Kansas City and Kansas City schools were good enough for their daughter.

"And I'm going to speak to Marino about getting into something, anything, so we can get out of Grandpa's house," she added.

Shortly thereafter, at a family conclave, it was decided that Harlean ought to finish the school year, since there were only three months or so left in the semester. But for Harlean this was too long, and one Sunday evening in March, 1927, Mrs. Bello received a dolorous telephone call from the headmaster's office: Harlean had been missing at room check the night before and had returned to school that afternoon to announce she and Charles McGrew had eloped to Waukegan. Of course Harlean could no longer be permitted to stay at Ferry Hall, and the school would appreciate the removal of Miss Carpentier's—or Mrs. McGrew's—belongings within the next day or so. The school disclaimed all responsibility. The headmaster's office could only say that Harlean had told the justice of peace she was nineteen, and the groom had given his correct age of twenty-one. Also, an annulment was out of the question, another reason for the bride's family to come for their daughter, who was being kept in isolation so other girls at school might not ask questions. If there was more Mama Jean never heard it, because the phone was snatched from her hand by Sam Harlow, who roared into the mouthpiece that he was a man bedeviled every day of his life by foolish, frivolous, unreasonable women and that the school was to send Harlean home at once, without her husband, whom he would horsewhip later.

Marino took the telephone from Sam Harlow's hand. "Is Harlean there?" he asked. If the boy's uncle was a stockbroker, he could be a valuable relative.

"Yes, in an outer office," the voice of the woman at the other end replied. "Would you like to speak with her?"

"Very much," Marino said, then covered the mouthpiece with his hand as he ordered everyone—and the ladies should pardon him—to keep their pants on. "Harlean," he said, "this is Marino. Now stop crying. You're married, so I'll wish you the best of luck. Where's the lucky man?" He listened, then reported that Chuck had been taken home by his family, a bad beginning for marriage and business. "Listen, can we trust you to come home tomorrow? Or better yet, Harlean, let me talk to the lady who's been doing all the talking."

Marino pointed out that Harlean was a married woman and entitled to the dignities of that holy state, then promised he would call for Mrs. McGrew tomorrow and take her home.

Late Tuesday night, on the train between Chicago and Kansas City, Harlean attempted to block out the memory of what she had done and of the stunned reaction of everyone, including Chuck, when his family had driven to Lake Forest to take him home. Chuck's uncle had sworn his nephew would be locked in his room for the rest of the summer. At Ferry Hall a housemother and a senior honor student had helped Harlean pack; no more had been said than absolutely necessary, and other students had been forbidden to talk to her.

Marino was the only person to treat Harlean with a sympathy she found reassuring. His kiss had been friendly, his hug paternal, and he had held her at arm's length to exclaim she was the most beautiful bride he had ever seen, next to her mother of course. He insisted that she wasn't to cry or be upset, because he would see what could be done with her family when they returned to Kansas City. And if her husband was a man, he wouldn't let anyone take his legal and lawful wife from him.

"I'd fight giants and dragons for you," Marino said as he dried Harlean's eyes, "so don't worry. We're pulling into the station, so you fix that pretty face and just keep smiling."

It was after midnight, but Sam Harlow was an angry prosecutor as he shouted questions at everyone and supplied answers to suit his outraged dignity. The school was at fault, and what sort of state was Illinois to permit a teen-age girl to get married even if she lied about her age? Marino's observation that Harlean was unusually mature for a sixteen-year-old girl, and that her husband was twenty-one, did not impress Sam Harlow at all.

After Harlean had been sedated and had fallen asleep, Mama Jean sat at the side of her daughter's bed and wondered if anything was worthwhile. She had spoken to Harlean, mother to daughter, and Harlean had replied as a married woman to a married woman.

"We spent the night in a hotel," Harlean said defiantly. "Where'd you think we'd go? To a barn or some park bushes?"

"Don't talk that way, Baby. Now's one of the times when you really need a mother's help."

"I sure do." Harlean rolled over to lie with her back to her mother. "Chuck seemed to like it, but I thought it was awfully messy. A nothing. But Chuck says it takes time before it feels good. He isn't full of hot air?"

"Go to sleep, Baby."

"Stop calling me Baby! And if you won't tell me I bet Marino will."

"I'll tell you tomorrow," Mama Jean promised with both hands clasped as if in prayer. "Go to sleep, please." She sniffled into her handkerchief.

Harlean sat up in the bed. The nightgown open at the neck had slipped down to reveal the fine flowing line between shoulder and throat. Her eyes were hard blue and also rimmed with red. "Is it just a lot of hot air?" she demanded.

"There's more to love than sex," Mama Jean said uneasily.

"*That's* hot air. Did you know that before I got on the train with Marino I tried to call Chuck at his house and they wouldn't let me talk to him? They had no right to do that." Harlean bounced up and stripped off the half-sleeved flannelette gown. Mama Jean turned away in embarrassment at the sight of her daughter's nude body and heavy breasts with their enlarged nipples that were—vulgar. "I don't want to wear anything that reminds me of school," Harlean explained as she slipped back beneath the sheets. She clasped her hands behind her head, stared at the ceiling and sighed.

"You know what bothered me most when he was doing it to me?"

"You ought to go to sleep," her mother said weakly.

"He wanted the lights on. At school the girls said that normal people do it in the dark. But I didn't seem to mind the lights, because I wanted to see too. So then I began to worry if we were normal, and of course I worried about getting a baby right off just like poor people do. But Chuck had something he called rubbers. I never saw things like that before. He let me look at one and when I giggled that made him sort of embarrassed."

"I'm embarrassed too, and you ought to go to sleep," Mama Jean said.

"But it was the ceiling and the wallpaper on it that really got me. Now I realize how silly it is to paper a ceiling. I kept following the design with my eyes, and maybe that's why I didn't get anything out of the other thing."

"Then maybe it didn't happen." Her mother's voice rose on notes of hope. "Maybe you think it did but it didn't and we could get a doctor—"

Harlean cut her mother short by waving both hands. "It happened." Her voice was dry. "Mama, you were married to daddy and now you're married to Marino. Tell me—"

But Mama Jean fled. Harlean fell back to the pillow and decided she ought to get some rest. Really, she didn't care about being married, because all she had really wanted to do was leave Ferry Hall. If marriage had failed *her* as an experience it wasn't Chuck's fault. Try as hard as she could, Harlean could not dredge up the least feeling of romance, and try as she might, she could not remember passion.

It was impossible to keep Harlean's return a secret from the people who mattered in a city the size of Kansas City, and the Harlow neighbors and friends could not be accused of unreasonable curiosity and interest in someone they had known from birth. There were personal visits and telephone calls at the Harlow house, and after one such visit by three women to whom Mama Jean would never speak again, Sam Harlow insisted the marriage might have been consummated in document and body but was null and void in spirit. No one agreed with him.

To the despair of Bello, whose letters were unanswered, the McGrews appeared to be quite willing to leave Sam Harlow in possession of the young bride. Chuck, with a reduced allowance that could not accommodate railroad fare or long distance calls to Kansas City, was sent east for a long visit to other relatives.

If ever Sam Harlow had needed proof of the incompetence of his wife, daughter, granddaughter, son-in-law and ex-son-in-law, he now had more than enough. In fact, he had had all he could stand.

In the summer of 1927, the Bellos and Jean arrived in Los Angeles. After the telegram of safe arrival to the Harlows, the newcomers to sunshine and orange groves rented a furnished two-bedroom apartment in the vicinity of Alvarado and Union Streets, close enough to the financial district of Los Angeles for Marino to get to the brokerages in a matter of minutes.

Summer in Los Angeles was much more pleasant than any in Kansas City, and to the small household there was no need to worry about tomorrow, because Sam Harlow had agreed to support them for nine months—long enough, he hoped, for Marino to find something suitable to his background, ambitions and talent.

As the exiled Mrs. Charles McGrew, who had lost eight pounds and taken up smoking, walked along the paths of Westlake Park, she ignored the whistles of boys and young men who called her Blondie and wanted to know if everything in the white silk dress was real. The sun felt so good on her face and head she could not care that her blonde hair was becoming lighter, almost white. There was so much to see!

It was difficult to think of her husband, to whom she

really should write. True, she didn't have his address in the East where he had been sent by his folks, and he hadn't written her more than one long letter while she was in Kansas City. Marino and Mama Jean had suggested she take off her wedding ring and forget about a marriage that would be terminated some time soon anyway. No mention had been made about her returning to high school, and the more she stayed out of sight of her mother and Marino the less chance they would have to think about books and what other sixteen-year-old kids did during the day.

Meanwhile, there were so many things to delight her: funny restaurants with the cutest names, exotic flowers, palm trees and banana plants, movies and stars. Also, there was a Chinatown near the Union Station and wouldn't it be exciting if she—an average American girl—were kidnaped into an opium den and just in the nick of time, before awful things happened to her, were rescued by—say—Richard Dix?

Chapter Six

"Every man . . . every man I know gets an . . . erection . . . Just by talking about her, other men get them. Arthur, didn't I have the right to think Jean could help me at least that much?"

The statement and anguished question could never have been used as a screen sub-title for a silent film. Western morality and its fear of words would have demanded that the actor substitute a more moral sounding paraphrase. *"Every man I know gets fire in his eyes—feels like a giant, a conqueror when he thinks of Jean! So why did she fail me?"*

The audience would read—some in silence, others with dramatic audibility—then see the actor attempt, through broad declarative gestures this side of ridiculous, to pantomime passion to match the printed title. However, if sub-titles were lacking and if the actor had to interpret in silence the agony of Paul Bern, the necessary gestures would have taxed the ingenuity of a mute Hieronimo, the most hambone Hamlet.

Despite the myopic awe of sanguine critics, most silent movies were awful. *The Cabinet of Dr. Caligari, The Last Laugh, Variety* and *Metropolis* were no more indicative of the quality of the average German film than *Paris Qui Dort, Nana* and *Therese Raquin* were indicative of French productions. And in the United States, *Greed, Lady Windermere's Fan, The Crowd* and *Salvation Hunters* had as little to do with average movies made for popular delight as *Marty* or the NBC *White Papers* have to do with *Dennis the Menace, The Beverly Hill-*

billies and television commercials where the most exquisite, antiseptic young people, unencumbered by alimentary tracts, engage in smiling, outdoor colloquy about the deep-down pleasure of cigarettes, the foaminess of beer, the strong odors armpits can produce and the irregularity of human bowels.

Almost all of the films of the early twenties were banal, unimaginative products which either portrayed sex openly by dragging it in by its round heels or offered it in stylish formal dress and undress, as in the spectaculars of De Mille, before he experienced a Great Awakening to become the Bible's most popular bowdlerizer and booster of the marble bath. Movie attendance grew steadily, and to accommodate the increasing millions pleased to languish in temples of euphoria, the moguls decreed that theaters become vast cathedrals complete with majestic organs able even to duplicate the tinkle of banjos. Movie houses became larger, more ornate temples of dreams, with lounges and restrooms filled with deep-pile carpets and thrones, and to build and maintain such theaters became increasingly expensive, especially if the purchase of prime real estate to locate such theaters had been made at prices inflated beyond reason or true worth. The popularity of older stars diminished, because active sex is still the burden of the young, and people in the sober, sour decades of life resented elderly men and aging women making fools of themselves in picture after picture—and at enormous salaries. Attendance was up but not as much as it should be, the maintenance of theaters after their initial investments was ruinous, and several film corporations found themselves confronted by severe financial crises.

Then—a voice was heard from the screen, a voice that could have said, *"Jean makes every man capable of love. Every man but me. Am I cursed?"*

Speech spoken by an actor from the screen meant the end of lugubrious pantomime. Seated, face covered by his hands, fingers stiff or knotted with tension, the actor could speak, moan, groan or lament his lines and the audience would react sympathetically to the oral agony. The actor could lie face down on a sofa or bed, stand with his head pressed against a wall, be photographed in darkness—even as a shadow, for his voice, not his body or features, had become the dramatic articulate instrument of ferment.

In 1927 a technological breakthrough was accomplished in *The Jazz Singer* and by 1929 almost all silent screens were gifted with speech and all the other sounds of reality; and if dilettantish defenders of silent pictures insisted that the stricture of silence had compelled the movie makers and actors to invent techniques that added to the artistry of films, if critical troglodytes insisted sound would destroy illusion, if stockholders deplored expensive theater modifications in a time of economic crisis, if prophets of taste forecast that sound was a costly novelty of which the public would soon tire, no one listened to them, for the public, whose theater admissions supported the industry, revelled in the sounds of film. Voices heard from the screen, music, storms, the most common ordinary sounds, the simplest of dialogue, all thrilled audiences, who reacted as if they had been born deaf and granted the aural sense only in 1927. The public raised its voice to demand that good voices on the screen convey the essential personalities of their roles, and important theatrical careers were cut short by the knives of scoffing laughter, hoots and whistles rising from theater seats. A great, romantic lover could never be convincing in scenes of seduction, anguish, or nobility if his voice was thinner than his mustache; a Western hero would be gunned down by audience yelps if his voice could only pipe "this town ain't big enough for the two of us." A divine mistress would be hooted if her voice grated or squeaked, or was for some mysterious reason unpleasant on the sound track. Heroes with the bluest eyes, heroines with the blondest hair were discarded by the industry if their voices failed to match their stereotypes. Even if he was compelled to wear lipstick, sound made a leading man of George Arliss, and it was sound that ruined John Gilbert and cut Greta Nissen out of an important film.

At the Metropolitan Studio at Romaine Street and Cahuenga Avenue in Hollywood, a picture begun by the Caddo Corporation in 1926, three years before, closed down again. There was nothing wrong with the exterior aerial battles—shot with Sopwith Snipes, German Fokkers, a Gotha bomber, British SE-5's and Avros—for these had been well planned and directed by Marshall Neilan, who had conceived the film's basic theme. When sound proved successful in 1927, all of the aerial dogfights had had sound dubbed in.

The outdoor aerial sequences brought World War I to Southern California. Stunt men and expert pilots flew daily from a Van Nuys airstrip, about twelve miles from Hollywood and Vine, where a ground crew of more than a hundred mechanics serviced the planes. After the planes flew in their rehearsals of mock combats, the pilots would relax by diving and strafing with blanks another set some miles from Van Nuys, where the producing company had built a replica of Baron von Richtofen's headquarters and field. Planes collided and crashed into houses, a loose propeller did headline damage to a bungalow roof in Los Angeles, but the rough cuts of scenes in the air were exciting and dangerous enough to satisfy adventure's most exacting critic. Ben Lyon's voice suited his role of a *carpe diem* aviator who drank, fought and leched with a cavalier disregard of consequences. James Hall, as Ben's more serious brother, was equally convincing on the sound stage.

Back at Metropolitan Studio, where the interior scenes of *Hell's Angels* had been shooting since October, 1927, everything was up in the air. Once again production had stopped because sound effects were not enough now—audiences demanded dialogue. More than a million dollars had been spent—which immediately tagged the incomplete picture as a major epic—a year's new film had been edited, and none of it could be used. It had been shot silent, without dialogue, and letters from distributors and exhibitors were proof of a nationally united demand for talkies. Howard Hughes ordered the people on the picture to speak up all the way, and loud. Fortunately, in the chaotic planning of the picture most of the close-ups of aerial dogfights and bombings had not been shot, so sound equipment was added to the cameras to record voices above the chatter of machine guns.

Actors and production units were working reasonably well, but the problem that really stopped the cameras was Greta Nissen, a good actress with an adequate voice, a conscientious professional and a beautiful woman not given to temperament. But Greta was a Norwegian who spoke English with a pronounced accent, and her role in the film was that of an English *fille*. The new remake of the picture was about to speak, but Miss Nissen, who had been paid $2,500 a week, could not speak her lines—at least not in accents acceptable to the ear of the audience.

A producer to whom movies was an industry and not a diversion would have struck his sets or dubbed Miss Nissen's voice, but Howard Hughes, whose hobbies were movies and planes rather than yachts and art, decided to finish the film his way. To accomplish this the men able to make minor decisions arrived at a terrifying but practical solution that had five related parts: scrap the old scenario, which was loose, rambling and tailspinning in all directions; write a tighter one to tell a story for voices; pay Miss Nissen her contracted salary and send her a bouquet of long-stemmed red roses; replace her with an American or British actress; and begin again. One day, when he was found camping out in his unfurnished Los Angeles mansion near the Wilshire Country Club, Howard Hughes agreed that a new, tight, all-dialogue screenplay had to be written and followed if the picture were to be finished.

MGM cooperated to the extent of ordering Joseph Moncure March to meet Howard Hughes and James Whale, the new director assigned to get the picture off the ground and into the theater. March was the author of *The Set-Up* and *The Wild Party,* narrative poems in staccato meters that reproduced graphically the swift, brutal atmosphere, mood and dialogue of people living by and for violence. In June, 1929, he had accepted a writer's contract with MGM, and a few days later, before he could be warned away from the project by more knowledgeable craftsmen, he found himself in a projection room at the Metropolitan Studios where for long hours he viewed the silent and sound hodgepodge of scenes shot for *Hell's Angels.* Then, with aching rear and tired eyes, March was compelled to read the silent scripts and random notes that had passed for the picture's continuity.

That night at dinner he told the assembled executives he could do nothing to patch the story—it would have to be rewritten, and if he could use the footage which had been shot as material for a scene he would do so; if not, new scenes would have to be staged. Hughes thought, shook his head several times, and—through James Whale—told March that he didn't care if everything had to be scrapped because he had already decided this was the thing to do. March was to write a new script and think only of drama, not costs.

In about two weeks March completed a new story and dialogue, and this script, with some minor revisions to fit the personalities of Ben Lyon and James Hall, became final for the film. It called for babels of talk. Trial scenes were shot with sound equipment, and, to the immense relief of a short, slender, sentimental man named Arthur Landau, the voice of Ben Lyon recorded well. Arthur Landau was relieved because he was Lyon's agent. But he was worried, too, because he was also Greta Nissen's agent.

Arthur Landau was less than five feet tall. This was not remarkable in a town where all the top men were little Napoleons, but what was remarkable was that Landau, shorter than the shortest producer, didn't wear the special shoes, trick suits and pompadour haircuts that movie executives employed to add to their visible stature. He didn't have to. He'd learned that lack of height had its advantages, especially in dealing with his clients; it enabled him to play Dutch Uncle, father confessor, foxy grandpa and thoroughbred watchdog to them, and they loved him for it.

Landau had suggested dubbing a suitable voice in Greta Nissen's scenes, and Ben Lyon and James Hall had advocated this because they had enjoyed working with Miss Nissen. But Hughes, once again on the scene and determined to be authentic, insisted that he wouldn't believe the picture if Greta were given a voice and pronunciation foreign to her. Find a new actress, he ordered Whale, and keep shooting other scenes until she was found. Whale shouted into the slipstream of Hughes' plane that at least two dozen actresses had been suggested and Hughes had vetoed every one of them. The plane disappeared in the sky, and the distraught director glared at Arthur Landau.

"You put Greta Nissen into the picture when you knew she couldn't speak English and you're responsible for our being stuck," Jim Whale accused Landau. "You should've had enough sense to know we'd have to shoot dialogue! Don't give me an argument—who's on your list? You represent Dorothy Mackaill?"

Landau shut his eyes and squeezed his temples. "I do and she's English. You know that Neilan saw her in a London show—"

"He told me," Whale said. "Get her over here. And be sure to tell her that Hughes makes these decisions. If he likes her, she's in. If not I'll kill myself."

"Dorothy'll do it," Arthur swore. "Now do me a favor and call the Warners and make the request official? I mean, it might carry more weight if you called."

"Call yourself," Whale said. "The most important reason that killing myself sounds so good is I wouldn't have to talk to anyone for the rest of my life."

While Landau drove to the Warner Brothers' offices on that fall day of 1929, he rehearsed what he would say to the studio executives: Dorothy Mackaill was between pictures, she hadn't been alerted for a part in any picture then in preparation at her home studio, and she was willing to play in the epic, which people now said would cost at least four million dollars—a staggering sum for the time. Her appearance in such an all-dialogue film, with special wide-screen planned for the aviation footage and one important scene shot in color—Hughes had decided to have everything—could only help Dorothy's career and make her more valuable to the home studio.

The Warner Brothers said no, not once, but many times and loudly. As long as their stars were getting their salary checks the problem of idleness was the studio's concern, not the actors' or their agents'. The Warners had made the first sound films and still thought of themselves as *conquistadores* of the new Hollywood. That year *Variety* had observed: "Sound didn't do any more to the industry than turn it upside down, shake the entire bag of tricks from its pocket and advance Warner Brothers from the last place (among the film companies) to first in the league."

No one could do better than the Warners, Arthur was told as the three brothers were about to dismiss him. "And if Dorothy wants to do an airplane picture, find one for us," Jack said to Arthur. "One with lots of sounds and a good writer. Then we'll talk to you." He propelled Arthur through the door and slammed it.

Driving slowly through Hollywood, then along Franklin Avenue and into the green restfulness of Griffith Park, Landau had to admit he had no one to replace Dorothy Mackaill and could think of nothing to help Jim Whale. Later that day he would telephone Sam Warner, the most reasonable of the three brothers, swear he was on his knees as he made the call and offer to humble, demean and degrade himself and to make any promises and keep them if Dorothy were permitted to take the test. Would Ben Lyon also be willing to call the Warners? Was there someone to whom the Warners felt indebted? No answers came to mind.

To offset his growing depression, Arthur decided to drive out to Hal Roach studios, where a comedy was sure to be in shooting. The antics on the set would amuse him, even though he wouldn't be permitted to laugh as in the old days, when the laughter of an audience on the set stimulated the comics to greater inspiration. Sound changed everything, Arthur reflected sourly, and right now, for him, the change was not for the better.

At the Culver City studios of Hal Roach the revolution of sound had made stars of Laurel and Hardy, comedians whose stage training and distinctive voices kept them before the cameras while some of their slapstick rivals failed the test of sound. This afternoon they were clowning with the crew as Arthur walked on the set. Hardy immediately put his derby on the agent's head, and everyone laughed as the hat fell almost to Arthur's chin.

"That's so we don't have to see a long face on a short man," Hardy explained. "Now what's new in pictures?"

"Accents," Arthur replied.

Hardy nodded solemnly. "I'd heard about that," he said.

"I can't see the difference," Laurel said in his British squeak. "A sexy voice is a sexy voice even if it has a Scandinavian accent. And personally, I'd rather have a voice like Greta's inviting me into a boudoir than most of the flat twangs you get these days—like the kid over there, for example."

Arthur looked where Laurel pointed and saw a girl drawing water from the cooler at the far end of the sound stage.

She was young, blonde, with high firm breasts that lifted the bodice of her sleazy green dress. But it was her astonishingly blonde hair, unnaturally light and brushed back from her high forehead, that fascinated Arthur as he watched the girl refill her paper cup. He whistled as she drank again.

"From here I can see she isn't wearing a bra," he said.

"She never does," Hardy said. "It's her advertisement."

"You know her?" Arthur asked.

Hardy struggled dramatically with his memory. "We've used her once or twice. Can you remember her name, Stan?"

"I've never tried," Laurel lamented as he screwed his mouth and eyes into an expression of misery. "We used her in *Double Whoopee*," he told Arthur. "She gets out of a cab and when I slam the door it catches her dress. When she steps away she's in a black chemise."

"It was a funny bit," Hardy laughed. "She follows us into the hotel and doesn't know she isn't wearing a dress." He sighed. "In a dress or out, it doesn't make much difference for that kind. She's still making the rounds and hoping."

"Can she act?" Arthur asked.

Hardy shook his head. "Not for our money. But out here, who can? And I don't believe that hair's real."

Arthur realized the girl had sensed she was the subject of discussion, because she brushed her hair back and stood in profile. Head flung back, hip forward and breasts high, she drank from the cup with her little finger stuck out in a gesture of elegance. The heels of the girl's shoes were extraordinarily high, and when she moved to rest her foot on a wooden box, her skirt hiked up to reveal her knee and a bit of inner thigh.

"It's the hair that makes me look at her twice," Arthur mused.

Oliver Hardy nudged his partner. "See, Stan, I always told you he was older than us."

Arthur waved as he continued across the sound stage. He

shouldn't even speak to this girl, he knew. It smacked too much of the corniest of Hollywood's mythical "traditions"—The Discovery. Industry morale throve on these stories—of girls discovered behind school books or counters, of future stars found in the uniforms of usherettes, of a teenager discovered while traveling with her family—how they were seen by a studio scout, tested, instantly propelled into fame and riches. Before 1920 movies still were in the novelty category and studio people and performers held the same status in Hollywood as their predecessors had in sixteenth and seventeenth century England: vagrant vagabonds subject to arrest unless they had placed themselves under the protective sponsorship of an influential courtier.

By 1920 the movies were an important local industry, the most glamorous tourist attraction in the United States and probably the best known and most widely reported of all American exports, and the rewards offered the lucky exceeded the fortunes made in the gold fields. The new rush was on, and every young man with a profile who had won a prize in a tango contest, every girl who had ever appeared in something that passed for an amateur play or even placed fourth or fifth in a local beauty pageant, bought a one-way ticket to Hollywood. By the early 1920's there were at least twenty-five thousand extras in daily clawing competition for jobs that never numbered more than a thousand. The number of beautiful girls that arrived in Hollywood was estimated at a hundred a week and the concentration of beauty, its willingness to undress for critical examination, its availability, the price it was willing to pay for a chance at stardom added up to a satyr's dream. And a new, important piece of furniture—the casting couch—was designed and became a standard office appointment. Most girls, if they were virtuous, never became more than waitresses or counter girls in Woolworth's; those who were pretty but less scrupulous often compromised their ambitions and achieved the status of party girls or regulars in a good establishment. But this girl undoubtedly believed in The Discovery—they all did for a while.

"I've been watching you," she said to Arthur as she offered him a cup of water. "And you looked like you were saying no-no-no to everything."

"I was." Arthur thanked her for the cup and continued to stare at her hair. The color was startling. "You'll become sick or probably poison yourself if you keep on using whatever you're using on your hair," he said. "I'm an agent. Arthur Landau."

"I've heard of you," she said nasally, then her voice changed to become artificially cultured in the worst tradition of the hick tea room. "My stage name is Jean Harlow."

And that was how he met her. She had worked for Laurel and Hardy, had appeared in some Christy comedies, and the year before had run across the screen in *Moran of the Marines,* starring Richard Dix and Ruth Elder. This year she had worked in a still unreleased Clara Bow picture, *The Saturday Night Kid.*

"As what?" Arthur asked.

"I really Charlestoned. The director—Mr. Sutherland, you know him?—he said I was a real hot number. Will you stop staring at my make-up?" The toniness disappeared and she sounded unhappy and desperate. "You're making me nervous."

"Sorry," Arthur said. "You had lunch?"

Jean shook her head. "I was counting on getting hired today so I left the house with just carfare. Mr. Landau, you've got some big clients, lots of contacts . . ." she paused and crossed her arms to hide the raveling seams in the shoulders of her dress, then pointed to the comedians. "I saw you talking to fat and skinny like you really knew them. Could you ask them to use me? I'm pretty good at pratfalls and they could work me into some business. Mr. Landau, I haven't had a day's work this week."

"And no lunch today?"

"No lunch. No nothing."

"You'll work tomorrow." Arthur extended his hand because Jean looked suspicious. "Let's eat now."

The hair fascinated him, but the girl's insistence that the shade was caused by the natural bleaching action of the sun made him smile. He had pointed out that if her explanation were the truth, she would have to spend hours each day in the sun to keep her hair the color of bleached straw.

"Okay, so I put a little blueing in the water when I wash my hair."

He was skeptical. "Is that all?"

"Look, stop looking at my dress—I know it's awful. I'm too hungry, too down in the mouth to argue, and if you want to believe what other people believe, I don't care. Matter of fact, Mr. Landau, if you buy me a steak I'll let you believe I'm a whore."

"Are you?" he asked.

She shook her head again, as if the willingness of people to believe the worst was something she had simply learned to acknowledge. "Don't you think I could've set up shop on a bed in one of the scene docks and made myself ten bucks without even trying? Believe me, Mr. Landau, I could work for Lee Francis if I wanted to. I've had offers."

"Which you didn't take."

"Which I'm gonna try not to take," she replied. "Now're you still taking me out to eat, seeing as the only thing I'm willing to share with you or anybody is a steak?"

Truth revealed the face of pathos. Under the awful make-up the girl was striking. Under the cheap dress she had a good body which she offered for pictures in the only way possible—still, she should have worn a brassiere. As they drove off the

Roach lot Arthur stared at Jean's high, firm breasts. Never before had he seen a connection between hunger and passion, but as she licked her lips in anticipation of food her nipples hardened until they were the size of marbles. But if this girl was something special, as his hunch told him, why hadn't some other salesman found her? It seemed more likely that he was wrong, that she couldn't act, that her voice was too harsh, too uncultivated to compete with the many stage professionals being brought into the city.

As an experiment, and to find someone whose advice he could almost trust, Arthur drove into the parking lot of the Green Mill and urged Jean to come along.

"How old are you?" he asked.

"I told you. Nineteen. I also told you I'm married, and as soon as I get the money I'm divorcing. Isn't this a speak?" she asked suspiciously. "I'm hungry."

"They serve food," he assured her. "And if you want a drink with your dinner it's there."

At the Green Mill, patrons with white cards were admitted to the dining room and bar and patrons with gold cards were permitted to pass through the door at the end of the bar into the small gambling room with its two crap tables, roulette wheel and bird cage. Arthur showed his gold card at the door and was disappointed that the slick-haired bouncer gave Jean only the most casual look—but it was directed at her hair. As the maitre d' showed them to a table where they could hear Fats Waller at his piano in the bar, several men at the tables nodded to Arthur and an actress waved, but no one looked twice at the girl. They probably thought he was sneaking in a matinee.

She ate ravenously, cutting and spearing and chewing pieces of steak, potatoes and tomato which she ate with little lip-smacking sounds and mews of animal pleasure. Once she paused to smile at him, breathed deeply with a hand on one breast, then returned to a strong attack on the steak. He was convinced she could be beautiful, that the hair, whether it was real or bleached with more than blueing, was original, and that she would look wonderful in a tank suit. Her voice, with its tones of harsh, common honesty, coursed shivers down his back. Mind made up, he excused himself from the table and telephoned Jim Whale. Quickly, he reported his inability to get Dorothy Mackaill, then said he wanted Whale to test another actress for the part.

"Listen, please listen," he pleaded to Whale's protests. "You want Helen to be believable? You've got Lyon and Hall, and people know who they are. But this is a picture about aviators, real planes and battles. So why not use a girl no one has seen, one who really looks as if she lived the part? Jim, let me bring her tomorrow for a test. If it's no go, it's no go."

Walking slowly back to the table, Arthur spread his hands in appeal to a phantom jury. Then he hitched at his coat, fingered his tie, and became an agent. The girl needed representation, and he would not proceed unless she agreed to this and promised to follow his advice and orders.

Because she had never been able to talk to an agent who was not a part-time pimp and producer of stag movies, she actually put aside her knife and fork, with a chunk of steak speared on the tines, and listened in wonder to the news that she was going to test the next day.

"In what?" she asked, clapping her hands. "When?"

"In a picture," he said warily. "Sometime in the afternoon. About two. I'll pick you up."

"And what'll I wear?"

"A brassiere," he said.

"I really don't need one."

"Then wear something that gives people the idea without actually showing them. And another thing"—he smiled, because he disliked hurting anyone—"just a little lipstick and nothing else. They'll make you up for the camera." His mind already had made the entry of a five-dollar tip to the Caddo make-up woman. "The important thing is to get a good night's sleep and not worry."

Jean lifted the fork, then replaced it on the plate. "You'll meet me at MGM?"

"Metropolitan Studio in Hollywood," he explained. "No, I'll pick you up. So anytime you're ready to go home . . ."

"You're really my agent?" she asked. "You want me to sign a contract?"

"We'll shake hands," Arthur explained. In all probability the girl would be unacceptable to Whale, and that would end their association. But a twinge of guilt compelled him to add, "If that's good enough for you."

"Couldn't you give me a contract? It'd mean so much," she said.

"Why?"

"Because it'll mean that you—it'll mean that I'll have confidence that you—" She paused to think of what to say. "It'll mean you don't believe I've ever gone out to the scene dock. That you're really kind. Why can't I explain it?"

"You have," he said. "I've some contract blanks in the car. Say we make it for—three years? Okay?"

She wiped at her eyes and turned away. "It sure is. I haven't been offered so much—or eaten so good—in an awful long time."

In deep now, Arthur drove Jean Harlow from Culver City to Oakhurst Drive, south of Santa Monica Boulevard, and into the maze of little streets that lay in the flatland below the Sunset Strip. He clucked sympathetically at the story the girl told him, no more nor less depressing than the hundreds he had heard, but with one major difference: the girl, her mother and stepfather had not come to Los Angeles to get into the movies, and she had only tried to get extra work because seven-fifty a day plus a box lunch was good money for interesting work that required little effort and no brains. Her mother had also gone to work when the Kansas City source of money had dried up. She had worked in several five-and-dime stores, had tried a job as cashier in a restaurant, and had failed at selling cosmetics from door to door.

"My mother has a beautiful complexion," Jean said with pride. "But she hasn't any confidence, and as soon as a door slams in her face she's through for the day."

"And your stepfather?" Arthur asked.

Jean grimaced and drew a finger across her throat. "He's a phony son of a bitch. I hate him about as much as my mother loves him. Her idea of heaven is his side of the bed."

"But why do you hate him?"

She sniffed. "Maybe you've got five thousand to invest? Or five bucks? Marino will sell you a half interest in a gold mine, silver mine, diamond mine, coal mine—you name it and he'll go out and print the stock." She sighed expressively and turned up the corners of her mouth in a wry smile. "Maybe you've got enough confidence in my future to loan me a hundred? No— make it fifty? If I don't get the job tomorrow I swear I'll go to work as a waitress and pay you back."

Fifty dollars was mentally entered in the ledger section devoted to bad debts. "Be confident," he said. "You've got the fifty."

The little gray bungalow with the green roof was home for the Bellos. Dusk moved along the street to soften the evidences of poverty, neglect, and hope so hobbled it was unable to indulge in grand, Aladdin-like sweeps of the imagination. Tired creepers climbed the broken lattices on either side of the Bello porch, and a sign that ordered ICE peered from an upper pane of a living room window. The shades in the front bedroom were pulled to the sill, but the windows were raised. Arthur accompanied Jean up the path and would have even gone into the house if they had not suddenly heard Marino's voice raised in anger. The cracked shade swayed in the slight breeze as Marino cursed Sam Harlow from hell to gone because the old bastard refused to send some money. What did he expect them to do—starve? Mama Jean was to get off her fat can immediately and write the old bastard if she knew what was good for her.

"Listen, don't I treat you right?" they heard Bello shout. "Don't I stay home with you and give you all the things you like when I ought to be out with important people? Don't think there aren't plenty of women in this town who wouldn't pay plenty for even half of what I give you."

"I'd kill myself!" they heard Mama Jean scream. "Don't let me ever catch you with another woman! I'd kill myself in front of you both!"

Jean turned to Arthur. "You still want to meet them?"

"I already have." Arthur backed down the path. "I'll pick you up at one. Be ready."

"Simple dress, face washed and just a little lipstick. If you want me to I'll buy a new bra," she said.

"Wardrobe'll lend you one if you need it," he said.

Next day he slept late, transacted some business over the telephone and convinced Jim Whale not to cancel out the test. There had to be a beginning for everyone and everything, he argued. Besides, Hughes had already scrapped more than a million dollars' worth of costs and effort for something new, so why shouldn't they be willing to test a girl who might be the answer to their prayers?

"She'll be good," Arthur promised. "Just you be fair."

As Arthur drove up Oakhurst he recognized Jean's blonde hair and saw her run down the path. He also saw the slightly heavier blonde woman and the dark, mustached man on the porch, waving to Jean to wait for them. Arthur understood and had the car moving in first gear before the girl slammed the door behind her.

"They wanted to meet you, especially Marino," Jean puffed. She smoothed her white skirt, which she wore with a white schoolgirl pullover that made her blondeness more startling. "Is my hair all right?"

"Fine. The test isn't until three o'clock, so we'll have a good lunch."

"I'm not hungry," Jean said. She pointed to a small paper valise at her feet. "I brought along an evening gown in case. That Marino"—she turned in the seat to look out of the back window of the car—"because I'm being tested he suddenly just-like-that became my business manager. And am I stupid!" she wailed. "I gave him the money to pay on the rent, because he's the man of the house, he says. And you know what he did?" she demanded. "He lost it in that card room where he always loses."

"Didn't you know he was going to do that?" he asked.

The girl closed her eyes. "I knew. But my mother began to cry that I was humiliating her lousy wop, and when she cries I just go to pieces. So I gave him the money. I must say, though," she added, "he must be becoming a better poker player, because it took him most of the night to lose the thirty. Usually he gets cleaned in less than an hour." She reached inside the sweater to adjust a strap. "I'm wearing a slip," she explained. "Honest, I would've worn a bra, but my mother just never got around to doing the laundry this week. And today it was just murder in that hell-hole I call home."

"If you want, we can stop and buy you one," Arthur said.

"Fine," Jean agreed. She continued to tug at the strap. "Usually I don't wear a slip, but wool against my boobs is just too ticklish."

☆

Chapter Seven

By 1931 the myth of Jean Harlow's discovery by the movies was ready for circulation in a conservative middle-class bible, and the September 19 issue of *The Saturday Evening Post* had an article by Frank Condon, "Kansas City Platinum," which offered an innocent, almost pastoral version of the legend:

> Not so very long ago she was a simple student. . . . a light-hearted schoolgirl, hurrying down the Boulevard with her books in a strap, peeking into shop windows and considering the general wisdom of having a chocolate ice-cream soda with vanilla cream. And now see what happened. . . .
>
> All the while Miss Harlow had this strange Kansas City hair, the like of which can be found on neither land nor sea. A director saw her, all of a summer's day. She was standing outside Kehoe's Drug Store, not far from the high school, hunting for a dime, thinking of nothing in the world but ice-cream soda in a more or less chocolate condition. The director sat up and said to his assistant: "Sweet spirits of Pomona, look at that hair! Go on over, Joe, and ask that girl would she like to bust into the movies, and get her name right."
>
> "Yeh, but that ain't no real hair," he re-

sponded gloomily. "I seen a lot of hair in my day and they ain't no hair like that."

Idling there in front of Kehoe's Drug Store, Miss Harlow continued to hunt for the dime, never conscious of the fact that she was being shanghaied into the fourth greatest industry. Her hat happened to be off at the moment, at home under some newspapers, and the silvery plume was visible for blocks. Joe stepped up and the thing was done.

The Condon history sufficed for the primitives of 1931, but within a year, when platinum blonde hair became an international trademark, the star required a more elaborate legend. So reporters, columnists, and staff drum-beaters transmuted leaden facts into myths of gold, and if details of divinity were lacking they were invented and presented with solemn but happy avouchments, to give to the millions of Americans whose only reading was comic strips, sports, movie news and sensational headines the details required to make them worshipfully proud of the actress they had deified. Constant repetition of the myth gave it the status of apocrypha, and constant citation of apocrypha gave it the divinity of gospel. And the name Harlow did sound enough like harlot to make of her the All-American dream Magdalene.

For students of history the following vital statistics may be instructive, since they appear to chart a line of evolution in defiance of all natural laws:

Jean Harlow	34	24	35
Marilyn Monroe	39	24	37
Jayne Mansfield	40	19	39

Great Britain has offered as evidence its share of well-upholstered, décolleté blondes: Sabrina and Diana Dors have proved themselves worthy of being considered as international competitors for the position of Telstar weather forecasters, but the awesome, thunderhead configuration of June Wilkinson, a British actress who has appeared in such cinema milestones as *Thunder in the Sun* and *Macumba Love,* offers a physiological challenge which may stand for some time, for Miss Wilkinson, also known as "The Bosom," measures in at 43–22–36.

If the Blonde Bombshell's endowments seem to shrink before this impressive march of mammillary history, one must remember her diminutive height, her fragile bones and small ribcage, and her lack of competition in an age when such cantilevered construction was reserved for dowagers and ducks.

At two-thirty, after a leisurely lunch, Arthur brought Jean to the stage where the Caddo Company was shooting. A distraught Jim Whale asked the agent to be patient, because the day's work had not gone well and he was anxious to get some solid footage of the scene in the mess hall somewhere in France. Whale was introduced to Harlow, shook hands with the nervous girl and was gone before Arthur could ask when the test would be made. It was almost six before Whale ordered the lights dimmed and Gaetano Gaudio, the head cameraman, prepared to remove his film from the camera.

"Put the film back," Arthur shouted. He pointed at Jean, who looked as if she'd been raped and left far from home. "Just a couple of minutes and you'll know this girl is the answer to your prayers. A couple of minutes," he repeated. "And we're tired, too."

In resigned silence Whale nodded, Gaudio loaded two cameras so the actress could be photographed from two angles, and Arthur ordered Jean to change into her evening gown. In a few minutes, lipstick freshened, cheeks rouged, false beauty mark in place, Jean entered a doorway on cue—and Arthur groaned. Her gown was awful, too tight across the bosom and with an impossible train that made her about as sexy as a dustpan.

Arthur ran quickly to stand before one of the cameras to wave his arms and plead with Gaudio for just another minute, because the dress and make-up were all wrong. Jean was in tears as Arthur removed the beauty mark and ordered her to scrub her face and put on the dressing gown and lipstick—nothing else. The test was made at a dressing table hastily brought on stage, where Jean spoke, smoked and nervously touched her eyes. About three minutes of film was shot, and after it was developed and run, Jim Whale agreed the girl might be all right for the role. True, her voice was harsh and scratchy, which might have been caused by nerves, but the test revealed a pretty girl whose facial features were good, whose albino hair was different, and who projected the quality of a girl who had become a hooker that very day and, anxious to keep her place in the parlor, was willing to do or attempt anything.

"I'll say yes," Whale told Arthur, "but you know it's still up to the boss."

Hughes saw the test at the studio, grimaced, then listened without expression as Arthur raved about the girl and the good impression she had made on Ben Lyon and James Hall.

"In my opinion she's nix," Hughes said at last. "But I'm making a picture about airplanes, not broads. How's she in the bomb department?"

"Big enough, believe me," Arthur said. "And isn't her hair beautiful? And different? Give her a chance," he begged. "Look at the test again and tell me if she doesn't look like a good kid."

"But we don't want a good kid," said Whale, taking his cue from Hughes' apparent lack of interest. "We want a pig."

"And what did she look like when she came out in that evening gown?" Arthur demanded of Whale. "She can be a combination of good kid and tramp. Why not? Isn't that what every man hopes he'll find some day?" Perceiving that he had found the right argument, Arthur paused for a moment. "She's a broad and willing to put out for the fliers. But she knows that after she's made them forget the war for a little while, they still have to take off and they might never come back. So her heart's breaking while she's screwing them."

Hughes nodded several times before he turned to Whale. "Think you can get a performance out of her?"

Whale also nodded. "I guess so."

"Then use her," Hughes said. "How much?" he asked Arthur.

"A little more than half of what Greta was getting," Arthur said. "Fifteen hundred a week for six weeks minimum."

Hughes shook his head. "I ought to keep you around for laughs. I'll give her fifteen hundred for the whole six weeks, and don't argue." His tone was clipped. "And she signs with Caddo."

"For how long?" Arthur said. "And does she get star billing under Lyon and Hall?"

"Why not?" Hughes agreed. "She's under contract for three years."

"At how much?"

"Two hundred a week if she's not working before a camera. Two-fifty if she does. There'll be fifty-dollar raises for the other years." Hughes stood to terminate the discussion. "See that she gets to work on time. When'll you be ready to use her?" he asked Whale.

"Next week," the director said. "Which'll give her time for wardrobe and time to learn her lines. We'll show as much as we can get away with."

The actress wept when Arthur told her the good news and wept more when she told him that immediately, right now, she had to have five hundred dollars because she had not told him the entire truth: the rent was really three months in arrears, they owed the butcher and the baker, the phone had been cut off the week before, her mother needed clothes and shoes, and Marino had his two good suits in the cleaner's and couldn't get them out. And Jean owed almost a hundred dollars that she had borrowed a dollar or two at a time from other extras.

"I'll pay you back a hundred dollars a week," Jean promised. "And I'll sign a paper that you handle the money to keep Marino on the sidelines. You'll take out your twenty-five for commission plus a hundred a week and that'll still leave me a hundred and a quarter," she concluded in wonder. "That's more money than I've had for years. And if he'll really pay me two hundred a week even when I'm not working, then you're covered."

"You've got the money," Arthur said.

Jean sighed. "Now if I could only get rid of the headache. Marino," she explained. "Wait'll he finds out."

If Arthur had not seen the unkempt yard or heard the disembodied voices through the bedroom window, he would have thought better of Mama Jean and Marino when he drove Jean home after the contract with Caddo had been signed. Jean's mother appeared to be a pleasant, overwhelmed woman, and Marino gushed friendliness and offers of cooperation—but only, he swore, if Arthur wanted them. The yard of the little house had been swept, the dead and dying plants had been removed from the porch, and the front rooms of the rented bungalow smelled clean. A fragrant pot of coffee percolated on the range. Marino wore one of the two suits redeemed from the cleaner's, frowned sternly at his pocket watch and looked at the telephone as if to keep it from ringing, no matter how important its business might be.

Jean's mother had visited the beauty parlor and had bought a new dress and shoes, and Arthur was impressed with her good appearance. Stars had parents, and some of them, like remittance relatives, had to be kept at a distance and bribed never to visit the movie capital. But it looked as though Jean would not have this problem, and Arthur only wished that the girl he had just signed for a lead in what was bound to be one of the biggest pictures of all time, if it was ever finished, spoke as well as her mother. Mama Jean's voice was well modulated and precise, and Marino's accent was so elegant that Arthur wondered if they *were* the two people he had heard in the bedroom.

Determined to be fair and firm, Arthur stressed how important it was for the Bellos to remain in the background, not give interviews and not become standard movie parents who made pests of themselves on a set. And he also told them the most important contribution they could make was to be patient, to demand little and expect less, because one picture wasn't a career. Jean was understandably nervous, overwhelmed and weak with exhilaration.

"No one'll know what Jean's getting because I won't tell them," Arthur explained. "So in a couple of days you'll start getting calls and visits from people who'll want to sell you everything from sheep dogs to yachts. People'll want to steer you onto big estates and someone else'll come around as exclusive agent for the Russian crown jewels. Then people will try to borrow money. Others'll ask you to give it to them outright." He looked directly at Marino, who opened and shut his watchcase in a sharp series of snaps. "Tailors'll be inviting you to come in for custom fittings and someone'll offer you a deal if you'll take two elephants instead of one. Buy nothing, please."

"And we're to go on living here?" Mama Jean looked at the worn furnishings and chipped linoleum rug. "Won't Jean have to entertain?"

"Not yet."

"Won't Mr. Hughes want to come here?"

Arthur smiled patiently at their concern. "If he did he'd never notice. You'll move when the time comes. Meanwhile, there isn't any real money, and Jean's asked me to handle her finances for her."

Mama Jean kept Marino seated at her side. "You're not taking Jean away from us?"

"Jean isn't leaving you now or ever. But she has to concentrate on making good. So a good home life'll help as much as luck."

They looked sad when he left.

The first day's shooting began disastrously. Because lines had raced through her head all night, Jean was unusually nervous. Although she knew every line of her part on the way to the studio, when she had dressed and appeared for her first scene with Ben Lyon and James Hall in the London barroom, she could not remember a sequence. The scene called for Jean to be half drunk and breezy, to appear amiably amoral rather than immoral. At last, when Jean felt she was able to remember her lines and rehearsed movements, her stilted interpretation compelled Whale to order the set closed for the day.

Desperately, Arthur suggested that one way to get the performance the director required was to get Jean really a little drunk. Whale stared, groaned, then agreed, and at the end of the day's shooting told Arthur they would keep the girl; not that she was the kind of professional he had in mind, but the picture had to be finished. The next morning after Whale saw the rushes he was happier with the scene. Jean saw herself on the screen, cried a little for being so awful, and promised she would do better.

Shooting continued close to the projected schedule. The actors around her were pleasant, but the crew took an immediate liking to Jean because she was sincerely grateful for their good wishes. She was beautiful in stills, but the one most important scene in her apartment remained to be photographed, and Jean began to lose confidence.

In Moncure March's censorious letter of March 23, 1954, to *Look* (March was protesting Stephen White's article about Howard Hughes, and its assignment of the dialogue credit for

Hell's Angels to Hughes), he reminisced at length about Harlow: "After Hughes had decided to give Harlow the part, it was up to James Whale to get a performance out of her, and this took all the skill and patience he had. . . . Harlow was quite aware of her deficiencies, and a lot of the time it must have seemed like a nightmare to her. Even her ability to be seductive was questioned, and in one scene which demanded considerable allure, she could not seem to please Mr. Whale. 'Tell me,' she said, with desperate earnestness, 'tell me exactly how you want me to do it.' Mr. Whale, his patience sorely tried, said, 'My dear girl, I can tell you how to be an actress but I cannot tell you how to be a woman.' "

Ben Lyon and James Hall were patient with Jean, and the working crew continued to give her their confidence. Her performance in the scene where she offered to take off her black negligee and change into something more comfortable so pleased Whale that he decided to reshoot some of her first scenes and improve the over-all quality of her performance.

The picture opened in June, 1930, at Grauman's Chinese Theater, and Jean received billing after Ben Lyon and James Hall. Daily *Variety* of June 4, 1930, devoted almost two full pages to their review of the film and called it the biggest air picture ever filmed and a natural for the censors.

A significant, portentous part of *Variety's* review observed that "The picture is to the brim with sex. It won't teach the modern youngsters anything, but it will certainly give 'em an idea of themselves in action." Of the leading lady's performance the reviewer said, "Jean Harlow wafts plenty of 'that' across the sheet and dresses to accentuate it. It doesn't make much difference what degree of talent she possesses here, for the boys are apt to go in an uproar over this girl who is the most sensuous figure in front of a camera in some time. She'll probably always have to play these kind of roles, but nobody ever starved possessing what she's got."

"It" was now "that." Hughes was satisfied with his picture,

and theater owners were eager to book the air epic because close-ups of the new hot number were more sensational than the planes. Why, she had a pair as big as the zeppelin in the film. Millions of American males had been knocked out by the Harlow look, the Harlow bombs. Every review of the film mentioned Harlow, her rich bosom, her startling, unusual blondeness and the bedroom huskiness of her voice, which gave stirring authenticity to her role of generous amateur whore. But the reviews also stimulated the antagonism of local evil-sniffers. There was a twofold result: people wanted to see the picture, but producers were afraid to employ Harlow because her appearance in another film might get it banned in too many key cities.

From the point of view of official and unofficial censors in all cities, Hollywood studios culled the most sensational, depraved headlines for plots to convert them into pictures that portrayed the seamiest, most disgraceful aspects of American life to all the world, and it was difficult to accuse a newspaper or civic body of a narrow patriotism if it protested a plethora of films that adulated the gangster, the crooked lawyer and politician, and the prostitute. There could be no reasonable argument for pictures that portrayed people engaged in senseless, brutal violence and flagrant adultery, pictures made to scoff at and ridicule American social myths and traditions. Sex and violence existed, and it was acknowledged that their principal purveyors were gangsters; but was that an excuse for showing this aspect of American industry to all the world—or even to ourselves? Nevertheless, in 1930 Hollywood's combined studios had enough gangster pictures in production to assure a release of fifty such films in 1931, so that the roar of bombs and stutter of submachine guns was heard throughout all the land. And where films had gangsters they also had gun molls, and where they had gun molls they had significant bedroom scenes, so that pictures tended to recapitulate each other and were distinguished only by variations in cast, not plot. According to the movies, gangsters got the best women and all the other rich fruits of the garden.

Hollywood, like any other industry, analyzes its markets and projects its product, and if gangster films were selling tickets, gangster pictures were going to be made; however, some anti-censorship insurance could be built into the product. Although some producers talked of using Jean Harlow and even communicated with the Caddo Corporation, the ire which this new star aroused among the Grundys and Comstocks decided movie-makers to cast less publicized stars in their seamy pictures. What did it matter if *The Literary Digest* reported that a national poll taken in 1930 placed Jean Harlow seventeenth in a list of the hundred best-known people in the world? Harlow was still an unknown quantity as an actress: she had lovely breasts and a great figure and looked as if she would perform as well as she looked, but her part in *Hell's Angels* could not be used as a measure of ability. Talkies were still new, experienced, proven actresses were available, and it was wiser to think of someone else for the part of a loose woman in a black negligee.

Arthur wrote to Hughes when he could no longer reach him on the phone and pleaded with the producer to start another picture with Jean, to keep her before an appreciative public. The letters were never answered, but through an intermediary Arthur was told that if he could arrange for Jean to go on a personal appearance tour in conjunction with the showing of *Hell's Angels,* and if the tour were successful, Hughes might put her in another picture. Ben Piazza and L. K. Sidney of the New York office of Loew's Theaters arranged Jean's tour —and she fell on her ass in Pittsburgh.

In 1954 Sam Bischoff at RKO Studios thought of making a screen biography of Jean Harlow, and on May 15, 1954, he received a letter about this project from Nils Thor Granlund— N.T.G.—a long-time impresario and working master of ceremonies of girlie shows. With good reason N.T.G. believed that he belonged in any history of Harlow, and much of his letter to Bischoff is interesting.

My dear Sam:

Congratulations on acquiring the Jean Harlow story.

I would very much like to work with you on this deal. I played a very important part in appearing for eight weeks in theaters with Jean. This was the turning point in her life.

It happened this way: I had seen Jean Harlow in "Hell's Angels" and thought she was the greatest I had ever seen. I had up to that time toured the Loew Theaters from Toronto to New Orleans with movie stars, individually and by trainloads, making personal appearances and opening new theaters, but no star affected me as did Harlow.

So when Charley Moskowitz phoned me and told me to go down to the Mastbaum Theater in Philadelphia and see Harlow, with a view to working with her on a stage show, it was the thrill of my life.

The situation was this: After "Hell's Angels" . . . . She was getting $250 a week from Hughes, and not working. She was given a ten-week deal, at $3500 per week, four weeks in Warner Theaters, and six in Loew Theaters.

She laid a big egg in the Warner houses, including Pittsburgh, where Dick Powell worked with her a week. Reports came to Nick Schenck that she was terrible, and he called on me. I understand that Nick or Marvin Schenck tried to buy her contract for $5,000. At any rate, she was a big flop at the box office, and the act she did was something awful.

I went down to Philadelphia, saw her show, which was worse than I expected.

The manager took me backstage to her dressing room, introduced us, and left. Jean flopped on a couch and broke into almost hysterical weeping.

She then told me that the end of the world, it seemed, had come to her. Pictures had turned her down, her act was a flop. She figured on $3500 a week for six weeks, but her debts were tremendous. After that, she thought, she would be out of a job.

I cheered her up, and two days later we opened at the Loew's Metropolitan, Brooklyn. The act was a riot, the crowds were tremendous. A week later we opened at Loew's State on Broadway. Again, a riot. Her six weeks were extended to ten, and later I went to Loew's Cleveland with her.

On the opening matinee in Cleveland, I asked Jack Dempsey, who had just lost his championship, to meet her, as he had been in town for an exhibition bout. She gave him a typical Harlow kiss, Jack collapsed, and Jean counted 17 over him. It was terrific. . . .

At the beginning of the tour, people who professed to be Jean's best friends were delighted at her failure; the thirty-five hundred dollars a week she was to receive for her personal appearances was paid directly to the Caddo Corporation, and the best Arthur Landau could do was convince the corporation executives that Jean was entitled to receive at least the two hundred and fifty dollars a week she would get if she were appearing before a camera. As another concession, the Caddo Corporation agreed to rent a wardrobe for Jean's appearances, but Jean would be personally responsible for the care of the dresses and furs. It was impossible for Arthur to accompany Jean on the personal appearance tour, and her twice- and thrice-daily collect-telephone calls of despair—audiences hated her, people actually laughed, Mama Jean was an idiot and Marino insisted on room service at the best hotels—prompted Arthur to tell Jean that she was not to worry, that he was willing to advance her up to five thousand dollars to cover the expenses of having her family along, but that she was not to tell them of this financial reserve.

Aware that new, professional material had to be written for Jean, and informed that N.T.G. had gone to Philadelphia to see the show, Arthur telephoned Granlund and told him to get some sharp writers to can questions and answers Jean might use in interviews. Max Lief, Edgar Allan Wolfe, and Al Boas were assigned to write material suitable for Jean, and N.T.G. worked out a new stage presentation. The actress stood on a dark stage and the lighting built slowly until a sudden fanfare revealed Jean in a bright spotlight. She wore a shimmering, form-fitting white gown, cut low in the bosom. Women stared at her light shining hair; men gawked at her firm breasts rising in joyous excitement. A claque was unnecessary because the applause was deafening when N.T.G. introduced "America's Blonde Bombshell." The bright little monologue written for Jean's fifteen minutes on stage suited her appearance, heightened the sensual illusion, and gave her the air of an accomplished performer. By the time Jean and Granlund arrived in Brooklyn, her act was polished and her brief monologue about airplanes and their joysticks delighted audiences.

One of Jean's most successful little jokes was found in a copy of a short-lived campus humor magazine. Jean would tell of visiting a local airport, and of a little old lady at her side who pointed overhead to call out, "Look at the mail plane!"

And Jean would simper, "No, dear, those are just the landing wheels."

As Jean's tour became more successful, a variety of publicity releases informed the American public that Jean always slept in the nude, that the touch of fur excited her, that Havelock Ellis was rewriting his sexological studies to focus them about the new Venus, that her Hollywood bed had been designed as a replica of the scallop shell in the Botticelli painting of the birth of Venus, and that at least twenty men, determined to be faithful in mind and body to Harlow, had undergone castration to make them useless to all other women. Young men were hired to spy on Harlow from nearby roofs, to attempt entries into her room through transoms, fire-escapes, even dumbwaiters. One college boy was delivered in a wardrobe trunk. Another had himself sealed in a specially constructed envelope and delivered by Postal Telegraph. A bootlegging mob in Detroit voted Jean Harlow the girl they would most like to hijack.

Writers turned out reams of bright answers to practically any question a reporter might conceivably ask, and Jean learned them well. And reporters, delighted at her witty, mildly lewd wisecracks, covered her press conferences enthusiastically for a public that never suspected the gems were not her own. (In a later day such scripts were written for another sex queen, Marilyn Monroe, and quoted just as widely by the press. Asked whether she had had anything on when she posed for her famous nude calendar, Marilyn—and her writers—replied, "Only the radio.")

At one such gathering, a reporter asked, "Miss Harlow, are today's young women immodest?"

Jean shook her head. "An immodest young woman is someone who would look better covered up."

"Miss Harlow, do you think sex activity outside of marriage is increasing among women?" another asked.

She shrugged and leaned forward for the photographers

to get a good shot of her breasts, which seemed to move with unusual freedom. "It would be sort of difficult for it to increase among women alone—wouldn't it?"

"Jean, would you advise a young woman to take a lover instead of a husband?"

"High enough?" she asked, raising her skirt. "To answer your question, I'd advise her to take what she can get—and to keep on shopping."

"Do you think a woman ought to forgive an unfaithful husband?"

Jean pouted, then looked astonished. "I can't imagine that happening to me."

"Some critics say you aren't a real actress," someone called from the rear. "How about that?"

"If audiences like you, you don't have to be an actress," was her answer, and it contained a truth that had made stars before Jean Harlow and will make them for years to come.

"What do you think of _____?" a reporter asked about an actress who had said that Jean was on her studio's layroll.

Jean spread her hands in a gesture of sympathy. "When snakes get drunk they see her." She laughed at their expressions of delight. "Too bad you can't print what she said about me and what I've just said about her. Poor thing," she continued, "no matter how she feels about me—I'll try to see her on visiting days."

"How about _____?" another asked. "She said some pretty sharp things about you."

"I know," Jean agreed. "She has a fine mind—but the rest of her sort of spoils things."

"Why do you think audiences like you, Miss Harlow?"

Jean winked. "The men like me because I don't wear a brassiere. And the women like me because I don't look like a girl who would steal a husband. At least not for long."

"But would you steal a husband, Miss Harlow?"

"Wouldn't that be like shoplifting in a secondhand store?"

"Are you wearing a brassiere now, Miss Harlow?"

"That sounds like a nearsighted question."

"Jean, how do you like to wake up in the morning?"

She yawned and smiled. "I like to wake up feeling a new man."

At this moment Jean's mother arrived to place her arm around Jean and say The Baby just had to rest. "You're tired and must go to bed."

Jean stood, stretched to make her tight dress fit like a wet skin and looked mournfully at the reporters and photographers. "That's one of the troubles with American women," she said to round off the afternoon. "They're always going to bed, but for the wrong reasons."

N.T.G. telephoned Arthur that people were reversing Howard Hughes' opinion—they were buying tickets for *Hell's Angels* to see the broad, not the planes. And Granlund also told Arthur that Jean Harlow was the girl to replace Clara Bow. "She doesn't have to act or try to be sexy," he said. "She *is* sex, and nothing sells like that."

Hollywood's Grail-quest was once again successful. Almost overnight, Jean Harlow had become a sex-goddess, an exotic confection of flesh, imagination and legend that had never existed before the invention of motion pictures and that has occurred only once in each generation since.

From Edison's invention of the Kinetoscope in 1889 to *The Great Train Robbery* of 1903, movies were a lower class entertainment of short films that averaged about ten minutes in length, with unsophisticated subject matter devoted to travelogues, animals, primitive stories of violence and broad comedies. As creative techniques grew and it was soon evident that more complex stories could be enacted on the larger-than-life screen, sex raised her skirt and lowered her bodice for everyone to get a good look. The search, more intensive and better organized than that undertaken by the Argonauts for the

Golden Fleece, was always successful; and Mount Veneris in Hollywood was a sacred shrine that attracted nymphs and nymphets anxious to serve as dedicated novitiates to Astarte.

C. A. Lejeune, in her article *Sex and the Movies* (1940) pointed out that as early as 1909 German film producers had realized the screen was ideally suited for stories of sex to be related straightforwardly or by means of symbolism. Several years later the potential was fully recognized and realized by American film companies as they developed women capable of appearing in uncluttered sex stories; symbolism and other artistries were left to foreigners and their primitive assembly lines.

In the history of the movies, from inception through 1937, there were three important sex personalities. In the year of Jean Harlow's birth, the first of these personalities slithered into the camera angle.

Theda Bara—her name a simple anagram for "death" and "Arab," both evocative of the mysterious, sinful East—was reputed to be the daughter of a French painter and his Arabian mistress. She delighted men of weak character by showing how difficult it was to resist the lascivious "vamp," a revelation that should not have come as a shock to any student of the American male's moral fiber. Most American men of weak character figured that they were damned anyway, so they might as well look forward to a hell that was pleasant, cozy and filled with the proper people. And the most prominent contemporary citizen of this select underworld, furnished as a Turkish corner with bearskin rugs for bareskinned love, was Theda Bara.

Movies that featured this wild-haired siren had greatest appeal when their backgrounds, sets, and *dramatis personae* were of the idle rich, royalty established by divine fiat, or merchant princes. To the man in the ten-cent seat, the movies for the first time gave him—in films such as *A Fool There Was, East Lynne, The Vixen, Her Double Life,* and *The Tiger Woman*—intimate access to castles, palaces, mansions and town houses. Movies made it possible for him to view close-up the costly furnishings, the bibelots, the dress and jewels of nabobs and their consorts. A dime admission made the man in the seat a secret, intimate spectator of the most private lives, lusts and raptures of the rich.

Naturally, the lusts of the rich were costly, too; legend was filled with tales of Cyprians whose price was more than a thousand ships or the towers of Troy. Thus, when Theda Bara, under contract to the Fox Company, played a select courtesan of history or mythology, she was not only gilded, lacquered, and garnished in super-colossal fashion, but she was dramatically established as a creature whose favors for the night were pegged at a price somewhat more than the cost in lives required to build the pyramid of Cheops and very much more than the annual budget of a fair-sized booming American city.

A fatal female, Theda Bara was presented in thirty-five millimeter as the crowning achievement of sensuality. This most exotic, mysterious, death-pale vamp, with her long hair, kohled, burning eyes and cruel mouth, had ruined countless titans of industry and peers of empire. Each of these urbane, worldly, cynical, jaded aristocrats, weary of and unmoved by other women, these absolute rulers of feudal fiefs and mercantile empires, knew that Theda was heartless, cruel, mercenary. They knew she despised those whom she relieved of honor, wealth, fame and fortune, before permitting them to expire after the most glorious of little deaths. They were fools who thought they heard the heavenly music of the spheres in the rustle of bedsheets, fools to be kissed during the course of a thousand and one secret delights known only to Theda and experienced in a single night of eternity before being cast carelessly into Theda's private boneyard. Destroyed beyond redemption, each of these ruined demigods gloried in his fall, accomplished in chambers reminiscent of Poe's *Ligeia*—a swan-boat bed with silken sheets so perfumed they made laundresses lovesick, a cloth-of-gold tent in the garden of Scheherazade, a barge whose poop was beaten gold, with sails of purple filled with scented winds—ah!—these were the heavenly, sensual hells viewed by the sighing, itching man in the ten-cent seat, for whom Theda and hell for a dime was more of a bargain than the best five-cent cigar. For Theda Bara a man would sacrifice his home, integrity, country—even the true-blue love of blonde pioneer women who had endured the heat of desert and cold of mountain passes to bring fat-fry cooking as far west as Catalina Island. Theda made every man an Everyman who occupied the swanboat bed, the silken tent, the barge of Nepenthe. And the beauty of it all was, for another dime he could peep and imagine and identify himself again as the fortunate sojourner in the Bower of Bliss.

Toward the end of her career Theda was costumed as a sensual sleepwalker, so her influence on the styling of street wear was negligible. Although women hated Theda enough to stone her, they never considered her to be a national threat, for she preyed only upon the very rich for her unhealthy triumphs, and most people at that time were not even moderately well-off.

For about three years after Sarajevo, Theda Bara, the goddess of sin, sex and death, officiated on earth as high priestess of the beast with two backs. She might have wielded influence after the United States proved its normalcy by electing Warren G. Harding as its president, but in 1920 she insisted, or may have been persuaded, to appear in a play. *The Blue Flame* was aptly named, for it proved to be Theda's funeral pyre. The reviews of her performance were disastrous—and Theda Bara's career was as dead as Woodrow Wilson's dream of the role the United States would play in the League of Nations.

However, what anyone else can do, Americans will invariably attempt to prove they can do better. Theda Bara was American, but this and her real name—Theodosia Goodman—were studio secrets. Until she was no longer slobbered over. It was now time to institute a quest for another woman to be identified with sex, and this time it would be a purely home-grown variety.

In 1920, the search went into high gear. The eighteenth amendment had just been passed, and now there was a law that anyone could break. The new personification of sex would have to be an image of lawlessness made good-natured, wholesome and attractive—in other words, American—and would have to know—no kidding around—all there was to know—you could bet your sweet life on that—about contemporary American love.

Poor Theda. To the Twenties, the decade of jazz, prohibition and emancipation from Puritan restraint, the pseudo-Arabian import was really a scream. On the other hand, America's new sex tootsie was as new as the night's batch of bathtub gin, as shiny as the firehouse-red roadster just driven from the showroom floor. Effervescent, giddy, with rolled-down hose to show her bee's knees, the new all-collegiate heroine drank, smoked, made love in cars and was as happy-snappy as bubble-gum. Taking note, the movie industry offered to the enthusiastic public its contemporary crap-shooting Aphrodite: Clara Bow, the "It" girl.

Boyish in physique, disproportioned by the new silhouette which flattened and almost eliminated the fine callipygian roundness of women, Clara Bow was associated with flip young men who drove fast cars and played kazoos and polo and tennis and ukuleles with cavalier facility. These young men wore raccoon coats and battered felt hats and were supported in excitingly alcoholic, collegiate-country club idleness by indulgent, stock-market-rich parents.

An ideal American product, Clara never took money from men nor accepted *really* costly gifts or engagement rings snatched from the fingers of heartbroken girls. But taking her out for fun and frolic was expensive, so she was still an upper-class date, far beyond the economic reach of ninety per cent of the male population. Then, there was the very real problem of age. Theda Bara, with her incense and musk personality, could be identified as an older, wiser woman, and if she were loved by a much younger man, a place could be found for him in the assemblage of older fools. But Clara was young and portrayed a girl in her late teens—occasionally she might be twenty, but that was as old as she ever became—so she could only be loved or romanced or seduced by men up to thirty-five. Men in their forties and beyond could only be considered as slobbering, evil lechers deserving of the horsewhip if they made love to Clara or any other college girl.

For everyone knew, because the movies were so written, that Clara might be a little wild, but at heart she was a good, patty-cake American kid. She might go joyriding, dive into fountains, laugh wildly in imitation of Zelda Fitzgerald and wink an okay at being invited to an apartment to see a collection of nonexistent etchings; once in the apartment Clara could be counted on to flop on the sofa and start sucking on a gin bottle, a social act that preserved her virtue. But if Clara proved to be a *demi-vierge* teaser with fancy garters, she also revealed herself to be a good girl, and this revelation was accepted and cheered by all clean-cut, happy-go-lucky football heroes, flaming youths, and their parents, for virginity in a bride was still an important norm of middle-class American culture.

Women were annoyed by Clara, for she had no salutary impact on fashion and her idea of love was a nervous spasm; by this time women conversant with Freud and Judge Ben Lindsey were certain they could achieve more. And a sloppy girl like Clara—chomping gum and swinging her beads as she swished her hips and stomped around in unhooked galoshes—was not an ornament to any downstairs room in a well-ordered home.

The addition of sound to sight brought an end to "It."

Clara was unceremoniously dumped from the roadster and told to walk home. No matter what direction she chose, it led to oblivion.

In 1929 Clara Bow made one of her last pictures, *Saturday Night Kid,* with James Hall and Jean Arthur as the feature players. Jean Harlow, nineteen years old and in pictures since she was sixteen, played a minor role as Hazel, a salesgirl in Ginsberg's Department Store. Her performance received no notice in the reviews, but her day was soon to come; she was to be the third of the American sex goddesses.

But the myth of Harlow, as developed, poses an interesting question: Why, at a time when the economic fabric had come apart at the seams and there seemed no possible way to stop the steady trickle of soup along breadlines, there was a national need for heroines and goddesses born of wealth, offers a nice problem for social psychologists and historians. And why, in 1962, at a time of full employment and high national income, when home swimming pools had become commonplace, the nation's current sex symbol, Marilyn Monroe, had to be presented as a girl of poorest circumstances—even if they were true—also offers the opportunity for productive speculation. Could it be that sociological opposites attract? It seems absurdly simple, but there may be no other answer.

The psychological and biographical parallels between Jean Harlow and Marilyn Monroe are striking. Both sex symbols made their marks in the concrete pavement court of Grauman's Chinese Theater and both blondes co-starred in their last pictures with Clark Gable, although Marilyn Monroe finished *The Misfits* and Jean Harlow's role in *Saratoga* was completed by doubles.

Both actresses had no more than tenth grade educations, and at sixteen both made marriages of immediate convenience: Jean Harlow married to get out of school and Marilyn Monroe married to avoid being returned to an orphanage. Harlow's second marriage was to a man granted by mythmakers the status of an intellectual, but Monroe's third marriage was to a genuine intellectual who did not require publicity or movie magazine authentication to prove his claim. Both women had problems with their mothers, both had difficulty in talking about their personal lives, and both memorized a fund of bright, risqué replies to make their interviews quotable. Both actresses were legends in their lifetimes; both were light, luminous heroines, usually virtuous but living in the darker shadow of sex.

The most striking similarity was that both women had some ambitions to be accepted as actresses; both were bewildered and hurt that sex, not ability, had made them important, and both hated and feared the emphasis placed on their bodies.

Marilyn Monroe died, most probably by suicide, on August 5, 1962. On August 6, Kim Novak, another blonde star associated with sex, had a television interview with Walter Cronkite of C.B.S., and a portion of the interview was repeated on Charles Collingwood's *Eyewitness* of August 10. The pertinent portion of Kim Novak's observations on the death of Marilyn Monroe was that any actress chosen for the sex build-up had to suffer agonizing indignity and corrosive emotional trauma. The publicity director of Miss Novak's studio had told her that she, Kim, was nothing more than "a piece of meat . . . that she was never to consider herself as more than this. . . ." She continued: "the studio attitude of sales, of bold criticism is designed to hurt and injure the ego. . . . I'm not opposed to sincere criticism . . . but the purpose of the criticism is crass commercialism. . . . and the worst part is that you're treated that way. . . . they are overdoing it and seem to delight in cutting you down. . . . it seems deliberate although they would say it's to keep you from getting a swelled head. . . . but I think it's their attempt to starve you in the heart. . . ."

Chapter Eight

The personal appearances might have gone on for at least ten more weeks, but Arthur used the notices in weekly *Variety* and local papers to sell the studios on a new fact of life: Jean was the greatest blonde package in all history, and the tour had given her poise, polish and the ability to deliver lines and a performance on schedule. All in all, Arthur succeeded magnificently: five pictures starring Jean Harlow were released in 1931.

Iron Man, for Universal Productions, was a fight story, and of Jean's performance *Variety* said, "Miss Harlow typifies a Broadway moll who . . . by no means can be classified as a good actress here. Woefully lacking in several spots but will likely aid the male reaction to the film with her proverbial low cut and flimsy raiment."

This film was followed by Warner Brothers' *Public Enemy,* now standard afternoon fare of independent television stations, and still an exciting story despite changing tastes. But Harlow's performance is a strong reason for youngsters to be quizzical of the enthusiasms of their elders.

Discounting the first shots of Jean Harlow on the sidewalk, where she is dressed in a fashion that must excite contemporary laughter instead of libido, her interpretation of whatever she is supposed to be defies adequate description. She claims to come from Texas, but her diction runs the gamut of pronunciation from Woolworth counter clerk to what she imagined would be proper for a woman loaded with diamonds and kept at the Ritz. As a blonde, easily kept, the psychological lesson she appears to teach is that if a man hoped to go to bed with someone like Harlow he would first have to become a gangster. *The New York Times* notes that "The acting throughout is interesting, with the exception of Jean Harlow, who essays the role of a gangster's mistress." *Variety,* the showbiz paper, was more critical. "The types are excellent, but Miss Harlow better hurry and do something about her voice. She doesn't get the best of it alongside of the Misses Clarke and Blondell, who can troupe." After the reviews several Hollywood snipers suggested to Arthur that he might make some arrangement to have Greta Nissen dub the voice of his blonde freak.

"Tits are tits, Arthur," one of his friends said. "But the best of them can't speak. And if Harlow did have a talking tit, people wouldn't expect it to win an elocution contest. But we've got a right to expect more of a voice."

Instead of arguing, Arthur slotted Jean for a film at MGM, the studio that polished actresses until they shone as stars. In *The Secret Six* Jean received fourth billing, beneath Wallace Beery, Lewis Stone and John Mack Brown—but above Clark Gable and Ralph Bellamy. Beery was always able to separate the expansive, good-humored bearishness of his screen characterizations from his personal life, where he permitted himself to relax by being tight-fisted, morose and unpleasant. He disliked Harlow at sight, took every occasion to insult her, and finally, when he could no longer stand for her performance as a gangland moll, told Jean that as far as he was concerned she was just a pain in the kehokas, and the next time her little wop of a father tried to put the arm on him for a loan he was going to break it off and ram it up his rear. Jean fled from the set, screaming all the way to her dressing room that Beery was a mean old son of a bitch whose grave she'd love to piss on.

The picture was finished in this spirit of theatrical camaraderie. Although Jean made other pictures with Wallace

Beery, her cold dislike for the man never thawed. In its review *The New York Times* commented that "Jean Harlow, the ash-blonde of several other such tales, once again appears as the girl in the case," and *Variety*, more kindly, refused to make any comment on Jean's performance in the picture.

Before any reaction could set in, Landau moved Harlow to Fox for *Goldie*, then pleaded with Hughes, through intermediaries, for some adjustment to be made in her contract with the Caddo Corporation. Despite Jean's performances, of which the best that could be said was that she was not hampered by talent, she had become the most popular, most photographed star in movie magazines, and her fan mail increased daily by hundreds of letters. Exhibitors and studios also received letters that demanded Harlow in pictures. Arthur now had no difficulty in getting Jean picture work, and Hughes used her burgeoning popularity to raise his loan-out price for Jean's services. Warner Brothers had paid fifteen hundred a week for Jean's services in *Public Enemy*, Columbia had matched this figure, and MGM and Fox were paying $1,750 a week, with the standard six-week minimum guarantee.

Jean's active status as a star had compelled her to move to a house on Club View Drive, and the expenses of proper wardrobes for Marino and Mama Jean, a day maid, entertainment and tips to studio personnel—for stars were expected to tip, distribute largesse and give pawnable presents to members of the crew when a picture was finished—had put Jean almost ten thousand dollars in debt to the Landau office. But Arthur assured the worried actress that an outlay of about fifteen hundred a month over and above her salary was no reason for financial concern, because she was playing leads, building up screen credits, and—no matter what reviewers said—gaining an important public.

"Look at the mail you get," Arthur told her. "Real mail that you don't pay for."

"But reviews of my pictures say I'm not very good."

"Remember and believe that thing you used to say to the reporters—about not having to be an actress if the audience likes you," Arthur said. "And things'll get better. I'm beginning to soften up Hughes."

Jean wiped her eyes. "How do you know that?"

"Because he didn't hang up on me," Arthur said. "He actually listened and said we'd talk about it."

"I'll never get outta debt," Jean moaned. "And Marino's driving me crazy."

"How's he bothering you?"

"By being mean to my mother. That kills her, and she murders me. You know he's just ordered three more suits and charged a dozen pair of chamois gloves and spats to match?"

"It'll get better," was all Arthur could say.

"For who?" Jean asked. "Him? I'm talking about me."

In *Goldie* a "first" was scored by the use of the word "tramp" to refer to an actress in the picture, and Jean was that actress. Of her performance in this remake of *A Girl in Every Port*, *Variety* said, "Miss Harlow is still high diving as a bad girl character. Here she plays a carnival performer in France. Far from being a good actress, Miss Harlow's appearance still counts with the boys."

Days after *Goldie* was finished, Landau negotiated with the Caddo Corporation for Jean to appear in two pictures for Columbia. Before she reported for work with Frank Capra, a director able to get a performance out of almost anyone, Jean's increasing popularity made her a fit subject for a magazine found in a majority of dental waiting rooms, among them Dr. Carpentier's. Frank Condon's article, "Kansas City Platinum," struck a responsive chord in the mind of Lincoln Quarlberg, a publicity man employed by the Caddo Corporation, and Quarlberg suggested that no matter what name Columbia had chosen for their Harlow picture, *Platinum Blonde* was a sock box-office title and the best description of Harlow's more-precious-than-gold hair.

It is difficult to find a reason for this title in a picture about newspapers and reporters and even more difficult to believe that a picture could be plotted for Loretta Young to take any man of sap away from Jean Harlow, but that is the way events were ordained. The picture was just another feature; aimed at entertainment, it achieved its commercial purpose only indifferently. But who cared? Without solicitation, theater owners wired Columbia the happy news that *Platinum Blonde* was one of the best titles to come along all year. And, strangely enough, Jean Harlow's not getting the hero was a nice plot switch, one appreciated by women. Men didn't care, because Harlow was still dressed in a way that put a strain on their buttons, if not their imaginations.

The film resulted in the founding of Platinum Blonde Clubs in at least a hundred cities. Beauty parlors were grateful for increased business in this time of economic depression; women of all ages began to imitate Jean's dress, make-up and speech mannerisms (in New York City and Chicago several voice teachers advertised that they could teach women to "talk as tough as Harlow"); and the publicity departments of studios for whom Jean had made pictures devoted more and more of their time to the sexiest thing to come along yet.

Platinum Blonde was followed by an arabesque that the publicity department wanted to call *Two Wise Girls and a Platinum Blonde,* but the title was rejected as too unwieldy. *Three Wise Girls* was a pallid compromise, and an even worse compromise was to assign to Jean the role of the good girl. *Variety* reported: "Jean Harlow has the lead—the girl who keeps straight. She does her best to suggest the innocent young thing and does better than might be expected, but she fails to be convincing and Mae Clarke takes the acting honors from her. . . ."

Reviews have always meant less than box office receipts, and pictures that showed Harlow as an *hors d'oeuvre* were making sufficient profit for Ben Piazza and J. Robert Rubin of MGM in New York to recommend to Mayer and Thalberg that Jean Harlow be added to the studio's roster of stars. Irving Thalberg informed Landau they were willing to put the actress under contract, but as a sober man he would not negotiate with Hughes.

A week of telephone calls at last prompted Hughes to meet with Landau, and the short agent told the tall producer that he was no longer prepared to finance Jean's career; if Hughes would not star her in a picture or sell her contract, supporting her, Mama Jean and Marino Bello would become the responsibility of the Caddo Corporation. Solemnly, Arthur showed Hughes an accountant's itemized statement of Jean's indebtedness to the Landau office and pointed out that Hughes was big enough to be liberal. As always, it was a matter of moment and place, of speaking to Hughes at a time when he was bored enough to find diversion in magnanimity, and he generously agreed to sell the Harlow contract to MGM Studios for a hundred thousand dollars. There followed two desperate weeks of negotiation, and at last Hughes accepted sixty thousand dollars and the right to use Jean in two pictures within five years at the salary she was receiving from MGM.

Landau worked out details of Harlow's contract with Eddie Mannix and asked for $1,500 a week for the first year, $2,000 a week for the second, up to $7,500 a week for the seventh and final year of the contract. The contract Jean signed gave her $1,250 a week for her first year and $1,750 a week for the second year; in her seventh year she would receive $5,000 a week. In exchange for Jean's receiving her salary for fifty-two instead of forty weeks a year, MGM had the right to exercise options for an eighth and ninth year at $5,000 a week. Also, the salaries of a full-time secretary, hairdresser and personal maid were the obligation of the studio. Jean also had at her disposal the use of any studio car, a uniformed chauffeur, and the studio wardrobe; the expenses of alterations were also borne by the studio.

To give the MGM publicity staff time to organize more Platinum Blonde Clubs, more fan clubs, more details of noble biography that would glamorize the new star; to give the studio photographers time to develop an album of shots that would make Harlow's breasts the most famous outside the Louvre or Prado; to give the wardrobe department time to design dresses with built-in brassieres that would contain and hide her nipples, which enlarged at any excitation including a change in temperature, Jean was put into a picture being produced by the Lord of San Simeon.

The loan of Jean Harlow to William Randolph Hearst's Cosmopolitan Productions, which headquartered at MGM Studios to make pictures for Marion Davies, aroused considerable speculation and hope among those reporters who wrote best about sensations. Was the millionaire journalist, who diverted himself by making political figures and movies, going to exchange one blonde for another?

Many responsible historians believe Hearst's inflammatory headlines had succeeded in involving the United States in its war with Spain; now Hearst had to cope with all the reporters of rival chains intent on provoking their own war. They probed, poked, suggested, and actually wrote copy they hoped would topple Marion Davies, the ranking star of Cosmopolitan Productions. They failed, and Hearst's *Beast of the City* was just another gangster standard, where Jean played her now-familiar but ever-pleasing role of a loose-living blonde charmer in the employ of a contemporary criminal gang.

"Another picture like that and I'll be telling people that the color of my eyes is shotgun blue," Jean told a reporter. "Honest, I don't mind being a heat wave, but there was a crime wave before I came along. Or doesn't anyone remember?"

Jean paused to open a button of her blouse to scratch

under an arm, and the reporters sighed and wished they could all lend a hand. In later years reporters noticed increasingly that Jean loved to touch herself, and they learned that she might, if challenged and if the circumstances were right, indulge in flagrant exhibitionism. Before she had signed with MGM, a young eastern banker had managed to persuade a New York friend of Arthur Landau's to speak in his behalf; he had come to Los Angeles on business, had been invited to a social dinner party on South Orange Avenue in Pasadena, and had wanted to prove to his host and hostess that he could bring a glamorous movie star to dinner. Assured that the banker had an impeccable reputation for sobriety and always kept his word, Arthur introduced the banker to Jean, and she accepted his dinner invitation. Arthur and Beatrice chose her gown, a garment of deepest blue with thin beaded straps. The gown fitted Jean to perfection, although Beatrice disapproved last-minute alterations which took in several seams and made it impossible for Jean to wear anything but a brief shadow slip.

The banker had not told his hostess who his partner would be, and his arrival with Jean Harlow was a triumph. After dinner the men were persuaded to move to the billiard room for brandy and cigars and the women grouped themselves around Jean in the library to ask question after question about the movies and their stars, which Jean answered with candid good humor. All the women were friendly except one, a woman in her late thirties with sharp angular features who smoked nervously and stared with open dislike at the blonde actress.

At last the hostile woman leaned forward. "Miss Harlow," she began sharply, so that all conversation ceased, "what would happen if one of the straps of your gown broke?"

Jean thought for a moment, then quickly tore the strap. A breast popped out of the dress. "That's what," she said casually before she pushed herself into the dress again.

In 1934 Max Lief, who had written some of the quips for Jean after her stage tour was taken over by N.T.G., returned to Hollywood for a writing assignment. Several weeks after his arrival Lief had lunch with her at MGM. At lunch they chattered pleasantly, and Max gave her some more bright comments she might work into conversation. After lunch Max walked with Jean to her stage, and as they stood before the building, Jean reached into her blouse and began to fondle her breasts.

"Got an itch?" Max asked.

"No," Jean replied. "I just love them. They're so beautiful."

At a 1931 press conference one reporter, hoping that he could get some comment from the star which could be slanted to make her appear to be in conflict with the studio, asked, "Then you're not satisfied with your parts?"

Jean looked at the reporter as her fingertips touched her breasts, then stroked her thighs. "Repeat that please?" she asked innocently.

"I mean—"

"You *are* mean to ask if I'm not satisfied with my parts." She sounded hurt.

The reporter flushed, then laughed with his colleagues. "I mean—have you told Mr. Mayer that you're unhappy with your scripts?"

"I've told him nothing he wouldn't like to hear, and I wasn't acting," she replied quickly. "I'm crazy about MGM. About everyone here. Especially Mr. Mayer, Mr. Thalberg and Mr. Bern. I love making movies and I'm getting twelve-fifty a week. Hundreds, not dollars." She traced the numbers in the air with a forefinger. "And if a man with kids is getting twenty-five bucks a week he's mighty lucky. Look"—she pointed at the assembled reporters—"if any of you try to get me in dutch with the studio I'll"—she paused—"get you bumped off."

She laughed, the reporters laughed and the photographers pleaded for just a couple more leg and bosom shots, because these were better for newspaper and human circulation than money in the bank.

"Why don't you say that I want to be a real actress?" she asked as a photographer posed her to show her high inner thigh. When his hand lingered, she slapped his face. "I know I can be one."

"Is that what your public wants you to be?" a reporter asked.

The question was cruel, but Jean held her smile and gestured for Arthur to remain silent. "The public—even the ones who don't like me—are my friends."

"Is that why you wear slacks and low-heeled shoes around the studio? So tourists'll think you're one of the boys?"

Her nymph's face was knowing and innocent. "That's not possible—thank God."

"Any romance you want to tell us about, Jean?"

"Sure!" She clapped her hands because the writers who did her material had anticipated most possible questions and she was learning to use her lines as if they were original with her. And she could see how everyone, even the photographers, were listening for her announcement. Now, now was the time to say it. "The one I'm having with the world."

There were some sighs of disappointment, but Jean's ingenuous smile made most of them believe she was sincere.

"What about marriage?"

"What about it?" she repeated languidly. "Get rid of it and what would happen to all those honeymoon jokes?"

The laughter at this sally was weak, and Arthur quickly ended the interview. Jean borrowed a studio car, one tastefully hung with signs that announced the driver was an honorary fire chief of Culver City, and drove home by herself.

She entered the house, yoo-hooed for her mother, and heard Marino call from the den that Mama Jean was out and for her to come in and see some of the new things he had bought that day.

On the wall hung an expensive antique chronometer and on the desk lay an array of open boxes with gloves, ties, black and blue silk hose with dark clocks, a sextant, a box of cigars in individual foil wrappers, a yachting cap, two pairs of binoculars and three little jewelry boxes, each with a pair of gold cufflinks.

"You've been busy today," she said.

Marino shook his head. "I really had to hurry to get home before you did. The maid's off today so we'll have to eat out. Want to?" He rubbed his hands. "I'm treating."

"I'm not hungry," she said. "You're going to have to send this junk back."

"Not a chance." Marino shook his head. "I'm thinking of buying a boat."

"Take all this back and you'll have enough for a rowboat and two pairs of oars."

"A yacht. A forty-footer that sleeps six and a crew is what I got in mind," Marino said. "I spoke to a boat broker this morning and he gave me some pictures." He pushed aside the wrapping papers to find several eight-by-ten photographs. "It cost more than a hundred and seventy-five thousand two years ago, and I can have it for forty thousand. The man who owned it jumped out of a window."

Jean threw the pictures into a corner. "Now I know you're crazy. And you'd better send all this junk back!" Her voice began to tighten. "I'm getting more and more fed up with—"

Marino's hard slap brought her up short. "Don't raise your voice," he warned his stepdaughter. "We don't want the neighbors around here to think we're not a happy family." He raised his hand again. "If you scratch my face and I give you a black eye—who's worse off? Because what've you got besides a pair of grapefruits and a pretty face? So let me show you something else I bought."

Pain filled Jean's eyes. "I don't want to see anything. And that stuff's going back, unless you want me to tell Arthur."

"Tell him," Marino said as he picked up a mahogany cane. With a quick, expert movement he twisted the top of the cane, withdrew a slender épée from the wooden sheath, and made two or three awkward slashes so close to Jean that she screamed.

"Nice, no? This cane's our little secret." He paused and rested the point of the bright steel on Jean's shoulder. "We don't want to worry Mama, do we?"

Jean shook her head.

"And I keep everything?"

"Yes."

"About the boat—"

"I haven't got the money! You know that! And Arthur won't lend you forty thousand."

"I got a feeling it can be bought for thirty."

"He won't lend it," she insisted. "And I'm not going to ask. No matter what you do. Cut or stab me and everything goes. This is crazy."

Marino smiled indulgently. "No more crazy than you being where you are," he said. "Still, my little toy'll keep you in line. You know we're not really related, and once you did like me. And you know how your mother likes me—especially that way. Aren't you ever curious about it?"

"Let me alone, please!"

Marino lowered the cane and ran the steel along her upper arm. "Aren't you curious? You play that kind of woman and I know you're not. But you know you're a lousy actress. If you let me, I bet I could show you how it really feels—the parts you play."

Jean threw up all over the desk and everything Marino had bought that afternoon. And when her stomach stopped churning, she was glad she had.

Chapter Nine

The wedding reception was carried off without a catastrophe. There was no excessive breakage, drunkenness or theft, no enmities engendered or blood feuds concluded, no affairs of the heart or body begun or terminated. And if the bride and groom seemed somewhat dazed, no one expected any less of them under the circumstances. Beatrice Landau was never more than two steps from Jean's side, and Arthur managed to stay in any group gathered around Paul Bern. When the newlyweds posed for pictures or thanked guests for their gifts and well wishes, Jean permitted Paul to hold her hand. If her voice and laughter were shrill and pitched too high, everyone agreed knowingly that a normal newlywed without sleep was a nervous newlywed. Still, Louella Parsons scolded Jean because the circles under her eyes betrayed too much work. She shouldn't be afraid to speak to Mr. Bern—the most sympathetic executive at MGM and just married to the loveliest girl—and ask him to do something about easing her professional schedule.

"You owe it to your fans to look well," Louella lectured Jean. "And I say you ought to take a long vacation somewhere with Paul."

"I'll think about it," Jean promised.

Louella shook a finger at Paul. "You're guardian of one of the world's most important treasures. Protector of one of Hollywood's most glittering crown jewels."

"I'm fully aware of it, dear lady," Paul said.

"You have a national responsibility," she continued in the throes of ecstatic inspiration. "I hope you understand?"

"Yes, dear lady." He pressed a courtly kiss to Louella's hand. Pale, perspiring so freely he already had changed his shirt twice, Paul complained of a nervous headache. "Jean, Louella." He bowed slightly. "You'll excuse me for a moment?"

"I'll take care of your beautiful bride," Louella said. "Such a lovely day. Thrilling occasion. And such a lovely man, Jean," she congratulated the actress, who had put on dark glasses. "Isn't it wonderful to see newlyweds, Mrs. Landau? Wonderful that they're Hollywood?"

Beatrice tugged at the broad brim of her hat so that it cast a shadow over her eyes. "Wonderful," she agreed.

"A lovely man," Jean repeated. "Really the nuts." She laughed at the unconscious overstatement, compelled herself to cough and took Beatrice's handkerchief. "Too much excitement," she apologized to Louella.

"Of course." Louella fluttered her fingers as she prepared to join Norma Shearer and Howard Strickling. "I'll expect a little private statement from you before I go. Something no one else'll have."

"You'll have it," Jean promised. "I'd rather give her Paul as a gift," she muttered to Beatrice. "But who'd take him?"

"Have a drink," Beatrice suggested. "It'll help."

"Nothing'll help somebody as stupid as me." Jean groaned as Mama Jean bore down on them. "If she hugs me again I'm gonna faint. I'm getting so stiff I can hardly move."

"Tell her not to be so emotional," Beatrice said. "Say you're warm and nervous and your hair feels as if it's coming down."

"Then she'll want to wash and comb it while everybody cheers. Beatrice, run interference and let her bend your ear while I hide out in the can for half an hour or so."

"Which one?" Beatrice asked. "In case you need some help."

"Master bath." Jean pecked at her mother's cheek and avoided an embrace. "Kiss Paul," she suggested to Mama Jean. "Make him feel really wanted by all of us."

By five-thirty the last guest had departed, the private police had shooed the last crasher and souvenir scavenger from the grounds, and Paul had told the Carmichaels not to worry about cleaning up—they could go to the beach or anywhere else for several more days. Marino and Mama Jean were given six splits of champagne and several jars of caviar and were persuaded to go home with their loot.

Two hours later Paul brooded in his den with a bottle of brandy, and Jean paced the master bedroom, chair braced under the knob. The first day of pretense had been successful, and Arthur had assured Paul that Jean would not file for divorce before a reasonable length of time. That would insure his not getting into trouble at the studio. But there were questions of masquerade that predated this wedding, and one that puzzled Arthur the most was—why had Paul gone to the expense of keeping a mistress?

"Think of me as Gregory Potemkin." Paul smiled cryptically.

"Who's he?" Arthur asked.

"Not a new director," Paul said. "Look him up in the library. Oh, don't bother." He took a book from a shelf, flipped the pages and put an envelope at the proper place. "Read it, Arthur. It'll explain better than I can. I'm not Potemkin and Hollywood isn't Russia. But a worm can bleed like a king. Read it and you'll get the idea. And thanks for everything you've done today."

"I wish I could say the same to you. Why're you drinking again?"

"I won't bother Jean," Paul promised.

"One more performance like this morning's and I'll have you committed to an asylum for life."

Paul thought for a moment. "You're tempting me. No,

Arthur, there won't be a repeat. Life's full of bad jokes, and I'm one of them."

"For chrissakes, Paul, be a man."

"Now, Arthur, *there's* a good joke."

"I'm calling for Jean tomorrow," Arthur said, ignoring him. "We're going to see my doctor. You're welcome to come along."

Paul shook his head. "I met Doctor Sugarman and thanked him too. Take the book," he said pressing it into Arthur's hand. "Read from where I marked. It's about Catherine the Great. A brilliant woman," he continued. "You know how she chose her lovers? Picked the biggest, handsomest men in Russia and made them take a physical examination before they got into her bed. But that wasn't all. Their powers were tried out by two of her trusted ladies-in-waiting. Catherine made political errors of judgment but she wasn't making any mistakes on the mattress."

"You'll be making a bigger mistake by not consulting Sugarman. Or is there someone else—another doctor you'd rather see?"

Paul continued to shake his head. "Go home, Arthur. I want to lock my door behind you."

Arthur took Paul's book straight to his den when he returned to his house. Removing Paul's marker, he plunged into the story of the Czarina of Russia's lover, Prince Gregory Potemkin. In 1783 he had taken the Crimea away from the Turks in battle, annexed it to Russia and sent glowing reports back home about the paradise he was building in the new province. Villages, cities, palaces, libraries, universities, cathedrals were going up to the glory of Catherine's name. Would she be kind enough to send a few rubles to pay for them? Delighted, she sent twenty million. But jealous rivals of the prince kept hinting that his reports were, to put it bluntly, lies. Catherine knew her Gregory, so she decided she'd better go and see for herself. But when she did, the villages, the cities, the palaces and the academies were all there, just as the prince had promised. There was so much to see that there was no time to stop and examine anything closely, so the Empress never suspected that, if she *had* stopped, she would have found every single building to be a hastily-slapped-together false front with nothing behind it but the endless Russian mud. Potemkin had attempted the most elaborate masquerade in history—and succeeded.

So that was it, Landau thought. With a talent like that, what movies that prince could have made! He was a man born out of his time. But Paul Bern was here and now. For the rulers of Hollywood, Paul Bern had created a false-fronted man who occasionally paraded in the company of beautiful and desirable women, who had maintained a discreet little love nest, and who, by a monumental coup, had at last succeeded in marrying the reigning sex queen of all the world.

It had taken Arthur four meetings in Bern's office, one every day, to persuade Paul that he was obligated to prove a real interest in his marriage, and that the most substantial proof he could offer would be a visit to Dr. Sugarman's office. Paul didn't want Jean to file for divorce until it was safe for both their careers, and he was even willing to stay permanently married to Jean if the arrangement suited her; in return he would forgive her bad language, malapropisms, awful mother and Marino. Of course he regretted the severe beating he had given his wife, but she shouldn't have laughed at him when he attempted to kiss her feet; she should have recognized his sincerity when he'd told her during courtship that in marriage a union of spirit and soul was superior, more lasting, than the contact of bodies. Potemkin had told this to Catherine, and the queen had understood.

He had lived as a man in fear, in daily anguish that his

secret would be discovered, that the woman sequestered in the little West Hollywood bungalow would decide she'd had enough of the façade and demand real activity. He had constructed elaborate situations, and his life depended upon them. But always there was the fear, the knowledge that he was supporting himself with an idealism that bordered on fantasy, because the woman in the bungalow was not Catherine, Jean Harlow was not Catherine, and neither woman possessed the intellect to understand his talk of soul and spirit. In most private, secret truth he did not believe in it himself.

"But you knew you were a fake," Arthur accused him during the fourth meeting. "She leveled and you didn't."

"If that's what you choose to believe, Arthur. Being different is not being a fake."

"Then you admit being a fairy."

"I admit being different," Paul persisted. "If you mean do I go to bed with another man—I don't. How can a man with one leg be a sprinter? You saw me. I'm not built for any kind of sex."

"But you did date," Arthur said. "You went out with Barbara La Marr. I'd even heard you were going to marry her."

"I had marriage in mind," Paul admitted. "But I'd rather not talk about a lady," he added after a moment's pause. "Even if Barbara behaved badly when she found out. I could've killed her. Instead I did about five hundred dollars worth of damage to her furniture."

"To prove what? That after all you were a man?"

Bern leaned an elbow on the desk to control his trembling arm. "Haven't you more pressing business to attend to?"

"This is my business, Paul. And it's got to be straightened out. I saw Jean before I saw you, and what you did to her a man doesn't do to a dog."

"So now I'm a man! You were just telling me I'm *not* a man!"

"How can I say that when you were keeping a broad?"

"She's not a broad. She's a fine woman who helped me play a part when I finally told her the truth, and Jean could've done the same!" Paul pounded his desk in rage. "Let me alone, Arthur. Just get the hell out of my life and take Jean with you!"

"I wish I could," Arthur said coldly. "It would be much better for Jean if I could. But for the sake of her career and yours she's got to stay." It was the agent speaking. "And I've got to admire you. Jean tells me you're behaving yourself at home."

"It's nice of her to let me stay." Paul took a flask from a desk drawer and drank deeply. "She even lets me sleep on the chaise, so that the Carmichaels won't get suspicious."

"You did give her the house," Arthur pointed out.

"And she'd better not give it away."

"Explain that," Arthur said.

"She wants to give the house to Marino so he can sell it and go into business. And then we'd move back with her folks. I'm telling you, Arthur, she'd better not do that. And you'd better do something about stopping that man from calling me twenty or thirty times a day!"

"I'll do everything if you'll see Doctor Sugarman," Arthur said. "Paul, he can't hurt you and he could help, I know. See the man," he pleaded. "Jean thinks he's wonderful."

"So she's told me when she takes the trouble to talk to me." Paul covered his face with both hands. "Is Saturday all right?"

"I'll make it all right," Arthur promised and compelled himself to pat the unhappy man on the shoulder.

Sugarman promised to be alone in his office, and Bern felt better because Jean had been almost pleasant that morning. She'd actually served him coffee and toast in the dining room, and with genuine compassion had told him not to be afraid of the doctor, a real darling who could be trusted like a priest.

Sugarman gestured for Arthur to sit in the waiting room. "We'll call you if we need you."

"For Jean's sake, Doctor," Arthur said, "make him well."

"And not for him, too?" Sugarman chided the agent. "He's very unhappy, Arthur."

"So's Jean," Arthur said. "And black and blue besides."

"She'll recover on all counts," the doctor assured him. "Without being technical, the plate showed a little bruise to her right kidney. We'll watch it and nothing will happen. Now I've a patient waiting."

Although Arthur had called Herman Sugarman to attend Jean Harlow and brought Paul Bern to the doctor's office, medical ethics would have prohibited discussion of the cases with Arthur if either patient had forbidden such confidence. Jean had no secrets from Arthur. Paul Bern's habitual reticence continued in Sugarman's office, but in his third visit Bern asked the doctor for advice, because he could no longer keep his secret and its agonies to himself. Sugarman was a professional, and Bern preferred to speak to someone whose interest in him was emotional rather than clinical. Right now he needed an understanding with at least one person—a friend—in whom he could confide with safety; someone who might become angry, but would never, never laugh at him.

"I should talk to Jean," Paul had told Arthur. "But I can't."

"But you can talk to me?"

"No," Paul said. "Not yet. But I've asked Sugarman to tell you whatever he thinks you ought to know. Which is about everything, I'd say. Then maybe you can help."

"How?"

Bern twisted his hands, opened a desk drawer and kicked it shut. "By coming in to see me every day. As often as you can.

I don't care if people are going to say you're cooking deals with me. Just come in to see me and check how I'm getting along. And the most important thing—"

"I've already told Marino to leave you alone," Arthur interrupted, "and Jean's not going to give your house to anyone. Matter of fact, I told her she ought to start thinking of refurnishing it."

In a series of swift little strokes Bern plunged a letter opener into his desk blotter to leave a pattern of punctures. "I know she's talking about me."

"She's not and never will."

"I want her to quit the studio. To give up her contract."

"Be sensible!" Arthur lifted his feet off a coffee table and sat erect in his chair. "If she quits you lose out."

"That's what you say."

"As often as I have to." Arthur looked at his watch. "And you'd better not say anything about Jean's quitting, because she'll stay and you'll be through. Finished forever." He paused for emphasis, then pantomimed a man blowing out his brains. "I'm meeting Sugarman for lunch. Are you sure you want him to talk to me?"

"Sure." Paul was weary. "I called him this morning and told him not to leave anything out."

"We'll have dinner tonight," Arthur said. "The three of us. Paul, listen, you kept things going all your life without anyone finding out. Now five people know the mistake you made. Jean, Beatrice, me and the doctor are four, and you can trust us. But we're worried about the fifth person."

Bern looked up. "My masquerade mistress?"

"She doesn't count," Arthur said, though he thought differently. "You're the fifth person. If anybody gives us away it'll be you." He pointed to the desk strewn with memoranda and scripts. "So do your work. Keep busy and find a good property for Jean." It couldn't be helped; business had to intrude on despair. "Have any idea what she'll be going into?"

"It's been set, I think," Paul said. "But I don't want to talk about her." He spun in his chair, then stared at a framed rendering of a musical set. "As disappointed as she is in me, I'm that much more in her."

"You've got your nerve."

"Talk to Sugarman," Paul said. "You might change your mind."

Herman Sugarman was waiting for Arthur at Musso Frank's in Hollywood. He assured the anxious agent that his afternoon was free and that Arthur could take his time and ask as many questions as he wished. But there were certain physiological conclusions Arthur, Jean and Paul would have to accept as final before they could proceed to a program of psychological therapy that might—only might—reconcile Paul to reality.

"Let's get this straight," Sugarman said. "We have to work with Paul's physical limitations. He can feel some passion and get what is for him an erection. He could possibly have an orgasm if he were in coitus. But he'd be afraid to try."

The doctor explained that emotional complications of sex result from the individual's response to whatever moral code he accepts. The Hebraic code of sexual behavior is strict, and even if Bern was not actively religious, the mores of his family, childhood group and religion were never discarded. In Jewish communities sex was accepted as God's mechanics to perpetuate his creation, and carnal abuse of sex, with a partner or alone, were major sins.

Until he was thirteen, Paul's natural modesty was respected without comment. A withdrawn child, Paul was unaware that he was different from other boys, and it was only when he entered his teens and boys in the high-school locker room began to compare physical characteristics and anecdotes that Paul felt the first guilt: He was small, and did not feel the same excitement the other boys did when they discussed girls or told dirty jokes. Attempts at the small boys' vice were dismal failures. Paul was physiologically semi-impotent. Even if all taboos and inhibitions had been removed, if the most desirable, passionate and willing women had been made available to the boy, his reactions and responses would have been unenthusiastic at best.

That this did not make Paul abnormal was something he failed to understand. Thus, in his middle teens, Paul felt an overwhelming sense of guilt because he lacked the normal sexual drive of his group. That lack, combined with feelings of shame, turned Paul away from normal social contacts when he realized that his secret might be discovered.

Boys his age swam nude in the East River. He was in daily fear that Italian or Irish boys of other blocks on their Jew-hunting expeditions might trap and cockalize him, an indignity accomplished by pinning the victim to the ground, tearing open his fly, and smearing him with axle grease or tar. What would happen if they caught Paul and discovered his secret? If Paul swam in the river, used the high-school locker room or ran with the boys on his block he had to be discovered, and the necessity to keep his crippling infirmity a secret compelled him to tell his parents that he had no interest in high school, that he wanted to study something he really liked.

At first Mr. and Mrs. Levy laughed when Paul spoke of the theater, until stubborn truancy persuaded where argument failed and they agreed to let the boy have his way. The Levys were simple people, and only knew that Paul had been a good, quiet boy who liked to keep to himself. Therefore, his determination to become an actor, where he would have to appear before critical strangers, was a choice of occupation so foreign to his personality it defied all explanation. And Paul was unable to explain that his daydreams did not take the form of usual sexual fantasies in which he knew and explored willing girls; rather he dreamed of being a bold, aggressive hero, a world-famous athlete, an armored warrior, a man renowned for his strength and body—a male desired but himself superior to such desire.

In his fantasies Paul traveled backward and forward in time, and in the secret of his room or on a rooftop, he assumed the shapes of Hercules, Jason, Robin Hood. The theater seemed the most likely place for these fantasies to become reality. If he was disappointed in his life in the street, on a stage he could perform roles of strength and bravery. And audiences might think he was the man he portrayed on the stage.

The brave dreams of an introvert seldom can be transmuted into real events. Paul's physique and appearance limited the characters he could play, and none of them were the types he preferred. Still, the egocentricity of people in the theater, their narcissism and colorful individuality was traditional, and Paul felt increasingly sure that his secret was safe, his aloofness a minor, unoriginal eccentricity. Another normal tradition of the theater was sexual idiosyncrasy, and if Paul showed no interest in women it was concluded that his interests were homosexual. As long as a theatrical person behaved himself and did not make passes at little boys and Western Union messengers, the aberration was accepted backstage. From time to time Paul repulsed the advances of known deviates, but these scenes were considered evidence that by choice Paul separated his social and professional lives.

The theater protected Paul but did not offer him the relief he hoped to find. Increasingly alone, withdrawn, fearing to confide in anyone, he wondered, then began to believe he was homosexual. And in this there was a great irony, for he still could not get or know the feelings of sex. Try as he might, the most pornographic books, pictures, artifacts, even nude women—or men—failed to arouse him. Desperation compelled him to attend several erotic circuses in which giant men whom he envied took many women, and he had even seen the performance of two Cuban girls and one dildo. After each circus he had vomited his disgust and wept hard against his pillow.

That he had not been found out did not mean he would not be found out. Restless, uneasy, Paul went to Canada, then moved on to Hollywood. In an industry that employed thousands more than the stage, the presence of more people would make it simpler for him to become lost in the crowd, to guard his secret. Then there was another, more naive reason: In the greatest concentration of beauty in all the world he might find the stimulus to arouse him. For there were girls of every nation, every beautiful physical characteristic, every background, and among them he might find the key that would unlock his passion.

So Paul prayed that by some psychological osmosis the medium he worked in would make him the man of his dreams. Motion pictures were dreams come true, and sex was the substance of the dream. There were cases—not too many and most of these were European—where the actors and actresses called upon to register passion for the public, commercial screen actually engaged in the act—with cameras focused upon the close-ups to film the dilation of eyes and nostrils, spastic muscular contraction and stiffening of limbs, rapid breathing, the tongue flicking at dry lips and palate, teeth biting into a shoulder. To add artistic symbolism for those who enjoyed such ornamental icing with their sex, the camera might intercut shots of a statue of a rampant stallion, the staring eyes of a gargoyle, the thick lubricous lips of a stone satyr, the striking of a huge bell, fireworks, the spume of a waterfall or sudden spurt of a fountain or geyser—and for those whose choicest fantasies placed sex in gardens, the pistil bent over the stamen.

Although men and women in formal dress and with penthouse or country estate addresses were the preferred characters in the sex fantasies, the movies made sex possible for all—beggar and king, lady and gamin—and through sex the miracle of love was always fulfilled.

Other miracles, too, were commonplace: Pictures were made where in full view of audiences the limbs of cripples were healed, the blind were restored to sight, the mute were given voice, whole towns threatened by bursting dam or avalanche were saved by the prayers of a small boy; an impoverished religious built a cathedral by prayer; wars were won by weary defeated soldiers in their trenches after they saw a vision of Christ walking the battlefield. Show an audience a sudden ray of light upon the screen and the audience knew that prayers had been heard and were to be granted. When a boy wept over his dog struck by a hit-and-run driver, then looked heavenward and prayed brokenly, almost drowning in tears, one could be sure that poor little Spot's paw would twitch, the pup would draw a short, tentative breath, then another, then bark sharply as a signal for the theater orchestra or the sound track to swell into full hallelujah as the boy kissed Spot and Spot licked the boy's wet eyes. Yes, there were miracles filmed about once a week, sometimes more, and Bern wished, then believed, that if he worked to create miracles, he too might be rewarded with a miracle.

"He was quite angry. Couldn't understand why God was willing to help a mutt and not him," Sugarman said as he raised a hand for Arthur to remain silent. "People who live and work with unreality begin to accept their circumstances as real."

"But that's crazy," Arthur said.

"Is it? You've seen the miracle of the little boy and the dog. Right? How did it affect you?"

Arthur placed a hand over his heart. "Everyone likes little kids and dogs. And sometimes kids think a dog is dead and it really isn't. So they think it's a miracle."

"Which means that adults don't believe in miracles? Don't want them to happen? Your finding Harlow wasn't a miracle? You're not hoping, wishing for miracles in your own family?"

"You're confusing me, Doc."

"It's unintentional," Sugarman replied. "But if unreality confuses you, think what it does to someone who believes in it."

The doctor sipped his coffee and idly tapped his spoon on the side of the cup. "Arthur, I can't do anything for him. Internal medicine isn't psychiatry."

"I don't believe in psychiatry," Arthur said. "And you've no right to discharge a sick man if he needs you."

"But all I can do is bolster his ego. Prescribe something that might make him sleep better. But he has to wake up, Arthur. Not only to go to work, but to reality. That little love nest was unreal. The fantastic strategem of a desperate man. And it's pathetic, Arthur. It's not unusual for children to invent imaginary playmates, and sometimes they actually begin to believe in them."

"But Paul isn't a kid!"

Sugarman looked sadly at the agent. "Really? Now you're confusing physical age with mental age."

"I don't believe it!"

"Neither does Paul." The doctor was patient. "But what would you think of a man who wrote to five or six companies— he admits it—that advertise in the pulps? You know, Arthur"— despite himself, Sugarman had to hide his smile behind a napkin—"companies that guarantee bust development for flat-chested women. Send a dollar and they send you a little plaster hand. Paul told me he knew they were fakes. Still, he wrote and asked them if they had something to increase the size of his organ. And one of them replied that they could get him a machine that would do the job. But it would cost a hundred dollars."

"And he sent the hundred dollars?"

"Two hundred, because they also had a deluxe model. I've seen it, Arthur. Paul brought it to the office. And I've a good mind to get in touch with the postal people, because it's an outrageous, disgusting, comic, yet brutal fraud." The doctor sighed. "I honestly wish there was such a machine. See? I'm indulging in fantasy."

Both men fell silent. Arthur looked at Sugarman and wished he would continue, but the doctor concentrated on adding several drops of cream to his coffee.

"Then what's to be done?" he said at last. "I can't tell Jean what you told me. She'd move out of the house and the scandal . . . we can't have it. Tell me, is Paul dangerous?"

"He's not well," Sugarman hedged. "And he's desperate because Jean let him down."

"I don't get it."

"Then you weren't listening, Arthur," the doctor said. "He felt that if Jean was the nation's sex symbol, the woman who could make every man bust his buttons if he just thought of her, then having her in reality, nude and willing, would do as much for him. And he hates her, Arthur, because he prayed so hard, and she couldn't make the miracle come true!"

"But no other woman can either!"

Again Sugarman raised his right hand. "But is Jean Harlow just another woman?"

"No," said Landau slowly. "But I think she's beginning to wish she was."

Chapter Ten

Jean and Paul Bern had come home in a cab driven by a too-friendly driver. When Bern slapped her, the cabby had stared first at him, then at Jean for a signal to haul off and hit the little balding bastard who resembled a stoolie in a gangster picture. But Jean had slipped out of the cab, spun on her high heels and clattered into the house. For several minutes Bern stood at the deep end of the pool and knew destruction, for his heart rioted as if torn free of the muscles that bound it in place. Being destroyed from within, nothing could save him from the exterior world and its cabdrivers who lusted to lynch him before they lined up on Jean. Nothing could save him, help him, unless he followed Dr. Sugarman's advice and took a leave of absence from the studio to go to New York, or Vienna, or Geneva, or even to London to see Dr. Ernest Jones, Freud's disciple. But he had revealed too much of his secret heart, turned himself inside out for Sugarman and, foolishly, had instructed the good doctor to share his knowledge with Landau. The odds were that his secret would soon be all over town. Then what? Could he count on people believing the truths were gross, delirious lies?

Of course, in vanity, he would continue to hope, but to protect himself against the suspicions of the world, Paul had begun to put into motion—for everyone to see and gossip about —evidences, acts and reactions to mark him as a jealous husband, possessive lover and complete, natural man. Therefore, at parties where men surrounded Jean, he behaved badly. And men always surrounded Jean to stare hard, defiantly, challengingly into her eyes and at her lips and tits—yes, they were tits to all men who stared at them.

There were times when he had joined Jean, taken her hand and attempted to squeeze so hard she would wince and cry out her submission. But her grip was stronger than his, and as their fingers contracted, their elbows locked and their arms grew rigid, the contest became a form of Indian hand-wrestling; and he had won because Jean feared ridicule and still wanted to keep her confusion, unhappiness and fear a secret. At several parties he had taken the center of the stage from his wife by bluntly criticizing her dress, her hair, her make-up, her jewelry, her diction; concluding that she didn't look, walk or talk as a lady; therefore he, as a gentleman, was taking her home. This attack was most successful; it inflicted the greatest hurt. Proof of it? In their secluded house Jean had raged, screamed, cursed, thrown things, then cried, and he had felt himself grow taller, stronger. But only from the waist up.

About a week before, while Jean and he were having dinner with the Bellos, he had slapped Jean at their table for speaking again of giving his—her—house to them! Mama Jean had gasped as if she had taken the blow, and Bello had half-risen from his chair, then relaxed, eyes twinkling with delight. Jean had left the table and gone home in a cab driven by a brute male. What wouldn't he give to be as endowed as the brute. . . .

As Paul had driven home, the memory of the incident, the way his palm had tingled as he had felt the slap, the way his temples had pounded at the fear—yes, terror!—he had seen in Jean's eyes made him feel momentarily faint. Jean's terror had been supplanted by a rage that had frightened him, but he had stood his ground, faced her eye to eye, and she had lowered her glance to make him feel victorious and manly. And—oh wonderful!—he had felt real passion, the actual need for a woman, and he had increased his speed and driven dangerously, delighted at his daring, through Benedict Canyon. But Jean had locked the door of her—their—bedroom, and the Carmichaels were in the house. How could he batter aside the stout door? How could he hope to break the lock and dislodge the chair Jean had probably wedged under the knob?

But the feeling of power had still raged within him, a power that made him sweat from head to foot so that he knew he smelled like an animal. Raging, begging, reveling in the odor and feeling of animal heat, he had slid to his knees to whisper hoarsely through the keyhole that he felt like a man and please please please wouldn't she open the door and let him in. Didn't she—oh, God!—understand or care for proof he could be her husband and lover this very night? All she had to do was open the door! Goddamn her hair and her lips and her tits and all of her to hell—didn't she care? But Jean had said nothing. Instead, she had knelt to spit through the keyhole into his face. Strength drained away, courage became a whimper, and he became a weeping child. That night, like a eunuch, he had slept before the door until he faintly heard Mrs. Carmichael's alarm clock. Panic gave him strength to hurry into his den, where he pretended to have fallen asleep in a deep club chair while reading a script.

Vienna? London? Geneva? They did not know, could not comprehend, what they asked of him. What excuse could he give the studio to justify a leave of absence? Thalberg, the understanding soul, might grant him the leave, might even arrange for him to receive his salary while away because he needed every cent of it. But there were other executives at the studio, men who didn't like him now that he—not they—had married *the* sex symbol.

Suddenly, standing by the pool with the cabdriver's angry face still before him, Paul embraced an oak as if to tear it from the deep black earth. A feeling of power surged through him again, but knowing the source, he feared it. He had slapped Jean again, before a crude man who was physically his superior, a man certainly not crippled as he was, a man quite capable, all the world would have said, of beating him into a jelly. Still, he had not been afraid. He had felt a jealousy normal to all men and had publicly, arrogantly punished his wife; now he felt like a normal man, powerful, angry, outraged, passionately hot, and anxious for the release found in the deep thrust into a woman. And he believed himself capable. Touched himself and knew he was capable.

The wonder of his feeling compelled Paul to embrace the tree harder, to revel in the roughness of bark against his arms and cheek. His feet pressed hard against the soil seemed to take root, and he felt it—he did!—the strength of the soil as it coursed through his body; felt the hardening of muscles. With a small animal cry he tore at the trunk. It did not move. He ran to a small, slighter tree—a young eucalyptus—and made it sway so that he was showered with leaves, dry twigs, scales of bark. Again he shook the tree with his new-found power, then stepped back to raise his head and arms as leaves and pods fell upon him, and he might have cried out in joy if Jean had not come up from behind to smack him across the head with a fly swatter.

"You little bastard, you just disappointed me again." She stood with the swatter poised. "I thought you'd squash like a fly."

Power, ecstasy, manliness drained from him, and he covered both eyes. "Go ahead, do it," he said.

He heard the crackle of leaves under Jean's feet and turned to see her about to enter the house. "Hurry up, dope," she called. "You got someone coming to dinner, I think."

"I don't remember," he said.

"Willis Goldbeck," she replied. "Unless you want to call and say you're sick. Which is no lie."

"I'm not!" he shook his fists. "Goddamn you, I'm not!"

"And I want to talk to you," she said as Paul approached

the door. "The bills're piling up, and as man of the house you're supposed to take care of them. Some gift, this house." She laughed and rapped the door with her knuckles. "Mortgaged to the chimneytop. What makes you think I want to keep making payments on this stupid old barn? I hate it."

"It's too damn good for you," Paul said.

"Really?" Jean held the door wide and mockingly invited him indoors. "Why won't you let me give it to Marino?" She stilled his protests by threatening him with the swatter. "Oh, shut up. What difference would it make? I'd have to keep on making payments on it. What a life for me." She pitied herself in a voice that quavered with laughter. "I'm supporting two men. One with too much balls and one without any. And if I have to go into that rainbarrel on the set once more there won't be anything for them to get out."

"I could speak to Thalberg and tell him Fleming just has to finish the scene. Are they keeping the water warm enough for you? They're warming the bathing suit before you put it on, aren't they?"

"I'm not wearing the suit. It's too much trouble to get into."

"I won't have you working nude!"

"Someone's gotta work." She slapped at a fly with the swatter and cursed because she missed. "And I don't care if everyone looks. I'm that tired of everything."

"You're a whore."

She laughed. "Oh, sit down," she said, gesturing to a chair. "It'll make you look more human."

"I hate you."

Suddenly her eyes were compassionate. "I'm sorry, Paul. I guess we've both had a bad day."

Paul rose to take her hand. "I—I guess if you're not wearing the bathing suit that means you're not worried about your back. I'm glad."

She squeezed his hand, then freed herself from his moist

handclasp and sank into the sofa. "Let's have a drink and get ourselves into the mood to play lovey-dovey at the table. But you shouldn't've slapped me," she complained. "Or maybe you're thinking of making it a Goddamn habit?"

Paul's hands trembled as he splashed gin into the highball glasses. "How're things going at the studio?"

He knew better than she could tell him. True, he had been out at least two or three days a week in the past three or four weeks, and last week he had only been at the office on two mornings. He had pleaded with Jean to keep him company, because being alone with his misery, his secret, with a mind that raced and skipped and refused him rest by day or night, was too difficult to bear. But Jean, to spite him, to leave him alone on his rack of anguish, had insisted on returning to work. The studio was delighted to star her, as Paul had suggested prior to their engagement and marriage, in *Red Dust,* a stage play written by Wilson Collison and bought several years before by MGM. Gable was her co-star; Bern had suggested him, but to go out to the set and see a real man enjoying himself by playing male to Harlow's female—while the slut worked in the nude because she would not wear the bathing suit—was more than Bern could bear.

"You might go to the studio and find out how things are," Jean said. "It gets harder and harder for me to look sorry when people say they're sorry you're not feeling well."

"Do it convincingly and you'll be on the first step to becoming an actress."

"Don't be funny," she said.

Paul seated himself on the flowered sofa and held the glass between his knees. "I'm not. Practicing emotion is the only way to gain control of the emotion. Try to feel sorry. Make yourself feel sorry."

"I can't for you."

"Tell me why," he continued patiently. "Did you ever meet anyone who wanted to be born ugly? Or stupid, or

145

crippled? I haven't. I'm not alone, Jean. There must be others like me—"

"I bet," she interrupted. "Do those other cripples go around beating up their wives? Chewing on them until they're ashamed? Slapping them around for no reason? Even in front of cabdrivers where the neighbors might see? If they do I don't feel anything for them either." Jean stood to smooth her hair with a nervous brushing of both hands. "Right now I don't feel anything for anyone."

"Should I call Goldbeck and tell him you're tired?" Paul suggested.

"And have someone else think the reason why we aren't having people over is because we can't get enough of it from each other? No, thank you." Her laughter became increasingly hostile, edged. "I'm going to shower."

Paul scratched at the stubble of beard on his chin. "I have to shower and shave, too."

"You want me to wait?"

He raised the glass and drank for courage. "I was wondering if you'd mind me joining you in the shower?"

"Why act when no one's around to see it?"

"Jean! Please! Enough!"

"Okay," she said carelessly. "Come along. I'll let you wash my back. And kiss my ass, too, if you want to. Maybe it'll make you think some more of what you did to me."

Pride compelled him to refuse, to shower in another bathroom.

Dinner was without incident, though Jean smoked grimly, lighting a cigarette, taking several puffs, grinding the butt into a large tray and lighting up again. Paul and Willis Goldbeck, a writer also experienced as a producer, discussed studio matters, pictures and grosses. They attempted to draw Jean into the conversation, but she replied in disinterested grunts, finally pleaded a headache and asked to be excused. After she left the dining room Willis stayed for approximately the polite twenty minutes, refused a second liqueur and left. Paul told the Carmichaels they could have the weekend off. For several minutes, while his heart attempted to pump courage into his hand, he stared at the knob of the master-bedroom door, then retreated to his den to sit at his desk in bitter misery while he wondered what to do.

He chose several records, then returned them to their paper covers. Music could not help him tonight. Only manliness could help him. Only by being a man could he shore up and save his marriage. Nothing was as important as empirical reliance on self; once again he would have to rely upon his own intelligence, ingenuity and strength to save what he really did not care about at all, except that the world demanded the elevation and ritualistic ass-pumping worship of its goddess, a bitch whose body could never be associated with or soiled by failure. Well, he would go to her. He would talk to her. He would reason with her. Perhaps he would hit her.

He rapped lightly. Sorrow made his eyes shy as he opened the bedroom door; hope enabled him to smile pleasantly because Jean was awake and reading her script in bed. She rested on an elbow, and her pink nightgown slipped low to reveal a shoulder. Deliberately, to taunt him, she stretched to free a breast and permit it to rest outside the gown.

"Fleming told me you know your part perfectly," he said with a smile.

"The more I read it the worse it gets." She put the script aside. "It's really a stupid story."

"For stupid people," he agreed. "I've come to apologize. For slapping you. For being moody. Everything."

Jean stifled a yawn and returned her breast to the gown. "Forget it. Get some rest. Or do you like to look awful?"

"And you look beautiful." He stood at the side of the bed and admired her. "I've been thinking that I might order some black sheets and pillowslips for this bed. They would really set off your beautiful blondeness."

"Stop crapping me and don't order anything I'll have to pay for." She pounded her pillow. "I've gotta get up early. Willis wasn't sore that I went upstairs?"

"No. He understands. You do have to get up early. After you finish the picture I'm going to insist you get time off for a trip."

She yawned again and stretched her arms. "There's no place in this world I wanna go."

"I've been thinking of Europe."

"I told you no before on that." She looked again at the script, then dropped it to the rug. "I'm getting used to putting on the act for us here," she explained without any inflection of malice. "But if we take a trip we'll have to be interviewed and all the rest of that crap, and it'll make it harder for both of us."

Paul picked at his lower lip. "Would you leave me if I had cancer or was dying of heart trouble?"

"Of course not," she said. "Paul, I've had a long, rotten day on the set, and in a couple of hours I've got nothing to look forward to except another long rotten day." Suddenly she was concerned, kind. "Get undressed and I'll fix you a drink. Then we'll go to sleep."

"Not to bed," he said. "There is a difference."

"That's not my fault."

"And I suppose it's mine? I wanted it this way?"

"I don't want to go into it again." There was only a touch of edge in Jean's voice as she fluffed her pillow again and turned away. Aware of Paul's weight as he sat on the bed, she sighed. "I don't see why they make us work on Saturdays. And we're working Sunday too because of Labor Day. I think it's just rotten. Come on, Paul. Don't be a baby in everything. Let's go to sleep."

A normal man could have foregone anger because he could

do so without being thought a coward. But if he acquiesced it could only prove that he was, as she had suggested, a baby. Reason told Paul that his wife was tired and did have two days of hard, wet work ahead of her. But Jean knew his secret and delighted in using just the words to make him suffer. At parties she frequently held him by a hair over the pit of insanity as she chucked his chin and cooed at him as if he were an infant. That was why he had begun to react as if he were jealous, which was all right with him because the world expected, even approved of reactions that could be construed as husbandly suspicion of all other strutting males delightedly willing to usurp his place atop the blonde Venus. Why, if he were to imprison Jean in a chastity belt the world might laugh and call him a dog, but it would approve his mangerish attitude.

With a tight curse of despair Paul tore back the covers and ordered Jean from the bed. "I've had enough of you," he piped in a childish treble. "We have to talk."

Jean pulled the quilt free, drew it to her chin and turned again to lie with her back to Paul. "All you want to do is talk. That's all you *can* do."

"Whore!" The word was whispered, but with such venom that Jean shuddered as she turned. Now she was held by his eyes. "You're a whore with no heart, no brain and a cold—" He tried to say the word and failed. "You're a fake!" he screeched. "And I'm going to see that the whole world knows it. They could forgive you for not being an actress, but—"

Paul's sallow features twitched as he struggled for breath to shout her down. None came and he pointed at Jean with a hatred she could not deride. Perspiration broke out along her spine and under her arms and she felt fear.

"You're not scaring me by looking like the Phantom of the Opera," she lied. "And stop calling me dirty names and saying dirty things about me. I get enough of that from my dear fans."

Paul rested on his knees. "You don't deserve any more.

And you like the dirty letters and pictures." He laughed. "What's the good of sending dirty pictures to a fake?"

Reason suggested that she remain silent; if she said nothing he would at last lapse into silence and possibly into some sort of self-control. But the imp of perversity dictated otherwise. With quick movement she kicked back the covers, peeled off the nightgown and fell back on the bed with her legs high and arms spread wide in the classic pose of erotic welcome.

"Come on," she challenged him. "I can do anything they do in a dirty picture. Let's see how good you are."

"Stop it!" He covered his eyes and turned away. "Cover yourself."

"Or maybe you wanna beat me up?" she asked, as she raised her legs again to wiggle her toes. "Oh, for chrissakes, Paul." She sat up and covered herself with the pillow. "Paul, what the hell do you want?"

Eyes to the wall, he stood in the corner of the room. "To die," he said at last. "I want that more than killing you."

"Now you're really funny. I mean none of this is real, because we're both tired and upset," she added hastily. "So I'm still telling you to go to bed. You can sleep here if you want to. Honest, I won't mind. Tomorrow night we'll have a long talk and figure out what to do."

His voice was hollow. "About what?"

"Us. Why don't you pick me up tomorrow when I'm through? Oh damn!"

Paul looked over his shoulder. "Yes?"

"Mama was on the set today and being her usual pesty self. Anyway, she wants us over for dinner Sunday night. And you'd damn well better keep your hands to yourself and off me."

"I don't put them on you. Not unless I want to feel dirty."

"Piss on you, too," she said. "Mama would like to borrow the Carmichaels."

"I gave them the weekend off," Paul said.

"So I'll give them the weekend *on* tomorrow at breakfast," Jean replied. "And Mama'll pay them."

"Which means I'll be paying them," he said.

"You mean I'll be paying them," she contradicted Paul, who had crossed to sit on the chaise. Then she waved her hand as if the matter were too unimportant to quarrel about at length. "Mama's expecting us," she continued kindly, in an attempt at conciliation, for there were times when Paul's unhappiness, despite her outbursts of contempt and cruelty, saddened her. "Paul," she beckoned, "be a good boy and come to bed."

"Damn you, I'm a man!"

"All right," she agreed. "So—"

"—don't say prove it. Not unless you want me to kill you."

She shook her head. "Come to bed, please." It was safe to say this and nothing more; it was safer, an assurance of longer life, to stifle the imp of the perverse before Paul tried choking it to death.

"Soon," he said. Fingers at his lips, Paul mused for a moment as he looked at Jean; when she stretched her arms in a gesture of friendship, he smiled. "I'll be right back," he promised as he walked toward the dressing room.

Jean moved to one side of the bed, smoothed the pillow and slipped into the nightgown. What to do? She wanted to telephone someone—Pops, Mrs. Landau, Dr. Sugarman, her mother—but she was afraid to use the phone because Paul, that solitary twisted creature, might be listening at the door. Something would have to be done, and soon, because she was not going to spend another night alone with a maniac. Tomorrow, after the day's shooting, she would have to speak to Pops and arrange to see his lawyer; or, they might secretly move a guard into the house. A man wouldn't do, but any big Irish nurse accustomed to handling drunks could take care of Paul.

From the uneasy safety of the double bed Jean heard Paul

shut the door as he returned to the bedroom and she turned to see him in a blue silk robe with black lapels. His feet were bare, and because she did not see his pajama legs, she wondered if he were going to be foolish enough to sleep in the nude— for all the good that would do him. Paul untied the belt of the robe and stepped out of it. He was nude. And Jean stared in amazement, her mouth slack and open, because strapped around Paul's middle, just above his true parts, was a large artificial penis and testicles. This formidable apparatus, harnessed around Paul's hips with a series of straps, appeared to be made of a soft, suede-like leather dyed the color of natural flesh—except that the enormous head was bright red. The testicles were huge, and from the sack extended a little bulb.

She wanted to speak, attempted to find words, realized there was nothing, no adequate comment to make, and finally the farcical quality of this awful dream compelled her to laugh. She gasped, snickered, tried to stifle the laughter which would not be contained. Hysteria defeated her weak attempts at control, and she continued to laugh until blinding tears came. Then curiosity compelled her to wipe them away. She beckoned Paul to approach her, reached out tentatively to touch the engine—and as she grasped it and was unable to touch the tip of her forefinger to that of her thumb, the conceit of the dildo's size made her shriek out in a fresh seizure. She touched the little bulb, pressed it, and as warm water squirted against a breast she covered her mouth with both hands, rolled over on her stomach and beat her feet against the bed in a still more violent paroxysm of laughter.

Above her own wild mirth she heard Paul laughing and, no longer in fear, wiped her eyes to look at him. He was strutting around the room, one hand on the dildo to hold it as if it were the staff of a proud flag, and as Jean continued to laugh, Paul began to gallop as if he were astride a horse and to utter crowing sounds in imitation of a cock. Now he stood as if he were a conductor on a podium and moved the dildo as if it were a baton; now he held it with both hands as if it were a fishing rod, and as he pantomimed hooking a fish and fighting to land it, Jean's laughter cheered him on. He ran across the room to ram the dildo against the door and attempt an entrance into the keyhole, an effort which racked Jean with such hysteria that spasms of pain stabbed her from the back through to the chest.

Piling conceit upon conceit, dancing, strutting, Paul burlesqued a worship of the phallus, then solemnly rotated his hips to imitate a cooch dancer. Gasping and choking, Jean rolled from the bed to the carpet, then bounded up to embrace him. Suddenly tears flowed again, and Paul began to cry too, and they clung to each other like children surrounded by an evil enchantment.

As a wife she helped Paul unstrap the dildo, and as he knelt before the commode, hacking away at the obscene object with a sharp knife and scissors, she helped him by pushing the flush mechanism. At last it was gone, and in silence they watched the water rise and settle. And when Jean took Paul's hand and led him to the bed, he followed as a child might his mother.

Later that night, just before dawn, Paul left the bed, slipped into his robe, and tiptoed downstairs to the garden, where, in utter loneliness, he stretched his arms and clawed for the sky and fading stars. How could he have debased himself this way? How could he have paid two hundred dollars for so shameful a thing? True, he had purchased with hope and been deceived, but how could he have worn it, paraded around in it? How could he have been so weak of mind, to have surrendered to a weakness he could only loathe? Here he was, married to a goddess, the most longed for woman in all the world, and he had worshiped her in the manner of the antic, corrupted idiot. There could be nothing more comic and nothing filthier than this new degradation of his spirit. He succumbed to a fit of bitter laughter.

Jean was startled from her uneasy slumber by Paul's laughter in the garden. What was the nut doing *now*? To cut off the sound, which made her uneasy, she buried her head under a pillow.

Maybe she would get a large dog house, one for a Great Dane, and tell Paul this was to be his home? Or, to keep the peace and give them some laughs, she might suggest that Paul buy another one of those big awful cocks. God, he had been funny.

But her situation was funnier.

Chapter Eleven

The note was devilishly clever, phrased so ingeniously that even if she had really loved Bern there was no time to mourn. Bello held Jean's shoulders to pin her to the bed and make her listen: Self-preservation demanded she convince the studio, Louis Mayer, the police and Paul's family of her sincerity, the majesty of her grief, and by some desperate act to prove her sorrow, divert them all from a probing, ruinous inquiry and examination of her married life. Query, investigation and revelation would absolutely destroy her career, and all this could result from the note—which might have been Paul's intent.

Marino shook his stepdaughter until she no longer struggled. "It doesn't seem possible that a man could hate you so much when he'd only been married to you a little while. But we've got no time for that now. So you just listen to what you've got to do."

To prove her desolation, to show that Bern's death made life without him meaningless, so great was the tempest of her love, Jean would have to take some dramatic action. So Bello suggested she make an attempt at suicide.

"You've been crying that you want to be a real actress," Marino told her. He paused to draw breath, then glanced again at a newspaper headline of Bern's suicide. He read the suicide note printed by the paper, swore, and placed the paper on the dresser. "You've got to try killing yourself. Of course I'll stop you in time. You've got my word."

"You're crazy!"

"Am I?" Bello pulled away the pillow under which Jean was hiding. "You want everyone to believe you loved Paul? That you still do and everything was all right? That all this talk of fighting about giving us the house isn't true? That it isn't true that I had a fight with that little Jew because he wouldn't put more money into the mine? Don't we have to stop that kind of talk? You want to be crucified for a little Jew? No?" Bello paused to draw breath and step back from the bed. "Then you got to run down to the end of this hall and pretend you're gonna jump from the little balcony. Don't worry, I'll catch you in time. Think you can do it?"

Jean blew her nose in the handkerchief and nodded. "You think it'll work?" She stared at him intently. "Maybe you won't stop me. Which'll be doing me a favor."

"And it'll be a favor for your mama? You're not going to kill yourself, my girl." Marino approached the bed again to speak directly into his stepdaughter's ear. "The only thing you got to do now is act. For the first time in your life, act, because your life really depends on it—and all of us wanna stay alive." Bello unlocked the door. "I'll start downstairs for aspirin and you suddenly come out screaming. Remember—screaming. So I'll hear you."

"I understand," she nodded.

The contemptible plan was as unreal as Bern's death. The little father confessor had really got even with her. Hollywood's "first gentleman" was stronger, more dangerous in death than he had ever been in life, and the knowledge of what he had done to her and how he had done it, so simply—with a bullet, pen and paper—made her nod again. Anything; she was willing to do anything if it would take the last laugh from Bern. It was incredible that the man could have hated her so. But she would be stronger in life than Paul was in death. Now she was ready. "Don't be too far downstairs because I'll be running like hell. The balcony door's unlocked?"

"Everything's set and it'll work," Bello assured his step-daughter. "When I catch up with you I'll be crying. That'll prove there's so much love around here you're willing to kill yourself to show it."

At any other time the little suicide scene certainly would have been reported in banner headlines; now, although noted, it was confined to secondary leads. Still, Jean had given a good performance, probably her best to date. She had darted into the hall and screamed that there was nothing to live for; that Paul, her lover, was dead; that she wanted to join her darling husband in death. When she had one leg over the balcony, a weeping Bello, as he had promised, pulled her to safety. Struggling with Jean, calling to the heavens for assistance, Bello had punctuated his prayers with cries for someone—a doctor or priest or Mr. Mayer—please to help his daughter. The crowd before the house and along the street had gasped, shrieked and keened in appreciation of the struggle on the balcony; two elderly women fell to their knees and prayed fervently until the rescue was successfully completed.

Newspapers dutifully reported Jean's suicide attempt, adding that she had been sedated and was now guarded round the clock by faithful friends to forestall another attempt. But Paul's little note still gripped the attention of the police, the studio and the newspapers. Even so, Marino felt the suicide attempt had had good effect because Mayer had telephoned to insist that better care be taken of Jean. Mayer's shouted concern gave Bello confidence that MGM was still interested in its blonde star. When Mayer began to scream for Bello to explain the suicide note, the wily stepfather replied that he was too overcome to speak now, especially since he had to comfort Mama Jean.

Exactly what did the note mean? And imply? Certainly more than it said.

Dearest Dear:

Unfortunately this is the only way to make good the frightful wrong I have done you and to wipe out my abject humiliation.

Paul

You understand that last night was only a comedy.

By firing a bullet through his head sometime between late Sunday night and early Labor Day morning, Paul Bern had once again become a national figure. He had prepared himself for death by removing all his clothing and had stood naked before the dressing room mirror, one gun on the dressing table, another in his hand. And, staring at his tormented body, he had pulled the trigger. The nudity added a sexual element to his suicide that encouraged a full spectrum of gamy interpretations of his farewell note.

Events of the last weekend were not difficult to reconstruct. On Friday evening, September 2, Jean and Paul had a dinner guest. Early Saturday morning, heartened by Paul's promise to speak to Victor Fleming about completing this scene, Jean left for the studio to take her place in the barrel. She had promised to wear a bathing suit and thanked Paul for asking the Carmichaels to forego part of their weekend and help her mother prepare Sunday's dinner.

John and Winifred Carmichael left Bern late Saturday morning; neighbors told the police they had seen the producer shortly after strolling along Easton Drive, carrying a stick he had used as a cane. Later, a neighbor saw Bern enter his garden. The neighbor had called a greeting, but Bern had only acknowledged by raising his hand, another proof of Bern's troubled preoccupation. With what? Well, according to the neighbors, eager to help the police without injuring anyone and their fine neighborhood, Bern had "become a changed man since his recent marriage." He had become reclusive and "seemed worried"; some burden apparently occupied his mind.

In their attempt to make the suicide note meaningful, the police investigators gave short shrift to the psychological conclusions of neighbors and concentrated again on their reconstruction of the fatal weekend.

Thus, to return to Saturday, September 3: Jean had completed the day's shooting and left for her mother's home, annoyed with Paul because he had not called Victor Fleming. Nor had he answered the phone at their house until eleven that night. The Carmichaels had been given the day but would be at the Bellos on Sunday, and Paul had told Jean he had been walking, sitting in the garden, even sleeping, and when he had been awake he had refused to answer the phone simply because he didn't care to do so. Now he was sorry if he had caused concern. For late supper he had managed half a cold sandwich, warmed over coffee and two fig newtons. Jean reported that their telephone conversation was pleasant, and that she had asked Paul to come to her mother's house, but he had replied, "It's so late, darling, and you have to work tomorrow. Why don't you stay there?"

Jean pressed fingers to her eyes, sniffed smelling salts and sniveled as she related that Paul and she had blown kisses over the telephone. Next morning she had left Mama Jean's for an unusual workday at the studio. Because it was Sunday, the crew, actors and director were unable to function, and after a day's unsatisfactory takes, Fleming had dismissed the company and walked off the set without wishing anyone a happy Labor Day. Bello had driven Jean from the studio to her home and left her there while she waited for the Carmichaels to pack a liquor hamper. According to John Carmichael, Bern said he would be along in an hour or so, after he finished a book, and Jean had replied, "Goodbye, dear, I'll be seeing you."

Pressed, prodded by the police, the Carmichaels were emphatic to the point of taking oaths that there had been no harsh words or evidences of hostility between the newlyweds. The meeting had been congenial and happy, the parting idyllic and lovely, worthy of film.

But the Negro gardener, Clifton E. Davis, disagreed with the Carmichaels' account of domestic harmony. Instead of sweetness and felicitous light, the Saturday afternoon had been an occasion for bitterness and shadow, for Bern had angrily dismissed his wife, practically ordered her from the house. Davis told the police he had been curious—how could any man be rude to Jean Harlow?—and Mrs. Carmichael had told him the Berns were not getting along, they were fighting and shouting at each other. No, not about other men or women, but property; Winifred Carmichael attributed the quarrels to Jean's desire to deed the Easton Drive house to her parents, and to Bern's objections to this. Still shouting, Bern had said he would not give away Jean's wedding gifts to him no matter what the provocation, and he expected her to show similar restraint.

In addition, according to Davis, there also appeared to be a difference of opinion about Bern's financing a so-called gold mine owned by Marino Bello. The gardener believed that Paul had made some investment to enable Bello to begin preliminary diggings; then, called upon for more money, the son-in-law had refused to sink another nickel into what he had called "a hole in the ground." There was some confusion here, Davis admitted, because he could not remember whether it was Bern or Jean who had objected to continued investment in the mine.

Marino indignantly denied that Mama Jean or he had any knowledge of Jean's projected gift of real estate and swore that nothing could have persuaded them to accept the house. As for Paul Bern's investing in a gold mine or any of Bello's business ventures, the suggestion was preposterous. "I have more money than Bern ever had," Marino told the assembled reporters and police officers. "There was no occasion for any financial dealings between us."

The police agreed that Davis' testimony was of minor importance, since it was denied in full by the Carmichaels and Mr. and Mrs. Bello. Turning again to classic police work, they continued to reconstruct Bern's last hours.

The Los Angeles *Times* of September 7 reported Bello as stating "he had been working at MGM studios and that between six and seven P.M. he drove Miss Harlow to her home and went immediately to his own. Some time later, he said, the actress and the Bern servants reached his home. It was his understanding that Bern was to come later for dinner. The producer did not arrive and Miss Harlow remained overnight with her parents. Bello said he left early Monday morning on a fishing trip and knew nothing of the suicide until his return home late Monday night."

What job or position Bello occupied at the studio has never been established, nor did anyone question his claim of employment, although there is no record of his ever having been on an MGM payroll. The studio did not deny or affirm his "working," although Thalberg later privately admitted his concern that Mayer might demand a showdown with Bello, a confrontation Thalberg believed was best avoided at this anxious time.

Jean, Mama Jean and Marino all agreed that Paul had telephoned Sunday night to apologize for not coming to dinner—the pressing work on his desk demanded all his attention. And once again Paul had suggested that his dear wife sleep at her parents' home.

Details of Bern's movements on Saturday night were supplied by Harold (Slickem) Garrison, a full-time MGM handyman and occasional chauffeur for Bern, and these were at odds with what Bern had told Jean when she had at last been able to get him on the telephone. Garrison informed the police that contrary to what the producer had told his wife, on early Saturday night he had driven Bern to the Ambassador Hotel. There, as instructed, he had waited in the car. Bern had returned about nine-thirty and asked to be driven home. Shortly after ten, Bern had dismissed Garrison but had instructed him to return the next morning about ten. They had jested that twelve hours of sleep was more than enough for any man if he was sleeping alone, and Bern had not appeared to be disturbed or preoccupied when he had dismissed the chauffeur. As usual, he had tipped generously.

Sunday morning, Garrison had returned to Easton Drive and been told by John Carmichael that Bern was still asleep and that he should come back Monday morning about eight-thirty. Garrison had insured his being paid by occupying himself with washing several windows and doing other small chores in the garden and around the pool, but during that time he had not seen the producer. He had left about four-thirty in the afternoon.

When the Carmichaels had left with Jean to drive to the Bello house, Bern had waved goodbye from the foot of the driveway; that was the last time they had seen him alive.

Monday morning Jean had breakfasted in bed and ordered the Carmichaels, who had also spent the night at the Bellos', to return to the Easton Drive house and look after her husband.

At about eleven-thirty John Carmichael had telephoned Jean to come quickly, for he had discovered Mr. Bern a suicide. Before Jean could scream twice Carmichael had hung up to telephone MGM. The operator at the studio switchboard had located Louis Mayer, who had telephoned Irving Thalberg to shout that his executive right arm was to protect the studio and its human properties; later, when there was time, Thalberg was to explain, if he could, what had happened to studio morale that one of its executives could kill himself.

With no further elaboration of his orders, Mayer left immediately for Bern's house, where he was relieved to find only people he knew: Ralph Wheelwright, from the studio's publicity department, and Whitey Hendry, chief of the studio's police force. Both men had been ordered to posts at the Bern house by Howard Strickling, and they had occupied themselves in calming the Carmichaels and preventing them from calling the police. To do so they had appropriated the telephone and called the Bello house, where they had spoken to Marino at length and advised him to keep Jean and her mother with him and not to return to Easton Drive.

Mayer thanked the Carmichaels for their cooperation and vetoed Hendry's suggestion that he look at the body; as executive head of the industry's largest and most active studio, one that had made its proportionate share of films with suicides in their plots, Mayer knew what had to be done first. There was no unauthorized woman in the house nor lacy garments left in hurried flight, and for this, at least, Mayer was grateful, since it left him free to concentrate every faculty in his search for a suicide note. In Metro films suicides always left notes and Mayer's disappointment in Bern was increased because the dead man, a well-trained production supervisor, had left a note which Mayer found easily but which he did not understand. Still, that was good picture stuff, too; later, before the big scene, the note would be explained and would resolve the several problems unreconciled by kisses.

Because this was a real suicide, with real blood, an actual corpse, and police *yet* to be notified, Mayer understood he could not wait for the unravelment to come to him in ninety minutes, the length of an average A-film; rather, he, the mountain, would have to go to Mohammed, in this case Jean Harlow because the note was obviously addressed to her, and demand her interpretation of the cryptic farewell and apology. In real life terms suicide was nasty, but not as bad as murder or spectacular adultery. Film production had also educated Mayer to the dangers of not telephoning the law within a reasonable length of time, so at last, reluctantly, because the people involved were his property, Mayer ordered the operator to put him through immediately to police headquarters. In the proper tones of awed and sorrowing bewilderment, he informed the officers of the tragedy. Propriety, diplomacy and showmanship demanded that Mayer wait until real life police officers and detectives arrived at the scene; then, apparently overcome with an emotion that thickened his voice and impeded his step, he told the busy officers that he had to leave them to visit his little blonde star. Old enough to be Jean's father, he would attempt to ease her bereavement and make proper funeral arrangements for her saintlike husband now among the saints. Shaking hands solemnly with the detectives from the West Los Angeles division, bidding them to be gentle with the Carmichaels—good, simple, devoted people—Mayer hurried off to get to Jean Harlow first and find out what this was all about. And God pity her if she'd been carrying on with another man—he'd ruin them both.

As he approached his car, Mayer saw Howard Strickling running toward the house and Wheelwright hurrying to meet his boss. Mayer paused to give his chief of studio publicity some orders. He was about to drive off when Strickling said he had been told by Wheelwright of the suicide note found by Mayer, and he wanted to see it. Mayer objected, Strickling insisted, Wheelwright withdrew. If Mayer was a student of films, Strickling also understood the medium, and in films people who concealed pertinent evidence from the police always got into trouble. Patiently, Strickling told his superior that the only course of action for Mayer was to return to the house and explain to the police how grief and confusion had shaken him so that he had neglected to give them Bern's note. After all, he had called the police, so why should he have reason to conceal pertinent evidence?

After crackling curses and purple protests, Mayer acceded to Strickling's suggestion and surrendered the note to the detectives. Later, when the note was published in translation in major newspapers throughout the world and an examination of Bern's body gave clues to what the reference to "comedy" might be, Mayer raged at the invasion of his studio's privacy and telephoned publisher Harry Chandler to scream that he wanted the case soft-pedaled. Mayer was becoming increasingly important in Republican politics, and his studio was a major source of news for *Times* readers, but later that day Chandler and William Hearst had to tell Mayer why journalistic tradition, obligations and circulation prevented the closing of their columns to the suicide. Still, they would do what they could. Chandler and Hearst reporters would cooperate to write of the Platinum Bombshell only as a bewildered, soul-stricken widow whose heart had been shattered by the lead of Bern's bullet. In friendly, sympathetic but emphatic tones both publishers told Mayer they would have to publish the note and all the facts, unless all other papers agreed to a cooperative censorship of so important a news item.

It was impossible to arrive at a treaty, so Mayer called together his top executives. Raised to an Olympian height by his thick rug and elevated by a passion of lamentation, he assured them that all their suicides performed over and over again could never propitiate his wrath, for at that time Mayer took a dim view of sexual irregularity even if it was undiscovered, a dimmer view of such social play if it was discovered, and the dimmest view if, when discovered, it affected MGM. And as his rage enlarged, Mayer resisted a stroke that would have toppled a lesser giant. A *fairy* had been employed at his studio! How, when and why? Had the executives no thought for the virile male stars contracted to the studio, stars who might seek to break their contracts because they had had to work in the proximity of and even under the executive orders of a sexual degenerate? At this meeting, which the Los Angeles *Times* of September 6 captioned "Bern's Chair Unoccupied When Executives Meet" and which the paper reported was an occasion for state sadness as the production executives mourned the "Father Confessor of Hollywood," Mayer was portrayed as chief, loudest, most unconsolable mourner, a man who rent his garments and wept as many tears as Jean Harlow.

In reality Mayer frothed, ranted and appeared ready to shake Thalberg by the throat as he demanded again and again to be told in yes-and-no terms if Thalberg was aware that the studio's brightest star had been married to a *fairy,* a treacherous little *pansy* whose wedding *and* reception they had attended and who had proved himself so ungrateful as to negate his only virtuous act by leaving a note designed to raise thousands of questions whose answers could ruin Harlow and everyone associated with the stupid blonde? And Harlow—was she so dumb that she didn't know the difference between a real man—say, like Gable—and a cripple? How could this be when she had been married before, or was the story of that marriage as phony as everything else written about her? In towering jeremiad Mayer flayed his silent executives, refused to permit all gestures of supplication and ordered them to die if need be for the studio—but scandal was to be avoided.

"Sacrifice, money are no objects," his fist pounded home this uncompromising dicta. "And bar Landau off the lot."

Bravely, Thalberg raised a hand, like a pupil with a question for his teacher. "Why?"

"Because Landau knew Bern was—the word disgusts me." Mayer's eyes glinted behind his glasses, and the men at the table nodded in unison to prove that they, too, were disgusted by psychopathology and its language. "And if he didn't he should've. So keep him off the lot and out of my sight until I say different. And one more thing—when you talk to reporters, to anyone, you'd better do nothing else except cry," Mayer warned his executives. "Your families, too. That'll keep all of you from running your stupid mouths off."

Mayer's concern was neither insane nor exaggerated. The scandals of William Desmond Taylor, Mary Miles Minter,

Mabel Normand, Fatty Arbuckle and Wallace Reid were still very live memories. Zukor at Paramount had almost a million dollars tied up in Arbuckle comedies that had to remain in the film vaults. Just by being associated with Taylor, the careers of Mary Minter and Mabel Normand had gone into decline. Yes, the memories were recent and painful to contemplate; eastern stockholders had no knowledge of the dangers of picture making.

"And one more thing," Mayer added. "Get him buried. Order lots of flowers and see that only nice things are written about the little rat. And for your own good see that nothing happens to Jean."

"Suppose we have to make a choice?" Thalberg asked. "Jean, or a little bad publicity for the studio?"

"Irving, don't be a fool," Mayer snapped. "Then we'll bury her, too. Something else—see that Bern's secretary also keeps her mouth shut."

Mayer need not have worried about Bern's secretary. Irene Harrison was so steeped in grief she was at present incapable of giving a coherent interview. Fearful of Mayer, no one at the studio would even make a statement of sorrow, so Mayer had to face the press. Equal to the occasion, though unhappy because of unreasonable telephone calls he had received from the company's New York offices, Mayer haltingly told reporters there had been so extensive a change in Bern's demeanor that he had personally brought it to Thalberg's attention. Sadly wiping his brow and sighing heavily, Mayer said Thalberg had answered that "Mr. Bern needed a rest and should be sent away for a few days. I had never seen him act so strangely before. He had the queerest look about his eyes and appeared to have something preying on his mind."

The Fourth Estate evaluated Mayer's statement as thinnest sheep dip and turned its attention to the office of the coroner. There, Assistant Surgeon Frank Webb described the hole in Bern's head as a "typical suicide wound," with powder burns inside the scalp. This too was petty news, as was the announcement that Bern was free of any malignant ailment or disease that might have prompted a despairing man to take his life. But—the autopsy did disclose a physical ailment that might preclude marital happiness! Now, at last, the suicide made sense! And what sense!

Now there was nothing Mayer could do to tone down the coverage or headlines; the papers continued to quote Jean without interviewing her, so that the man in the street must have been convinced the actress was as he had suspected: beautiful, brainless and incapable of guile. One quotation attributed to Jean was so artless it subjected her to hours of interrogation, for the police investigators refused to believe that anyone, even a blonde, could be in real life that simple a Lorelei Lee.

"Paul often talked to me of suicide as a general topic, but never once did he intimate that he himself contemplated such an act," she was quoted. "There was nothing between us that I can think of that would have caused him to contemplate such an act. There was nothing between us that I can think of that would have caused him to do this."

In summary, the newspapers continued to ask editorial questions, though some were credited to the police:

"Was jealousy the underlying cause that induced Bern to end his life?"

"What was the 'frightful wrong' Bern believed he had done the screen actress?"

"Was it really a 'comedy' enacted at the Bern home . . . or was it prelude to a tragedy of death?"

"Did neighbors hear a powerful car roar away from the Bern home at 3 A.M. Monday, and if so was someone present when the film director (sic!) fired the fatal bullet through his brain?"

The question about the powerful car was quickly dropped because the neighbors would not stand and be identified, but as a final drop in the overflowing cup of conjecture, the Los Angeles *Times* commented: "Reports that several members of Bern's immediate family had died by suicide were denied by attorney Ralph Blum, who has been retained by the Bern family. Blum said that his investigation had revealed that the only members of Bern's family who had died suicides were an aunt and cousin."

Now Irene Harrison was reached for an interview, but when she spoke the public was disappointed, for Miss Harrison would say only that she could not believe her boss—that wonderful, gentle, perfect man and saint—was dead. Such news dispatches were judged to be pallid, wanting in sensation and lacking in prurient detail.

At the Easton Drive house, crowds milled in the street, questioned one another, and appropriated several ornamental mailboxes as souvenirs of pilgrimage. A plague of quidnuncs invaded the Bern grounds, peered into the house, stole potted plants, clothespins, and an antique iron bootscraper set outside the service porch door. In retaliation the property was floodlighted to aid the special guards in their identification and expulsion of petty thieves, children, necromancers and necrophiles, and a variety of erotic types who had to be beaten out of the bushes and the garage.

Repulsed at Easton Drive, the crowds regrouped before the Bello house until the street was clogged with cars, several of which locked bumpers; threats were made, curses flung and fists beat against noses and eyes until the good burghers on Club View Drive burned up the telephone lines to the police department with demands that their street be cleared of human trash, ice-cream vendors, newsboys hawking their latest editions and several itinerant photographers who were doing quite nicely by photographing people before the "Harlow suicide house."

But the sturdy, belligerent crowds before the Bello house

were in a holiday mood and were determined to resist banishment, especially as their idol Jean was in an upstairs bedroom, probably naked in bed and under guard to keep her from attempting suicide again in the nude, as Paul Bern had done. At last Mama Jean appeared to make a personal maternal appeal. Madonna-like, holding fast to her well-thumbed copy of *Science and Health,* Mrs. Bello pleaded that all of Jean's loyal, loving fans disperse to their homes to pray for her daughter's recovery from such tragic sorrow. Some of the curious, sentimental by nature, were moved by Mama Jean's tears and left, but more calloused spirits refused to go until the sorrowing mother signed their autograph books. The next morning the gardener discovered and without apology reported the theft of the garden hose, hedge clippers and a sack of fertilizer.

The reporters, desperate for new angles, snapped to life at the news that Henry Bern, Paul's brother, was coming by air to Los Angeles. Interviewed in the Kansas City airport, where the plane had landed for refueling, Henry Bern of New Rochelle, New York, would only make a short, unsatisfactory statement: he was on his way to mourn his brother, attend his funeral and "help with the investigation," because it was difficult for him to conceive of his brother as a suicide. However, because the fact of suicide was apparently incontrovertible, he added that "any man will commit suicide with provocation." Pressed to offer his opinion of what might have been his brother's provocation, Henry Bern's reply was vague. "He lived under tension always. Tension, tension, almost unbearable tension. I have seen him work. I know. Motives? I know none. Most of the things that have been said about motives are untrue."

At this point Henry Bern refused to elaborate on what motives had been suggested that he could brand as falsehoods, but hastily assured the reporters that his brother had loved Miss Harlow. "She on the other hand could have married any marriageable man she chose to take. She had youth and great beauty. Nothing was misrepresented. I know it was not. He did not misrepresent his financial condition. It was good."

Alert reporters telephoned their papers that they had not asked questions about the dead man's finances—was this angle worth following? Editors did not think so and instructed their reporters to find more inspiration in the suicide note and the coroner's report. Bern's body lay in the Price and Daniel mortuary in Sawtelle; Jean was still mute under heavy sedation and, to the relief of her family, agent and studio, was still the object of sympathy; Henry Bern continued on his flight to Los Angeles.

A rush of reporters to the Bello house only elicited the unsatisfactory information that Jean was still too withdrawn in deep shock. Marino Bello swore again, on his honor, that his stepdaughter and Bern had been ideally mated, and that anyone who dared slur Jean's reputation would have to answer to him on the field of honor. An interview with the coroner proved no more newsworthy, for Mr. Nance would only say that he intended to hold a formal inquiry into Bern's death, that witnesses of all degree would be called, and that the mourning widow would have to testify under oath, because on September 8 she had been served with a subpoena.

Arthur Landau knew it was time to turn to counsel for advice and for preparation of sound statements Jean might make to the press and police. The physical report on Bern and the suicide note were damning, and Arthur feared that an unknown witness or witnesses, some unknown *voyeur,* might reveal himself as having been privy to the course of the hymeneal rites, or to the horrid scene of the past Friday night which Jean had revealed to him, but which his mind still refused to accept.

Although she insisted it was all truth, that Paul had pranced around dressed only in a dildo, he could not credit her story. He told Jean she was hallucinated, suffering from

171

morbid fantasy; she had substituted a photo received in her mail, one Arthur remembered he had seen and commented on, for the true facts of her bedroom. He would not, could not accept her fantasy; furthermore, if she insisted on repeating it to others the story could ruin her career, her family and her associates, and could cause harm to her studio, possibly to the entire industry. In desperation, because Jean refused to consider his advice, Arthur gambled on a psychological play. He called Bello into the bedroom and dared the actress to repeat her account of Friday night. While Jean sobbed and beat the bed with her fists, Arthur told Bello that Jean was sorry she had left the dinner table to retire early, and that Paul, feeling slighted and humiliated by her discourtesy, had killed himself two days later. Marino ordered Jean to keep her stupid mouth shut and agreed with Arthur that counsel was required to represent Jean's interests in Bern's estate. Marino had heard some reporters ask if the producer had really left a half million in insurance; furthermore, Bern had earned fifteen hundred a week at the studio, so there should be a pile somewhere.

It was up to Arthur to get an attorney, and Mendel Silberberg was retained to represent Jean. The attorney was introduced to Miss Harlow, and he assured her that she would be protected, and that she had no reason, he was sure, to fear the coroner's inquest. She was persuaded to drink a cup of hot coffee spiked with brandy and helped to her bed to sleep and await the arrival of Henry Bern.

The intelligence that a fretful, petulant Greta Garbo was invalided in her island home near Stockholm was given an inch of newspaper space. Far greater coverage was devoted to the arrival of Henry Bern, who alighted from the Transcontinental and Western plane in a dark suit, dark mourning tie and Panama hat, and was photographed with his hands in his pockets and Irene Harrison at his side. As the secretary began to sob, Henry offered her his sympathies and all the family's appreciation for her grief, then told the reporters he was simply a man come to the funeral of his brother. Apologizing for looking and feeling ill, Henry Bern explained that his first flight had been an exhausting experience.

Pressed for some statement for readers everywhere, Henry promised to speak freely but said he wanted "to confer with relatives before agreeing to a statement of any kind." A phalanx of MGM police in plain clothes maneuvered Henry and Irene through the crowd to studio cars. Miss Harrison was driven home, and Henry Bern was taken to a restaurant. At about ten that night he was driven to the Bello house for a first meeting with his widowed sister-in-law.

At the Bello house Henry was welcomed by Mama Jean, who dampened his collar with tears while Marino pressed his hand. Followed by a cordon of studio attachés, Louis Mayer offered offhand sympathies, then began a tirade because Jean had been served with a subpoena to appear at the coroner's inquest, which was to be held at the undertaking parlors where Paul's body lay. The ghoulishness of this arrangement had so unstrung Jean that she had begged for another try at suicide, and it had been necessary to reinforce her sedation and to fill her bedroom with fresh cascades of flowers to prove to the actress, as she lay in deep, induced slumber, that all the world loved her.

Almost as if on cue, Jean awoke and insisted upon seeing Henry. He was to come to her room alone, she insisted, and as Henry entered the bedroom and began to wheeze in reaction to the floral attar, Jean began to wail. She had loved Paul so, she moaned, and she could not believe he had chosen death. Now she, too, had attempted death, so she could join Paul and ask him why, why, why? If she had known their marriage would have caused Paul's death she would never have married him, and even now, this very minute, she would lay down her life for his. Did Henry and his family hate her? They shouldn't, because she did not hate them.

The actress' grief became increasingly bathoscopic, and Henry was able to calm her only after he promised not to believe whatever an evil, lying world with a sick, dirty imagination might say about her.

It was almost midnight when Henry left the house with Louis Mayer. To the nocturnal reporters Henry promised a brighter tomorrow. "I want no secrecy veiling the matter of my brother's death," he said. "He would not have had it that way in life. I wish to do as he would have done. He never had secrets from anyone."

Two young women dressed as nurses were unmasked as imposters just before they gained admission to Miss Harlow's bedroom.

Chapter Twelve

As the reporters left the Bello house with Henry Bern's statement in their pads that his brother "never had secrets to hide from anyone," the prevalent feeling among the journalists was that they would have to wait for Jean's recovery from her extended swoon and her appearance at the coroner's inquest before spicy seasonings could be added to the rich, lip-smacking ingredients that make the basic mulligatawny of scandal. True, the suicide, the cryptic note, the post mortem revelation of Bern's singular insufficiency—not an heroic accident as in the case of Hemingway's Jake Barnes, but a rarer physiological shortening of natural detail—and the widow's operatic attempt at suicide, at least what had been seen of it, could, with only minor reservations, be believed. At MGM studios the usually affable and generous publicity staff was grouchy, niggardly in detail, even reluctant to give out standard still photographs of Harlow and Bern. Then the staff became determinedly silent. Irene Harrison was no longer available for comment, and attempts to see her were rebuffed by a cold studio statement that she was too overcome by grief to say more than she already had, and that her private mourning had to be respected. The dignities of sorrow continued to be planned, and the decreed theme for Bern's funeral, as befitted the shy retiring nature of the man whose death would be an irreplaceable loss to his wife, family, friends, studio associates and the entire world, was grave solemnity without great fanfare. And private rites would be a comfort to his wife, who could not be forgotten. Her suffering had been evident to everyone; after all, a man linked to heavenly figures, saintly virtues and intellect had killed himself for love of her.

The temptation to invent, to make logical projections and fantastic summations challenged papers and their staffs, and their hesitation to take this tempting approach could be attributed less to their dedication to truth than to their educated guesses about what Mayer could and would do to a paper and its people if he found their coverage offensive. Because at that time Mayer was living his moral phase, and though his concern with morality, right living and the puritan virtues were congealed opinions and standards that might be laughed at by a Mencken, for average adversaries Mayer was best not challenged. He could bar a paper and its staff from his lot, and it was not beyond the Culver City margrave to call his peers in the industry to inform them how singularly displeased he would be if the gates of their demesnes were not closed tight against the men and information distributors whose vagrancy had offended him.

But just as in the best made movies, the waiting did not take too long, for the wonderful journalistic miracle occurred: It was discovered that for ten years, until the first months of 1932, a "Mrs. Paul Bern" had been living in New York City at the Algonquin, a hotel famous for its literary round table. (Adela Rogers St. Johns in her *Liberty* article in November of that year, which purported to tell the reader all that Jean Harlow had told her, made an interesting dissent about the Algonquin: she referred to it as "A sanitarium for mental cases.") Literary coffee house or convalescent hospice, the Algonquin had now come to the attention of readers everywhere, because it was quite possible that the Hollywood suicide had also been a bigamist, a man smart enough to keep his wives a continent apart. And if Bern had been bigamously married for ten years, the supposition about Bern's sexual inadequacy could no longer serve as the foremost reason for his suicide.

The Los Angeles newspapers soberly reported that the woman identified as "Mrs. Paul Bern" was about "thirty-two years of age, with flaming tresses and described as 'bookish' and of Bern's own intellectual type." Hotel attachés informed delighted scribes, once again able to record *news,* that the woman of the flaming tresses had received substantial fortnightly checks from Bern and had paid her bills with them. And Bern had made at least one annual visit to Mrs. Bern, usually in the autumn, for at the turning of the leaves he went to New York on business. Paul's last visit to the lady in residence at the Algonquin had been in October, 1931.

Chided for his lack of candor, Henry Bern told the injured newspapermen that it was quite true Paul had supported a woman with whom he had been friendly many years before, and that there was nothing unusual or remarkable in such philanthropy.

Patently aware of their responsibility, the reporters were careful to quote Henry Bern in full, and went to the unusual length of checking their transcriptions with rivals. "He had no secrets from anyone," Henry Bern stated again. "His only secret was his last one. He was never married before he wed the screen star, Miss Harlow, but he lived with a woman once, a long time ago. This woman had a nervous breakdown, a derangement. Paul had nothing to do with it, but he took care of her just the same, as though she were his wife. He had been keeping her in a sanatorium. Miss Harlow knew of it because Paul told her. He concealed nothing, but lived openly. Nothing was misrepresented when he married Miss Harlow. I know this."

Dorothy Milette was the maiden name of the woman the newspapers insisted upon identifying as Mrs. Paul Bern—with cause, because this *was* the name under which she had been registered at the Algonquin. Henry told the newsmen how his brother, as a young man in the New York theater, had met and fallen in love with Dorothy. They had lived together for several years. Then Dorothy had become seriously ill, and in 1920, as Mrs. Paul Bern, she had been admitted to the Blythewood Sanatorium at Greenwich, Connecticut.

"Paul was heartbroken," Henry continued. "The man went around like a shadow. He mourned. He would not think of putting her into a cheaper sanatorium, although he could not afford to keep her in such an expensive place."

The costs of Dorothy's convalescence were many, but Paul provided generously at an expense, Henry observed, "that might have been warranted had he been a millionaire."

When Paul decided to move westward, it was impossible for Dorothy to leave the sanatorium. Then, after eight months of treatment she was discharged "not as entirely cured, but because her condition was not dangerous." Fortunately Paul had prospered, so he had arranged for his convalescent friend to move to the Algonquin and register there as his wife. And so she had lived for ten years. The Los Angeles *Times* of September 9 reported Henry Bern dating his brother's last visit to Dorothy Milette in October, 1931, but the *Times* of the next day reported that, when Henry met the press in his dead brother's office at MGM, he now stated that "Paul saw her at the most four times during all this period of time. Every time he saw her he came away actually sick. The last time he saw her was about four years ago."

This interview also established other facts about Dorothy Milette. In early 1932 she had telephoned Henry Bern for advice: should she move to California to enjoy its salubrious climate? Henry had not believed that Dorothy was interested in climate or travel, but, reluctant to disturb her delicate emotional balance, he had agreed that she might make the move if she felt a change of scene would be beneficial. In the latter part of April, 1932, Dorothy arrived in San Francisco, a city of many distinctions but certainly not noted for its climate, and moved into the Plaza Hotel. Henry Bern's recital was interrupted at this point by Irene Harrison, who informed the assembled reporters that she had arranged for Miss Milette to stay at the Plaza Hotel.

When this story appeared, two anonymous tipsters—a man and a woman—telephoned the police and every newspaper in Los Angeles to suggest that Miss Harlow be asked what she was doing in San Francisco on August 18. Could she have gone there to meet Dorothy Milette? The studio immediately issued a statement that Jean had visited the northern city to purchase some clothes and had registered at the Mark Hopkins Hotel with her parents.

Questioned further, Henry Bern told the press that his brother had never been to San Francisco to see Miss Milette, and that Dorothy had most certainly not been disturbed when she read of Paul's engagement to Jean Harlow, for the sick woman desired nothing more than to live in quiet surroundings. The most that Dorothy and his brother had ever been, Henry insisted, was good friends. He would say it again: good friends.

But another classic messenger entered from the wings to play his role in this Senecan drama by contradicting Henry. George Clarken, an insurance agent, told the press that he had always believed that Paul Bern had been legally married to Miss Milette. Some time in 1921, Clarken had written a small insurance policy for Bern with the New York Life Insurance Company; Paul had described himself on the company form as a married man and had named Dorothy Milette as his wife and beneficiary.

Urged by the press to elaborate on the important matters of relationship and nuptial contracts, Henry preferred to discuss the nature of Miss Milette's illness, which he described as a religious mania. "You could talk to her for half an hour and realize the keenness of her mind. Mention religion and the conversation was all over." Paul had provided for the quiet woman by sending her at least $350 a month, which, Henry observed, was a substantial sum. Henry had attempted to tele-

phone Dorothy at the Plaza, as had certain enterprising reporters; to everyone the desk clerk at the Plaza said that Miss
Milette was not in her room, and that the management had no
knowledge of her whereabouts.

Henry and other members of his family attended the
simple funeral services at Inglewood Cemetery. Approximately
a thousand curious spectators crowded the chapel doors to see
Jean Harlow, a veiled blonde widow, helped from her limousine by Marino Bello. Her mother got out alone. The actress
sobbed and covered her face with several handkerchiefs, and
Marino glared to silence the throng around the chapel steps.
Arthur Landau offered to help the actress, Marino refused any
offer of assistance, so Arthur and Mrs. Landau gave their attention to Mrs. Bello, then moved to the second row of pews.
About fifty people were communicants at the services.

Jean, weeping hard, was led to a small room connected
with the chapel by an archway hung with somber purple
draperies. In a similar mourning room on the opposite side of
the chapel, members of Bern's immediate family gathered
around Paul's sister, Mrs. Friederike Marcus. Her lamentations
could not be controlled. Earlier that day she had made an
attempt to learn from Jean what might have caused the
suicide, but the meeting between the women had only resulted in a commingling of tears. After she had left the Bello
house, Mrs. Marcus told reporters that to her Paul had been
"more than a brother. He told me many of his secrets. I think
he was a good healthy man, and if he found life unbearable
now, then let him rest and sleep as he deserved to sleep. . . .
There is nothing to forgive. He had never sinned. His affair
with Dorothy Milette twenty years ago was never a secret to
anybody. Everybody knew about it. He brought her into the
family as his wife."

Everyone noticed that this statement of relationship was
in direct contradiction to the statement made by Henry Bern,

and a choleric Mayer countermanded his edict of banishment and ordered Landau brought immediately to his presence. If everyone know about Dorothy Milette, it was everyone except Louis B. Mayer. As a reasonable man, he could understand why this confidence had not been imparted to him by Irene Harrison, for Mayer spoke to no secretaries except his own. But *Arthur,* an *agent* whom Mayer had respected and treated squarely, and who was being punished now for his own good, as a father punished a son—Arthur certainly should have told him about Bern and his love affairs. Yes, Mayer had at last been made aware of the little bungalow—and he now hoped that *this* wouldn't be found out, and he appointed Arthur as a committee of one to get the kept woman out of town. But why hadn't Arthur known about Dorothy Milette, who could certainly lay claim to being one of Paul Bern's *two* widows?

"You're the worst kind of dope," Mayer accused. "You're not handling merchandise, but a flesh and blood woman with a golden body to match her platinum hair. Or don't you understand that?"

"Almost as well as you," Arthur said.

"If that's so how come she didn't confide in you?"

"I suppose she confided to other people things she didn't know herself? I suppose she confided in you?" Arthur replied.

"Let's go to the funeral and look sad for him," Mayer said. "But I'm not through with you yet. If you want me to think better of you, Arthur, figure out some way to make everyone connected with this terrible scandal deaf and dumb. Tell me," he demanded, "how does a girl like Harlow, a temple of sex, wind up married to a fairy bigamist? Tell me!"

In his short, restrained eulogy, Rabbi Edward F. Magnin of the Wilshire Temple compared Paul to an innocent child lost, wandering in a naughty world of grown-ups, a reference which Mayer felt was an oblique dig at him. The rabbi went on to bid farewell to the dead man before he offered the comforts of religion, the strength of the living and the virtues of the dead to the bereaved widow. A short Hebrew prayer concluded the temple services, a violinist performed, and a chosen few wept at the bier. Mayer helped Jean advance to the open coffin for a last farewell, then took her to a limousine. He ignored Bello's hand but ordered the handsome Italian to stop telling people he was on the MGM payroll, to take care of Jean's mother and not let her talk to anyone, and to lose himself at the bottom of his deepest gold mine.

Shortly thereafter the corpse was cremated. And Henry Bern collapsed when he learned that upstate police were dragging the Sacramento River between San Francisco and the state capital, because they had received a report that on Tuesday, the day after Paul Bern's suicide, a woman answering to the description of Dorothy Milette had thrown herself from the deck of the *Delta King,* a river steamer plying between both cities.

While police crews dragged the river, other members of the San Francisco department interviewed the manager of the Plaza Hotel, and that distraught gentleman informed the investigators that Miss Milette was seldom seen and only appeared in the lobby to get her mail and room key. A quiet woman, a perfect lady, she never addressed anyone and replied simply, eyes downcast, to direct questions. The manager agreed that Miss Milette bought a daily paper, and he remembered having remarked upon the Bern suicide, but Miss Milette's manner betrayed nothing; she had only said that she hated to read or hear of death, especially if the people were young. The woman's hotel bills were settled by checks drawn on either a Los Angeles or San Francisco bank, and all her checks had been honored by prompt payment. As a matter of fact, the hotel was surprised to learn that Miss Milette was missing, for she had made no mention of checking out and a trunk and bag were still in her room.

Although the disappearance and probable suicide of the other woman in Paul Bern's past was good copy, no more could be done with it for the time. To the despair of Mayer and other studio officials, the press turned again to Harlow and her family for news. The coroner, determined to honor his oath of office, had again served Miss Harlow with a notice to appear at the inquest. Also, Henry Bern had again visited the bereaved star, had spoken to her in private for almost two hours, and then had met the press with tight lips to say he had "nothing to say." Patiently, with good will, reporters reminded him of the statement he had promised after the funeral, when he was to speak again with Jean. Bern offered no apology and would only say that sometime, some day, he might have some comment to make; then again, he might not, because his concern was not with the circulation of newspapers.

Jean was near collapse again, medical bulletins were discouraging, and it was quite impossible for her to answer any questions, especially those of a coroner. It was obvious that she would not speak to the press; in fact, her attorney urged that Henry Bern be permitted to deal with the press and make whatever statements he felt were relevant to an unraveling of the mystery. The press believed that during the second meeting between Harlow and Henry Bern the actress had offered her explanation of the "Dearest Dear" farewell note, in which Paul had written of his "great wrong" to her, his "abject humiliation," and the night that "was a comedy." But neither party to the interview would offer any interpretation of the note and the reasons that had prompted it.

In despair the press turned northward again to San Francisco, and they were cheered to find a new revelation from that quarter. Letters from Bern to Dorothy Milette had been found in her room. But the reporters were doomed to disappointment again; the letters would not be released by the police until their contents had been evaluated.

Another possible source of information was explored when a waiter at the Ambassador Hotel in Los Angeles informed the police that he had served dinner to Bern, another man and a woman in one of the hotel bungalows. This checked out with Garrison's statement of having driven Bern to the Ambassador, and hotel records further proved that Bern had rented the bungalow for the day and had ordered dinner. But the waiter could not identify Bern's guests, could not remember Bern calling them by name, and his descriptions were vague, applicable to countless thousands of men and women. In desperation several photographs of Dorothy Milette were shown to the waiter. After viewing them carefully, holding the pictures to the light and at arm's length, the waiter declared he could take an oath that she was not the woman he had served in the hotel bungalow. Questioning of Harlow, her agent, her attorney and the Bellos about the dinner party given by Bern also led to dead ends. Marino's challenge, then plea, for Bern's mysterious dinner guests to make themselves known was forever ignored.

Bern was dead, and arrangements were begun for the widow to share in the disposition of Bern's estate. First stories that the producer had left assets in excess of half a million dollars, with insurance policies that would make the estate worth more than a million, proved to be the wildest exaggerations. A totaling of Bern's effects revealed that he had been covered by approximately $50,000 in life insurance, that he had also left several minor parcels of real estate of negligible value, and that the house which he had deeded to Jean, a house worth sixty thousand dollars, was mortgaged for exactly that sum. Four days before he had shot himself, Paul had applied for an additional $85,000 worth of life insurance and passed a physical examination, but the application had not been fully processed.

A search had been made of Bern's papers, at home and in his office, but nothing pertinent was found. Neither was a secret diary, which reporters had hoped for and Mayer had prayed against. Later, Irene Harrison remembered that Bern had had a safe deposit box. He had placed previous wills in the box, and she remembered adding a new, amended will to these. She was also quite certain that Jean Harlow had been named as his principal beneficiary. Problems of opening the box were left to the interested attorneys.

The next day the papers reported that the San Francisco police had made public two letters typed on MGM stationery and found in Dorothy Milette's room, letters which proved the close ties between the dead producer and the vanished woman.

The first letter, written on March 29, 1932, before Bern's marriage to Jean Harlow, had been addressed to Dorothy while she was still at the Algonquin in New York.

> Metro-Goldwyn-Mayer Studios
> Culver City, California
> March 29, 1932

Dear Dorothy:

I was very happy to get your letter of March 17.

I have been desperately trying to get away from here for both vacation and change of scene for the last year but so far it has been quite impossible.

I read with great interest that you are contemplating a trip to San Francisco. Of course, I cannot give you any advice because you yourself can be the only person to know what is best. If you do go I hope that it will be a happy change.

I understand that the Plaza Hotel is a fairly reasonable and attractive one.

If you do change to any other place we will find some way of supplying you with funds in a manner convenient to you.

My love and best wishes always,

> /s/ *Paul*

P.S.

The Clift Hotel is, I believe, quite fashionable and not very expensive.

The second letter provided details of the financial arrangements made by Paul for his common-law wife and handled by Bern's secretary. This letter of May 13 was addressed to the Plaza Hotel in San Francisco.

Dear Miss Milette:

According to the arrangements agreed upon, I am enclosing a money order for $160 due on May 14.

Mr. Bern has already left on his vacation, but I am at the office in the meantime, and if I can help you in any way at any time, please don't hesitate to ask me.

I hope you are comfortably and happily settled in your new home.

Sincerely yours,
/s/ *Irene Harrison*

The search of the countryside around San Francisco and Sacramento continued, all leads were checked to their negative conclusions, and the dragging of the river continued—but Dorothy Milette's body could not be found. Henry Bern remained at the Beverly Wilshire Hotel and refused to see any reporters, and L.B. Mayer's office suggested that it would be wise, decent, humane if Jean were permitted to mourn in dignity and if nothing more were written about the tragedy until Bern's will was read.

By grieving, attempting suicide and fainting at each revelation about the secret life of Paul Bern, his widow gained increasing sympathy, and telegrams and letters continued to arrive by the sackful. And each letter of sympathy helped keep

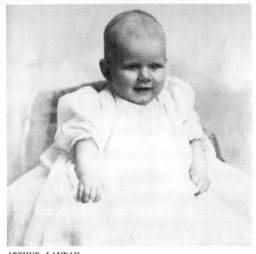

Harlean Carpentier, then known
as "The Baby" and later somewhat
better known as Jean Harlow,
in shots from the family album:
at six months *(above left)*,
six years *(above right)*,
and a wistful nine *(left)*.

Some of the famous Harlow allure is already apparent in this snapshot *(above)* of Harlean at twelve. Two years later *(below)* adolescent Harlean inscribed this thoughtful portrait: "Heaps of love to the dearest grandma in the world."

CULVER PICTURES, INC.

CULVER PICTURES, INC.

(Left) Harlow in her Charleston costume from *Saturday Night Kid* (1929) with Clara Bow, and out of her costume *(below)* in the famous slapstick scene from *Double Whoopee* with Laurel and Hardy.

Harlow in the famous
gown and pose
that stole the show
from the bombers in
Howard Hughes' World
War I epic, *Hell's Angels*
(1930), with Ben Lyon.

As a daughter of the underworld in *The Secret Six* (1931) *(below)* Harlow was billed under Wallace Beery but over Clark Gable (Mary Caryle is at right); both men shared her spotlight as leading men in later films. That same year four other Harlow films were released, including *Public Enemy* with James Cagney *(above left)* where she again played a gangster's girl, and *Platinum Blonde* *(above right)* which made her name—and her hair—world famous.

Harlow was haunted by the similarity of the roles which she was required to play. Here, as the bad girl with a heart of gold, she gets paid off by Chester Morris in *Red Headed Woman (above)*, Franchot Tone in *Girl From Missouri (below)*, Spencer Tracy in *Riff-Raff (opposite above)*, and Wallace Beery in *China Seas (opposite below)*.

CULVER PICTURES, INC.

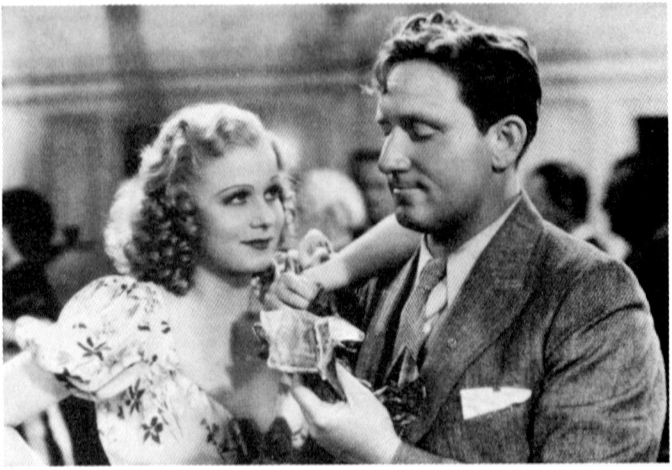

CULVER PICTURES, INC.

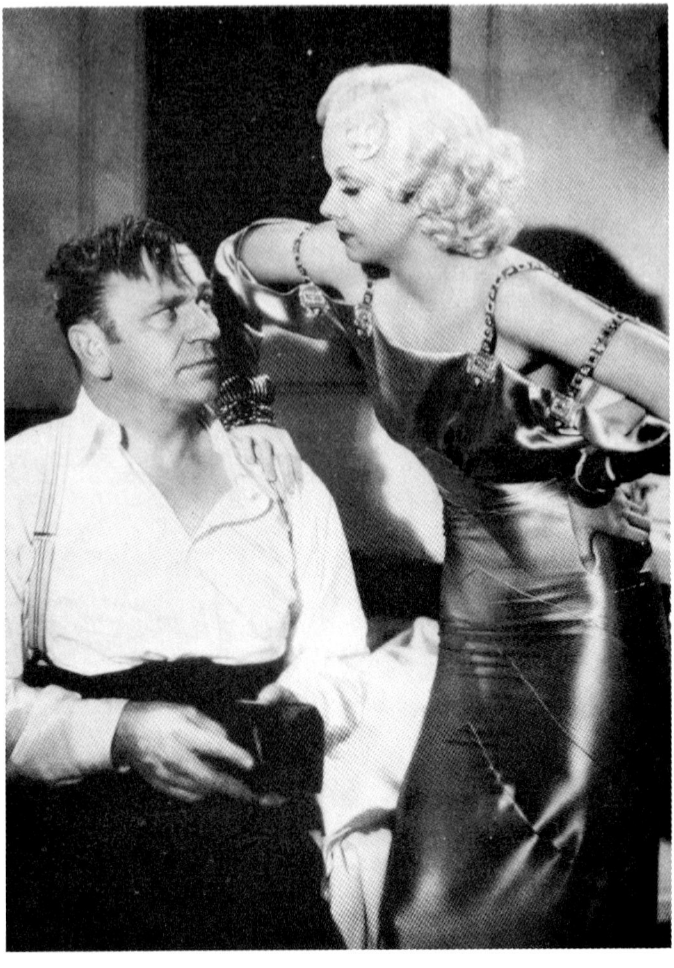

ARTHUR LANDAU

A valued MGM property, Harlow strolls on the lot with Louis B. Mayer and his right-hand man, Eddie Mannix. The inscription reads: "Jean:—Affectionately, Eddie."

In 1931, as an up-and-coming MGM star, Harlow attends a premiere escorted by studio executive Paul Bern, the man she was later to marry.

Mama Jean and "The Baby."

Bathed and refreshed, the stars of
Red Dust engaged in a wrestling
match that was said to raise movie
house temperatures ten degrees
wherever it was shown.

Harlow and her last love, William Powell *(left)*, during rehearsals of Harlow's only musical, *Reckless* (1935), after which it was decided that "the singing was best left to Jeanette MacDonald." The latter-day Harlow image *(below),* in a shot taken on the set of *Wife vs. Secretary,* co-starring Myrna Loy and Clark Gable (1936).

(Right) in a lighthearted
scene from *Suzy,*
Harlow atilt over
Cary Grant's
shoulder (1936).
(Below) with Robert
Taylor in her
last completed
picture, *Personal
Property* (1936).

The house, a press agent's dream in white satin and gilt, brought Harlow little happiness, though she did brave the threat of sunburn for an occasional dip in the pool.

CULVER PICTURES, INC.

Harlow makes a gallant effort at the President's Birthday Infantile Paralysis Fund festivities which she attended with Mrs. Roosevelt in January, 1937.

DAILY NEWS

FINAL ★★★

NEW YORK'S · PICTURE NEWSPAPER

The net paid circulation
for May exceeded
Daily — 1,700,000
Sunday — 3,000,000

Copyright 1937 by News Syndi-
cate Co. Inc. Reg. U. S. Pat. Off.

Entered as 2nd class matter
Post Office, New York, N. Y.

Vol. 18. No. 297   New York, Tuesday, June 8, 1937*   56 Main + 4 Special Harlow Pages   2 Cents IN CITY | 2 CENTS Elsewhere

BEAUTIFUL
JEAN HARLOW DIES

———Story on Page 3

BORN: Mar. 3, 1911, Kansas City, Mo.   **DIED:** June 7, 1937, Hollywood, Cal.

-Page Harlow Picture Section In Center Fold

Jean among the stars of MGM. Some of the letters were from private detectives, seers and clairvoyants, but most of the communications assured Jean that the nation grieved with her. About half of the sympathetic letters suggested that Jean share her secret with their writers, devoted fans and persons of absolute trust. All in all, a large sampling of the letters and telegrams heartened Mayer, Thalberg and Strickling.

Mayer countermanded his order to exile Bern's West Hollywood mistress from the city, because the woman so far had proved her trustworthiness by not making any public pronouncements. She had not asked for a job or other reward, and it would be easier to check on her if she were not moved to another city.

An analysis of the column space devoted to the affair convinced Mayer that the worst might be over. The county coroner had not, for almost a week, made another unreasonable attempt to summon Harlow to an inquest hearing. Get the girl back to work, Thalberg suggested. So, a week and a day after the discovery of Bern's suicide, "to forget herself in work," Jean returned to the studio for continued shooting of life in a rain barrel.

Accompanied by Marino Bello, her mother and Miss Ada Wilson, a trained nurse, Jean parted tearfully from Arthur Landau at the studio gate, but swore to reinstate him or she would not continue in the picture.

Every effort had been made to make the star's return as commonplace as possible, and strict orders were in effect to keep the streets to the set of *Red Dust* clear of loitering employees and sightseers. The stage was ordered closed, and as Jean was helped through the door, which was barred behind her, she was embraced by Victor Fleming, then kissed by Clark Gable, Mary Astor, Gene Raymond, Donald Crisp, Harold Rosson, the picture's cameraman, and all the members of the crew. Henry Bern was kissed by the actress, although Marino Bello made it a definite point to snub the New York mourner.

After several hours of pointless shooting, because Jean performed poorly, Fleming was informed that Jean would have to be at the bank the next morning, when Bern's safe deposit box would be opened before witnesses. Fleming agreed to shoot around his star.

At ten in the morning Jean, her parents, her attorney, Henry Bern and a variety of other witnesses met at the Culver City branch of the Bank of America with Theodore L. Pettit, deputy state inheritance tax collector. Proper waivers and documents were signed and witnessed, the box was opened and two "wills of a sort" were found. The first was a six-page document prepared in New York City on June 12, 1925, which left an annuity of $2,500 to Dorothy Milette and bequests to other members of Bern's family. It was immediately evident that the witnesses of signatures to this will had been written in by Bern, and that the document would have no validity in any court. The second will, dated August 14, 1927, was one brief page which left $2,500 to Miss Milette as her total inheritance. There were small bequests to members of Bern's family and cash gifts to six actresses whose names could not be learned by the press. This will had apparently been typed by Bern, had never been witnessed, and had been phrased so ambiguously that any of the principals or persons who felt they should have shared in the estate could have made impressive challenges.

A sealed letter addressed by Jean to Paul and dated some days before their marriage was also found, but the will which Irene Harrison swore had been prepared by Bern's lawyer shortly before the producer's marriage to Miss Harlow was missing.

The Los Angeles *Times* reported that "with the missing will deepening the mystery of the already unusual case, Miss Harrison was summoned for a conference with Louis B. Mayer . . . and Mendel Silberberg . . . and after they had been closeted for some time Silberberg quoted the secretary as declaring she 'may have been mistaken about where the document had been placed.' She said further, according to the attorney, that it is possible she may have placed it in her own strong box and that she will 'search her memory' and make efforts to locate the instrument today."

Two days after Jean's return to the studio, Dorothy Milette's badly decomposed body was recovered from the river at the Georgiana Slough near Walnut Grove, about thirty-one miles southwest of Sacramento. The body had been sighted by two Japanese farmhands who were fishing in the river; a search of the body failed to reveal a suicide note, and further examination indicated no foul play. Arthur Landau sent a telegram to the Sacramento police that his client would pay for the burial and that everyone would be grateful if the interment could be kept dignified, quiet and without publicity.

Chapter Thirteen

On March 22, 1953, over twenty years after Paul Bern's suicide, the Des Moines *Sunday Register* carried a "My Hollywood" column of Hedda Hopper devoted to "The Death of Jean Harlow's Husband." The column was an excerpt from Miss Hopper's book, *From Under My Hat,* published that same year.

A significant portion of the article observed that:

> Paul would do anything for a friend. A happily married producer, who had never broken his marriage vows, suddenly conceived a mad passion for an actress who was working in a picture for him and who reciprocated his feeling. The obsession became intolerable to him, so he went to Paul for guidance.
>
> "Get the urge out of your system," said Bern. "I'll help you. Tell you what we'll do. I have a bungalow at one of the hotels which I use for story conferences among other things. I'll invite the lady to have dinner with me. You come in about nine o'clock, take over, and I'll quietly make my exit. You can tell your wife you're having a conference with me and not to expect you home until morning, and I'll back you up."

The producer said, "That will be perfect. She knows I have to stop at a writer's house for a story conference about noon, and that will give me time to gain my composure before going home."

It was the perfect alibi.

Everything went according to Paul's plan. It was a beautiful Monday morning in September, 1932, when the producer said goodbye to the beautiful actress, left the hotel bungalow, and stopped off at the writer's house for his conference.

He was surprised to find Hollywood's big brass there. Their gloom could have been cut with a cleaver. Never during the greatest picture crisis had they looked so unhappy.

"What's going on here?" asked the happy man. "Did someone die?"

They could have struck him in the face.

"Haven't you read the papers? Don't you know that Paul Bern is dead?"

The perfect alibi shattered by a bullet.

The producer, the first friend Paul Bern ever failed in his life, ran out of the house and was violently ill on the front lawn.

Many times you've read that this or that event rocked Hollywood. But the town really shook on the morning when we read of Paul's death. The newspapers called it suicide. It's still one of our town's three unsolved mysteries. Along with the murder of William Desmond Taylor and the death of Thelma Todd, Paul Bern's "suicide" has never been properly explained—to my satisfaction, at least.

Poor producer retching on the front lawn, how could he have read of Bern's suicide in Monday's paper if accounts of the death first appeared in Tuesday's editions?

In the November 26, 1932 issue of *Liberty*, an indulgent magazine that told its readers the length of each article, to make possible the better budgeting of intellectual time, Adela Rogers St. Johns reported that Mrs. Bello believed the woman who had dined with Bern in the bungalow at the Ambassador Hotel was Dorothy Milette. "Is it possible that she was really Mrs. Paul Bern and that her poor brain, already in the grip of dementia praecox, evolved some threat which menaced the happiness of Paul's new wife, and that Paul believed his death would render that threat ineffectual? Or is it possible that the comedy was some meeting between Jean Harlow and Dorothy Milette?"

Having asked the question, Miss St. Johns turned to Harlow for an answer and was told by the actress that she had never met Dorothy Milette nor heard of her until Paul accomplished his suicide.

The article is interesting because of the author's soliloquy on Bern:

> Strange little man. He told me once that he was twelve years old before he knew what it was to have enough to eat and that his childhood was haunted by his little brothers and sisters crying for food.
>
> How much of the suffering he attempted to console had he absorbed? For all his charity and his brilliance, he was cursed with a morbid curiosity about death and suffering. He insisted on wearing every crown of thorns that he saw. Hypersensitive, introspective, his masculine vanity must have been an open wound. *He* knew

his own tragedy. Was that why he sought out and was seen with exotic women famous for their sex appeal? Barbara La Marr—Joan Crawford—Estelle Taylor—Nita Naldi—Jetta Goudal—Jean Harlow?

The question was rhetorical and after a reader's pause, Miss St. Johns observed that: "You see, I knew long ago all that the doctors told. . . . [and] . . . what Jean Harlow discovered only when she had been three days a bride."

Twenty years later, on February 4, 1951 Miss St. Johns did a piece for *The American Weekly* entitled "Love, Laughter and Tears," which also concerned itself with Jean Harlow. In this latter seasoned recital of circumstances there are some significant changes of incident worthy of full quotation:

> Barbara La Marr projected me into the middle of Jean Harlow's marriage to Paul Bern, Irving Thalberg's right hand man at Metro. Barbara was dead then but the things she'd once told me lived in my memory. Paul had wanted to marry Barbara once upon a time. She'd refused. The night she married Jack Daugherty, Paul tried to drown himself. Jack Gilbert and Carey Wilson saved him, but plenty of gossip swept Hollywood. It was then that Barbara told me what kind of person Paul was and why she wouldn't marry him.
>
> When Harlow announced her engagement to Paul, therefore, I was on a spot. I didn't know what to do, so I consulted Jean's greatest friend, Marie Dressler. "Why did a thing like this have to happen to her?" Marie said.
>
> Born of a fine family, with tradition, position, wealth, she'd been the idol of her grand-

father, a highly-respected gentleman of the old school.

. . . .

When I went to see her after her engagement was announced, I learned that Paul hadn't told her about himself. I told her.

"Then it's true," she said, and began to cry. "Paul loves me as he says he does, for my mind, my spirit, my companionship, for me. He's paid me the highest compliment I've ever had. No man has ever loved me before for what's best in me."

So she entered into a marriage that would be a marriage in name only.

For a biographer time moves in mysterious ways to alter historical sequences. In Miss St. Johns' *Liberty* article of 1932, Jean Harlow is told by Paul of his infirmity *three days after her marriage.* In *The American Weekly* of 1951, the facts of Paul's disability are given to Jean by Miss St. Johns *during the engagement.*

In her 1953 article Miss Hopper hinted at some sort of foul play in the death of Paul Bern, and in 1959, while Ben Hecht was writing his version of the Harlow legend for Jerry Wald, the producer often observed during story conferences that the property's dramatic values would be doubled if Bern's suicide could be revealed as a murder. Hecht finished his assignment in November 1959 and the treatment was set aside for later consideration by Wald, who was then engaged in producing a series of screen tributes to William Faulkner, with an emphasis on lively Mississippi folkways.

If Miss Hopper hinted, Ben Hecht did not. For in November, 1960 *Playboy* Magazine published a reminiscence by Hecht with the longish title, "If Hollywood is dead or dying as a moviemaker, perhaps the following are some of the reasons."

The article was a résumé of Hollywood history and a lament for dead giants among producers, directors, performers and writers. In his reminiscence of Harlow, Hecht wrote that "Jean took her fame seriously. She wore no brassiere under a white satin blouse. Before making a public appearance, she would rub ice on her nipples to improve her appearance."

About Paul Bern, Hecht was also so specific that his article could not be ignored:

> Paul Bern, remembered for having committed suicide as the impotent bridegroom of Jean Harlow, the great cinema sexpot, did no such thing. His suicide note, hinting that he was sexually incompetent and had therefore "ended the comedy," was a forgery. Studio officials decided, sitting in conference around his dead body, that it was better to have Paul a suicide than as the murder victim of another woman. It would be less a black eye for their biggest moviemaking heroine, La Belle Harlow. . . . It was a delicate point of the sort that is only clear to the front office theologians of a great studio. The weird details of this "suicide whitewash" are in the keeping today of director Henry Hathaway, who was Paul Bern's protege.

Between 1951 and 1960 Southern California suffered from a great drought; however, even when it does rain in the Los Angeles area, thunderstorms and lightning are a rarity. But Hecht raised a storm worthy of the Ark. Several local papers thundered the charge of murder in headlines larger than those reserved for the downfall of political enemies or the death of an international playgirl. District Attorney William B. McKesson called attention to a quirk of law that kept the crime of murder from falling under the statute of limitations, and members of his staff went into high gear to acquaint themselves with a suicide a quarter of a century old. Henry Hathaway was ordered to make available to the District Attorney the "weird details" of the "suicide whitewash," and the bewildered director sought the counsel of his attorney; together, both men met with Brad Morris, an investigator for Mr. McKesson, and the director proved that Ben Hecht's saying so did not make it so. Of course the writer of the article was interviewed by the District Attorney himself, and what might have been an explosive investigation, with the governor's mansion as one of the possible prizes, ended as a dud. The District Attorney returned the records of the suicide to their files and closed the case. A spokesman for Twentieth Century-Fox would only say that a screen biography of Jean Harlow had been considered, but the project was now dormant.

But whatever interest contemporary and later columnists and other writers had in the affair, the principals were, despite important antipathies and conflicts of interest, seemingly united on one theme: to close the matter forever.

Although Jean's attorney saw no reason for an inquest, inasmuch as the police and everyone concerned appeared to be satisfied that Bern had taken his own life, the coroner still insisted on the formality. The hearing was held, but the coroner cooperated to the extent of holding it quietly, without publicity. After Jean, Marino Bello, Irving Thalberg, the Carmichaels, Clifton Davis, Harold Garrison and M. E. Greenwood (MGM's studio manager), were questioned, the jury foreman, William W. Witenham, returned his verdict of suicide and declared that he could not give credence to a report made by one of the witnesses that Bern had threatened Jean or himself with violence if his wife insisted that he accompany her to the Bello home for Sunday dinner.

To the relief of Mayer, Landau, even Jean and her

family, it was that time of the four-year cycle when newspapers, no matter the murder or scandal, began to increase their coverage of news pertinent to the national contest for the presidency, so the coroner's report received scant attention.

At last, every facet of the mystery suicide appeared to be exhausted. Because the Blonde Bombshell insisted she could not give any logical reason for the tragedy, newspapers expanded their coverage of the Hoover-Roosevelt campaign, for which the motion picture industry was grateful.

Furthermore, a telephone and telegraph poll of exhibitors and theater managers throughout the country proved there was a heightened interest in Harlow. Because he wanted her new picture in the theaters before a strong adverse reaction might set in, Mayer ordered *Red Dust* rushed through to completion. Additional telephone calls were placed by the studio to various key distributing areas and the information gained was always encouraging: Harlow was still popular, for the most part public sympathy was with her, and any pity extended to Bern was now minimal. The revelation of his bigamy, which had seemed to make a fool of the movie-goddess, increased hostility toward Bern, and his reduction of bequest to Dorothy Milette tended to make of the sad, vindictive suicide a niggardly, seemingly disloyal man.

On September 15, two short days after Jean had returned to work in *Red Dust,* Miss Harrison found Bern's third will, which he had composed on July 29. The will, drawn by Attorney Oscar Cummins and witnessed by Mr. Cummins and an associate, Harry C. Cogen, consisted of two short paragraphs that left Bern's entire estate to Jean and named her as "sole executrix and administratrix of this my last will and testament, to act with bond." In this last document there was no mention of any family bequests, and Dorothy Milette was ignored. Of the three wills left by Bern, only the last had been drawn by an attorney and would have been recognized by a court. Meanwhile, Jean's attorneys again stated, after filing the newly discovered will, that Bern's estate would exceed $10,000, which proved to be an optimistic evaluation.

While Jean worked in *Red Dust,* the problems of Bern's estate multiplied. The house he had deeded to Jean was mortgaged for its full value. She had no desire to live in this empty reminder of scandal and death, so the mortgagor was persuaded, reluctantly, to take it. In return, Jean was asked to cooperate by vacating the house without delay, so the property could be placed on the market while it still had some notoriety value. A horde of gulled and clamorous tradespeople descended on Jean to demand payment for long overdue purchases made by Bern.

The shock and wonder of the young widow mounted when she realized that her husband had earned $1,500 a week for some years, had not had to pay any agency fees, and had left mountainous debts and virtually no cash. All in all, after the dead man's debts were consolidated, the best settlement that could be arranged amounted to almost thirty thousand dollars. And his cash assets, including his salary for the week in which he had shot himself, were still less than two thousand dollars.

Where had his money gone? His personal extravagances, gifts and generosities still did not come to a third of his annual earnings. No answer was forthcoming; and the supposition everyone arrived at was best not voiced loudly. But in guarded statements it was agreed that Bern might have been a blackmail victim; that his guests in the bungalow at the Ambassador Hotel could have been his blackmailers; that he could have pleaded with them for mercy and been refused; and that this disappointment, combined with other disappointments and blows to an already sick ego, might have been an added incentive for him to solve his problems through suicide.

Whatever the complex of motivations that prompted the suicide, the insurance companies refused to honor the policies, which had a face value of $48,000, claiming that suicide invalidated the death provision. Although there was no clause that specifically ruled out suicide as an acceptable cause of death, the companies were willing to test their assumption in the courts. Several of Jean's advisors suggested patience; haste to collect Paul's insurance might cause a bad public reaction. Meanwhile, they would continue to negotiate with the insurance companies until some acceptable, face-saving compromise could be reached.

"Don't worry about the money you owe," Arthur told Jean one evening when she insisted they drive to Santa Monica where they could see the moon upon the ocean, lovers on the sand, and poor people living on the beach in little tents. "In fact I've some plans for you to owe more. You need a house to suit a star," he continued rapidly, before Jean could protest. "So I've carried through on the option."

She had no memory of an option, and carefully, as if he were preparing her for another misfortune, Arthur reminded Jean that she had authorized him to make a deposit on a lot he had recommended, a one-and-a-third-acre parcel offered for $9,500. After Jean had returned to work on September 13, Arthur had decided to buy the lot; if Jean refused to build, he might do so.

"And you laid out the money?" she asked.

"It's a good investment," he said. "The deed's in your name."

"So I own the lot? And suppose I decide not to pay you? What can you do about it?"

Arthur shrugged and wondered if he would have to build. "Even if I could I'd do nothing."

"Because you're way at the end of the line," she laughed at him. "There must be at least fifty, maybe a hundred people ahead of you screaming to be paid. How could a man owe sixty thousand on a sixty-thousand-dollar house?"

"I'm not going to break my head thinking about it," Arthur said. "Just give thanks you're rid of the house."

"He even owed for the gun he killed himself with! For

the bullets! What did he do with his money?" she demanded in a fury of frustration. "What did he spend it on? He couldn't have spent it on whores like some of the people around here do! Or did he?" She paused to press her cheek against the glass of the car door. "Are we going to pass it? I mean the lot."

"It's on a hill and really nothing to see at night," he replied. "By day you'll see what a beautiful location you bought."

"Where is my lot? If I own it I ought to know where it is."

"We can go there tomorrow."

"No," she insisted. "That means Mama and Marino'd have to come along. I want to see it alone. Now."

Arthur calmed the actress and returned along Sunset Boulevard until he turned south into Beverly Glen Drive, made a U-turn and parked before a dark hillside close to the east gate of Bel Air. The hill had been partly cleared of shrub vegetation, trees and unkempt bushes, and a "sold" sign had been placed on each end of the lot. Pulling themselves up by grasping the wild ivy, they climbed the steep slope for more than a hundred feet until they reached the level hilltop. Arthur pointed out the advantages of the site: the area would prove to be as good or even better than Beverly Hills, and the novelty of planning her house would give Jean a healthy interest. All in all, land, house and landscaping would cost about fifty thousand dollars, plus another ten or fifteen for furnishings— but Jean would have a hard asset of real value in keeping with her position as a star.

"With what I've got to settle up for Paul that'll mean I'll owe more than a hundred thousand dollars! How'll I ever pay it?"

"Out of your salary," Arthur said. "Don't worry."

"Why not? You'll do it for me?"

"I'm willing."

"Worrying is one thing, owing is another. What'll I do

when they get after me for the money? And I don't want a big house. With a big house Mama and Marino are going to be part of the place. No," she shook her head. "Not for me. I'd rather have an apartment. You paid for the lot, Arthur. So put it in your name. And I'll buy *you* a swell house gift."

As they continued their drive to the beach Jean smoked nervously and lamented that she would never have believed it possible for one person to accumulate so much grief in so short a time.

"What did Paul do with it?" she asked again and again. "Sometimes I actually think more about the money than the beating he gave me. I don't want a dime of his, but I also don't want to pay his debts. And I've got to. Because of the publicity. No one ever expects a great lay to pay all the bills. So why do they expect it of me? Is it because I'm not a great lay?"

"I'm glad that nobody else hears you talk this way," he said. "At least I hope nobody else does."

"And my back hurts!"

"Then you should see a doctor," he said, concerned. "Why haven't you said something?"

"Who'd listen when there's so many more important things about me? And I don't like the way nurses look at me."

"What nurses?"

"All nurses. As if I'm something hanging on a butcher's hook. Or that's where I ought to be hanging."

"Stop making things up," Arthur said. He made a mental note that Jean would have to see a doctor. "People really are on your side."

"Jesus! Every week he'd get that fifteen hundred dollar check—more than me, the slimy little bastard!—and when I'd ask him what he did with the money, you know what he'd say?"

"I'm listening," Arthur said. He wondered how long he could continue to be patient.

"He might say he bought some more phonograph records. But that might be five or ten dollars, and since he charged them

I've been getting the bills! So I'd say that records were only a couple of bucks, and he'd give me one of his sick smiles and walk away. I guess we'll never know unless the people he gave it away to tell us. Some fat chance," she muttered.

"Jean, listen," he said, trying to break her mood. "Come Monday I'm being let back on the lot. We'll have lunch at the commissary."

She clapped her hands and kissed his cheek. "Then you'll be able to get me into another picture."

"Not just another picture." Arthur laughed with her. "Something big."

"Don't ask for more money," Jean advised as she rolled down her window to hear the boom of the surf. "Just keep me working until I'm confident."

He continued to smile. "That you're not going to have your contract canceled?"

Jean sighed as she took a fresh cigarette from his case. "I've got to keep working to pay back what Paul owed. The only good thing out of all this is that that crazy Marino knows he's got to forget about gold mines and treasure ships and all his other junk until I get myself out of the hole. And now you want me to pile up more debts. How come you don't own a house?" She blew out the match and threw it in his lap. "How come you're free as a gypsy?"

Cracking her knuckles, drumming on the door, kicking off her pumps then putting them on again—all were signals of her restless, uncertain state. Daily since her return to the studio, many times within an hour, she tested the script girl, hairdresser, maid, everyone on the set; and she weighed their responses, deliberated their every word, inflection and gesture. When she could find no evidence of insincerity she was still unable to believe fully in the people whom she had queried. And she could not believe in her future, that she wouldn't again become one of the anonymous hundreds in the little rooms and bungalows of Hollywood courts.

But after Arthur returned to the studio, he was able to show her a memorandum from Thalberg's office, which suggested that directors and production supervisors think of a story for Jean. She had finished *Red Dust,* which was slated to open on November 4 at the Capitol Theater in New York. Previews of the picture had been good and the studio was eager to follow this certain hit with another. Jean drew more cheer from the memo than she had from all Arthur's assurances.

And the building of the house pleased Jean. She spent most of her leisure time inspecting the progress or playing with toy furniture, arranging it on a scale floor plan presented to her by the architect. During the early part of October, when *Red Dust* was receiving its last polish, Jean at last could believe that the studio was planning another picture for her and her contract was not going to be canceled by Mayer. For Mayer might be pleasant, interested, fatherly to her one morning, and rude as a mule the next.

After a snub from Mayer, which Jean swore was deliberately insulting, she insisted that Arthur remain in her dressing room. Lips chewed raw, she locked the door, examined the walls for peepholes, adjusted the blinds, and looked in the closet; then she drew the stool of her dressing table close to Arthur's chair and whispered that there were times, usually at night, when she had a pain in her back, just about where Paul had beaten her with his cane. And the pain was always aggravated when Mayer was unpleasant to her or at that particular time of the month. Could there be some connection? She rejected Arthur's insistence that she visit a doctor. How could she when there were so many more urgent things?

But there was something else, something she could mention to no one but Arthur. She was haunted by the memory of Paul begging for a chance to prove that, for once, he really could make love to her. He had called her his goddess, and what had she done—except put her lips to the keyhole and spit in his eye? It was her mother's fault and Marino's. It was

Arthur's fault and the studio's. And it was also the fault of the pictures she made, the publicity she received, the letters and pictures sent her, the jokes about her. She had been made notorious. It was not sexual admiration she wanted to attract, but understanding. She needed it, required it, but it was a hunger no one paused to notice. And she was unable to make anyone notice.

No, she did not object to admiration, worship; she could reconcile herself to the knowledge that thousands, millions of men wanted her—until she would remember her mother and Marino, and be frightened. And disgusted. In all her experience she had never seen a woman so dominated by a man—not even Grandmother Harlow—and Marino's superiority was not achieved by any manly or intellectual quality she could admire, but by sex. Since their arrival in California, even in that first year, Marino had indulged himself in occasional affairs, never serious. But, more often than not, as if to boast, Marino was deliberately careless; Mama Jean would go through his pockets and wallet, would discover evidences of the affair and go into a collapse. Not that she threatened to kill herself, but she would lie in bed and sob for days, rejecting all food and only taking a little tea or juice. At last, when spirit and body demanded that she move or die, Mama Jean would crawl from her bed to Marino's feet, embrace his legs, weep, beg him to be true and never stray again.

Of course Marino would promise, and that night Mama would be an acrobat in bed. The next day, despite the dark circles and puffiness around her eyes, she would be fresh, vibrant and joyous again. There might be long periods, sometimes six months or more, when Marino would be faithful, and Mama Jean's complexion and brightness of voice and manner would be the envy of women younger than she.

Jean had attempted to speak to her mother about Marino, to discuss sex and enslavement with her, but Mama Jean would only laugh and say primly that Jean did not understand and might never understand that a woman could never love the act as a man did. If Jean thought that it was sex that kept her in love with Marino, it only proved her daughter's inexperience. However, she didn't deny that Marino made love the most wonderful of all experiences.

"Really," she had once said to Jean, "I shouldn't be so angry with Marino when he goes outside. He is an unusual man and I'm selfish for wanting him all for myself."

"It's a pity he can't prove that royalty crap of his," Jean replied. "Then we'd have papers on him and you could charge a stud fee. That'd give you an income of your own."

"I won't take another cent from you!" her mother wailed.

Jean sighed. "If you'd only keep that promise."

Still, a strange fascination drew her to talk to her mother about Marino. She kept hoping that some day her mother would describe not what Marino did or said, but her own state of mind when she knew that they were going to make love. Could desire be stimulated by thought? Could wishing make it so? Was the expression of the women in the dirty pictures real or feigned? Why, when she was supposed to live only for passion, could she not feel joy, only fear and depression? If Bern had been the little father confessor, the St. Francis of Culver City, the first gentleman of Hollywood, she was—all the interviews and fan magazines and mail told her—the most passionate and abandoned woman in America.

"You've got to listen, Arthur." She moved to stand before the door. "Why does thinking about it make me sick?"

"Then don't think about it," he replied.

"And what'm I supposed to do?" she demanded of him. "Do without it? Especially when all I do is play it in the pictures I make? You know somebody's going to ask me to marry him."

"Who?"

"I don't know," she said. "But someone will. And I'll say yes. And then there'll be another first night and everyone all over the country and especially around here will be slobbering like pigs. And every woman who's just got her hair bleached or is thinking of doing it'll be wondering if they're going to feel the kind of feelings I'm supposed to feel. And for their sakes I don't want them ever to feel like that!"

Arthur poured her a glass of water. "I think you're going to have a nervous breakdown."

She slapped the glass from his hand and the shards scattered across the carpet. "I want you to find me a man."

"You're really going crazy," he said.

She pointed at him. "I'm giving you an order. You'd better go find me a man who'll really show me why everyone thinks it's the greatest thing in the world. You'd better."

"And if I don't?" He would have to speak to Sugarman and tell Thalberg that Jean wasn't ready to go to work, that she needed a rest, even hospitalization. "You ought to be ashamed of yourself talking that way. No one would believe it."

"Would they believe it that I've never had a good screw? That I've never even got close to it?"

"You've got to stop talking that way!"

"Then find me a man," she said as she flung herself across the sofa. "I've gotta stop thinking I'm a fake."

"You're not."

"I am," she insisted without looking at Arthur. "And if you don't help me out—you know what I'm gonna do?" She pounded her temple with a small fist. "It's so crazy that it scares me. But if you don't help me out, Arthur, so help me God, I'm gonna climb into bed with the man I really hate most in the whole wide world."

"I won't listen!"

"You don't have to," she sobbed. "Because you already know. So help me, Arthur, I'm gonna get into bed with Marino!"

206

Chapter Fourteen

During one of Jean's public appearance tours she had been kissed by Mayor Frank Edwards of Seattle, and newspapers reported that Mrs. Edwards had approved her husband's surrender to temptation; Seattle, therefore, might be a good city for Jean to start a new tour to publicize *Red Dust*. The tour could only be a success because the studio would make it so. Claques could be engaged—not to stimulate applause, of course, just to direct it and to prove to Jean and her fans that she was still popular. This was what Landau told Thalberg, every time he could buttonhole him in his office or in the studio commissary.

But his insistence that this was the only way to reinforce Jean's ego, her box office appeal *and* her new film, made the studio hesitate. The executives observed the cardinal rules of industrial survival: never to acknowledge or make use of any suggestion from the outside; never to trust anyone; if possible, never to give credit to anyone; and to be ever vigilant against petitioners, for they might be spies and character assassins. So the studio had been willing enough to send Jean on tour, until Landau insisted this was the only logical course. Then the studio had begun to wonder if a tour was wise. Landau insisted, Thalberg stalled, and Jean drove through the city streets at night.

Alone in a touring car with raised side curtains, a dark scarf over her head or a broad-brimmed hat hiding her face, she would drive from Main Street to Santa Monica. Engine in gear, she would stop before speakeasies, low saloons and dance halls, then sit in the car unable to do what she had sworn and felt impelled to do: pick up a man. The threat she had made to Arthur had been so awful it had made her ill, made her worry about her sanity. For she recognized in the threat an envious, expressed hatred of her mother, because the older woman had found in sex a delight seldom granted to women and by rights—all the movie writers for magazines, newspapers *and* pictures said so—reserved for a goddess.

She knew; she had begun to listen for sounds, movements, rustlings, sighs and words; and she heard, because Mama Jean never failed to cry out in ecstasy when she was being bedded by Marino. That this vapid, almost simple-minded woman, made famous only through association with Jean Harlow, should be so happy in marriage, so in love, and so fulfilled physically and emotionally, made her the envy of her famous daughter. It also frightened her famous daughter.

Fright, not consideration, kept Jean from going to bed with Marino. Not that there would ever be a divorce or a scandal to ruin her career, for Mama Jean would have kept the secret rather than risk her position. What kept Jean from so unnatural an act was the fear that Marino would enslave her sexually as he had Mama Jean. If she had not despised the man she might have gone to bed with her stepfather—she was a goddess, and therefore above mortal conventions—but enslavement to someone like Marino would have destroyed her.

Aimlessly, without direction, anguished by desire and revulsion, she drove by night to find another man, saw men that made her slow the car, which made the men approach her. But each time as they came within steps of the car, Jean realized she could not escape recognition—and with recognition there could come blackmail. And each time she jammed her foot to the gas pedal and drove off with a hard clashing of gears. Sometimes she even saw their faces and knew they were handsome, but the fear of subservience to a man who could please her, or blackmail her, made her drive home with no other thought than to get into bed, alone. She was determined not to court the possibility of a second blackmailer until she had rid herself of the first. . . .

For the little quiet woman, the bit actress Paul had established in the West Hollywood bungalow, had informed Arthur that she had always nurtured ambitions to be either a writer or rich. She knew that any of the New York tabloids or any of the large chain newspapers in California would pay handsomely for her memoirs as the secret mistress—in name only—of Paul Bern. It had been an odd, lugubrious, horse-laugh arrangement; once she found out—the quiet little woman told Arthur—she had agreed to the masquerade, because Paul was liberal and she had hoped that he would get around to doing what he had promised: give her enough money to open a speakeasy or party house or a small convalescent home for rich drunks and rich women recovering from abortions. He had promised, but now they all knew the worth of his promises.

Arthur had reasoned with the actress, swore to her that Paul had told him she had never demanded anything more than support, but she had denied this and ordered Arthur out of the bungalow. At the door Arthur had paused to see her picking up the telephone, and when she asked for a downtown exchange he had crossed to the phone to break the connection. Yes—she was telephoning a newspaper to make an appointment. He had dared not doubt her, and reluctantly, because Arthur knew that the promises of a blackmailer are also worthless, he had asked if she had really written her memoirs.

With some ceremony the actress brought out two bookkeeping ledgers, opened one, skimmed the pages and showed him an entry that graphically described Paul in the nude; the style was not literary, but its vigor and able detail were evident. Casually, as if he were unimpressed, Arthur asked if he could look at other entries. After reading at random several other pages, he smiled to indicate the diaries were worthless.

Nonchalantly, he offered her a hundred dollars for both ledgers.

"I know you're kidding," the actress said. "Unless you mean a hundred dollars a page. That's what you mean," she continued rapidly. "A hundred dollars a page. There's a hundred pages in each of them. Twenty thousand." Again she paused for more mental arithmetic. "That's not enough. I was figuring each of these is worth twenty-five thousand. If you think they're too expensive for you, you can buy one and I'll sell the other to someone else."

"I could have you arrested or barred from the industry," Arthur huffed, puffed and bluffed. "Honestly, you don't look like a blackmailer."

Now the actress smiled tolerantly, because she knew that her ledgers were as solid as a house built of brick. "I'm not interested in the industry," she said. "And I'm not demanding that you buy. Let's understand that, Mr. Landau. I'm not demanding that you buy. If you don't understand that then I think you'd better go."

"I understand," Arthur agreed.

"Good. Now I hope you understand that I'm giving you first refusal. If you don't buy we're still friends. At least I won't have any hard feelings."

"How do I know you haven't made copies of what you want to sell—"

"I haven't."

"—or that you haven't made up everything in those ledgers? Why should people believe you before they believe Jean?"

"Because you and I know people," the actress replied. "Why believe good of someone when the worst is always more interesting?"

Thinking, attempting to sort things out, Arthur's mind came back to a facet of the financial problem that puzzled

Jean: what had Paul done with his money? Could this pleasant little woman have milked Paul during his lifetime?

"Bern gave you plenty," he accused her. "Tens of thousands."

The actress put aside her cigarette holder. "Are you crazy?" she asked. "Do you know there were lots of times when I had to lend him back the money he gave me to keep this place going? He gave me a hundred a week in cash," she continued. "And more on the first to pay the rent. What do you think a place like this rents for?"

"Twenty-five dollars?" Arthur hazarded.

"With utilities," the actress said. "And some of this furniture was mine to begin with. All right, so Mr. Bern would give me a couple of dollars more around the first to cover the rent. Look at it, Mr. Landau," she challenged. "For someone earning his kind of money it's obvious he wasn't a spender."

"So?"

"So," she replied. "I'd like to get paid now. Better late than never is the attitude I've got to take."

"Then you haven't been reading the papers?" he asked. "His estate is worth nothing."

"I don't believe everything I read," the actress said patiently, "and neither do you. He didn't spend any money," she insisted, her voice rising slightly, "and he made fifteen hundred a week." She paused to take the ledgers from Arthur and place them in a drawer of the china dresser. She locked it and put the key into her brassiere. "Fifty thousand," she said. "And I don't care if it's all in singles."

"Publish," Arthur said. "Because we can't pay fifty thousand."

"It's nice to know you see things my way," the actress said. "You're lucky that newspapers are published every day," she added. "That's why I'm willing to wait two weeks."

"Happy waiting."

"Thank you," she said. "But you don't have to go, Mr. Landau. I was just going to fix some coffee. Tea if you like. I'm a fan of Miss Harlow's. Really. Poor girl," she reflected. "If I'd known her I'd've told her not to marry him."

Curiosity kept Arthur at the door. "After Bern was married—what did he do about you?"

"Nothing!" For the second time Arthur heard her voice rise, saw color mottle her cheeks. "I never heard from him again. Not even a 'thank you, goodbye, it was nice knowing you and here's a couple of dollars for the road.' I'd just about decided to give him another month. So I guess, Mr. Landau, if he hadn't killed himself I'd be speaking to him instead of you."

The actress proved her willingness to cooperate by holding off when, on October 20, Herman Koch, the Public Administrator in Sacramento, claimed that he was about to reveal a will made by Paul Bern which designated Dorothy Milette as Paul's wife. A Mr. Henry Uttal, an attorney in New York City, had informed Dorothy Milette's sister in Ohio that he had prepared a will for Bern which named Dorothy as his wife and sole heir.

So many attorneys in the hunt for wills and treasure made it mandatory that another be entered in the contest, and Albert Sheets of Sacramento was retained to represent Jean Harlow's interests in assets that might rise to the surface. While he attempted to find documentary proof of more than a common-law marriage, the Public Administrator announced a public auction of Dorothy Milette's effects—trunk, luggage, clothes, foreign language dictionary, playing cards and other items. The proceeds of the auction would be used to purchase a headstone, because Miss Harlow had failed to make arrangements for such a memorial when Arthur had wired money for funeral expenses.

There had always existed a suspicion in Southern California that the northern, more sophisticated part of the state was jealous of the importance that had accrued to Los Angeles, an orange grove and picnic ground that had become the world capital of films. San Francisco reporters and columnists delighted in writing of the buffooneries and falls from grace by Hollywood's stars. The community malice that had made a disgraceful tragedy of the Fatty Arbuckle trial was still a frightening memory, and opinion was firm that if a similar accident had occurred to someone prominent in the Bay City, or for that matter to anyone from a city other than Los Angeles, the entire matter and trial would have been conducted and reported in kindlier vein.

Mayer screamed at Jean that although the studio and he were sick, tired and fed up with insanities of her private life, he had ordered money wired for a monument. As Jean described this encounter to Landau, she swore that Mayer had smiled all the while, which was proof that he delighted in tormenting her. Just thinking about it agitated her into a two-hour emotional tantrum in her dressing room, and it was necessary to call on the services of a nurse and male attendant. The attendant was Canadian, about thirty, a former lacrosse goalie whose nose had been broken twice and badly set, and as he carried Jean from her dressing room to the studio car that would take her home, Jean clung to him and attempted to run her hand inside his shirt. The attendant insisted that the nurse sit with Jean in the back seat of the car. As they drove from the lot, he told the actress, who was succumbing to sedation, that his wife was really a fan and that he hoped when Miss Harlow was feeling better she would autograph a picture or two. But she was not to worry about his telling his wife that she had been upset, because this would be violating a professional confidence. Jean sobbed her way into the induced slumber.

For the next several days she insisted on eating in her room, refused to speak to her mother or Marino, telephoned

Arthur constantly to demand that he do this as she countermanded that. Once she insisted that he meet her to discuss getting her into a picture where she could play the part of a school teacher or a nun. Patiently, Arthur explained that she was not the type to play such roles, that the public would not accept or pay to see her in such a part. His sympathy exhausted, he asked how many girls would be willing to trade places with her and to suffer, if need be, more than she had? Thousands, he answered.

"And that's what I owe," Jean replied. "And more's to come."

"All right, so you owe thousands," he said wearily. "But you're earning thousands. And no one is closing in on you."

"That bitch," Jean said switching suddenly to another problem. "I'm not going to give her fifty thousand dollars! As far as I'm concerned let her publish her junk. People won't give a damn and everyone knows anyway. And if Mayer, the bastard, has so much weight, let him tell his newspaper friends that he won't like their buying what she has to sell."

"But suppose she takes it to New York?" Arthur asked. "I know she could sell it. But for how much?"

"Let her find out, because I don't care. It's a rotten world and I don't owe it anything." She shrugged her shoulders and continued to autograph photos to be mailed to her fans. "I'm in it up to my neck." She altered a photo by drawing a dunce cap over her platinum hair. "So who cares?"

She refused to confirm the information Mama Jean had telephoned him that morning: that Jean was going out at night alone and returning as late as two or three in the morning. Arthur remembered Jean's tirades about her sexless life and her threat to steal Marino from her mother. It was easy to deduce that Jean, convinced that she was a moral bankrupt, prowled at night to search for a man. He would have been willing to arrange some parties at which Jean might have met men, but the conventions of mourning demanded that Jean not attend social functions. Why, there had even been some criticism because she had not returned to work at the studio in widow's weeds! True, she could have been invited to small dinners and get-togethers, but the truth was that Arthur had begun to doubt the emotional stability of the platinum blonde star.

At last, when he had several items of good news to celebrate, Arthur took her to lunch alone. Item one: she was going on a limited tour, because she was to begin work with Clark Gable in a story and script written by Anita Loos. The tour would include a stop at Kansas City, and the studio was willing to help make Jean's appearance into a civic holiday. Item two: the attorney for Paul Bern's mistress had agreed to a realistic price of eighteen thousand dollars for her diaries. Item three: the contractors had assured Arthur the house would be finished by the first of November.

"You can give a little housewarming," Arthur suggested. "We'll make it a refined party that'll move you back into the social picture. Then you'll start seeing more and more people and everyone'll soon forget it."

"Bastards," Jean replied. "I'll feed them poison at the party if I give a party. They don't deserve anymore." She paused, her mouth twisted in a bitter smile. "Did you say I'll be working with Gable?"

"Yes."

"How nice for him."

"I'm not going to argue," Arthur said patiently. "Now there's one thing I want you to do for me."

She began to laugh. "Right here on the table?"

"I want you to give up your claim to Paul's estate. There's nothing there but lots of bad publicity. Let's just make a formal announcement that you're relinquishing all your claims to whatever he left over, but you hope his family will use the assets to take care of any claims that come up. I don't think that when the estate is settled it'll really amount to anything, but it'll make you look good in the public eye."

"I'd like to spit in the public eye," she replied. "And I'm not giving up anything. That little bastard caused me enough trouble, and anything I can make him pay back'll help."

"You're being foolish," Arthur said.

Jean autographed a menu brought to her by a waiter. She acknowledged his gratitude with a smile, then turned to Arthur. "No, by God, I'm not giving up the estate if there is one. I'll fight them tooth and nail and use up every cent there is to pay for lawyers. Then win, lose or draw, they'll get nothing."

"But if there's nothing in the estate you'll have to pay your attorneys."

"So I'll owe them," Jean said. "Like I do everyone else. I'll go to Sacramento to fight them if I have to." She laughed again, then tilted her head archly. "And when you work out my hotel reservations, I want you to schedule good-looking bootleggers and good-looking bellboys. I'll be careful, Arthur. You see, I won't tell them my name."

Chapter Fifteen

By the second week in December, the Beverly Glen house was completed and partly furnished. Landscaping of the lily pond and installation of the little bridge were left for last. The exterior brick had been painted white, the chimneys at either end of the house had been topped, and the roads had been graded to permit cars to drive into the four-car garage; negotiations were under way to buy a V-12 Cadillac limousine and a Pierce-Arrow touring car with wire wheels. Roses had been trained over the trellised entrance to the lily pond and the showers in the pool-house and cabanas at the far end of the swimming pool were tested and passed by building inspectors. Masons were completing the barbecue and chimney in the center of the pool-house, and florists had brought up the potted boxwoods which would stand at each corner of the pool. Throughout the city shopkeepers waited for the order to deliver foods—for the refrigerator was a walk-in room.

At last the brick steps to the classic recessed doorway were completed, and Marino carried Mama Jean and a magnum of champagne across the threshold. Mr. and Mrs. Landau applauded this gallantry and Jean blew a razzberry on a kazoo as she waved a bottle of Gordon's. However, exclamations of joy were tempered, because Marino did not conceal his disappointment that Jean, who had evidenced no constructive interest in the house, who had refused to cooperate in choosing the furniture, plants, even the automobiles, who had done nothing but complain and bitch that the costs of construction, furnishings and maintenance were going to ruin her, now insisted upon occupying the master bedroom suite! Also, Marino's plan for a secret staircase between the bedroom and his den had been dismissed with scornful laughter, although Mama had found the idea charmingly wicked. To balm Marino's feelings, already crushed under the full weight of the national economic debacle, which had caused a shortage of solvent investors willing to develop a superior gold mine not far from Death Valley or in a jungle not far from Vera Cruz, Mama bought her nobleman a five carat diamond ring and three pairs of garters with all the metal parts made of gold.

Numbed by bills, by her mother's weeping that Jean was drinking too much, by the appearances required of her at the studio, Jean was indifferent to the arrangements and told her mother to take the master bedroom. She'd take the bedroom beyond the common massage room. No, she didn't care what her room looked like; whatever Mama and Mrs. Landau did was just fine with her. Anything, so long as they didn't bother her. So Mrs. Bello and Mrs. Landau threw themselves into furnishing the new temple of the goddess.

It was agreed that photographs of Jean would dominate most of the rooms in the house, but the architect and studio decorators suggested that the large spacious rooms with their paneled walls and ceilings and graceful curved doorways would show a combination of French and English period pieces to advantage. Antiques were the order of the day, and only antiques that had been owned by the rich would suffice. Both women spent full days, even several weekends, in decaying mansions along Adams Boulevard, the antique shops along Los Feliz Boulevard and in the Glendale Thieves Market. (Many years later Mama Jean had her own antique shop in Palm Desert, and she was happy there.) The longer trips took the ladies to Redlands, long known as the Southern California community favored by eastern millionaires. The depression had closed many of the homes, their furnishings were for sale, and the women bought several carloads of furniture, some of which they used, much of which they discarded. Other adventurous treks to Pasadena, where some suffering among millionaires was also in evidence, enabled the two women to acquire some choice marble busts and a superb eighteenth-century drawer chest with a bow front that was just perfect for Jean's room.

As if to prove that a bedroom could be a place of joy, most care was lavished upon the chamber The Baby would occupy. Amidst the easy chairs, the Empire sofa with its deep pillows and side bolsters, the graceful tables, consoles and lovely screen with mirrored inserts stood Jean's throne—a bed placed between two windows of the handsome bower. The bed was large, with a headboard upholstered in quilted satin and a graceful canopy to make anyone in the bed a princess. On either side of the bed were night tables with tambour receptacles for books, sleeping pills, liqueur bottles and a buzzer system for Jean to summon her mother or the household help, if she chose not to leave her bed. The profusion of mirrors reflected a plethora of Jean's photographs: as a child, as an actress, as a sexual nymph. After studying the remarkable room, Marino presented his stepdaughter with a bedpan. Jean used it for a camellia bowl until Mama donated the appliance to the Salvation Army.

Indifferent to all the excitement; complaining only of bills, the press, a multitude of nameless aches and pains in her back and elsewhere; snapping at Marino and her mother; cursing Arthur at least once a day to his face and more often on the telephone; weeping that Mayer hated her, everyone hated her, and she hated everyone; threatening to sue everyone and to involve the state of California in litigation that would bankrupt it and make it the laughing stock of the entire world—

Jean refused to like anything bought by her mother and Mrs. Landau.

It was at this time that Jean chose to make perhaps her most pathetic decision. Willfully determined to prove how little she was impressed by the house, the group about her, the studio, her future, her career, the Platinum Bombshell went to work on her own body, the sex shrine of a nation. She hacked her hair into a boyish bob, darkened her brows and lashes, took a black wig and simple hat, coat and dress from the studio's wardrobe and went by train to San Bernardino.

There she permitted herself to be picked up by a salesman, down on his luck and reduced to peddling soap, toothpaste and other sundries from door to door for beans and flophouse money. Of simple mind and weary with disappointment, the salesman accepted, with clucks of sympathy, Jean's story that she had been ill with typhoid fever and lost all her hair. When he promised to make no effort to remove her wig, and not to ask any really personal questions, Jean paid for the room at a small hotel near the depot and spent two nights with the peddler.

As Jean defiantly told the story to Mama Jean, Marino and Landau, the itinerant had complimented her, had said she was not bad, not bad at all; perhaps a little tense, which kept her from really getting all the good possible out of it, but not bad. And if business had been better, so that he could have afforded to spend the time with her, or if he were the gigolo type—a sad hint that Jean ignored—he would have taught her some of the fine points of screwing. Then she could have got herself a pretty good job in a whorehouse somewhere back East. Because Jean was pretty, and he was not saying this just because she was good to him. There were hundreds of pretty women who couldn't get into good houses, but Jean had something special in her favor. Besides her good looks, sexy body, strength and remarkable nipples, she was bald! The salesman swore that he meant no offense, but a woman with a beautiful body and astonishing nipples and a bald head would be an exciting addition to a high-class joint. And if Jean played it smart, she could probably marry some rich customer.

There were going to be other men, Jean swore, there was going to be no secret about it—if she wanted to she would even bring the men home.

"And they won't be anyone any of you'd be proud of," she challenged Arthur. She jerked her thumb at Marino. "They'll all be bums like him."

"You're aching for a slap in the mouth," Arthur said to her. "But you're not going to get it."

"Why?" she challenged her agent.

"Because you don't deserve it," Arthur said. "Let's get out of here." Arthur signaled for Marino to help him lead Mama Jean from the bedroom. "The place stinks of ingratitude."

Later that night The Baby lay in Mama's arms and wept, remembering how it really had been. The salesman in San Bernardino had been neither handsome nor strong; in fact, he might even have been less than average in appearance. And he had had the awful nervous habit of trying to pull his thumbs out of joint. But he had been able to perform like a man as often as Jean had demanded—after she had bought him a good dinner and some ten-cent cigars. Once she had almost felt complete passion, but the fool had stopped to ask her if she was enjoying herself, then had left the bed to adjust the closet door so that the mirror mounted on it would face the bed. She had looked in the mirror, seen herself, seen Mama and Marino, seen all the letters and pictures that she received through the mail—and she had wanted to die of shame.

But revolted as she was, she had continued to look, and suddenly she had looked so funny in a tangle of arms and legs, her black wig askew, that she began to giggle hysterically. The salesman had thought that her gasps and cries were ecstatic, so he had been doubly proud and done his best to pound her through the bed.

The man was really stupid, a miserable nothing with his valise filled with cheap nothings, a clod who even tried to pull his thumbs out of joint while they lay in bed nude and she explored him—yet she knew that poor, darling, dead Paul, that son of a bitch, would have sold his soul to the devil to be able to do what the salesman did so easily.

Repentant now, revolted, sick with herself, she began to dread the moment when she would have to face a distraught hairdresser and an irate director to discuss her role in *Hold Your Man*. And to make things worse, she could not remember if the salesman had always worn a condom. There had been dozens of them in one of the sales valises, and she was quite certain that he had used some several times, but the act, the liquor, the close confinement of the room, his tales of all the other women he had shagged—all of this made it impossible for her to remember whether the salesman had always been armored. For Mama Jean's benefit, she insisted that she did not care whether she was pregnant, venereal or both.

Suddenly Jean freed herself from her mother's embrace to scream that she hated Mama: it was all her fault that she was an actress, a notorious woman that men couldn't think about without slobbering. If Mama Jean had had the sense, the decency, the maternal responsibility to remain married to her *real* father, a prince of a man much too good for her mother even on the day he had married her, she might have this very day been living in Kansas City, married or going steady with some nice normal boy, and she would never have seen San Bernardino and its skies through the window of a gray hotel room. Now she had need of love—a love distinguished from sex—and the only man who had wanted to give her such love was dead, and she had killed him with her cruelty. She still hungered for love, but no man could ever give her the love she needed, because publicity had made it impossible for them to think of her as anything but a female sex machine. But only Mama Jean, Marino, Pops and she knew the truth—that she was a lousy lay, hated hated hated it, and hated most the people who enjoyed and derived pleasure from it.

Although they had spoken of a leave of absence and agreed that this was best for Jean, Arthur knew rest and vacation could not be had without the studio's permission. She still had to have her meetings with Sam Wood, who was to direct *Hold Your Man*. The studio might have forgiven Harlow everything, all of her disgraceful conduct in San Bernardino, but the ruin of her hair was another matter. Arthur telephoned Irving Thalberg at his home, informed the tired executive that the matter was one of life and death and could not wait until the morning, and arranged to meet Thalberg for a late supper in Santa Monica.

While they ate, Arthur told Thalberg that Jean's problems were unusual; she had really loved Bern, so much so that she had done a foolish thing.

"She got the idea that Jewish women cut their hair when they go into mourning," he said at last.

Thalberg placed his fork on the side of the plate and primly folded his hands. "You're not going to tell me . . . ?"

"She did," Arthur said. "She can't cry any more and she wants to keep on mourning him. It's cut real short, Irving."

"But she has to get over it," Thalberg said. "What am I talking about, feeling sorry for her!" he exclaimed. Aware that he had raised his voice, the slight executive drank a glass of water at a full gulp. "I'll murder her before I get murdered by Louis. We're getting ready to mount a new campaign just based on the hair on her head! What's the matter with you, Arthur? Why didn't you stop her?"

"Because I don't go to the bathroom with her," Arthur replied. "It isn't so bad. If you'll just listen."

After some preliminary remarks about the two hours re-

quired each and every morning to dress Jean's hair and the
two hours Jean needed to set her hair before retiring, Arthur
suggested cautiously that the studio's hairdressing department
make up two wigs for Jean. The wigs would be made in the
greatest secrecy, and when Jean arrived at the studio a combed
wig would be delivered to her dressing room. Then, at the
end of the day's work, a second wig would be delivered and the
first wig made ready for the next morning. This would save
hours of personal hairdressing and eliminate much of the star's
discomfort. Arthur doubted if the secret would be revealed.
He had taken the liberty of sampling the feelings of the little
people at the studio, to determine how they felt about Jean,
and not one had anything but sympathy for the unhappy
widow. To swear some hairdressers and messengers to secrecy,
and to hold them responsible for this secrecy in this time of
major unemployment, would insure the studio against leaks.

"In any case," Arthur finished, "if you expect Jean to step
on a set, she needs hair. And she hasn't got enough of her own.
Later on, Irving, when her hair grows back, if you still don't
like the idea of the wigs, we'll get rid of them."

"But people might see that she's wearing a wig," Thalberg protested.

Arthur shook his head. "They didn't in *Red Headed
Woman,* not even when she wore the wig for her personal appearances. Whatever MGM does looks real. I really don't have
to tell you that."

"No," Thalberg agreed, "but I'm glad you did. All right,
Arthur, I'll give orders to make up the wigs. Two?" he asked.

"Make four," Arthur said after a moment's thought.
"Then there'll be one extra and one for the studio beauticians
to work on to develop new hair styles."

"And what'll we do meanwhile?" Irving asked. "What we
need will take a couple of weeks. And Sam was complaining
again today."

"So you'll ask him, as a personal favor to all of us, to go

out to see Jean at her new house. He ought to go over there anyway. And I'll pick up the wig Jean wore in *Red Headed Woman*. If you don't trust Sam, tell him that she likes to get away from herself by wearing the red wig—that it helps her to think of Paul."

"That doesn't make sense," Irving said.

"Admitted. But if you tell me what does, I'll do it. You've got another suggestion?"

"None," Thalberg said. "But let me tell you something, Arthur, and you can tell it to Miss Harlow." He became aloof and formal. "At the studio we make pictures about life and death, but we've no time to waste on them in real life. I hope you understand."

"I do," Arthur said.

"Now it's up to you to see that she does. We'll call Sam Wood tonight." Thalberg gestured for the waiter to fill his glass again. "And someone will deliver the red wig."

"Make the someone someone who can start measuring her for the new wigs."

"Naturally. Meanwhile, Arthur, I've got something I want to discuss with you. Mr. Bello's been bothering our accounting people. He said *he* should be given Jean's check, not you."

"Bar him from the lot. Mama too," Arthur suggested. "I won't be jealous if you treat them as well as you did me. And I'll keep picking up her check. Soon, I hope, we can start getting ahead. The house cost a lot. You ought to go up there with Mrs. Thalberg. Jean would appreciate it."

"I don't think she'd care," Thalberg replied. "And Norma and I would visit the house only if we could be sure none of that miserable family was there."

Arthur shut his eyes. "I didn't know you didn't like her, Irving."

"I like her as a property," Thalberg replied. "And in our business none of us can ask for more."

The wigs proved a well-kept industry secret. Until the end of her career Jean wore only wigs in her films, and for most of her public appearances. The grooming of her hair excited international admiration and gave rise to a new crop of stories that her hair was the rarest texture, with certain unique qualities never spelled out.

Work on the house continued daily, and the more important movie reporters were invited to visit Jean in her all-white bedroom, where she received them in slacks and white tennis shoes. Sam Wood and Anita Loos visited Jean to discuss the new picture, and one evening Jean entertained Clark Gable, Stuart Erwin and Dorothy Burgess, who were to appear with her in *Hold Your Man*.

It was decided to begin shooting after the inauguration of Roosevelt. Who knew? He might be good for business.

Although Jean wanted to visit San Francisco without her mother and Marino, they insisted upon going with her. However, they agreed to leave her alone there for at least a week, because they were going to Caliente for the races. Meanwhile, Marino insisted and Landau agreed, that Jean should have the protection of her family during her conferences with her attorney in northern California or with public officials in and around Sacramento. Even Marino had swung around to the position that it would be wisest for Jean to surrender all rights to the litigated estate.

The adventure in San Bernardino had sobered Jean, and she began to take some pleasure in the house and the increasing beauties of the grounds and garden areas. She delighted in the first of the completed blonde wigs and swore that the hair was prettier than her own. But with all of these compensations, she refused to give up her rights to Bern's estate; she would fight Dorothy Milette's heirs *and* Sacramento County, because anyone else would have done so and she was no less a person than anyone else. To prove this she smashed every dinner plate on the dining room table. MGM, pleased that they had persuaded

Jean to make so many concessions, notified their distribution and exchange executives in the Bay City to create an atmosphere around Harlow that would enhance her public image, and to screen out anyone of the press who might be unfriendly.

Jean, her parents and her secretary registered at the Mark Hopkins Hotel on Tuesday, December 27, and found their suite decorated with an elaborate tree, stockings hanging from the mantle and elaborate bouquets that bore tags from fan clubs as far east as Columbus, Ohio. But all of these had been paid for by Landau and MGM. There were bouquets and baskets from the studio and from other Hollywood stars, and the hotel had placed a dozen white roses on the dresser of Jean's bedroom. All the interviews were held after Jean had rehearsed appropriate statements: she had always loved San Francisco and admired its cosmopolitan atmosphere; she certainly bore no one in San Francisco or Sacramento any ill will; she did not intend to visit the Plaza Hotel or the cemetery where Dorothy Milette was buried. What purpose could such visits serve? She would rather visit an orphanage and distribute presents to children. She looked forward to her new picture and enjoyed working again with Clark Gable. She let the reporters read the telegram he had sent to her. Gable had also wired flowers and candy, and Jean opened the box and insisted that everyone help himself. It was a successful interview. There was also a bouquet and a basket of fruit from Harold Rosson, and Jean told the reporters that he was the best cameraman in the world and she intended to telephone and tell him so.

It was after midnight before the last visitor was dismissed and after one before Marino finished the last bottle of champagne he had brought in the hamper from Los Angeles. Jean lay awake in her bed, unable to sleep, her memories alternating between outrage and shame. She recalled the salesman in San Bernardino, and her mind drifted on to the nagging possibility of pregnancy. Suddenly she sat erect. If she was pregnant, she had become so only months after Bern's death, and she would permit the pregnancy to show, insist that she bore Paul's child, and then go abroad where money could arrange for her, she was certain, a predated birth certificate! Then, in triumph, she would return to Hollywood and confound her enemies and make Louis B. grovel—by God, she would make him godfather of her child! She would prove herself to be the best mother in the world by doing no more than booting Mama and Marino out of the house, out of her checkbook and out of her life. She would show them all what kind of woman she could be!

These fantasies were so delicious Jean could not sleep, and she stood at one of the windows in her hotel room to see the city shake off the night. As dawn began to wash the city, her pulses quickened at her first view of the harbor and its magic bay. The city was interesting, as she imagined European cities might look, different from most other American cities she had seen, especially those in the west, all of them so alike in theme, purpose and appearance that they might have been ordered by number from a mail order catalogue. The sights and sounds of San Francisco stimulated and rested her. If she was not pregnant she would say she was and to succeed in her deception she would make Pops get her a baby somewhere; possibly in Europe, where she would go to complete the hoax. She began to hum a little lullaby, stopped to listen to the fog horns in the bay. Without effort she combined the mournful notes in chords and bars of music, eerie yet soothing; and she understood the horns because they were on ships, as she, lost and seeking safe harbors.

Bright flowers in wooden boxes lined the paths of Union Square, and Jean ordered the cabdriver to circle the square several times. As they passed the St. Francis Hotel, she looked out of her window and wondered in which of the rooms Fatty Arbuckle had met his tragedy. She had dressed quietly, left a note for Mama that she had been unable to sleep and wanted air, but that she would call later and return in time to keep all the scheduled appointments. The elevator operator and doorman had been kind, especially after dollar tips, and had told her that she looked just as lovely in her dark wig.

The cab drove up Powell, turned east into the city's bohemia, for Jean was curious to see where the artists and writers lived, and chugged up the hill with its narrow sidewalks, cobbled streets and crowded little houses, most of them converted from poor flats to poorer studios that were often unoccupied because their modest rents were beyond most artists. Some of the houses had been elaborated with carpenter's Gothic around the doors, windows and every other available surface; others, indifferently painted, were topped by red, blue and yellow roofs that gave a Mediterranean air to this northern California city. The cab drove past little Italian groceries and barber shops. Spanish signs identified a poolroom and a notary public who wrote personal letters, dabbled in real estate and offered advice on all legal matters and private and public relief procedures. Halfway up the hill a clenched fist and *Up the Rebels!* painted on a store front identified a Sinn Fein headquarters six thousand miles from Dublin; a bum and his empty bottle slept in the doorway.

"Sixty, seventy years ago this used to be a mighty rough neighborhood. Now it's filled with free-lovin' artists," the cabdriver told Jean. He attempted to see her in the rear view mirror, but she had moved out of his line of vision. "Don't ever drink any booze up here," he continued.

"Really?" she asked.

"It's all made in dirty bathtubs." The cab was at the crest of Telegraph Hill and the driver shifted into neutral and applied the brake. "You meeting someone up here, lady?" Jean shook her head. "Then you want me to wait? This is a mighty rough neighborhood."

"I'll manage," she said and tipped him generously. Then she changed her mind. "All right. You can wait for me a block away and come back for me in a half-hour or so."

The cabdriver scratched his head. "You're not thinking of doing something to yourself?" He glanced quickly at the good clothes, the large sunglasses and broad-brimmed hat which hid most of her features. "A good-looking lady like you—I hope you're not in trouble? If you want a drink I know a place where the stuff's safe. Or maybe you'd like to hire me for the day? I could go home and change clothes and really show you the town."

"Come back in half an hour," she said. "Then we'll talk."

Fisherman's Wharf and Alcatraz, still the Army prison, were easily seen. Looking down the eastern slope of the hill, she wondered at the crazy catwalks between the old wooden houses on the hillside. Beyond them, the whitecapped blue waters of the bay were becoming streaked by stronger lights of morning. Grouped on the peninsulas were the skyscrapers, these proud, grave temples of commerce in which few worshiped but from which an occasional human sacrifice would, they said, leap from a window or turret. Hills dominated the city; houses, crowded together, were colorful terraces that descended to the sea and streets were narrow clefts that tied the hills to the great piers where unemployed hundreds stole food and sleep.

As Jean turned from the sea to stare at Russian Hill and Lombard Street in the distance, so steep and narrow that its descent was a series of hairpin switchbacks, she exclaimed at the beauty and felt, again, the wonder of this unique morning. But this was a greater wonder! Now, for the very first time, she felt adult, a true woman, capable of knowledge and affinity with all the people who slept in the rows of boxlike houses that descended the hill.

New York was too far away from the studios; but why could she not live here? The house on Beverly Glen meant nothing to her, she had no affection for it and could leave it without regret. But Mama and Marino would not leave her; the studio would never permit it; Pops would think she was crazy; and choosing San Francisco, of all places, would make her apostasy unforgivable. She would have to return, but even understanding this added to the new feeling of adulthood. And now, as an adult, she realized fully all the benefits she could gain by being pregnant, the power pregnancy would grant her. If she were *not* pregnant, there were other men in the city—the cabdriver for one—far better looking than the salesman she had picked up in San Bernardino. As she ticked over the appointments for the day, she knew she would be free after three.

As she walked down the hill toward the cab, Jean decided to leave the matter open. The driver would call for her at the hotel at three-thirty and tell the doorman that he had arrived as ordered. If Jean were free she would leave the hotel and go home with him while he changed and got the other car; if not, she would now give him enough money to compensate for his disappointment.

As she entered the cab, Jean told the driver her plan and paid him. Now she was at last able to lean back in the leather seat and understand that she no longer required sex to stimulate her imagination. As an adult, she still wanted to know passion and desire, but she would always be their mistress. She no longer cared what parts the studio gave her or whether she would ever be thought of as an actress, for her ultimate ambition stretched far beyond such minor accomplishments. Her ambition was to triumph over three people she loathed: Mama, Marino and Louis B.

And she might do this through a baby. She just had to become pregnant quickly.

Chapter Sixteen

As soon as he discovered the way things were, at about six Thursday morning, Marino ordered the cabdriver out of Jean's bed and threatened the man with death and destruction if he ever revealed the graces granted him by one of the greatest stars of all time.

The cabdriver, though, was glad to have several photographs autographed to "A kind friend and guide. Best wishes and good luck for the New and all the Coming Years." He assured Marino that he, too, was of Latin ancestry and a man of honor and swore that he had not recognized Jean when he had first picked her up as a fare and that he still could hardly believe that Jean Harlow had been so attracted to him that she had been willing to give him . . . and if he told it to the other drivers in the garage or on the hack stands he worked, no one would believe him anyway. Still, did Mr. Bello think there might be a place for him in movies? The cabdriver had heard from reliable people that short men were photographed on boxes, that make-up could alter noses, and that lights and shades and angles could change a man's appearance so that his own mother wouldn't recognize him. And, if the cabdriver said so himself, he had a good build and some sort of personality, otherwise why would someone like Jean Harlow have picked him to shag with?

Noting Marino's scowl, he abandoned that line—but he had one last question. He was clean, in perfect health, but movie stars had . . . well, reputations. If Jean was sick he would appreciate knowing it so he could take precautions as soon as he left the hotel. Marino's reply was a slap across the cabdriver's mouth, and the driver abandoned voice for fist to drive it deep into Marino's stomach and crumple him across Jean's rumpled bed. Jean was so delighted she gave the cabdriver another twenty dollars, kissed him again, her tongue deep in his mouth, swore she was healthy and promised to speak to her agent and see what could be done. The driver did not believe her, but wished everyone the happiest of New Years, apologized to Mama and Marino, gave them the address of a good Italian restaurant where they could get some really good old wine, and left, an excited, bewildered man.

While breakfast was served in the suite, Jean sat at a hotel typewriter and pecked out a note to Landau to assure him that she was enjoying every moment of her stay. "Everyone has been so kind and each moment has been filled with delightful experiences."

Because Marino and Mama insisted that they leave for Los Angeles immediately, Jean added a line about their Pullman reservations for that night: they would "arrive home Friday morning, then your blonde child will have a shampoo and about two o'clock said child WHOOPEE Mother and Marino start [for] Caliente to stay over New Years."

On the way to the station Jean rebelled, threatened to leap from the moving cab or kick out the windows and slash her wrists on the broken glass if Mama and Marino did not return to Los Angeles without her. They had no choice but to permit Jean to leave the cab on a Market Street corner. In her dark wig, glasses and broad-brimmed hat she waved goodbye, thumbed her nose at her family and disappeared into the crowd.

The holiday season of 1932 was unusually festive. The election of Franklin Roosevelt created a new administration that might be able to break the grip of depression, and more to the point, it was quite certain that one of Roosevelt's first executive communications to the Congress would recommend a repeal of the Eighteenth Amendment. Most people got busy celebrating repeal in advance.

For Jean the weekend was an alcoholic haze of people, bars, noise, music, booze, groping hands and creaking beds. She remembered once even on the floor of a closet, twice—or was it three times?—in the back seats of speeding cars. Most of it she never completely remembered, except for one thing: no matter how much she drank and laughed and raced about, no matter how many men she gave herself to or how violently they took her, she could not blind herself to the sight of Paul prancing about like a satyr, dressed only in the ridiculous dildo.

Thursday night, Friday, all of Saturday and even Sunday night were a round of bars and pickups and parties and fast drives in automobiles all over the peninsula. Had she been in Carmel for an hour or so? She wasn't sure. But she was certain of awaking nude Sunday afternoon in a Geary Street hotel room, with her money and jewelry gone.

She telephoned Los Angeles collect and asked Arthur to send her five hundred dollars by Western Union. No matter how she demanded and swore, Arthur refused to do more than to pay for her Pullman fare and to wire her fifty dollars. Jean pleaded to speak to Beatrice, Arthur refused and Jean hung up in a rage. A minute later she telephoned again and asked that the ticket be left for her in the name of Jane H. Smith of Kansas City at the Southern Pacific ticket office. She would pick it up that evening. But a hundred dollars was the least she would accept; otherwise Arthur might as well not send the ticket.

"Of course, Pops," she said, "I guess I could earn a hundred without even trying."

"I'll send it," he said. "But only to stop you from talking that way."

"Then make it the five hundred," she said. "Unless you want me to tell you how much of it I've already given away for nothing. Holiday spirit, Arthur," she laughed, "so this piece of earth was showing her good will to all men. And what besides grief did Santa bring you for Christmas?" She switched to her tough voice, "Arthur, listen. I want three hundred if you're going to send the ticket. Otherwise, forget everything."

Three hundred dollars gave Jean the funds for two more nights of alcohol. She picked one man up outside a theater which was showing *Red Dust*, and he told her that she looked like Jean Harlow and advised her to go to Hollywood, where she might get a job as a stand-in or double. Indifferent sex was now indulged in only in her own hotel room, where she had taken the precaution of removing all the electric bulbs. She insisted on darkness and, toward the end of her orgy, no longer bothered to remove her clothes. She told considerate men that she wore a pessary and that they shouldn't worry about what was her problem. The determination to become pregnant possessed her; this was the fantastic explanation for her debaucherie that she gave to Arthur and Beatrice, who met her at the depot in Los Angeles.

Most of the long taxi ride to Beverly Glen was completed in silence, except for some casual questions from Jean as to whether the studio was prepared to have her return from her vacation so soon. Mama Jean and Marino had not gone to Caliente, but it was of no interest to Jean. Before they arrived at Beverly Glen she insisted on a stop at the Landaus' for coffee. There she attempted to explain to Beatrice and Arthur the dramatic, subtle reasons for her promiscuity: in a child she would not only have the satisfactions and revenges she desired, but she would have a weapon to force MGM to use her in other roles that demanded she do more than walk into a scene and look provocative. Besides, she would really love a child. She would deny Mama and Marino the privileges of being grandparents, but Pops and Mrs. Landau, who should not think too badly of her, could play these roles with Jean's beautiful, beautiful child.

The thing was a *fait accompli,* so it was pointless to berate her. And actually, the ridiculous plan could have some exploitable features, but nothing could be done until pregnancy was established. Meanwhile, wearing her wigs, Jean continued in *Hold Your Man.* The shooting progressed on schedule and even gained several days, which pleased Thalberg and Mayer. Exchange managers were informed that a new Harlow picture would be ready for the theater engagements in July. The new publicity campaign to be built around the picture would emphasize Gable's raffish charm and Jean's brave determination to continue with the career that Paul Bern had planned; "on with the show" was her monument to his beloved memory.

By the end of March, Jean was willing to admit that she was not pregnant, that continued promiscuity was not likely to make her pregnant, and that in any case, an illegitimate child would ruin her career. But in desperation she visited several doctors, all of whom agreed that she was not pregnant. Bitterly, she realized that she could be sexually promiscuous and never worry about human consequences; as a goddess, she could be indiscriminate, flagrant, outrageous, and it would not matter because she was sterile. Therefore, she could never really be a citizen in the community of women.

The news made her despair, but certain mature ambitions she had felt in San Francisco enabled her to hang on. Her plan at best had been, as Arthur had insisted, ridiculous. Although the studio had been able to squelch most of the vague stories of the wild holiday she had enjoyed in San Francisco, hints and generalized innuendoes of Jean's excesses appeared in the columns of some minor writers unfriendly to or out of favor with the studio. To dam off the trickle of dangerous news items, MGM made available to reporters and magazines a plethora of managed new stories, photographs and interviews.

The studio was so friendly and democratic in its general *rapprochement* to all the press, even the hostile columnists, that as a matter of courtesy most columnists and reporters continued to present Jean in a sympathetic focus.

By studio appointment Landau was made responsible for Jean's cooperation, and on April 3, newspapers throughout the country were favored with a picture and story layout of Jean Harlow and Gene La Verne, "a famous dance creator and teacher," who had "evolved the Hollywood Tango," which gave "women of the silver screen and their escorts a terpsichorean exercise that is new, novel and the epitome of grace." Jean illustrated the tango in her wig and a full-length ballroom dress that was high of neck and low of back. The photographs were so well received there was at least five hours of executive discussion about the advisability of sending Jean on personal appearances with a tango partner, for it had been firmly decided by the studio that, as soon as Jean completed her major scenes in *Hold Your Man,* she would go to Chicago to begin her three-week westward tour. This was to include a triumphal return to Kansas City, where her personal appearances could be combined with a good, old-fashioned, American old-home-week. A tango partner was vetoed because of the San Francisco rumors, and Arthur was informed that the Bellos would accompany Jean as chaperones.

Jean's cheerful cooperation made the studio worry for her health, but Arthur explained the tractability of his platinum client as the onset of maturity, a philosophical realization that she had, despite her tragedy, much to be grateful for, and he pleaded with Thalberg and Strickling to start the tour. On weekends, at his own expense, he would visit Jean wherever she might be; he would work closely with MGM men in the field to make the tour a success and keep the Bellos as cooperative as their daughter.

Casually, as if the matter were of no consequence, Arthur asked what other properties the studio had in mind for Jean, and what long-range plans were under consideration to increase the magnitude of their bright star. And mightn't it be a real, pleasant and profitable surprise to everyone if Jean proved herself as an actress? He had heard that the script of *Dinner at Eight* had been completed, and judging from what critics had said of Jean's performance in the rough-cut screenings of *Hold Your Man,* she deserved the reward of appearing in a picture that would star Marie Dressler and the Barrymore brothers. With kind impatience, Thalberg suggested that Jean might find herself in waters beyond her depth. But Landau insisted that Jean be permitted to read for George Cukor, assigned to direct the film, and personally assured Thalberg that Marie Dressler—also his client—would not be opposed to working with Jean.

Jean left for her tour, reports were favorable, and most of the weather and press cooperated. Landau showed Thalberg a letter from Mama Jean in which she said that Jean's arrival in Chicago had been splendid; although tired by travel, Jean had agreed to everything, even to an appearance at a press luncheon arranged by the Chicago representative of MGM and held, of all the ridiculous places, at the Horticultural Building of the World's Fair. She had regretfully declined an invitation to visit Cleveland because, in truth, she was eager to return to the studio, which she missed, and she was eager to know what projects the studio had for her.

Mayer, who was in New York, had deliberately avoided a stopover in Chicago and had instructed Thalberg that he did not, for the present, want to be bothered with anything that concerned Harlow. Decisions about the final version of the picture were to be the responsibility of his executive producer.

Thalberg and Landau attended another screening of *Hold Your Man,* where some hearts and flowers scenes dropped on the cutting-room floor had been restored to the film to make it more palatable to local censors. (Jean played one of the girls in a "flathouse," and Gable was cast as a small-time crook, running from the police, who entered the house and took refuge in Jean's bathroom while she was in the tub. A barrel in *Red Dust,* a tub in *Hold Your Man,* and the same principals . . .) There were also sequences with Jean as an inmate of a woman's prison, and in one troublesome scene Jean and other inmates attended services in the prison chapel and sang "Onward, Christian Soldiers" in such a way that spontaneous and un-solicited comic elements had been added to what had been planned as a scene of sentimental but sincere redemption.

At the end of two screenings Thalberg agreed that this was the best performance Jean had ever given and decided to make a master print of a more forceful version of the picture—hearts-and-flowers out, Christian Soldiers and bathtub in. Before Arthur left the studio Thalberg assured him that Jean would get a good part in some new all-star picture, and that by the end of the week they would both speak to Cukor.

This good news required a direct telephone call to Jean. It was entirely possible that she would get a role in *Dinner at Eight* without reading for Cukor, so nothing else mattered for the moment except to be cooperative and to put herself in a psychological mood that would make the rest of her tour a success. Her return to Kansas City had to be a triumph the studio could not ignore.

"And I hope you're behaving yourself," Arthur said.

"I sure am," Jean replied. "I only laid the cutest bellboy once. But I won't do it with anyone in K.C., Arthur. I promise, honest-to-God."

Despairing, Arthur hung up, canceled his flight to Chicago, and got gloriously drunk.

Jean and the Bellos went on to Kansas City, where, to prove she was humble and a true Kansas City prairie flower unspoiled by Hollywood, Jean stayed with the Harlows and insisted upon sharing her room with Mama, which meant that Marino had to sleep by himself. Such a show of mastery de-

239

lighted Jean's grandfather, who reciprocated by posing for friendly pictures with Marino. Jean addressed a local drama group, encouraged the girls to work hard at their profession, assured everyone that she missed Kansas City and could always be called upon for advice, and accepted a plaque from the Kansas City Beauticians Association for her contributions to hair styling.

A triumph in a former place of defeat can be so stimulating, the envy of those once envied so heady an elixir, that while they held court in Kansas City Mama Jean insisted she be permitted to dictate an arrogant message to Arthur Landau. It was about time that he and other hirelings were put in their places. It was improper, outrageous, that he had Jean's financial confidence. This would have to end. People even had the discourtesy to discuss in her presence, and Marino's, how Arthur had found their daughter and made her a star as soon as she had become his client. Elated with her reception and weary of Mama's complaints, Jean returned to Hollywood.

The first salvo in the campaign to force Arthur from the field was a telegram sent to him on June 22 from Kansas City.

> Please wire immediately by Western Union that
> our return tonight imperative. Advise servants
> also Strickling our arrival Saturday evening.
>
> Mother

The telegram was a confusion of imperious commands. Why should the presence of Mama and Marino be required in Hollywood? Because they had tired of Kansas City? Jean had already reported for work in *Dinner at Eight* and was doing famously. Living in her dressing room at the studio, eating at least once a day with the crew and other "little" people, and being cared for by Blanche Williams, her newly hired and loyal personal maid, Jean was having a grand time.

However, it required no great sophistication for Landau

to see all the implications in the peremptory little telegram. That afternoon, as he examined his ledger sheets on Jean's earnings, commissions received, and sums advanced to Jean, Marino and Mama, he realized that Jean Harlow now owed him almost twenty thousand dollars. If Jean were to join in with her mother's plan, most likely suggested by Marino, he would not attempt to keep Jean as a client. He was too weary, and the situation had become too distasteful. In addition, he felt overwhelmingly burdened by the weight of secrets he now bore, and if things ran true to form, he could expect to be burdened by more. If Jean wanted to leave, he would regret it. For, looking at the whole situation—Mama and Marino, the desperations Jean insisted upon practicing, her refusal to see a doctor although she complained almost daily that her back hurt and that she was getting a calloused seat from going to the john every minute on the minute (this was an exaggeration, but four or five times an hour was not unusual for Jean)—the future could at best, if one insisted upon being optimistic, be a disaster. Arthur decided that he would dismiss Jean and her family before they could do this to him, but all loans and advances would have to be repaid before he agreed to a termination of contract between them.

However, if he was annoyed with the telegram from Mama, the one sent by Marino later that night was downright insulting. It demanded that he proceed immediately to secure Marino memberships in either the Bel Air or Los Angeles Country Clubs, preferably both (Rosson, the MGM cameraman, had casually mentioned golf to him a month before). Further, Arthur was to arrange for several of the best tailors to be on hand with swatches of fabric suitable for plus-fours, slacks and sport jackets. The telegram was simply signed with the initial M, as if Marino's full name were like Yhwh's, never to be written in full, read nor pronounced by a mere man.

Arthur, stuttering with outrage, swore and swore again that he was going to drop Jean in the morning. The money she owed him could go with her too; the debt would stand as an effective barrier between Jean, the Bellos and him, and he would once again know peace. Then good sense overcame passion and Arthur decided to return the telegram to Bello with his own letter of demand for full payment of the debt. He had mentioned the debt to Jean on the phone that day; now the letter to Marino would prove that one client did not make an office, and that he would survive if he did not represent Jean.

Short hours after the Bellos returned to Beverly Glen, Arthur presented himself with the telegram and his letter of demand and gave them to Marino, who was lording it about the room in a weighted silk robe and puffing a Turkish cigarette through a gold holder.

Marino tossed the letter aside but waved the telegram at Arthur. "How come you didn't follow my instructions?"

"Because you can go to hell," Arthur said. "The people I do business with always get paid. That's the way it's always been and always will be."

"My business is none of your business," Marino said.

"And that's the way I want to keep it," Arthur said.

Arthur waited for Jean to speak, but she sat cross-legged on the living room carpet and practiced revolving movements to keep her pectoral muscles tight so that she could continue to do without brassieres. But the set of Jean's eyes and fix of her mouth warned Mama to remain silent.

"You want to owe people," Arthur continued, "that's your business. Mine is a cash business. Cash for the talent I represent. That's the way my clients demand we conduct our business."

"I'm not complaining, Pops," Jean said. "I told you myself not to do anything about my salary until everything blew over." She pointed at Marino. "And you shut up. Because this is between the two real money people in the room."

"Correct," Arthur agreed. "That's why I'm here to talk about what you and your family owe me."

"You've no gratitude," Mama Jean said tearfully. "Look at what our little Pink Bunny has done for you."

Arthur rubbed his ear to hear better. "Pink Bunny?"

"The Baby," Mama pointed at her daughter, who had rolled over to lie on her stomach. "Our Pink Bunny."

Jean sighed and rose slowly, dusted the knees of her slacks and stretched herself on the piano bench to continue her exercises. "Since when am I a pink bunny?" she asked her mother. "You know," she continued without waiting for a reply, "I think you've got a head full of feathers. And don't you say how dare I talk that way to my old lady," Jean warned Marino as she sat erect and banged an elbow into the piano keys. "Arthur, let's stop playing games. I owe you lots of money."

"Correct," he said.

"But you didn't come here because of the money. You came because of the way that greaseball struts around. Because my mother thinks she's the Queen of England or something. All right," she slapped her knees, "if you say the word, Arthur, tomorrow morning I'll tell the studio I'm authorizing them to make out all my checks to you except for a hundred bucks a week to me. That's until you're paid off. Would that be satisfactory?"

"If it is to you," he said.

"Go to work if you need money!" she screeched at her mother and Marino. "This Pink Bunny's had enough of being your chicken."

Mama compressed her features to form a giant tear. "If you don't like to be called Pink Bunny I won't. If you insist, I'll even call you Miss Harlow. Or Mrs. Bern, if it suits you better."

Cheeks sucked in, Jean took a step forward as if to

strike her mother. Then she wiped at her white face and hooked both thumbs into the belt of her slacks. "Mrs. Bello," she began slowly, "why don't you and Signor Bello go upstairs and climb on each other? You look as if you're in the mood." Suddenly she ran to the fireplace and grabbed a poker to stop Marino in his tracks. "Go ahead, Mr. Bello," she challenged her stepfather. "You haven't got your cute little cane now. But if you want to get it, fine." Suddenly she laughed and waved the poker as if it was a saber. "Arthur, I want to show you something."

Urging Arthur to follow her and not to ask questions, she ran to Marino's den. As Arthur and the Bellos watched, Marino with narrowed eyes, she poked around in the umbrella stand in one corner of the room, found the cane and fiddled with the handle. A little yelp of triumph escaped her lips as she discovered the lock mechanism, pressed it, and withdrew the slender steel blade from the deceptive wood sheath.

"How do you like it?" She waved the sword, then made a slash at Marino. "That's what he threatened to do to me, Mama Jean. Didn't you, Marino?"

"Put that down," Marino said. "You know I was joking."

"Some joke." Jean continued to point the sword at Marino, but she noted with delight her mother's open-mouthed amazement, the way Arthur stared at the weapon and Marino's desperate attempts at composure. "Some damn joke. He was gonna slash my face, Mama, if I didn't let him keep on spending money faster than I made it."

Cursing eloquently, she opened a desk drawer, slid the blade halfway into it, closed the drawer and pressed down on the handle of the cane. The steel snapped off at the hilt, and with a cry to match the snap of the steel Mama Jean flung herself at Marino and raked his cheek with her nails. Then she crumpled herself into an armchair and sobbed that she still loved Marino, that she also hated him, that she was so confused she wanted to die.

Jean flung the handle of the cane into a corner of the room and wiped her hands as if they were dirty. "Arthur, come upstairs. I want to talk business to you. Agent-client business."

"I want him out of the house!" Marino roared. "Out of my home!"

"I wish you'd order me out, too." Jean laughed at him. "Say it to me and I'll see you get a thousand bucks tomorrow. You've got my word."

Door to the massage room locked, door to the corridor locked, Arthur listened as Jean, flushed with triumph, padded between her bathroom and the chaise, not even closing the bathroom door as she used the toilet several times. Never pausing in her tirade against Marino, but raising her voice to be heard above the flush of water, she told Arthur that she expected from him the frankness and confidence he had always had from her.

"But you don't have to tell me," she said as she returned again to the bedroom and zipped up her slacks. "Mama and that bastard want you out of the picture."

"Correct," Arthur said. "And unless things change, Jean, it'll be better all the way around."

"It'll change," Jean mumbled thoughtfully.

"I don't like what you did in Chicago," Arthur said.

She looked at him, then winked in the hope he would laugh. "The bellboy?"

"And don't tell me you were kidding."

At her dresser she passed a bonehandled brush from hand to hand. "I wasn't. But I've been on good behavior since I've been home. Ask anyone."

"Fine," Arthur nodded. "But what about the future?"

"I won't promise anything." She approved of herself in the mirror, inhaled sharply and opened her blouse to stare at the reflection of her full breasts. The nipples were erect and hard. "I'm so damned pleased that you came over, Arthur, because it started things going. Did you see what Mama did to her wop? Honest, that's why I'm so excited. You know, I feel better now than any man's ever made me feel. Honest."

"Pull yourself together," Arthur ordered. "We still have to talk."

"There's nothing to talk!" She threw the brush and it struck one of his raised elbows. "Don't think you're going to leave me with the two of them!" She reflected. "Arthur, maybe we can get Mama to divorce him somehow?"

"That's between them and none of my business," Arthur said as he replaced the brush on the dresser.

Jean embraced him and laughed when he tried to avoid her naked breasts. "And then, Pops, you'll figure out some way maybe I can divorce Mama! You can, Pops. You can do anything."

"Except get you to a doctor," Arthur said after he managed to free himself.

"Because I pee a lot?" Jean continued to laugh at him. "Don't worry. I only use clean johns. And no one dies from peeing, do they?"

Chapter Seventeen

Movies can succeed at the box office despite the critics, but when the reviews are good, everyone is happy. *Hold Your Man* opened at the Capitol Theater in New York City on June 30, 1933. It was applauded by *Variety* for many things, among them skilled interpretations of unoriginal roles by all the principals, with Jean Harlow given the nod for expert performance. *Variety* observed primly that there was "nothing wrong with the ethics of the situation in which both principal characters start as unworthy, for it is the honest love they find in each other that works out their regeneration. That outline ought to be censor-proof."

It was. The audience-wide approval of Jean Harlow overwhelmed the voices of Bible Belt Comstocks. In 1933, when the national population was a hundred and twenty-five million, eighty-eight million people went to the movies to dream better than they did when asleep. A Harlow film would average, during its first and subsequent runs, between fifteen and twenty million adult theater tickets.

Although Jean felt under the weather and began to drink more than she should, during filming she was prompt and cooperative and worked to the best of her ability, which she knew was little. Even at a time of low costs a day's shooting involved a budget of between $7,000 and $9,000, and if three minutes of usable film was shot in a full workday of eight hours, the work accomplished was a success.

In a six-day week, although Saturday was a short day, if

fifteen minutes of film could be canned, a nine reel film could be completed in six weeks at an average A cost of $350,000 for the filming; other costs might bring the full total to a half or at most three quarters of a million, but such films, which would cost under a million dollars for prints, advertising and distribution, would gross several millions and more. It was a profitable and most enjoyable business; and what made it even better was that Jean Harlow and Clark Gable were stars but only receiving the salaries of good feature players.

David Selznick, married to Louis Mayer's daughter but determined to prove that nepotism had nothing to do with his success, finished *Dinner at Eight* on schedule. A film that starred Marie Dressler, John and Lionel Barrymore, Wallace Beery, Lee Tracy, Billie Burke, Edmund Lowe, Jean Hersholt, Madge Evans and Jean Harlow could not fail. Directed with flair by Cukor from a script co-authored by Frances Marion and Herman J. Mankiewicz, with additional dialogue by Donald Ogden Stewart, the film was a sound adaptation of the play by George S. Kaufman and Edna Ferber. If the film was not as dramatic as *Grand Hotel,* it was still a brilliant showcase for the studio's top stars, and it proved that Jean—who had been determined to prove to Wallace Beery that she was an actress— could, with proper stimulus and direction, hold up her pages of the script.

The picture opened at the Astor Theater in New York on August 23, 1933, and a week later *Variety's* Rush could write that this flick was "By long odds the best thing Miss Harlow has done to date." The role was a change of pace; Jean had been responsible for lines that demanded intelligent delivery and coordination. The part had given her the opportunity to concentrate on the role she played, giving her some relief from brooding about family and financial problems.

Although she did not wish to discuss finances there were two problems that Arthur had to solve for her: a $1,009.50 claim by Jetta Goudal and Paul Grieve for furnishings Bern had ordered for the Easton Drive home and a small claim of $330.10 which MGM had billed her for floral wreaths the studio had ordered for Bern's funeral, to make that event more impressive. The first was settled, but the second Jean rejected in a tornado of oaths that Landau did not criticize. The bill was withdrawn by the studio, but not before some unfriendly reporter had got wind of the demand and had managed to insert a straight notice of it in at least one edition of one local paper published on July 26, 1933.

After these small alarums Jean demanded peace and insisted that Arthur take at least five hundred dollars a week from her check over and above his weekly commission, which made it, even in a year when the dollar had real value, a triumph of good housekeeping to maintain the house on Beverly Glen, an establishment that required two full-time gardeners, a chauffeur, a full-time cook and kitchen day maid, three full-time maids, a laundress two days a week, and Blanche Williams, who was instructed by Jean to be courteous to her parents but always to be too busy doing something for Jean to do anything for them. To make Mama feel she was not neglected, Jean bought her an ermine lap robe which Mama loved so that she used it to drape the elaborate French corner in her master bedroom. Propped up by a bed chair upholstered in satin, the robe over her lap, Mama made it a point of honor to devote at least an hour a day to the writing of letters of instruction to Landau and MGM executives. Occasionally she even mailed them, but they were never answered.

At that time it was not studio policy to pamper its stars by permitting them long periods of inactivity between pictures. Before *Dinner at Eight* was completed Jean was notified that she would play the lead in *Bombshell,* to start within a week after her work with Cukor. The new picture would be like old home week: the *Bombshell* script had been co-authored by John Mahin, Hal Rosson would be one of the two cameramen and Victor Fleming would direct this story of a sexy movie star

—Jean's role—and her wacky life in Hollywood. The story also gave her, for a real-life touch, a parasitic and stupid family. Lee Tracy was assigned the male lead role, a press agent who loved and plagued Jean with his stunts. Franchot Tone, unhappy with the studio for wasting him in minor parts, would play another romantic lead. The part was one Tone hated; he thought his dialogue was silly, especially when he had to say to Jean, "Your hair is like a field of silver daisies. I'd like to run barefoot through your hair."

Shooting continued on schedule. Jean enjoyed making a picture about a medium she knew, and the cast around her were delighted to interpret roles they also knew all too well. And her good humor and truly cooperative attitude lessened the problems of photographing her. At all times the camera had to be controlled, aperture and film grain checked and lighting sharply defined and focused, for the lens had a tendency to soften Jean's good jaw line and to make her cheeks appear pudgy. Increasingly, Hal Rosson had the responsibility of key-lighting the star, and daily rushes proved that when he made a little fuss with the camera before he shot a scene, Jean gave a better performance.

In August the company moved to Tucson for the resort scenes of the film, and the cast was in a holiday mood; working on location was always an adventure. Tucson was still hot at the end of August, and this slowed production because so much time had to be given to keeping the stars fresh and comfortable for their outdoor scenes. Most of the shooting was done in the early morning or late afternoon, where natural light could still be used without the addition of lamps or reflectors that were uncomfortably hot. No matter the temperature, which was often above the mid-nineties, the stars looked cool and airy, and Rosson worked carefully to make Harlow crisp and lovely in his shots.

Most evenings the cast enjoyed the clear nights and cool

horseback rides across the desert or dips in the pool under the stars. As they relaxed in wicker chairs on their hotel patio with cold drinks in their hands, the man whose company Jean began to seek most often was Harold Rosson. With him, listening quietly, nodding attentively as she told him—in expletives —what she thought of scenes performed and scenes to come, she felt increasingly secure, even began to feel that she could think again of some permanent arrangement, though it was still too difficult, too damn frightening, actually to think of marriage.

But as she sat and talked with Rosson, squeezing his hand for emphasis, seeing him nod or smile appreciatively, sensing that he treated her as an average woman, not as a movie star with a dark scandal in her recent past, she began to look forward to the good-natured kidding of the members of the cast and crew, who loudly wished *they* were in Hal Rosson's shoes.

On the last day of August Jean's paternal grandfather, Abraham Carpentier, died in Wichita at the age of 91. She had only the vaguest memories of the man, but she sent a long telegram of love, affection and condolence to her grandmother. Then she telephoned her father at his Kansas City office, spoke to him for some minutes and asked him to come west and visit, assuring him that he would not have to see Mama if such a meeting would upset him. The quiet dentist thanked his daughter, hoped she was well and happy and told her to write if she ever needed advice, comfort or even—he laughed to prove he was sincere—money.

The Labor Day weekend continued to be a difficult time for Jean. On the anniversary of Bern's suicide she drank steadily most of the day, felt sorry for herself with tears and curses, and avidly gulped the sleeping draught that bound her to the bed through Tuesday morning. When she got up she had such a headache that Fleming, quite sympathetic, made no protest at having to shoot around his blonde star.

251

Jean awoke Tuesday night in time for dinner, which consisted of a cup of bouillon between two cups of iced black coffee, and spent the rest of the evening lying on her back, speaking in a monotone to Arthur and Beatrice. She had a confession to make. She was in love with Harold Rosson, but she wondered if he could love someone with her past. The agent and his wife assured her that, although Paul's suicide was discussed, people increasingly sympathized with Jean. She was young, a star with a brilliant future, and it was now time to bury her memories of Paul and stop thinking of the past. She had been in mourning for a year; more was not required of her. If she decided to marry, everyone would wish her well.

"Has he talked about getting married?" Arthur asked her.

Jean thought for a moment. "I wish I were sure."

"Why aren't you sure?"

"Because he's so nice."

"Meaning what?"

"I don't know," Jean said after a moment. "How can I give him Mama and Marino as in-laws?"

"They wouldn't bother him, I'm sure," Arthur said.

"They bothered Paul."

"They can be talked to."

Jean crossed both wrists over her eyes. "Talked to, yes. But do they listen? You want to know why I'm doing so good in this picture? Because I'm really, in a way, playing myself. Matter of fact, I gave Ralph Morgan some tips on how to play my father. He thought they were great, but all I did was tell him how Marino acts."

Arthur sighed, waited for Jean to speak again, and only nodded at her silence. "Don't worry about things," he said at last, lamely. "You just rest and we'll be looking in on you. If you need us, just call our room. And Rosson's a fine man." For a moment Arthur wondered why Jean was attracted to men so much older than she, but psychologically the answer was quite plain.

"We'll see you later," he said. "Now stop mourning and think of living."

"I'm not mourning," Jean said sharply. "Maybe it's a sin, but I hate him more than ever. He should've died before I met him."

The airport at Yuma was an indefinite outline in a stretch of desert cleared of mesquite and sage. At one end of the field was a small tin-roofed hangar, a small maintenance building and a smaller administration shack. The landing strips were situated far enough from the hills to make take-offs safe and easy. But there was no tower or guidance system to bring planes in at night, and no pilot would have attempted a landing at Yuma after dark unless the emergency was major.

It was almost three in the morning on Monday, September 18, when Joe Redondo, manager of the Yuma airport, heard the healthy drone of a small single-engine plane at about a thousand feet and realized that the plane was flying in a large circle as if the pilot were attempting to locate the field. Stepping quickly into his work pants and slippers, Redondo grabbed two flashlights and hurried outside. He ran toward a strip, waved the flashlights in slow arcs and wondered if the pilot would know that he was standing at the head of the strip and would come in over his head. The engine sounded strong, there was no sputter or miss that he could hear, and he wondered why a plane would choose to attempt so hazardous a landing in the dark. There was no time for further reflection, because Redondo heard the plane just overhead. He ducked instinctively as the dark mass of the plane, its engine exhausts glowing red, dipped low toward the field. There was only time for the briefest prayer before he heard the wheels touch the strip, heard the scrape of the tailskid and knew, without really being able to see, that the plane had come in for an expert landing. Waving his flashlights as guidance beams, he signaled the small plane toward the tin-roofed hangar.

Whatever questions, instructions or complaints Redondo was about to utter were caught in his throat when one of his flashlights revealed the face, the famous crown of hair and the fabulous body of Jean Harlow. The pilot, Allen Russell—well known as Hollywood's "air-cupid"—helped her from the rear cockpit, where she had sat with Harold Rosson. The actress greeted Redondo breezily, twinkled that she was glad to be in Yuma and hoped she might be able to see it sometime, then introduced the still startled manager of the airport to Rosson. She adjusted the silver fox fur-piece around her throat, remarked that it was cold and asked if coffee was handy; champagne for everyone would come later. They had taken the precaution of bringing several bottles in the plane, and they would all drink to Hal's happiness and hers. Russell said that Miss Harlow and Mr. Rosson were eager to get married before full sun-up. Matter of fact, this was an elopement, and a successful one so far. But the knot had to be tied before Russell could return the deliriously happy couple to Los Angeles, where they would face the newspapers and well-wishers.

Other notable couples had flown to Yuma for hasty weddings, but Joe Redondo could recall no bride who had ever been so gay and radiant at so unnatural an hour or had made so dramatic a landing. The field was left in the care of a mechanic routed from his tent behind the hangar, and in Redondo's small touring car they all drove merrily into Yuma and the office of Donald Wisener, the county clerk. Awakened from a sound sleep by a phone call from the field, Wisener had boomed his cooperation and assured everyone his office door would be open, the welcome mat out.

At four-thirty in the morning, as dawn began to dilute the night, as the desert and the hills assumed pattern and configuration, the brief nuptial ceremony was performed by a yawning Justice of the Peace, E. A. Freeman, with Redondo and Russell as the proud witnesses. Justice and witnesses claimed the privilege of kissing the bride before the wedding party drove to a small cafe hastily opened for the occasion where everyone shared a Western breakfast. Later all hands would celebrate with the champagne left as a gift of the bridal couple and toast them a long life and a happy marriage. Redondo waved as the plane, Cupid's silver arrow of love, streaked into the sky and banked toward sunny California.

Minutes after seven Russell began his landing pattern over the United Airport in Burbank and dipped his wings toward the field. The word had already spread, and the crowds were out. Mama shed more than the required number of tears, Marino pumped Rosson's arm in hearty congratulation, and a platoon of photographers asked Jean to push the little shrimp —meaning Landau—out of the way so they could get a picture of blushing bride and groom.

"I wish I could blush," Harlow called to the photographers, "but I'm too happy. How do I look?"

"Radiant," replied a reporter with a flair for description.

"You said it," Jean replied as she clutched Hal's arm. "How long've we been going together? When did we plan this?" She repeated the last two questions thrown at her, looked at her husband for permission to speak, and smiled because he had nodded. "We've been friends for nearly two years," she continued in a bubbly voice noted and reported by the press. "Several months ago our friendship became love. We decided last night to elope to Yuma by plane and get married because we are both so busy right now with our film work. I—we just can't imagine how all of you found out. After all, it *was* an elopement!" She looked about to see if she could discover the culprit who had betrayed their secret, shrugged and kissed Rosson again, which pleased the photographers.

The Los Angeles *Herald* reported later that day that it had telephoned Justice Freeman, who had reported that Miss

Harlow's name on the license appeared as Jean Carpentier Bern, age 22, and that Harold Rosson was sixteen years older than his bride. The story continued:

> "Miss Harlow had little to say," declared Judge Freeman. "They seemed to be in a hurry, but neither Miss Harlow nor Rosson was nervous.
>
> "I was particularly impressed with Miss Harlow's graciousness. She was certainly very nice and looked awfully pretty.
>
> "She wore a dark blue traveling suit, but was hatless. I think she also wore a fur, but I was too excited to notice much.
>
> "While we went through the details of filling out the proper papers before the marriage there was a lot of 'small talk,' but I didn't hear what was said.
>
> "The bride and bridegroom seemed to be very happy and were smiling when I finished marrying them.
>
> "They didn't announce their future plans to me."

At the airport, the reporters saw that Rosson was annoyed that the story had leaked, so they turned to Russell, obligingly posing for photographers with one hand on a propeller blade.

"The trip up and back took six and a half hours," Russell told the reporters. "It was smooth flying all the way."

"How did they act on the way back? Did they bill and coo?" Russell was asked.

"Well, naturally." Russell went on to relate that he had been aroused shortly before midnight and told to hurry to his plane for the elopement; it was just about midnight when the plane with the pilot and two lovers took off and sped south.

Jean terminated the airport interview when she heard

Relman Morin, the cinematters editor for the *Record,* observe that the new groom, who sported a small mustache, resembled Paul Bern and was almost the same size and age as the recently deceased husband of the blonde sex bomb.

The next day, when Jean read Morin's account of her wedding, her fury went beyond the bottle-throwing phase. He had not resisted adding inches to his article with an enthusiastically detailed account of her marriage to Paul Bern, the suicide of that unhappy man, a restatement of his suicide note and some veiled sentences to remind the reader that there were still many details of sexology and suicide which had never been explained.

Louis Mayer, the real lion of MGM, roared when he read the morning papers, and demanded to know why he had not been informed of the elopement so he could show up at the airport to welcome back Rosson, whom he liked, and Harlow, whom he was beginning to despise with a passion that gave him the healthiest morning appetite he had enjoyed in years. The damage was done, he had been ignored. The star and the people around her would have to be instructed in the facts of life—that they were not bigger than the studio—and he would mete out judgments and punishments at the proper, most dramatic time. Meanwhile, as Mayer showered, he shouted commands to be delivered to Strickling's office. When he left his shower, swathed in a thick, monogrammed robe, and paused for his valet to dry his feet and fit them with polished bath slippers, a Cheshire smile turned up the corners of Mayer's mouth. Graciously, he patted his valet's head, then ordered that Strickling be telephoned again and that Landau too be commanded to appear before the royal presence.

Landau was directed to sit on a low hassock, where he looked like a man in mourning, but Strickling was permitted to rest on a chair of normal height.

"It's about time we had a straight-from-the-shoulder talk."

Mayer directed each clipped word at Arthur. "What's the matter with that stupid *shiksa* of yours? Didn't I personally give her an order not to get married again without first getting my permission? There aren't enough Christians in the world that she has to go around marrying Jewish boys? Paul wasn't a real man, but he never got into trouble until he married your *shiksa*."

"Dorothy Milette was Christian," Arthur said.

Mayer brandished a clenched fist. "It was a common law thing, and I don't recognize living together as being the same as being married. Why do you upset me so bright and early in the morning, Arthur?"

Head bowed, Arthur touched his forehead. "I'm sorry."

"I'm all for religion." Mayer addressed himself to Strickling while he permitted Arthur to stew in the vinegar of penance. "Some of my best friends are Christians. And I know a couple of fine, refined niggers I'd have a cup of coffee with and I wouldn't be offended if they picked up the check. But I don't believe in mixing things up. Jews should get married to Jews. Russian Jews to Russian Jews. German Jews to German Jews. And Christians should marry Christians."

"Mr. Mayer, please," Arthur raised his head. "I'd like to say—"

"Speak when you're spoken to," Mayer cut him off. "What was I saying?" he asked Strickling. "Oh yes, Christians should marry Christians. Chinese people should marry their kind. That's the way that's best for everybody. And another thing, Howard, in Jewish homes we seldom have divorces. We don't have drunks and run-arounds and we don't have divorces," he stated proudly. "And I don't like to see a nice Jewish boy's heart broken by a divorce."

"Rosson's not Jewish," Arthur said. Mayer gasped, but Arthur continued to nod vigorously. "He was born in England and baptized in an English church." He raised his right hand. "It's true."

Mayer turned to Strickling. "Is he telling the truth?"

"He is," Strickling said.

"So why doesn't someone tell me?" Mayer asked his ceiling. He paced back and forth, contemplating this new development. "Anyway, I don't know if I like Jean being married," he said. "When a good boff is married it takes her out of circulation unless she's a tramp, and we have no room in the industry for genuine tramps. So it ruins them, like people finding out that Frank Bushman was married killed him at the box office." He paused again. "One thing for sure," he added. "It'll be a long time, maybe never, before anyone'll ever say that Mr. Mayer approves of mixed marriages. They are against God."

"Aren't you glad to find out that Jean didn't commit a sin?" Arthur asked.

Mayer stepped behind a screen and returned moments later in a fresh BVD. "Still, I want you to fix the little bitch," he ordered Strickling, rubbing his hands together as if to warm them for the haft of an ax. "From me, beautiful flowers and pronouncements and the rest of that crap. The full treatment."

"I understand," Strickling said.

"No you don't," Mayer said. He paused to approve a shirt, collar, tie and cufflinks. "I want the publicity so sweet and kind and stupid that it'll make her sick. I want stuff written that'll make people laugh at her without exactly knowing why."

Strickling protested, Arthur clasped his hands in supplication, but neither man could budge Mayer from his decision, although the publicity chief pointed out that Harold Rosson, a fine man who was innocent of any wrong-doing, might suffer if every reporter were encouraged to write like a sob-sister. Everyone at the studio liked Rosson, and the new groom deserved better at the hands of the studio he had worked for long and well.

"Let me read you what's bad enough right now without encouragement," Strickling said, picking up a copy of the *Herald.* He took a deep breath. " 'Rosson photographed the star in all her scenes in *Red Dust*. And the fingers that handled the whirring camera so delicately and carefully trembled with love. Before him stood the beauteous girl that Rosson desired as Rosson sighted over the camera at the dazzling blonde's love scenes with another man.'" Strickling dropped the paper. "It's sickening."

"Agreed," Mayer said. "And to tell the truth that article —real garbage—gave me the idea."

Chapter Eighteen

It was dangerous to dilute Mayer's orders, but Strickling made it a point to give every reporter a biography of Rosson that could only reflect credit upon Harlow's groom. Rosson enjoyed a reputation as one of the best cameramen in the industry; for years until he moved to MGM, Gloria Swanson would not permit herself to be filmed except by Harold Rosson, whose understanding of angle, focus, sharpness and lighting imparted a luminous glow to her face. *Manhandled, Zaza* and *A Society Scandal* were three of the pictures whose photography delighted Miss Swanson; now, for Jean Harlow, he had also solved the problems of key-light and angle. Prints of his work were studied and praised by other directors and cameramen. Furthermore, Harold could really claim to be a member of a respected and honored film family. One of his brothers, Arthur Rosson, had directed Douglas Fairbanks when that athletic actor had made western films; Richard Rosson was a director for MGM and had recently returned from the Arctic where he had filmed *Eskimo* for the studio; a sister, Gladys Rosson, had for many years been secretary to Cecil B. DeMille.

No matter how Strickling tried, the reporters could not help but elaborate on the studio handouts, all of which crossed Mayer's desk. The *Examiner* of September 19 reprinted a handout without any correction; only paragraphs were rearranged.

"He is MY man," said Jean, simply.

"For years," said Rosson, "I have admired

her. For months, I have loved her. And now she is mine."

"We are happy," they chorused. "We will be happy always."

Reading it, Arthur Landau groaned. A little lower down in the article was sweet Jean's reported account of the romance, all of which had been written and rewritten the night before until Mayer agreed that the final version, which he approved and ordered distributed internationally, gave him "a good unhealthy throwing-up feeling."

Her love for Rosson is the one great emotion of her life, Miss Harlow declared as she strolled with him yesterday in the gardens of the home she built following Bern's death and which was completed six months ago.

"I believe," she said, "that I have reached the point where I know what I want. And I want Hal. He is, I think, the finest, kindest, most sincere and most honorable man I have ever known. . . .

"We were on location in the desert near Tucson last week, completing 'Bombshell.' One night, after we had finished shooting, Hal and I went for a walk.

"We stopped beneath a giant saguaro, silvered in the pale desert moonlight. Hal looked at me. I looked at him. We knew, then, that we would be married."

. . . behind the "No. 1 Camera" was Hal Rosson. He it was who obliterated the shadows of grief that played upon Miss Harlow's face as she whirled through the boisterous, rollicking part she played in "Red Dust." His was the

kindly, quiet voice that guided her through difficult scenes. His was the hand that steadied her
when she seemingly was about to collapse. . . .

"I am sure," Jean predicted, "that the difference in our years will not matter. I have
always known people older than myself. Besides,
Hal and I like the same things—another reason
for our love. We play together like a couple of
kids.

"He is just old enough to enable him to be
my mentor. I respect him, so I'll always heed his
advice."

"Oh," she added, fervently, "I know that
ours is one Hollywood marriage that will last."

. . . . "Now," said Miss Harlow, "it is up to
me to repay Hal's kindness. I can and will do so.
I consider him the ideal husband, lover, golf partner and cameraman. I will try to be the ideal
wife."

"She is, already," murmured Rosson.

Mayer loved the articles, though he wondered aloud if
Rosson was guilty of the statement, attributed to him in the
Record of September 18, that his platinum bride was "the
only beautiful star at Metro-Goldwyn-Mayer studio." This
sweeping judgment had raised eyebrows and hackles, and
Mayer's office had been swamped with calls from irate actresses
threatening broken contracts and suits. However, pleased with
what he read, Mayer ordered the publicity department to write
more such releases, but to see what it could do about sup-
pressing further mention of the Bern scandal which was receiving a disproportionate number of column inches. The
affair was dead, and it was an evil, sinful thing to exhume a
corpse; but what could one expect from newspaper people who
were without morals?

"You want proof?" he asked Arthur Landau. "They print the garbage we give them and ask for more. Newspaper people are worse than vultures feeding on the dead. They've got no right to print those stories about her and Bern!" he shouted. "And I'm warning you, Arthur, there'd better not be another scandal by your bum. One breath, Arthur—just one breath, and she's through in pictures! I hope you understand?"

"They're in love," Arthur said.

"Sure," Mayer replied, but his voice gave no hint how this reply could be interpreted.

In the big house on Beverly Glen—which Relman Morin compared to "an ice cream confection, perched atop a hill"— the broken glassware had been swept into the trashcans, the chair Jean had broken as she had attempted to pound it through the floor had been placed in the garage, and Jean sulked while her husband sat quietly, patient and reserved, waiting for his wife to make up her mind.

Although the newspaper accounts portrayed Marino as one of his closest, most intimate friends, a man with whom he had played golf for years, Harold did not feel put out. He understood the uses and abuses of publicity. But they were newlyweds, Harold pointed out, and he felt it would be better if they ran their own household. Mama Jean immediately took this to be a polite request that they move out of the house, Marino's eyes smoldered as he stroked his mustache, and Jean was about to observe, with great delight, that she agreed with Hal—it would be best for Mama and Marino to bill and coo elsewhere. But Harold quietly told his bride that he wanted *them* to move out of the big house, not her parents.

For months Jean had threatened to leave Beverly Glen, to leave Mama and Marino with the big white barn and all its bills and demands, but without fully realizing it she had become increasingly fond of the house. Now it rankled that she, a star and married to a real man she respected, would have to

264

leave the house to a pair of dogs who had taken over the manger. They had no rights to the house, and it was time that Marino went to work and her mother got off a rear that was becoming hefty. Jean did her best to persuade her husband that they should stay in the house; if there was anything in the house that displeased Hal—furniture, wallpaper, carpeting, any-thing—why it could be changed. Hal shook his head and told Jean it was a beautiful house, handsomely appointed—but they would take the apartment.

"You may wear slacks," he said, smiling, "but who's going to wear the pants in our family?"

"You," she replied without hesitation. "But you'll let me come along when you go apartment hunting?"

"Of course," he replied.

She was sad, and she sulked, but her pain at leaving the house was lessened because Mama and Marino wanted them to stay, and anything they wanted seemed immediately less desirable. Mama said she loved them both, Marino swore he loved them both, but Jean knew their love, if sincere, was fired by the fear that without her they could not maintain their style of living and the house that inspired it.

On the morning of September 20 the newlyweds went apartment hunting, and both were delighted to find that the morning's papers had given them little coverage—just enough to report that Hal Rosson was to be assigned as cameraman to *Viva Villa,* to be shot in Mexico, and that Jean would accom-pany him there. Actually, although Mayer agreed that at most *Bombshell* required no more than a half-day or so of insert shooting and that Jean had been the least temperamental of all the stars in the film, he refused to say definitely that she could go to Mexico. News of her marriage had stimulated exchange orders for her old films, and the studio had concluded that it would be good business to cast their platinum star in another film, which would rule out a trip to Mexico. But if Mayer had not made up his mind, there was reason for optimism, so Hal drove cheerfully through Beverly Hills toward the Sunset Strip where there were many vacancies in the newest apartment buildings, many of them completed just at the time of the crash.

The Chateau Marmont stood within bottle-throwing distance of Nazimova's Garden of Allah, and in less than an hour Jean and her husband had chosen a third floor apartment that overlooked the southern sweep of the city. From the living room window they could see the swimming pool in the Garden of Allah, and Hal told Jean they could have dinner in the Garden's dining room and the hotel would be delighted to extend pool privileges to Jean. The furnished one-bedroom apartment had the bathroom at the far end of the hall, which would make getting there first a sporting event, and the living room was of generous size with a cozy fireplace. There was a small dining room, large enough to invite no more than two people to sit-down dinner, and a kitchen which was so small Jean would have to keep her lovely figure if she wanted to turn around easily. The Marmont also provided maid service at nominal cost, the address was good, and rent—only two hundred and fifty dollars a month—was a pittance.

Jean agreed to take the apartment and next morning was convinced that life would be good if she always followed the advice of her husband. Her tractability had been noted in heaven, and Louis Mayer—blessed archangel—was moved to tell them that he was going to give them the nicest wedding gift of all: Rosson would not have to go to Mexico to photograph *Villa,* and bride and groom could plan to leave the studio in a fortnight for a Honolulu honeymoon. Jean was so delighted she just had to embrace the studio president and kiss him on both cheeks.

The honeymoon of Jean and Harold Rosson had not even begun before the idyll with Louis Mayer came to an end. For on Sunday, September 24, three days past the first of autumn, when Jean had been delighted at Mayer's present of time for a honeymoon in Hawaii, Alma Whitaker wrote about her for the Los Angeles *Times*. The article said, in part:

It's all very well, but when a glamorous Jean Harlow, arch-siren, who pretty well has her pick of the sex, chooses a Hal Rosson "for better or worse, till death do them part" we want to know how he did it.

"He's no Apollo; his best friends wouldn't call him a lady killer, but he obviously reeks of lure, so tell us, lovely Jean, what is it that won you?" I craved.

Jean, in cute brown slacks, curled up in a big chair, took two puffs at a cigarette while she pondered.

"The physical means nothing to me," she said. "If you love a person he or she automatically becomes beautiful. Yes, I know exactly what won my heart. It is Hal's exquisite quality of friendship, his vast capacity for loyalty. Without that nothing else counts. Friends, you see, have been very important in my life. Then there is his divine sense of humor. However do people get through life without humor?"

"So this one is forever?"

"Well," said Jean, smiling a little reproachfully, "when you care for a man enough to marry him you always hope it is forever, don't you?". . . .

"I could never do anything but respect him highly," said Jean earnestly, so I was to get the reproachful smile again when I flippantly remarked that "respect is an awful thing for a husband to live up to."

"Not for Hal," she dimpled. "It is I who am
likely to have the hard time living up to him."

The next morning Jean yowled, raged, swore she would
sue the *Times*, Alma Whitaker, the typesetter and anyone who
dared mention the awful column, and insisted that the quotation attributed to her—"It is I who am likely to have the hard
time living up to him"—was filthy gutter innuendo. She was
going to telephone everyone she knew and insist they prove
their friendship by canceling their subscriptions to the paper.
And she was going to take her attorneys off the stupid suit for
Bern's paper estate and put them to work on something sensible: suing the Los Angeles *Times*.

"Then you'll really be batting your head against a wall,"
Arthur advised her. "I say forget the whole thing."

"But I never met the woman!" Jean swore and turned
toward her mother to keep her quiet; Mama had insisted on
going with Jean to Arthur's office. "I never met her and never
spoke to her. Not even on the phone! My fingers got actually
sticky from reading her slop. I'm ashamed to look at Hal."

"I'm sure he understands," Arthur suggested. "He's been
around a long time and knows how these things are."

"But it makes him look like a fool!" Suddenly she snapped
her fingers. "I've got it, Arthur," she crowed. "Hal and I—
we'll go to Mayer and tell him we want the *Times* reporters
barred from the lot."

Arthur sighed and locked both hands across his middle.
He swung his chair about to complete a full circle, faced Jean
again and shook his head. "No good," he said quietly. "I'm
taking a chance on your being grown up, so I'll tell you. Those
ridiculous stories were written on L. B.'s orders. That's right,"
he continued as Jean's lips tightened. "He was angry that you
got married without his permission."

Jean exploded. "He can go screw himself! Even God
doesn't require you to ask permission for marrying or having

children." She paused as if imprisoned by a binding sheet of pain, rallied and moved to stand with one gloved hand resting atop a low bookcase. "He's not God." She trembled to control her voice. "Who the hell does he think he is?" Frustration compelled her to beat the shelftop. "It's a good thing I don't have to ask him for permission to go to the can because I'd be wetting my pants at least ten times a day!"

"Sit down!" Arthur said sharply.

Arthur waited until Jean joined her mother on the sofa and had blown her nose in a small silk handkerchief which she gave to Mama to throw in a wastebasket.

"It's time to be sensible. Forget this Whitaker woman and what you're going to do to Mayer," Arthur said.

"You can't stop me from hating him," Jean insisted.

"You'll have to get at the end of a very long line," Arthur said. "When're you moving to the Chateau?"

Jean removed a glove and began to knot the fingers. "At the end of the week. By Sunday, I guess. It's mainly clothes. Hal and I'll be sleeping there a couple of nights this week."

"I'm taking care of the kitchen," Mama said. "Marino and I are shopping for china tomorrow." She patted Jean's hand. "We'll pick something nice."

"It can be not-so-nice as long as you pay for it," Jean said.

"Ladies," Arthur said, "let's keep it polite. Listen," he said to Jean, "what *about* this kidney business. Are you all right?"

"I think so," she said.

"Why don't you let me take you back to Sugarman? Or some kidney specialist?"

Mama shook her head. "There's nothing wrong with Jean that Science can't cure."

"Let's not discuss religion," Arthur said. "I think Jean ought to have a real medical checkup. Do you still have pains in the back?"

Jean put aside her purse and placed the heels of both

hands over her kidneys. "Sometimes they both hurt. I can't even exactly remember which one he bruised."

"I think you should see a doctor," Arthur said again.

"And I think Jean should really start taking an interest in Science." Mama looked righteous and prim. "Science has as good a record of cures as medicine and the other healing arts."

"Will you both please shut up?" Jean exploded again. "I come up here to discuss that lousy paper"—she pointed to the *Times*—"and I find myself involved in a discussion of my *kidneys!*" She jumped up and leaned over Arthur's desk. "Like you've told me, Arthur," she said, her voice under fair control, "you can't fight city hall, and I've got a new and good life to lead with Hal. So I'm not going to make a stink any more because Mayer played us a dirty trick. But I'm telling you, Arthur, I'm not doing one Goddamn thing more than I have to on the set. And I want more money. Not for me." She pointed to her mother. "For her and her lousy lover."

For the next three weeks Jean busied herself with the apartment, straightening the closets, assembling a library of cookbooks and keeping Mama at home. She and Harold continued to make plans for their Hawaiian vacation: they pored over hotel brochures, planned itineraries of the islands, even debated the wisdom of going on to Tahiti, where Hal might photograph the island and its people in color. It was romantic dreaming, but it relieved the tedium of the last shots for *Bombshell*. Jean also utilized the time to build her reputation among the little people of the lot by being one of the boys while she continued to be hailed, without challenge or rival, as the ranking goddess of sex. On the job, she made white her trademark; and in slacks, white tennis shoes and sheer blouses— now worn with a brassiere because she was married—Jean captivated the people she worked with whose salary was less than a hundred dollars a week and proved again that, although she earned fifteen times as much and felt she was worth more, she could still practice democracy—and what was more amazing, believe in it. Nevertheless, she pressed Landau at least three times a day to get a radical rewriting of her seven-year contract with the studio. Right now she wanted a minimum of three thousand dollars a week, with salary increases every six months until, at the end of the seventh year, she would be paid ten thousand dollars a week for forty weeks a year. In the remaining twelve weeks she wanted the right to negotiate for an outside picture.

Her agent told her the initial demand was so preposterous that it offered no room for negotiations. He advised her to complete her contractual year, during which he could use the box office success of her films to prove how miserly fifteen hundred dollars a week really was. Meanwhile, as Arthur pointed out, her economies were rapidly reducing her debts, and in another year she would be solvent. But this happy state could only be realized if she continued to work, received a check every week and did not antagonize the studio to the point of ordering her suspension, which was always the severest form of punishment since it cut off the essential flow of money. Now was not the time to be contentious, Arthur advised Jean. He told her he was surprised that she was giving any ear to Marino, who reported to her several times a week that he was in touch with private investors who would back Jean in her own company if she could free herself of the MGM contract.

In his daily discussions with Jean, Arthur found an ally in Hal Rosson, who also advised his wife to play by the rules and to concern herself only with finding good parts and interpreting them so that critics would respect her as an actress. And, by the way, she should also do something about her voice. Jean listened, grumbled and continued to report to Arthur the extravagant propositions that Marino said he could put together. But she also listened to and heeded the advice of her agent and husband and made no commitment that would antagonize Mayer. After several tries, Landau was granted an appointment with Mayer and told the lord of MGM that he could guarantee Jean's loyalty to the studio, but that Marino was badgering her daily with offers of her own company. Mayer barred Marino from the lot, ordered that no explanation be given him, and threatened Mrs. Bello with similar exile if she dared call his office again. Loyalty to Marino kept Mama Jean away from Culver City, and Mayer was delighted, he said, to be rid of the parents.

To prove his displeasure, Marino made only a token appearance at the ceremonies held in the courtyard of Grauman's Chinese Theater on September 29, 1933, when Jean's hands and high-heeled shoe prints were immortalized in concrete. Arthur and Beatrice Landau left for New York immediately after the ceremony to attend to business in the East and had to miss the première of *Bombshell* held the next night at the Chinese Theater. Marino refused to attend the première, so Jean and Hal Rosson reluctantly permitted Mama to accompany them. Some days later Arthur received a letter from Mama describing the gala night.

Popa darling, this will please you.

Bombshell was a SENSATION, a WOW, a SUCCESS and what an evening.

The wires poured in here and Hunt Stromberg sent the Baby a huge box of roses with this note "To my favorite actess, with my appreciation for a perfect performance. Love Hunt." Which made the Baby cry with gratitude. A huge box of cut orchids from Jules Furthman (from his own greenhouses) with an exqyisite note of appreciation for the most perfect performance he had ever seen and that NO one could have done what Harlow did, and how proud he was to have his name on the sheet with hers. Wasent that lovely?

We are so grateful and happy for the Baby.

L.B. sat in front of us and when he and Mannix came in the[y] did not EVEN speak to the Baby ONLY nodded. When it was over and the audience was WILD L.B. stopped at the Babys side and started to explode he caught himself and said "God [Lee] Tracy has great lines." Now Pops if I had not heard it I could NOT have believed that. Not even "Jean your work was nice." Not one word except JUST what I have told you. CAN you imagine such a fool as to think he could intimidate three people like us with such childish tactics. Really those people must think we are of very limited intelligence and of very lowly birth to accept such childish tactics. BUT Pops if I had anything to do with the situation I would make that gentleman pay in blood for the insult.

Yesterday the Baby finished the concrete at the CHINESE and we are so proud to have her name among the biggest of the industry.

I have only met Miss Dressler once but Pops will you please tell her I am a really devoted fan of Dressler the magnificent woman as well as Dressler the great actress? I adore her.

Tell Mrs. Landau when she returns I will have to hear all about the pretty new styles.

Love to you both.

Mother

Two weeks passed, and Marino sulked amidst his treasure maps and spoke gloomily of suicide. Early Saturday afternoon, October 15, Mama Jean called her daughter to insist that Jean, Hal and Arthur, still in New York, do something immediately to lift Mayer's humiliating order. Using her tears for fullest effect, Mama was broken-hearted that her daughter had become so callous; Jean, anxious to leave for the Southern California-St. Mary's football game at the Coliseum, promised to drive directly from the stadium to Beverly Glen, where Hal and she would stay for an early dinner before they returned to their apartment to dress formally for a night on the town. At dinner they would discuss the ban. Jean was sorry, but Hal had only two tickets and she wanted to see the game with only one rooting companion, not three.

Southern California won, and in rare good spirits and slightly hoarse because of the cheers she had led, Jean and Hal drove to Beverly Glen, where she spoke throughout the entire dinner about nothing but the Hawaiian trip. Gulping a cup of coffee, kissing her mother hastily and waving at Marino, promising that she would speak to Mayer, Jean dragged Hal from the house and thanked him for being so patient.

This evening at the Beverly Wilshire was to celebrate four weeks of marriage, and, for Jean, the longest period of happiness in that condition. But at about eleven Jean complained of weariness, slight nausea and a hot pain in her stomach, so Hal paid the check and drove his wife to their apartment, where he suggested that they call a doctor. Instead Jean answered the ringing telephone. It was her mother, and Jean told her that she felt ill. Shortly after midnight Mama telephoned Arthur that he was to fly home immediately to make Jean listen to reason; Jean was ill, in pain, and Arthur had to order The Baby to harken to her mother.

"Meaning what?" Arthur asked.

"I want to call a Reader!" Mama screamed over the phone. "We'll join in prayers and by morning Jean will be as gay as a lark."

"She could also be a dead duck," Arthur said before he hung up.

For only a moment did Arthur know cowardice, then he telephoned Mayer, explained that Jean was ill and begged the busy man to take charge because her parents were incompetent. When Mayer telephoned the Marmont and spoke to Rosson, Jean was unconscious with pain. Mayer ordered a doctor brought in immediately.

Dr. Sidney R. Burnap arrived, diagnosed the illness as acute appendicitis and advised an emergency operation at the Good Samaritan Hospital.

Marino and Rosson agreed with the doctor, but when Mama Jean held out for Christian Science, Dr. Burnap called Mayer, who asked that Mama be put on the phone.

"I want you out of that girl's life," he ordered Mrs. Bello. "She's under contract to me. She's my star, and if you don't want to take care of your daughter I insist on taking care of my investment. So I'm ordering you to go home."

"You're ordering me to violate my religious beliefs," Mama wept.

"You're crazier than anyone I've ever talked to," Mayer replied. "Now put the doctor back on the phone."

Jean was operated on within the hour and came through surgery without complication.

Chapter Nineteen

1933 OCT 17 AM4 24

ARTHUR LANDAU
    HOTEL DELMONICO NYK
DEAR ARTHUR WE ALL THANK YOU
FOR YOUR WIRE BABY PROGRESSING
RAPIDLY EXPECTING HER HOME IN
TEN DAYS AS USUAL SHE WAS A BRICK
STOP AS SOON AS SHE OPENED HER EYES
AFTER THE EFFECT OF THE ANES-
THETIC VANISHED SHE STARTED TO
MAKE FUN OF US AND WISE CRACK STOP
IF BABY WOULD NOT HAVE FALLEN ILL
YOU WOULD HAVE SEEN US IN NEW
YORK ON THE WAY TO EUROPE SO THIS
WILL HAPPEN AS SOON AS SHE RECUPER-
ATES LOVE FROM ALL OF US
                            MARINO

The ebullient arrogance of the telegram annoyed Arthur almost as much as the visit he had had that morning from the public relations representative of a prominent eastern gangster who was willing to cut Arthur into a little business venture that could net as much as a quarter of a million dollars. All Arthur had to do was guarantee that the little tufts of blonde hair enclosed in little gold mementos had been shaved from Jean's pubic zone just before her operation. As politely as possible Arthur declined the deal, which compelled the portly, perfumed young man to observe that Arthur was a little crumb liable to find himself wearing a cement hat if he ever told anyone the hair in the gold novelties was not genuine. Then, shifting from threats to the sincere interest of a fan, the gangster invited Arthur to lunch because he was just crazy about Harlow. Pleading a prior engagement, making promises he never kept to send an especially autographed photo of Jean plus a genuine lock of her downstairs hair, Arthur saw the fat young man to the door, hurried through his business and returned to Los Angeles.

Jean gained rapidly, convalesced without complications, and ignored her agent's telephoned suggestion that now was the time to have the attending physician evaluate her kidney condition.

Jean laughed at him over the phone. "Come on over, Pops. I wanna show you my scar."

On October 30, two weeks after she had entered the hospital, the *Citizen* carried a two-inch inner-page item that "Jean Harlow Leaves Hospital for Home." Readers were informed that "Miss Harlow, recent bride of Harold Rosson, ace cameraman, is no longer confined to bed, but is permitted to spend some time each day sitting up and walking in an effort to regain her strength. The surgery interrupted honeymoon plans for the pair who had expected to spend the last few weeks in Hawaii."

Every sane reason for Jean to convalesce in her apartment was swept away by a tide of maternal zeal; from a publicity point of view, it was callous to ignore Mama's loud protestations of love and affection for the Pink Bunny. Furthermore, Mama was not convinced and never would be that Science would not have been more efficacious than surgery. Why, if a proper ceremony of prayer had been permitted, her daughter would now be up and about—swimming, golfing and playing tennis. A hospital bed was moved into the mansion, and Mama bought herself a silk nurse's uniform and cap, though she refused to wear nurse's shoes because they were too business-like and prosaic. In high heels Mama tiptoed around Jean's bed and made life difficult for the professionals.

The European trip Marino had mentioned in the telegram was off. The promoters who had pledged to put up the money to send him to London to meet with the Korda brothers, supposedly willing to put up a million pounds if Jean would make a color film for them, had been arrested by two postal inspectors. All very embarrassing, a silly charge of mail fraud, but they swore to Marino that their agreement with the Kordas was an honest reality. Jean had agreed to pay for a cablegram and reply, and it was as she expected: the brothers Korda had no knowledge of the men. They were interested in making a film with Jean, but they would not negotiate with anyone except a representative of MGM, and they were unwilling to pay even fifty thousand pounds for her services. However, they were willing to negotiate the matter further, especially if something could be done about her voice.

Shamed at having proved himself a sucker again, Marino gloomed in his den, began to write his memoirs and ordered his food to be sent in on trays. At the end of his retreat Marino had gained eight pounds. Mama mewed piteously at the closed door for assurances that her bad boy was all right and, as she began to feel active desire, pleaded with the silly to open the door and let Mama Jean in for a long talk. Love in a nurse's uniform was so novel that Mama began to wear the silk dresses to bed instead of nightgowns. Until Mama's divorce almost two years later, Jean borrowed a variety of costumes from the MGM wardrobe for Mama to wear to spice her evenings—one night Mama wore the pantaloons and metal breastplates of an Egyptian belly dancer while Marino, caparisoned as a prince of the sands, strutted around the house in riding breeches, polished boots and burnous, and the phonograph wailed *The Sheik of Araby*. Life was clinically concupiscent and therefore normal for the senior members of the household.

By the end of November the first volleys of battle between Jean and her studio were duly reported by correspondents. Jean refused to appear for wardrobe fittings for her part in *Living in a Big Way*, and she gave notice that she would be nursing her health until her salary was increased. To speed her convalescence, Mayer ordered Jean's salary suspended, because the rich diet of money had made her giddy. Jean accepted the challenge—her husband was still drawing his salary—but paused briefly in her campaign to express sorrow at the passing of her paternal grandmother, Mrs. Diana Carpentier, who had died on November 29 after a decline in health attributed to the death of her husband in August.

The brief newspaper squib was still long enough to report that "Miss Jean Harlow said yesterday, on receipt of word of her grandmother's death, that her motion picture contract was such that she would be unable to go to Kansas for the funeral." The cynically crisp notice, sent nationally over the AP wire, subjected Jean to the first full broadside of unfriendly mail ever addressed to her, much greater and much more violent than any she had received before and after the Bern scandal. The executive offices also received letters from the forces of decency complaining that it was cruel, unfeeling, inhuman and an evidence of Jewish hatred of Christians to have kept Jean from attending the services for her beloved grandmother.

Responsible studio officials—meaning Mayer—decided to ignore the matter of the funeral, and even went so far as to deny with laughter the report published on December 2 that Jean and her husband were parting. The Rossons left for San Francisco for "what the platinum blonde star termed her 'appendix vacation' . . . 'Claudette Colbert set the vogue,' said Miss Harlow apropos appendices. 'Now everyone's doing it. Maureen O'Sullivan is the latest.' "

After reading this vacuity Arthur decided he could no longer risk another barring of the studio gates against him. If the studio even planned to ban him, Harlow would have to find another agent; there were too many Landau clients at MGM to risk their leaving his office for other agents with access to the lot. Losing Harlow meant his acceptance of a loss of some forty thousand dollars in loans, and the severance of a relationship with a girl in desperate need of human warmth, but the wrench would have to be endured. In the long run this might be best for Jean; there had to come a time when she would have to stand or fall on her own decisions, would have to decide just how much family she could carry on her shoulders.

Apparently Jean was not ready to unload Mama and Marino, because she agreed to pay for and attend the New Year's Eve party they planned to give. Jean had accepted the invitation without consulting her husband, who had made other plans. Rather than quarrel with his wife, Rosson canceled his plans, attended the party and spent most of the evening in an upstairs bedroom of the Beverly Glen house, where he dipped into the books available to him. Shortly before midnight he put in an appearance to mingle with the other guests, kiss his wife at one second after midnight, and exchange formal pleasantries with the Bellos.

Marino, in expansive mood, attempted to play the genial father-in-law and invited Harold to come to him with all domestic problems, no matter how trivial. He had recently discovered that shortly after Jean's marriage to Harold they had signed an agreement whereby each partner was to retain individual properties and earnings. This was wrong, bad, Marino insisted; a husband and wife should pool their resources.

"Look at me," Marino twirled a brandy snifter. "I pay more than my share to make this house a home. If it wasn't for what I contribute, Jean and her mother could never afford to live this way."

Rosson escaped without comment to the upstairs bedroom, where he waited for Jean until she was ready to leave for home. The drive at dawn to the Chateau Marmont was chilly.

As if she were determined to muck up matters completely, Jean did not disown her mother and stepfather when Marino gave an item to the newspapers on January 9, 1934, that he would never sanction Jean's return to her studio unless she received immediately a salary of $10,000 a week, a far greater tribute than was paid to Greta Garbo. True, Marino admitted, the studio held a contract which entitled it to five more years of Harlow's services, and legally she could not make a picture elsewhere. However, Marino boasted, he depended upon an avalanche of letters from Jean's loyal fans to make a lamb of the MGM trademark. There *was* some unlettered mail from the unwashed, but the studio just sent out Jean's old pictures to keep the dreams simmering. It now amused Mayer to have Arthur come to his private office so he could twit the agent about his idle client.

"Just the other day I actually unbent enough to put in a call to her," Mayer said genially. "You know, Arthur, I'm quick to anger and just as quick to forget. So I decided to talk to her like she was a little child, which she is, the stupid. So I had a call put to the Marmont and they said she was at Beverly Glen. We telephoned Beverly Glen and were told she was on the way back to her apartment. That's when we gave up."

"What did you want to talk to her about?" Arthur asked.

Mayer admired his manicure and paunch. "What does a father talk about to his children? Important and unimportant things. I just wanted to find out if she had enough to eat and a pot to piss in."

"She's managing," Arthur said.

"Don't tell me she has Harold supporting Beverly Glen?" Mayer asked.

"She'd never ask him to," Arthur said. "Mr. Mayer, if there's anything special you'd like to say to her, I'd see she got your message. There must be some way to work this out."

"Naturally," Mayer rocked gently. "My way. Which is exactly like the contract way. Imagine a girl refusing to work for fifteen hundred dollars a week! Fifteen hundred," he repeated heavily. " And personally, between us, for what? For not having class," he answered. "Which makes her not my kind of woman." Mayer thought for a moment, then pressed the key of his squawk box. "Make a note, please," he ordered, "for a title and variations. My Kind of Woman. His Kind of Woman. Their Kind of Women. Pass them around by appropriate memo for star and story suggestions." He released the switch and thanked Arthur by touching an eyebrow. "It's a good title for your tramp, right? So tell her to come back to her senses."

"She's bothered because you ordered Mama and Marino kept out," Arthur said. "She considers that insulting."

"And the trash that lowdown wop gives to the papers isn't?" Mayer stood, the better to accuse Arthur. "Ten thousand a week. Even if she was worth it I wouldn't pay. And I'll tell you why." He jabbed with a forefinger. "Because that miserable Roosevelt only gets seventy-five thousand a year for sitting in the White House. And before him, when there was a real president in Washington, Mr. Hoover, whom I'm proud to call my friend, he showed that he's a friend of everyone by taking a salary cut of twenty per cent. And I dare you, Arthur, to compare Harlow to Hoover! Or for that matter even to Roosevelt. Go ahead, I dare you."

"I won't compare," Arthur said.

"She should be down on her knees"—Mayer knelt to illustrate remorse and supplication—"from the moment she wakes up, thanking God that it happened to her. Friends she needed after that miserable rat killed himself and friends she had. Deny that. You don't dare." He paused to gaze fondly at a still photo of a puppy being nuzzled by a duck. "No, Arthur," he continued, "when someone doesn't work for me and insists upon behaving like a silly child, I certainly don't want her *paskutzveh* family around. When she decides to come back to work she'll be welcomed by publicity with open arms. Then, when she's behaved for a while, we can talk about other things."

"But if you'd only say they could come back. Let me say that they can come back if she goes to work," Arthur begged.

"I'm not bargaining." Mayer concluded the interview by offering Arthur his choice of a dollar cigar or the photo. Diplomatically, Arthur chose the photo. "My office is like her home." Mayer was half-way sincere. "If she comes back to work she won't be chasing around getting nowhere. Meanwhile, keep your eyes open for another sexy blonde." He stopped Arthur at the door. "Tell me, what do you think of Jean Howard?"

Arthur knew she was a minor blonde actress, very pretty, under contract to Universal, and there were rumors that Mayer was romantically interested in her. "She's not Harlow," he said carefully.

"I'd throw you out of here if you said she was," Mayer replied. "She's an innocent child and a lady. No," he sighed, "she's not your freak whore. But you can keep your eyes peeled, like I said, for a replacement. And on the way out see Ida." Mayer referred to his executive secretary, whom he prized because she had been employed by Herbert Hoover. "She'll tell you why we tried to call Jean."

Ida Koverman had suggested a temporary truce because the March of Dimes campaign had planned a Birthday Ball to be given for President Roosevelt on January 30. MGM was sending Robert Taylor to the affair and Senator Hiram W. Johnson, the state's Republican senator had suggested that Jean Harlow be sent as the studio's first female representative. Politics, philanthropy and publicity demanded the truce, and the studio was even willing to pay the expenses of the Bellos if Jean would go to Washington. She went.

In the capital Jean was photographed on the Senate steps with Hiram W. Johnson and William Gibbs McAdoo, at that time the Democratic senator from California. Regal in a mink coat and black turban decorated with a jeweled platinum buckle, Jean stood between both senators while Marino stood behind the trio, boutonniered, elegant and solemn as befitted a man who had only minutes before suggested that both California statesmen prove their grasp of international affairs by recommending him for some ambassadorial post where his command of Italian and knowledge of diplomacy could be put to the service of his beloved adopted country. To prove how close was the relationship between the actress and her stepfather, another photo was taken of them together, and Marino's finely tailored suit, capeskin gloves, cane and Borsalino homburg completed an attractive family portrait.

During her visit, Jean and Robert Taylor were photographed with Eleanor Roosevelt in front of the White House, and the MGM stars had a short private visit with the President in his study. He congratulated them on being lovely and handsome representatives of young adult America. At the ball, Jean graciously signed dance programs and danced with notables. She could not be criticized for her dress, because she wore it with undergarments. The trip was a success, and would have been a delight if Harold had been able to accompany her instead of remaining in Los Angeles, concerned with an editing matter at the studio.

Arthur met the train and Jean at San Bernardino and immediately reported to the actress the seriousness of her financial situation. She was advised to make the most of the good will engendered by this trip, to capitulate and return to work, and to make one of the conditions of her return the continued banishment of Mama and Marino from the studio. In private Jean admitted this was what she wanted, but blood was thicker than water and she could not abandon her mother. The truce ended and the operetta war continued, with Arthur serving as messenger between both camps. Jean had just borrowed five thousand dollars from him; now her indebtedness stood at forty-five thousand. It was no way to do business, especially since the Los Angeles Collector of Internal Revenue, John P. Carter, had just notified Harlow that she owed the government $2,654.00 in income taxes for 1932 and that a lien would be levied against her if the debt was not paid. (The notice was ignored, in March the lien was levied and the amount owed plus penalties was collected from the actress when she returned to the studio.)

Suddenly the battle moved to another field. Herman A. Koch, the public administrator of Sacramento County, appeared for his day in the branch of the Superior Court located in Los Angeles and filed a petition for one half of the estate left by Paul Bern. In the case of "Miss Milette vs. Estate," it was stated that in July, 1932, Bern was married to a woman not named in the suit—Jean Harlow. According to Koch, he had communicated with Viona Milette, of Longview, Washington, a sister of Dorothy's, and with the attorney for the estate of Mrs. John Hartranft, recently deceased in Finley, Ohio, about their rights as heirs. Inasmuch as Miss Milette had decided to do away with herself within Sacramento County, the one-half of Bern's community property that might have been her share of the estate should go to the state if the heirs did not press their claims.

Meanwhile, the financial situation had become desperate, and, without consulting Jean or her family, Arthur informed Mayer that his client had capitulated in an unconditional surrender and was ready to return to work. But her salary would have to be raised to two thousand dollars a week, and she would have to be advanced four weeks' salary to take care of immediate and pressing bills incurred by Mama and Marino. In a sweep of generosity Mayer agreed. He ordered Jean put into *Eadie was a Lady,* later retitled *Girl from Missouri,* which was scheduled to begin shooting on March 29. Now Arthur told Jean his own integrity and career were at stake at the largest studio in the city, that if she did not appear for wardrobe fittings and the first day's production it was likely she would never work again, and he might have to close his office.

"There's no time to talk to Mama or Marino," Arthur told Jean in her apartment. Hal sat quietly, staring at the ceiling, but Arthur knew he had the silent man's sympathy. "You either report or make a liar out of me."

"That's putting me on the spot!" she shouted. "I had a right to expect more from you!"

"So did I from you," Arthur replied. "Mayer'll let your folks back. But if you show them that you're ready to go back to work without them—what'll they do? Mama'll cry," he continued. "Marino'll tell you I'm a double-crosser. So what? Does it really matter? Not to me."

She bit her lips in sulky silence. "What sort of a part am I getting?"

"Jack Conway's the director and you're getting Franchot Tone as a leading man and Lionel Barrymore," Arthur replied.

"He's cute and refined," Jean said. "Very rich and educated. And what'm I supposed to be? The same old whore?"

"The part's good and a lot better than you deserve," Arthur said. "Jean"—he looked at his watch—"I want to call the studio in five minutes. Are you going to be in the picture or not?"

"Drop dead," Jean replied. She ran from the living room to the bedroom and slammed the door loudly behind her.

Arthur telephoned Bernard Hyman, the producer of the picture, that Jean would be in his office before nine and that parade activities of welcome would be appreciated by the star; Arthur would contribute a hundred dollars for the purchase of flowers for her dressing room, but she was never to know they were his contribution; the flowers he would send would bear his card.

To make the fans believe that Jean's absence from the screen had not been a strike and that her return was not surrender, it was decided that the press should be given one big story instead of a series of elaborate puffs. This story would, it was hoped, add dignity to the image of the blonde Venus, who would be revealed now as a challenger to Minerva in the realm of reason.

JEAN HARLOW TURNS AUTHOR

The future billing for the screen's platinum blonde may be "by Jean Harlow" as well as "Jean Harlow in—"

Out of films for six months, Miss Harlow returned to screen life today and said she had been in seclusion for six months writing a novel.

It was the hardest job she ever tackled, she said, even more difficult than attaining film stardom, but she got a "thrill" out of it. The book will be published soon. The plot does not concern her life and the characters are fictional, with New York the setting. She did not divulge the theme of the story.

Having ventured into literature, she had decided to extend her studies and has taken up French and music. She wants to play the piano purely for personal pleasure.

Talking of her varied interests, she revealed that she did not like to shop, her mother buying most of her clothes. She said she wears white most of the time because colors are not suitable to her. She likes slacks and "hates" formal clothes.

Eager to talk, she said she liked her role in "Bombshell" better than any other and disliked that in "Hell's Angels" more than any other one. Marriage was touched upon and she said her third romance is a "huge success." Her husband is Harold Rosson, film cameraman.

Chapter Twenty

The cultural notice and affirmation of connubial beatitude appeared in the *Hollywood Citizen* on March 30, 1934. On May 6, at the wedding of Carmelita Geraghty and Carey Wilson, Jean served as the bride's matron of honor, and her lack of escort focused more attention on her than on the bridal pair. Why had she not come to the wedding with Harold Rosson? Next day all the local papers headlined the same explanation: Jean and her husband had parted. Jean had returned to "her abode with her mother and stepfather," and Rosson had moved into the Hollywood Athletic Club. The marriage had lasted eight months, which, for Jean, was a record. Harold, as a gentleman, left all statements to the lady.

To mourn this announcement properly, production was struck on the *Girl from Missouri* set for one day while Rosson was replaced by another cameraman. Jean broke her heart for the press, as duly noted by Louella Parsons, still the ranking begum of Hollywood exclusives and related pillow intelligence, whose column was moved to the lead page of the Los Angeles *Examiner*. (It should be noted that the *Examiner*, because of William Randolph Hearst's personal interest in films, always featured movieland news with the importance it deserved. Thus, on September 3, 1949, the *Examiner* appeared with a two-decker banner headline across the entire first page: MILTON BERLE NEPHEW INJURED BY BOULDER. Certain prophets of doom masquerading as sociologists, psychologists and educators have suggested that such headlines make it difficult for the reader to judge and evaluate the relative importance of current events and national issues, and tend to encapsulate the American reader in his mythos of dreams and, occasionally, of ignorance.)

Miss Parsons noted that at the wedding of her friends Jean had "never looked more beautiful. The wistful look on her face as she heard the minister pronounce the words that made Miss Geraghty the bride of Carey Wilson was not a stage expression. Jean felt really sad and sorry, she said, that her marriage had turned out unhappily." Before she went into standard biography, which included a strong mention of the Bern affair, Miss Parsons felt called upon to quote Jean directly, which made Rosson's silence more golden.

> "Yes, it's true," she told me, "that Hal and I have separated. I shall seek a divorce. It's the only way out for both of us. I feel other people have made mistakes, and it's wrong for us to live together when we are obviously uncongenial. Hal can probably find some other woman who will make him happier than I have done.
>
> "I have always felt i[t] sounds so silly when a husband and wife make up their minds to seek a divorce and they announce that now they will be better friends than ever and will probably see more of each other.
>
> "Our marriage is finished. There will be no reconciliation, nor will we see each other every day. I will say, however, that Hal is a fine man. I regret more than I can say that our marriage has been such a failure. We simply were not meant for each other. There is no other man or woman."

All the local papers gave the story the prominence it deserved, and all added to its length by referring to the Bern matter. The following day atmospheric highlights were added by rumors that Jean Harlow, the blonde Venus, would marry Max Baer, the Mars of the prize ring, after she had shed Harold Rosson. But at orders from the studio, Jean denied the report as ridiculous, then denied herself to the press. The announcement of her separation and planned divorce had been received dourly by Will Hays, who had telephoned MGM's New York office—he was not speaking with Mayer that week—to inform Nicholas Schenck, MGM's ranking Gotham executive, that he was the last man in the world to insist that a married couple without children remain married when they were unhappy or incompatible with each other, but Miss Harlow had involved herself in a nasty affair still strong in the public's memory, the ridiculous suit over the nonexistent Bern estate kept her before the public and there were rumors circulating throughout California about certain emotional escapades which involved the actress; a star whose popularity was bluntly tied to sex should certainly show more mature judgment in what she did and the time she chose to do it. Hays also pointed out that the Legion of Decency had made its official appearance in April of that year and that its officers and members would react badly to overtures of cooperation with the MPDA if the Hollywood self-censoring organization did not take notice and censure men and women important to the industry and the American way of life. Movies could be a moral force, Hays continued in a pulpit voice that lost much of its sonority over the telephone, and in this time of economic depression the hope for America's future lay in moral courage, the good life and optimistic musicals like *Footlight Parade*; it was outrageous to announce a separation and divorce one day and a romantic report the next day with a free-living and free-loving prize fighter whose manager, Ancil Hoffman, had observed that Baer was "'that way' about every good-looking blonde in the country."

Baer blushed over the romantic story, Jean termed it preposterous and Mayer ordered a police watch established over the sexy truant from the studio kindergarten.

At that time Mayer was planning to go to Europe with Mrs. Mayer (Jean Howard was to come along on another ship), and he was too preoccupied to throw his usual tantrum. So Jean was advised—not threatened—to emulate the silence of Rosson and to leave personal statements to the studio. And she was advised to get ready for meetings with Jack Conway and Ray June, the new cameraman, who would attempt to duplicate the filming technique established by Rosson.

Jean was warned to behave, to speak to no one and to avoid any direct meeting with the press not arranged for by the studio, and she was helped in this regimen by her friendship with Kay Mulvey, a bright woman recently assigned by Howard Strickling to the position of MGM's magazine editor. Miss Mulvey, a divorcee, lived with her young son in an unpretentious house at Playa del Rey within sound of the ocean. At MGM she had been given the job of getting news about the studio and its stars out of the movie pulps and into the slick magazines bought by moral women and families. In Kay's company Jean could relax and escape from Mama and Marino, so she began to spend as much time at Playa del Rey as she did in the Beverly Glen house.

Jean adored Kay's five-year-old son, Dick. She played with him, attempted to spoil him and appeared to express through the youngster the maternal fulfillment she would never know. After Kay's son was put to bed, both women would relax in the living room and Jean would daydream aloud about her future. She was going to demand that the studio assign her to Louisa May Alcott roles, and then she would alter her hair style and dress and do something about her sound-track voice, which she knew was awful. She would insist that Kay be assigned to the creation of a new image of Harlow. And then she would adopt one, several, a dozen children and prove to everyone and herself that she could be as good a mother as any biological parent. She knew from her own sad experience what was good and bad for children. Given the chance, she could succeed as a mother. Meanwhile she could relax in Kay's modest home and be accepted as an aunt by Kay's son.

Harold Rosson was stricken with poliomyelitis in June, two weeks after Jean had completed *Girl from Missouri* and some six weeks after her announcement of divorce. Throughout their separation she had racked herself to discover a means to save this marriage, but all approaches were blocked by the parasitic figures of Mama and Marino. Frustrated, embittered, Jean admitted to her agent, her attorneys and Kay Mulvey that any man capable of putting up with the Bellos was not a man she, or any woman, would want in marriage.

Hal was treated at the home of his sister. The attending physician felt that the disease was being overcome, but polio was a treacherous ailment that might strike at other limbs. All medical resources were concentrated on inhibiting the spread of the disease, which was localized in Hal's arms and shoulders, and in overcoming its crippling effect on Rosson's upper body. A quarantine sign kept visitors from entering the house, but papers noted kindly that although she refused to make any direct statement to the press, Jean called several times a day for news of the invalid. She wanted to be at her husband's side, wanted to deny the newspapers that wrote "that she felt sorry for her estranged husband but his illness would in no way alter her plans for divorce." But, to return to Hal, to have to be quoted as determined to stand by her husband and to nurse him back to health so that they could grow old together, would be translated into banal prose that could only be insulting to a man in the grip of a malignant illness.

In addition, Jean was haunted by one of the myths about her own youth—when she supposedly was prayed well from her own paralysis. The telephone rang constantly in the Beverly Glen house and anonymous voices asked, demanded, implored that Mama be called upon to work another miracle: what she had done for her daughter she might be able to accomplish for her son-in-law. There was pressure from members of her denomination who saw in the illness a great missionary opportunity. Within a week Mama was certain she had been called, was even convinced she had as clear and bright a vision as any ever granted to Joan of Arc. For several days she paced deliberately about the house, her eyes veiled, mysterious, as if she saw the broad horizon of all eternity, and she spoke in the low dramatic tones of a sibyl. Marino had to warn Mama that she looked, sounded and behaved like the traditional aunt hidden in the attic, and it was quite likely that she would be arrested if she led a prayer team to the door of Gladys Rosson's house on Highland Avenue.

Weeping into a martini pitcher, Jean knew that her Hollywood environment created chains that bound her natural sympathies and desires, that her mother and Marino were added shackles. And, worst of all, she knew that even if she selflessly, miraculously nursed Harold back to health, her marriage was still beyond salvage.

By the middle of July, Harold was well enough to be transferred to the Orthopaedic Hospital, where he could receive the best physiotherapy available. By the end of the month Jean was able to tell Kay that Harold had been discharged from the hospital as completely cured; she had seen him briefly before he left for New York and London, where he was going to photograph a picture for Alexander Korda.

In loud dudgeon Marino announced that it was his initial negotiations with the Kordas that was responsible for Rosson's assignment, but very few people listened, least of all Jean, who had left for a short vacation alone at the Del Monte Lodge, some three hundred miles north of Los Angeles. Alert reporters found her there in the company of William Powell. Both actor and actress admitted they had played golf and bridge together, had dined, danced and gone swimming; but both denied any romantic significance to such companionship with the stock Hollywood phrase: "We're just good friends."

Before Mayer left for Europe he approved the rough cut of *Girl from Missouri*, approved its immediate distribution, and ordered that another starring vehicle be found immediately for Harlow. In all of 1934 she had made only one picture, and jealous MGM actresses had complained that Jean was being pampered while they had to emote their brains out in three, four, even five pictures a year for the studio.

But Jean herself was not feeling particularly well. Her stay at the Del Monte Lodge had exposed her to the sun, and an attending physician had advised the actress that her skin was too tender to tan; she would have to reconcile herself to the knowledge that she had become a heliophobe, and that she would be subject to severe burns and skin poisoning if she did not exercise the greatest care. She was also informed that the studio would have to be very careful in its use of lights. Fear compelled her to communicate this to Landau and Kay Mulvey, but both people were bound to secrecy because Jean feared for her career.

The studio was bracing itself for Mayer's return from Europe, where his attempts at courtly romance had been frustrated by the marriage of his lady-friend. Advance dispatches from abroad and New York told of a very snappish Mayer indeed. At such a time of trial everyone swept his problems and grievances under rugs and practiced smiling happily for the return of the chief. There would be speeches and testimonials; problems and complaints would be taken up at a later date.

However, Jean's problems escaped Mayer's concern, because his return thrust him squarely into a political crisis that affected the entire state: The governor's chair and many seats in the state legislature were up for election, and Upton Sinclair, with his dangerous program of social reform and relief for the little man, had enlisted more and more adherents to his banner. Mayer saw the banner as red and vowed that the ex-Socialist, muck-raking author whose books could *not* be made into wholesome American films had to be stopped before he made a Bolshevik bastion of California. Furthermore, Mayer was determined to stop the passage of a state personal income tax—championed by Sinclair—which threatened every comfortable individual in California. Also, there was a more direct threat against the movie studios, against which Sinclair intended to levy heavy taxes.

It was impossible to hide the economic distress throughout California; Los Angeles County, with a population of 2,490,000, had almost 400,000 adults with familial responsibilities unable to find work. The California sun shone alike on rich and poor, but the poor could not get out of the sun and into the shade and could be arrested for loitering if they sought the shelter of a tree or plucked rotting oranges.

On many counts Mayer did not like Frank Merriam, Sinclair's opponent. The man was an Iowa farmer from a state so notoriously antisemitic that even as late as 1955 Jews were not permitted to join the Great Books Club at the Mason City Public Library, and he also had a reputation as a practicing, preaching, believing prohibitionist and reformer who had stumped briefly to nominate Anthony Comstock for president. Definitely not a man to invite to dinner or for a dip in a pool decorated with bathing beauty starlets. However, forced to choose between a man who was a symbol of moral bigotry and a man who campaigned for taxes to be paid by those who could afford them, the motion picture industry had only one possible choice: Merriam.

Everyone at the studio with a salary of more than a hundred dollars a week was taxed by Mayer for a day's pay as a contribution to the Merriam campaign to keep taxes out of California. Jean paid without protest, even signed her name to a piece of scurrilous campaign literature that compared Upton Sinclair to Lenin, Genghis Khan and Ivan the Terrible, then permitted herself to be photographed as she delivered her "voluntary" assessment to the Merriam headquarters. After Mayer was certain that everyone at the studio had contributed to the Republican campaign, he busied himself with offering suggestions for the improvement of the bogus newsreel about Sinclair that Thalberg had begun before Mayer returned from Europe. *The Inquiring Reporter* served as a Machiavellian primer to succeeding generations of Republican candidates in California, Maryland and Wisconsin; distributed free and even ordered into theaters, it purported to show the decline and fall of California, which would be sacked by Okie and Arkie vandals if Sinclair and his un-American program to End-Poverty-in-California were victorious at the polls.

Upton Sinclair lost the election on November 6, 1934, but the state was safe only briefly from taxation; then Merriam betrayed his class and party by plumping for a state income tax, which was passed the following June. But during the week of November 6, Merriam's victory, for which Mayer took full credit, made the film czar so ebullient that he did nothing more than shrug when the Los Angeles grand jury decided to reopen the Bern case. The jury, which was investigating certain irregularities of office of District Attorney Buron Fitts, previously indicted for perjury, and his sister, Mrs. Berthal Gregory, with whom he had been indicted for their involvement with a Hollywood love mart and shenanigans related to the sale of a ranch in which they had an interest, had subpoenaed all relevant records and files held in Fitts' office, including those on the Bern case. Foreman John P. Buckley of the 1934 grand jury refused to make any editorial comment and declined to say whether Jean Harlow would be compelled to appear for renewed questioning in the matter. But it was quickly remembered that her appearance before Buron Fitts had been private, brief and mysterious, with only one other member of the jury present with Fitts when the actress was interrogated at the Ambassador Hotel in 1932.

Now the records were turned over to C. E. Memory, auditor for the grand jury. But the increased heartbeat of rumor did not bring on a coronary of scandal, because it soon became evident that the grand jury was more interested in the district attorney's secret service fund and how much had been spent in investigating the bizarre suicide than in the suicide itself. But the mention of Harlow and Bern by the newspapers assured the conditioned Pavlovian response which demanded the publication again—by all the papers—of the sad little note of farewell. Later articles reported that review of the maze of evidence presented in the secret investigation of the 1932 grand jury revealed that the actions of at least "one individual" had never been cleared up to the satisfaction of the police or jury, and that the testimony of the seventy witnesses called to the hearing had revealed some astonishing stories about Bern and persons reputed to be closely associated with him. The ghost of Dorothy Milette was also raised, because evidence taken at the secret inquiry had failed to account conclusively for her whereabouts during the Labor Day weekend.

In the next several days the national press dutifully reported "Miss Harlow Grilled Through Night by Probe Group"; "Mystery Clings"; "Transcript of Session Mysteriously Gone, Inquiry Bares." The new investigation revealed that a transcript had been made of Buron Fitts's examination of Harlow, but it was missing. Strangely, the stenographic notes had been saved and filed, which made the disappearance of the official transcript even more puzzling. However, when the parts of a problem are available, the whole can be reconstructed, and it was revealed that Jean's questioning by Fitts and a representative of the 1932 grand jury had not dispelled the mystery which shrouded the famous "comedy" death note written by Bern.

The grand jury proceeded to the testimony of Clifton Davis, which they thought was composed of real meat.

During the course of his testimony Davis had been asked: "Do you think Mr. Bern committed suicide?"

"I do not think so," Davis had replied. "I knew him too well. He had no reason to commit suicide. I have thought it was murder from the very beginning."

In other relevant paragraphs of his testimony Davis revealed his discovery of a small pool of blood near the swimming pool. He had also seen droplets of blood on the steps leading to the house and he had washed the steps. Later he had found a broken cognac glass near the swimming pool and shown it to officers who were investigating the grounds. They had concluded that someone had cut his finger. In his testimony Davis approved this theory.

But elsewhere in his testimony Davis said he had conversed with John Carmichael after the inquest and the butler had said: "If I had it to do over again I would tell the truth."

Davis could not tell investigators what Carmichael meant, and later, when Carmichael was questioned, he denied making such a statement.

The filet of Davis' testimony proved to be gristle and hambone, nothing more, and the 1934 jurors searched through the records for the testimony everyone really wanted to read. But it was quickly learned that Jean had only been questioned once, briefly and privately, and no written transcript had been made of questions asked and her replies. Why? Possibly to keep down the expenses of the investigation was one theory offered to the curious, but no one could say for sure.

Hopefully, reporters turned to William W. Widenham, foreman of the 1932 grand jury that had conducted the Bern probe, but he considered the case closed. "I was satisfied that Bern's death was a suicide," Widenham declared. "And I see no reason to change my stand now. Miss Harlow appeared during our investigation and we talked to her for several hours.

She answered all of our questions and seemed more than anxious to present the facts and clear up the case. She gave a satisfactory account of her movements on the night that Bern died and we closed the case after hearing her testimony."

Guarded by her lawyer, agent and parents, Jean made two statements for the press. The first was that she intended to begin divorce proceedings against her husband, which she had delayed because he was still in London. She did not know when he intended to return to California, but if he did not commit himself to an early return she would instruct Oscar A. Trippet, the attorney who would represent her in the divorce action, to file by the end of November.

The second statement was that she had nothing to say about the Bern matter.

"I did not talk about the case before," she read from a prepared statement, "and I see no reason for discussing it now. If it would do any good, and any new information could be obtained, that would be different. The case was thoroughly investigated once and became a closed one. Authorities were perfectly satisfied with the evidence. I have no personal knowledge of what is going on now, and I have not been asked to make an appearance before the grand jury. My personal wish is that some day the matter will be dropped for all time."

"What about Davis' testimony?" a San Diego reporter persisted.

"No comment," Arthur spoke quickly. "That's all," he signaled for Mama and Marino to shelter Jean from more questions, because the actress had tightened her lips and appeared about to flare into a snit that would be photographed. "Jean says thanks and God bless you and all her loyal fans. Please print that."

No one did.

There were several more days of rehash until on November 12, the grand jury decided it was no longer interested in any phase of the two-year-old suicide and returned to its investigation of Buron Fitts and his sister. And it was on this day of surcease that Jean was informed she would appear as the star of *Reckless*, which would be directed by Victor Fleming, in whom she had confidence, and produced by David O. Selznick—proof enough that she was in good grace with the studio. Other stars to stud this musical epic were William Powell, Franchot Tone, May Robson and Rosalind Russell. As Landau pointed out excitedly, the film would also use Allan Jones, and Jean would be given the opportunity to warble songs composed by Jerome Kern, Oscar Hammerstein, H. Burton Lane and three other competent men of music. And she would get to dance in numbers created by Carl Randall and Chester Hale.

Another actress would have been jubilant at the opportunity offered her, but Jean stared coldly at Landau until his new mustache began to perspire.

"If you were bigger I'd punch you in the mouth," she said.

"Thank you, friend," he replied.

She began to gather a head of steam. "You must think I'm pretty damned dumb. Maybe because I don't vote and I let them write that ridiculous story about me that I'm studying French—the language," she added pointedly, "and that I'm writing a book, you must think I'm dumb. But I read the script, Goddamnit, and I know where those writers got the idea for the story. And what recent newspaper business gave everyone the idea of putting me in it. If I was Libby Holman I'd sue Mayer for at least ten million."

"She has enough money of her own," Arthur replied lamely. "She doesn't have to sue."

"For chrissakes I visited her a year ago last April or May when I was back East!" Jean shouted. "I was her house guest in Wilmington and she treated me great! How can I do this to her? It's one friend stabbing another in the back! Maybe that's normal for out here, where everyone walks on his friend—but not for me!"

Swearing, stamping and screaming, Jean continued to rage at Arthur for his participation in a deliberate, vicious and calculated outrage as bad as anything Mayer had ever done to her. To put her in a story obviously, even admittedly, based on the mysterious suicide of Zachary Smith Reynolds II, heir to the Duke tobacco fortune and husband of Libby Holman, proved to Jean that she was friendless in a wasteland. But she was not going to take it with a whimper while her reputation was destroyed in a banging of news presses.

"You couldn't find me a property until now," she accused Arthur and the calendar on his desk. "Then on the same day that lousy grand jury digs into a case that's two years old and none of its business . . . With all my troubles and problems do you have any idea what it's done to me? Marino's said right along you're a lousy agent, and I'm beginning to believe him."

"Continue," was all he dared say.

Her eyes were wide and bright as if she would have delighted in some signal that he was hurt, but Arthur only clasped his hands and pursed his lips.

"I'd been hearing things, so I was ready for you when you called and asked me to come over to hear some good news. But I was wise to all of you, Arthur. So I'd called for a couple of scripts, and I asked for that one, too." She pointed to the script she had thrown into the wastebasket. "How dare you?" she screamed at him.

"Dare what?" he said.

"Reynolds was found dead in July, 1932, and you know how the papers wrote up the case. They hinted all sorts of things—that he wasn't exactly a man, that it might've been murder! Does that sound familiar? And you know Paul killed himself just a couple of months later. And there've been more than hints that in Paul's case it was murder and flat statements that he wasn't a man. Look how close the circumstances are! Where the hell is your heart?"

Arthur tapped a temple. "Lucky for you, up here."

"So how could you let me get mixed up in that kind of picture?"

"Because it's a picture with a big supporting cast and lots of production values. And you like Powell."

"Who'm I supposed to be playing—Libby Holman or Jean Harlow?"

Arthur took the script from the wastebasket and turned to the page that gave the names of the characters. "You play a nightclub singer named Mona."

"Not Libby?" she laughed. "Aren't those writers original! They actually have the talent to change names. Maybe I ought to have the writers work in that Friday night skit where Paul ran around with that thing strapped to him."

"I'm warning you," Arthur said as he signaled for Jean to lower her voice. "Keep talking about that and someone's bound to hear you."

It was time for maudlin tears. "First you stick me into *Bombshell*—"

"Which everyone liked."

"—where the whole world gets to know what my family's like, and now you stick me into a picture where I play out Paul's suicide for everybody to see."

"No one really identifies pictures with real life," Arthur said, and shuddered.

"I won't make the picture," Jean said.

"If you say so," Arthur said wearily. "But the least Louis B. will do is take you off salary."

She hesitated, stared at the script, then dropped it once again into the wastebasket and sat down to draw on her high-heeled pumps. "All right, Arthur." She would not look at him. "You sold me out. I'm firing you as my agent."

"Suit yourself. But not until you pay what you owe this office. It's still over forty thousand."

"I'm getting a business manager who'll see that I pay it off quickly. Then we're through?"

"Word of honor, if that's what you want," he replied. "I can recommend some good business managers."

"Marino'll do nicely, thank you."

"Now you're really crazy!"

"Am I?" She stood at the door, blonde, beautiful and brainless. "And since when does that hurt in this business?" She breathed deeply to lift her breasts, then opened her mink coat to show him the red silk lining. There was an inscription embroidered in Spenserian script: "To Jean, With Love."

"Very nice," Arthur said. "Coat and sentiments. I suppose the coat's new?"

"About a week old," she admitted, her smile malicious. "That's my going price now. Think you can afford it?"

"Get out of my office," Arthur said. "The script in the wastebasket is too good for you."

Jean began to take off the coat. "It's worth more than a thousand. Take it for Beatrice and knock five hundred dollars off my bill." She laughed raucously. "For you, knocking me off will only be another five hundred."

"Out!" Arthur pointed to the door. "And quick!"

Chapter Twenty-one

In December, 1934, events connected with the filming of *Reckless* were as ridiculous as the charges filed by Jean against Harold Rosson in her divorce suit. David Selznick was the producer appointed to guide *Reckless,* a dancing, singing, magnolia-scented melodrama, from sound stage to box office. As Mayer's son-in-law, with good reason to believe that some day he would fill Mayer's shoes, Selznick had the power to get things done.

At any rate, to establish his authority, to assure everyone connected with the film that he was a no-nonsense *graf,* Selznick summoned Jerome Kern, the distinguished composer of *Sunny, Showboat, Roberta* and a score of other musical shows, to his presence.

He yawned and pointed at an upright piano. "Jerry," he said, "how about playing one of your tunes? You see, I'm not too familiar with your recent melodies."

Kern strode to the door and turned. "Mr. Selznick," he said with exaggerated politeness, "I'm sorry, but I don't give away samples."

Selznick later defended himself by telling people—who did not believe him—that Kern was offended because he had been asked to perform on an upright rather than a full grand. Whatever Kern's reason, in *The Ascap Biographical Dictionary,* where a life of Jerome Kern occupies a full page, the titles of films to which Kern contributed music are listed; neither *Reckless* nor his song of that title are included.

When the picture was released and reviewed in April of 1935, the title song, "Reckless," by Kern and Hammerstein, was as undistinguished as the vocalizing and dancing of Harlow. She was poorly photographed, an obvious failure on her twinkletoes, and no better as a songbird. Efforts to make Jean into a musical star, which would have added dimensions to her personality, were flatly disappointing. Distributors who saw the film were quick to point out that, despite the pains taken with staging and sets and the expert talents employed to create tunes and dances, the footage of Harlow as a singer and dancer could improve the picture—if it were cut out. The public was still solidly behind Harlow as the ideal pillowmate, and as long as her dialogue was loaded with sex, sex, sex, that was all that mattered. Singing was best left to the birds and Jeanette MacDonald.

Reckless was the studio's problem; divorce from Harold Rosson the problem of Jean's attorney, who could not persuade her to follow his advice and make her charges of mental cruelty vague and indefinite. Mr. Trippet's advice was sound, but Jean had notified Marino that he was her business and personal mentor, and he had advised her that vague charges would make people think Jean was at fault. She had to be specific, incisive. Jean probed her memory for incidents to prove Harold's lack of manners or courtesy, but nothing came to mind that did not prove his self-control. If he was rude to Marino, one could only admire his restraint. If he was indifferent to Mama, it only proved his polished good manners; most people were downright insulting.

Knowing all of this, Jean still persisted in filing specific complaints. They were howlers. Her first and principal charge was that Harold read in bed until late hours, "much to the detriment of her art as an actress, for the next day, after losing sleep, she was unable to play her role to the best of her ability." This produced guffaws in the movie colony and astonishment among readers everywhere. But there were other charges: that her husband was "the original 'gloomy dean' around the house," that he was rude to her friends, that he was sullen and irritable, that "his ungenerous character constituted in effect continuous brutality," and that he had caused gossip when he had refused to attend the Geraghty-Wilson wedding. There was no request for alimony.

Blanche Williams, Victor Fleming and Kay Mulvey all telephoned Jean's agent to speak to his client, but Arthur, although he regretted the published follies, was quick to point out it was at Jean's insistence that matters between them were strictly business. Still, he had gone to the studio to arrange Jean's salary increase for 1935, to raise her earnings to $2,750 a week.

Because Marino refused to take or return any of his phone calls, the only direct meeting he had had with Jean was an accidental one in the MGM commissary. Peremptorily ordering him to accompany her to the backlot, then to her dressing room, she had cursed him roundly for all her misfortunes; then she told him how she had redecorated a room at Beverly Glen.

"Not exactly my bedroom," she told Arthur. "But the little massage room just off my bedroom. I've done it over and made it my dream room."

"Very nice," he replied.

"If you weren't so all wet you'd see," she persisted. "I mean my *dream* room. Get it?"

Arthur continued to shake his head. "I'd rather not. And I'm busy." He stood to go. "We must have lunch sometime."

But she would not let him leave, not until she had described in fullest detail the new "dream" room. New locks had been fitted to the door of this room and the windows had been shrouded by heavy draperies. The floor was covered with a carpet of deep white pile, and there were several night tables of white wood with lamps and shades of white. There was a white dressing table and a chaise of gleaming black silk. The walls and ceilings had been mirrored so that she saw dozens of Harlows. Securely locked in, dressed only in gold jewelry or one of the mink or sable coats in her collection of prizes, Jean would posture herself on the chaise and abandon herself to stream-of-consciousness monologues.

"A psychiatrist would give a million dollars just to hear me," she told Arthur.

"I'm just your agent," Arthur said. "And you still owe me about forty thousand. Paying your debts would be better business than acting out your dreams. Still, if you know a psychiatrist that would give you a million, let me make the deal. I'll take my forty thousand as commission and you'll be rid of me in every department."

"You're every lousy thing Marino says you are," she said.

Arthur opened the dressing room door. "So don't bother sending me a Christmas card," he said.

If Jean was unhappy, Marino and Mama were not. As financial administrators for one of the most famous women in the world, both Bellos imagined themselves persons of consequence. They were wooed by stockbrokers, automobile salesmen, mining engineers and financiers of dubious antecedents, all with important things to sell. Then, too, it suddenly looked as though Marino might actually be useful to the industry. Craft unions were raising their heads, and making demands on the studio. Some executives wondered in whispers whether the studios might not be able to enlist a little protection against the pressure of organized labor—*professional* protection. But where could they find it?

Then it was remembered: Marino Bello had migrated from Italy to Chicago, he looked Sicilian and dangerous, and he occasionally mentioned—mysteriously of course—his past but close association with the gangland aristocracy of Chicago and Detroit. At late private suppers Marino was questioned about the gangsters he really knew, and within a very short time Jean began to complain that Abe Mankovitch, Necco Brown, Willie

Bioff, George E. (Three-Fingers) Browne and Benjamin Siegel were not the kind of men she wanted to see at ease in her home.

But if she was concerned about the reputation of such guests, Mayer was not. Soon thereafter Mayer and Joe Schenck met Bioff and Browne in the vicinity of the Chinese Theater to negotiate labor "peace terms." A hundred thousand dollars was exchanged for a no-strike guarantee. Marino claimed ten per cent as a finder's fee but settled for a nudge between the shoulder blades with a barrel of a police special, a box of cigars, and a one-night stand with a geisha en route by yacht to Rafael Trujillo.

To the disappointment of the studio executives, Marino soon proved himself unacceptable to Bioff, Browne or Siegel as a negotiator: they could not trust a man who tried to borrow money from them at business conferences. However, the fact that Marino was on a first-name basis with men of murder gave him some temporary status. And, because gangsters, as other men, enjoyed the company of starlets, Marino's little black book was deemed as valuable as a Shakespeare First Folio. Proud, arrogant, enjoying the drunkenness of power, Marino appropriated all of Jean's check, except for the agency commission which Landau collected directly from the studio. In full charge, Marino mismanaged Jean's affairs with a sweep of prodigality that gave him a name for infamy and Jean an increased reputation for stupidity.

It was not only money that he spread around. In the city of stars the bungalow courts were filled with young girls willing to do anything to come to the attention of a producer, a director, a star or talent scout, willing to endure the body of a phony in the hope that some day or night they would feel the genuine breath and heartbeat of someone really able to get them into pictures. Marino Bello was the father of a top star, a man photographed with the famous, a man seen on golf courses and yachts and in the executive dining rooms of great studios. And Marino Bello was handsome; in fact, in the opinion of many he was the most impressive-looking member of the Harlow ménage, the only one with natural grace and at least the appearance of character.

The telephone rang often for Bello, and occasionally when Mama answered the phone the party at the other end hung up immediately. Mama's beauty parlor friends delighted in telling her—as if it didn't matter and they were making the idlest conversation—that they had seen Marino having lunch with some sweet young thing, no doubt the daughter of an old Kansas City or Chicago friend entrusted to the Bellos to keep her from trouble in this wicked city.

Now there were more frequent scenes in the house. Mama had begun to rifle Marino's pockets and find little evidences of dalliance. Once she had punched pinholes into a supply of condoms she found in Marino's vest; later, when she ascertained that the box was empty, Mama revealed her stratagem. Marino had been furious and had spent most of that night talking to mysterious people, among whom Jean had caught the name of a well-know abortionist. Delighted, she had telephoned Arthur and several other friends to give them the full details of the scene, and she was angry when no one appreciated its humor.

The only New Year's resolution Jean made for 1935 was to speak to Landau—he was still her agent and collecting his commission—and have him explain to the studio that she wished to be groomed for other roles. There were actresses on the MGM roster who had been call girls before they entered the movies (one star was rumored to have spent more than a hundred thousand dollars in her endeavor to buy up stag films in which she had starred when she was broke and hungry) but Jean's reputation had been without blemish until she had married Bern, a studio executive. Therefore, the studio owed her something, a chance at something with more class, and she would demand that she be considered for the roles given to such stars as Jeanette MacDonald, Constance Bennett, Greta Garbo, Norma Shearer, Helen Hayes and Joan Crawford. It was still too early in the year and she still felt too blue and hung over to realize that these starring actresses could sing, dance and act, that they had important executive connections, and that they had not made the mistake of being too democratic at the studio.

Later on Jean wondered whether she ought to take a leave of absence from the studio and devote a full year to study, poise and diction. Deliberately, and alone, she ran some of the films and winced at the stridency of her voice, the clumsiness of her acting: instead of making an exit, she flounced out of a room; instead of reclining gracefully on a sofa, she flopped; she moved her arms as if they were uncoordinated pistons, walked with a stride, whined nasally when she wished to be intimate. Secure in the small projection room, whose door she had locked to make sure she was not disturbed, she wondered at herself on the screen, tried to see what men saw in her—and failed. Attempting to see why she was popular with women, why her hair style and coloring were copied, why her make-up was so popular, why girls imitated the tough, splayfooted, hip-thrust way she stood, she only saw and heard herself as a bray-voiced tart.

But there was no fighting success. As soon as she finished *Reckless* and had a short rest, she was scheduled to go into *China Seas* with Gable, Lewis Stone, Rosalind Russell, C. Aubrey Smith, Robert Benchley *and* Wallace Beery, who would share starring honors with her and Gable. What was her role? The same old standard gilded lily of the fields pursued and pollinated by Clark Gable: in *Red Dust* she was known as Vantine, in *Hold Your Man* as Ruby, in *Girl from Missouri* as Eadie; in *China Seas,* where Gable would again be the bee in her bonnet, she would be regionally identified as China Doll. It was enough to make her heave every fortune cookie she had ever eaten.

Meanwhile, everyone was busy at Beverly Glen: Marino was negotiating again for the purchase of a yacht to sail to Treasure Island, Mama had bought a ledger to keep accounts and to tabulate Marino's comings and goings, and fans were always being shooed from the grounds. Evenings that Jean spent in the house were enlivened by three-way arguments in which Mama, with increasing vehemence, accused Marino of infidelity, Jean accused him of being an outright crook, and Marino accused Mama and Jean of being two insane women allied in determined conspiracy to keep him from making them millionaires.

These at-homes became so stormy that Jean spent more and more time with Kay Mulvey, at whose house she slept, and with William Powell. At first she had not liked Powell, because his mustache, debonair polish and charm reminded her unpleasantly of Bello. But she soon realized that this was where the resemblance ended, and in his company she found a sympathetic listener who advised her to make a clean break with her family if she wished to be healthy in body, mind and soul. Quietly, logically, patiently willing to listen to sense and nonsense, Powell permitted the distraught actress to rage at length, then quietly asked her what she intended to do about the situation. Until she was capable of doing what she would have advised someone else to do, until she was capable of accepting her role at home and in the national mind for what it was, she would be unable to function as an adult, unable to free herself from a fear of what gossip columnists and movie reporters *did* say about her.

Despairing, miffed with Powell, she turned to an accomplished Hollywood writer, Carey Wilson, for advice, and he could only point out that her early youth, if examined objectively, gave little evidence of unhealthy passion or temperament. Now she was famous for her appearance, her hair, the roles she played in films, the interviews she gave, the clothes she wore and refused to wear, the cloud created by her second marriage and its melodramatic conclusion. If her fame was based on an image of reckless nymphomania, if she was the focal figure in every dirty story told about Hollywood and actresses, if she was rumored to have had affairs at the tenderest age, if she had become, in the mass mind, the woman on every other dirty picture that circulated here and abroad, there was a reason—but it was not in herself. She had to realize that all these—myth and commercial product—were manufactured, distributed and sold to a mean world eager for sensation and only too ready to believe the worst of its sexual goddesses. Her altar and temple were a bed, thinking of her a ritual, and there was nothing she could do about it. No studio, anywhere, would change her image; the public would not accept an alteration in its worship.

These were handicaps, Carey admitted, but Jean had some positive assets apart from her blondeness and body: at times she gave evidences of positive, assertive character; she responded wholeheartedly to friendship; she was respectful of learning and willing to be guided in her craft; she was genuinely democratic because she enjoyed the natural rather than the artificial. If she was unhappy because she lacked the love of a real family, she could still give strong evidence of an ability to appear cheerful and unaffected by a salary, importance and adulation that would have turned the head of most people. It was time, Carey advised her, to take that year off instead of just talking about it. And she should see a doctor to correct the continuing pains in her back and her constant use of the bathroom. Furthermore, when she finished with the doctor she should see an analyst capable of strengthening her ego until she could disassociate herself from her family.

"But I guess I'm wasting my time," Carey said at last. "Because the people who come for counsel don't want your advice. They just want you to agree with them."

"I listened to everything you said," Jean protested.

"But you didn't hear," Carey replied.

Ruefully, Jean nodded that this was true.

Reckless was finished by the middle of February and Jean girded herself for the ordeal of divorce in March. Although half-a-dozen other Hollywood couples were also having their circulation restored by a public thawing in court, public interest was focused on Jean's sad appearance before Judge Elliott Craig.

When she appeared in court, suitably garbed for grief in a black crepe dress, brown sable coat and brown hat, Jean had expected she would have to do nothing more than answer in one word the judge's question as to whether she wanted a divorce: automatically, she thought, the decree would be granted. Judge Craig, however, asked for particulars.

Prompted by her attorney, Jean told the judge how Rosson's sarcasm had harried and distressed her and impaired her health. Pressed for details, she unfolded a specimen narrative or two: Rosson had been surly at the New Year's Eve party given by her mother and had only appeared at midnight to make some disparaging remarks about some of the guests. At another party, when she had asked some young chap to sing, Rosson had sat glumly through the song, then said something like "phooey." Warming to her theme, the actress revealed that Rosson's sarcasm had been directed at her within twelve hours of their marriage.

"He was jealous of my friends, of my time and of my position—of everything I had," she declared. "He belittled my profession and I never knew how to take him, he was so sarcastic. It got so bad, his jealousy and his sarcasm, that it affected my health and my work. I could stand it no longer. So we parted."

Mrs. Bello corroborated her daughter. The judge was informed that Mr. Rosson was in London and had not entered any rebuttal in the suit, and that no property or alimony were involved. A default was filed for Rosson and Jean was divorced.

One of the first of Hollywood's celebrities to congratulate Jean was William Powell. The entire cast slated to make *China Seas* with Jean (with the exception of Wallace Beery, who pleaded the discomfort of his obedient dyspepsia) hosted her at a dinner party; they encouraged her to think positively and wished her well in any future marriage she might make. She was still young, only twenty-four, and there was a long and happy future in her life-line.

If this was true, when would the present end and the future begin? Would it be when she moved into one of the new star bungalows then under construction on the MGM lot? The studio, perhaps inspired by the federal government's massive housing program for the underprivileged one-third of a nation, had decided to build these little houses for its leading stars. Bungalows were to be constructed for Garbo, Jeanette Mac-Donald, Joan Crawford, Myrna Loy, Luise Rainer and Jean Harlow, and two bungalows were to be reserved for visiting stars. Each would have a living room, dressing room, wardrobe and bath, and a small kitchen. Jeanette MacDonald's bungalow would be decorated in powder blue and pink, Garbo's in red and white, and Jean's would be all white. Similar bungalows with more masculine appointments were to be constructed for leading actors.

Jean had made another resolution and was keeping it: to sell the house. Although there were no signs before the house and no advertisements (it was unbecoming to offer a temple for sale), the property was being offered by several brokers. She had finally faced Mama and Marino with the harsh fact that the drain of maintaining the house, along with Marino's unfortunate losses on gambling ships anchored outside the continental limits, were too much.

The pressure of *China Seas*, because Jean considered any picture which included Beery a challenge, kept her from cursing Marino at length. Several days before, he had refused permission to a real estate broker to take a rich Canadian through the house, then had told the embarrassed broker the house was no longer on the market. Mama seemed relieved, because she loved the house, but Jean telephoned the broker that she alone was mortgaged to the house and that, if he would meet her at the studio the next day, she would give him a set of keys and a written authorization to enter the house five minutes after he telephoned.

To assist the broker, Jean ate her pride and telephoned Arthur for assistance. He had many friends, many clients, and among them there had to be several rich or vain enough to assume the responsibilities of a beautifully furnished house. She would remove the mirrors from the walls and ceiling and restore the massage room to its original appearance. The conversation between them was strained and polite, and only at the end did Jean unbend enough to ask Arthur when he and his wife were going to invite her to dinner. Maybe they could get together—just the three of them—to discuss their future.

"Everyone says I've got one," Jean said. "I wish I could be as sure."

"You're whining," Arthur told her. "Call in the Bank of America and tell them to take over."

"You don't even bother telling me to see a doctor anymore!" Jean screeched at him. "You're only concerned with your money."

"Get back to work. I'll be over to see you soon," Arthur said.

"Thanks for nothing," she retorted and hung up.

It was the worst kind of unsatisfactory situation, but nothing could be done for the time being. Jean was busy with *China Seas,* and the cloud of her recent divorce still hung over her. Until her life settled back into some kind of normalcy, it would be impossible to untangle the messy business and personal relationships surrounding her.

Meanwhile, Marino's increasing unfaithfulness had now become so brazen he had begun to bring his more attractive young ladies home with him. As he told Mama, while his eyes twinkled, he was thinking of becoming an actor's agent. It would be only a sideline, of course, but he knew that he could be as successful as Landau, and he would persuade Jean to break her contract and join his office. Weren't the patio and poolside the best places to talk business with actresses he hoped to interest in his services?

"Some services!" Jean heard her mother screech. "Some services, indeed!"

By the second week of May, *China Seas* was close to completion, and the studio was enthusiastic about the film. And—for a real coup—the New York offices of MGM had hopes of having Jean on the cover of an August issue of *Time,* shortly before the picture would be released. It was impossible to overestimate the publicity value of a *Time* cover, and the prestige that accrued to the person so honored. Moreover, since the founding of the magazine in 1923, *Time* had portrayed only thirty women in more than six hundred issues, and before the decision was made to install Harlow on the cover, only twelve citizens of the movie colony—seven movie actors, three actresses and two producers—had been thought important enough to be displayed on the cover of the weekly news magazine. All the Hollywood studios were impressed. Jean, however, was not. She pointed out that she had made the *back* cover of *Time* on October 19, 1931, when, in a slinky gown molded to her famous body, she had endorsed Lucky Strike cigarettes.

Her indifference to *Time* was linked to a long-nurtured hostility toward the magazine. Its 1932 review of *Red Dust* had panned the picture, described her as "Harlot Harlow," snidely reviewed the Bern affair and concluded—as Jean described it—with a kick in the ass when she was down: "Audiences at *Red Dust* watched her face for traces of tragedy, found none."

Ignoring her hostility, the studio ordered her to smile for the photographer. Swathed in protective layers of treacly kindness and blessed with telephone calls from the Schenck brothers in New York, Jean pledged herself to fullest cooperation and good behavior. To insure her, and the studio, against mishaps, the publicity people and studio police were charged with keeping everything unpleasant away from the actress, with stress on reporters not connected with *Time*.

The responsibility was observed but, alas, the Associated Press picked up a story in Little Rock, Arkansas, and distributed it nationally to give the studio a red face and the Blonde Bombshell a black eye. For the Independent Theater Owners of Arkansas, in annual convention at Little Rock, had unanimously adopted a resolution against Jean for her attitude toward fans and admirers "who have made her what she is today," and sent their notice of censure to the district distributors for Metro-Goldwyn-Mayer. Telephone wires hummed, voices screamed and Mayer raged at Harlow's too-dumb-blonde stupidity.

It seemed that on Saturday night several dateless coeds of the Pi Beta Phi chapter at the University of Arkansas had gone to one of the Fayetteville theaters to see Jean Harlow in *Reckless*. To the sheltered coeds the film had been wonderful. Their delight continued from the theater to the sorority house, and they decided to telephone Jean to tell her of their enthusiasm for a picture which reviewers had disliked but they thought great. They pooled their money to telephone MGM in Culver City, and the call was referred to Jean's home. The girls held the line, felt their hearts beat more rapidly as they anticipated speaking to their favorite star, and were shattered to have the long distance operator tell them that Miss Harlow had said she "didn't know anybody in Arkansas and didn't want to talk to anybody in Arkansas."

Next morning at breakfast the girls told other members of their chapter of Harlow's snootiness, and a committee of girls visited W. F. Sonneman, manager of three theaters in Fayetteville, one of which was showing *Reckless,* to tell him what had happened and that their sorority chapter intended to boycott all future Harlow pictures. They would also tell everyone they knew how awful Harlow was.

Pi Beta Phi sorority, founded in 1867, was one of the leading undergraduate social organizations in the United States, with more than ninety chapters, about seven thousand undergraduate members and considerably more alumnae members, many of them women distinguished in American life. Mr. Sonneman realized this was not a time to trifle with cash customers. He forwarded the girls' complaint to the theater owners' convention, which certainly—until this lucky break for them—could not have passed any resolution worthy of national attention or coverage. So the complaint was received with enthusiasm, acted upon with enthusiasm and probably acclaimed with rebel yells.

The mills of MGM ground as fine as those of the gods, but more speedily. Howard Strickling wasted no time in going directly to the stage where the final scenes of *China Seas* were being shot to demand an explanation of Jean's monumental stupidity and to prepare a statement that would explain, if possible, Jean's *gaffe.*

"Snub a Harlow fan? Preposterous," Jean was quoted. "The only thing I know about the matter is that on Saturday night, sometime after midnight, the studio operator reported that she had a collect long distance call from Arkansas from a man named Smith who said he was my manager and also a blood relative."

"The same Saturday night that the girls called?" a reporter asked.

Jean thought for a moment and nodded after a glance at Strickling. "Yes."

"What city did he call from?" the reporter persisted. "You can ask, you know."

"It didn't occur to me," Jean replied. "Since I have no manager in Arkansas and no blood relative there, I naturally referred the call back to the studio. Matter of fact, there's no one named Smith in our family. It was all a mistake, you see. No one is more appreciative than I am of the interest of my fans. And if the fraternity—I mean sorority girls want me to talk to them, I'll be glad to do so."

"Jean is going to telephone the girls tonight," Marino added. "And if they think she should apologize she will."

True to Marino's promise, Jean made a person-to-person call to Roberta Henderson. She told the chapter president how sorry she was to have misinterpreted the source of the call and that she was unaware, until she read it in the papers, that the sorority members had even attempted to reach her by phone.

The Associated Press dutifully reported the apology. It also reported Jean's reversal of the long distance charges, so that it cost the chapter $6.25 to have its feelings soothed.

At a later date, when the contretemps was discussed without malice or hilarity at Hollywood hearths, opinion was always divided as to what had prompted Jean to telephone Fayetteville collect. Chronic knockers insisted she was ignorant, or so confused by family and finances that she could not have added a double column of ten numbers. Champions swore that to make the girls of Pi Beta Phi bear the cost of talking with the star was a clever ploy Jean had used as the final reason for demoting Marino from her financial manager to her mother's kept man.

That Jean should charge him with failure to advise her of the impropriety of collect calls so astonished Marino that, for the first time in the memory of his acquaintances, he was speechless. To have charged him with waste and spoilage of her assets, with gambling, extravagant indulgences, ridiculous investments which had put Marino on major sucker lists in the United States, Canada and Mexico—these Marino could have understood. But to have Jean go to the bank and inform the officers that his signature was no longer to be honored was the grossest, most damaging insult. A more headstrong man would have abandoned Jean and her mother to the fates they deserved, Marino told some new drinking cronies. But he understood women and was not surprised by their lack of character and appreciation. He would stand by patiently until called upon for assistance.

"They'll need me." He spoke loudly enough for most people in the bar to hear him. "Just wait and see."

Arthur met with Jean, kissed her in truce, and agreed that financially she was a foundering wreck, but not beyond salvage. The house would have to be sold furnished, and Arthur instructed the brokers to advertise the house as "Glamor Star's New Ancestral Mansion For Sale." The closest computation Jean could arrive at was that the house, furnishings and added improvements amounted to a hundred thousand dollars, but only the antique furniture had been paid for in cash. All the articles that Mama had bought because she could not resist a good bargain were sold as a unit to an auctioneer for a little more than storage charges and the cost of cartage. The house was now publicly advertised at an asking price of a hundred and fifty thousand dollars. Mama and Marino were given a combined allowance of a thousand dollars a month, payable bi-monthly; merchants and restaurateurs were advised that Jean would not be responsible for anything charged by her parents, and plans were made to get Jean free from litigation, so that legal fees and retainers could be eliminated from her expenses.

Although the outflow of money was dammed, it was at best a temporary arrangement. Jean still owed more than sixty thousand dollars on the house and new furnishings, and she still had to maintain the house, two automobiles and the

household staff. By the most charitable of estimates, Marino
had squandered and lost $85,000. Jean's gross annual salary
was $143,000, a sum that rolled sonorously off the tongue, but
her savings account had less than a thousand dollars in it.

"Cry in your swimming pool," Kay Mulvey advised Jean.
"That'll give you perspective."

"Mama and Marino don't talk to me when I come home,"
Jean complained.

Kay shrugged. "Isn't that what you always wanted?"

Although Mayer could not find anything to criticize in
China Seas, he still refused to congratulate Jean because of
her stupidity in telephoning fine American college girls collect.
For several days after the Pi Beta Phi telephone comedy Mayer
wondered aloud if Jean was worthy of the cover of *Time.*
Cautiously, he suggested that Garbo or Crawford might be
better choices, but the New York office advised him not to
tamper with the magazine's reporter assigned to write Jean's
biography.

Strickling's problem was to make *Time* swallow the Harlow legend of discovery, glamor and sex. Unbelievably, the
Time man bought the myth of Jean reporting to work in a
limousine driven by Marino in uniform and the story of Ben
Lyon's discovery of Jean as a spectator on the set of *Hell's
Angels* and his suggestion to Howard Hughes that she replace
Greta Nissen. Other stars on the MGM lot were envious, even
outraged that Jean had been chosen for honor by *Time,* and it
became a police problem to keep the tattlers and malcontents
disciplined and dumb.

To determine whether Jean could work with other leading men of rugged appearance, it was decided to give her the
lead in *Riff-Raff* opposite Spencer Tracy, whose stage reputation was secure, but who needed an important sexual exposure
to quicken the pulsebeat of ladies in the audience. Tracy
would play a conceited fisherman, and Jean would be a
beauteous wage slave in a tuna cannery. It would be Jean's

misfortune to marry Tracy, bear his child, and, as a final sacrifice, go to jail for her husband. To lend reality to this farrago about her labors in the cannery, Jean exchanged her standard platinum wig for one of light brown, but the simple dresses worn by a girl who worked dockside would assure the audience that the superstructure had not been altered. Once again, she would not be called upon to act. (Neither, apparently, was Tracy. In its review of the film in January, 1936, *Variety* criticized his performance as being "just this side of a psychopathic case," and queried: "What has a tuna fisherman got to be conceited about?")

Meanwhile, Arthur had given her some confidence that she might see economic solvency within a year. The studio, she was told, would do everything possible to soft-pedal *Time's* treatment of the Bern affair—although it had to be mentioned in a news magazine. So Jean, feeling better, flew for a solitary vacation to a dude ranch in the McCloud River district some 250 miles north of San Francisco. There she rested, slept late under sedation, rode trails that kept her out of the sun, read, attempted to think positively and succeeded so well that she refused to read the special delivery letters from Mama. The ranch was in a valley miles from the nearest telephone line, which also pleased Jean; her recent misadventure had made her suspicious of Bell's invention.

When Jean returned to Los Angeles at the end of July she felt well and rested, and as she disembarked from the United Airlines plane in Burbank, she was so pleased to see William Powell, she managed to be tolerant of her mother. Powell kissed Jean and she returned the affection, but she hastily told the reporters that they knew as much as she about any plans she had for another marriage, and whether such plans included Powell. She added that it was a little early to discuss marriage, because she was still in the interlocutory phase of her divorce. However, she would not deny her romantic interest in a certain handsome, debonair and talented man.

Time tied its August 19 cover and story about Jean to its cinema section, where two introductory paragraphs rated the new crop of pictures the major studios were going to release for the fall season. Paramount was riding DeMille's *The Crusades* and RKO was banking on Booth Tarkington's *Alice Adams,* with Katherine Hepburn, Fred MacMurray, Hedda Hopper and a Hollywood ending designed to bring in the customers. Marion Davies would be seen in *Page Miss Glory,* with Cosmopolitan unique in that it did not care if its movie showed a profit. Charlie Chaplin would be seen on an assembly line in *Modern Times,* Fred Astaire and Ginger Rogers would dance in *Top Hat,* Will Rogers, recently deceased, would sail in *Steamboat Round the Bend* and Jean would take a longer but more familiar and exciting voyage in *China Seas.*

Familiar as the theme and principals of MGM's sex and he-man stock company might be, the picture had been advertised for two months on billboards all over the United States, and if there were moviegoers uncaring of rough stuff, romance and sex, the advertising mentioned that the film had cost a million dollars; certainly anything that expensive was worth seeing. For the snobs and penny-pinchers who refused to go to the movies but still wanted to know what was going on, *Time* noted that in *China Seas*:

> . . . . All the action takes place on, in or near the *Kin Lung,* bound from Hongkong to Singapore. Experienced cinemaddicts need not be told who is on board the *Kin Lung.* It is the same hardy little group of characters who have been regularly encountered in railroad depots, country inns, trains, cross-country buses and every other public place except a comfort station for the past four years: the bad girl with the heart of gold; the dipsomaniac writer; the hero pining for his lost love who makes her appearance in time's nick;

the shady financier; the cuckold with his wife and her dishonest lover and all the rest. However, in *China Seas* this familiar crew has a new and entertaining bag of tricks to display.

China Doll (Jean Harlow), in defiance of the Legion of Decency, has apparently been the mistress of Captain Gaskell (Clark Gable) for six years.

The rest of the article was devoted to Jean as "the foremost U.S. embodiment of sex appeal," an emphasis which pleased everyone but the subject and other stars of her sex. Nor was Jean delighted with the emphasis placed upon her mother as the guiding genius and mentor responsible for her elevation to stardom. The story had everything to make her sick: rich-Cinderella elements of her canned biography; the mention that at a recent party where she had made a bright remark, the person to whom she was speaking had asked, "Who did you hear say that?"; and the smooth account of the Bern affair, which reported that her second husband had been called by his friends "a motion picture Christ."

"What friends?" Jean demanded after she had burned a dozen copies of the magazine in the incinerator. "A motion picture Christ!" she harangued her cook, personal maid and chauffeur. "The next thing we know people'll be saying that Paul had disciples! Maybe blackmailers, but no disciples!" She paused, bit down on her tongue, and waved her arms as if she wished to erase from the memory of her household staff what she had just said.

"Doesn't Jean look lovely on the cover?" Mama said as she entered the sun room and invited the household help to admire her divine daughter in revealing negligee, feather boa and come-hither look. Jean was seated on a large quilted chair backed by a thick round pillow, which did resemble a throne of love. Disgusted, Jean returned to the studio, where she spent most of the morning counting her lines in the *Riff-Raff* script to determine if she was getting her fair share of dialogue.

Later, rereading the magazine article in her dressing room, she voiced her approval of one paragraph in which the writer had noted: "If there is a fly in the scented ointment of Jean Harlow's current celebrity, it is her occasional dissatisfaction with the character which her appearance and her mother, by a sort of conspiracy of nature and circumstance, have built up for her." But the article had also mentioned that she was good-natured and had a good sense of humor, and everyone who had called her that day, including William Powell, had thought the article a good one.

She was about to telephone Powell and ask him to take her for a drive when the phone rang. The receptionist at the main desk informed her that a man claimed to have an appointment with her.

"He says his name is Smith and he's from Arkansas," the receptionist said carefully.

"Send him over," Jean said. "I'm waiting."

She used the minute to wash her face and run a comb through her hair. The private detective she had employed to get evidence of adultery against Marino deserved to see her as a woman important enough for the cover of *Time*.

Chapter Twenty-two

So energetic was Jean's approach to her *Riff-Raff* role that everyone associated with this documentary of love, labor and tuna was convinced of her enthusiasm for the part. But what made her study her lines until she could deliver them without fault was a determination to get through the day's shooting early to rendezvous with Mr. Smith of Arkansas and hear his latest report. Marino was careless, and tailing him was an amateur assignment, Mr. Smith reported. Whenever Jean wanted him to close in with camera and witnesses, she just had to say the word.

Although Jean wanted to trap Marino in the hay, it had to be at a time when all the circumstances were in proper conjunction: Marino and Mama had to quarrel bitterly about his seeing other women; Mama had to feel disgusted and humiliated; the news had to be relayed to Jean that Marino was entertaining at night; the assignation had to be in a shabby hotel or apartment from which Marino could not escape when Jean and the private detective pulled the raid; Mama had to be persuaded that she had to go along and see Marino's unfaithfulness; and finally, the woman with Marino had to be an unattractive two-bit whore, to keep Mama from forgiving Marino's eye for beauty. Of course, it would help if the girl trapped with Marino became vulgar and cursed Mama, or even tried to bust her one. And if Marino could be trapped in surroundings so seedy that they would belie his fastidiousness and claims to nobility, the humiliation would make him easier to handle.

At last Mr. Smith telephoned Jean that all the unities appeared to be in chime, and she remembered with glee that at breakfast Mama had used strong language to describe Marino.

"I'm getting fed up with that creature," Mama had admitted after he had been gone all night. "I know he's with another woman."

"Then do something about it," Jean suggested.

"Exactly what?"

"Find him with the woman," Jean said from behind the newspaper, to make it appear as if she were cruelly indifferent to her mother's dolor.

"All the money I've lavished on him," Mama continued. "All the affection—"

Jean belched in her fist and rose from the table. "I'm going," she announced with formal politeness. "If you're gonna cry so that everyone'll be sure to ask you questions, don't bother coming over to the set today."

"If I could lay my hands on that man! If I could just find him with another woman!"

When Mr. Smith telephoned Jean late that afternoon, Mama was in the dressing room and still angry with her errant husband. At the raid Mama was in the vanguard, right behind Mr. Smith as he entered the seedy hotel on Figueroa Street. The woman in bed was a Mexican tart who spoke no English beyond the four-letter words, but a good slap in the mouth by Mr. Smith reduced the frightened girl to a lumpy outline under the gray sheets. Photographs were taken, Mama identified Marino before witnesses as her husband, and Jean admitted he was her stepfather. Marino smiled, shrugged and invited the detectives and photographer to help themselves to drinks from the bottle on the dresser.

"If you'll leave I'll get dressed," Marino said in dismissal. "But I'll be home later to talk business."

"You heard that," Jean said to the detectives.

"You want us to shove him around on account of he threatened you?" Mr. Smith inquired. "But if you ask me, I'd give him a couple of bucks so he can pay the bum. And don't let him in the house. Just dump his clothes and a couple of suitcases on the lawn."

Several days later Marino appeared at the house and forced a French window, because all the locks had been changed, and politely informed Jean and Mama that he was there to discuss his share of their community property.

"That's simple," Jean said after a good laugh. "You keep your gold mines and treasure maps, Marino. You can also keep all the companies you've promoted. We'll manage to get along with what we have."

"If only you were as funny on the screen," Marino continued quietly. "I want fifty thousand dollars."

"You're crazy!" Jean shouted.

"No, you are," Marino corrected her. "For arguing with me and losing even more of my good will than you already have. Good will is very important in the industry."

Mama ignored Jean's command to remain seated and walked toward her husband. "Meaning exactly what?" she asked haughtily.

"That I was devoted to the two of you. That I humbled myself by dressing as a chauffeur—"

"You know that's a lot of crap!" Jean interrupted. "That never happened!"

"Now you're calling *Time* a liar," Marino replied. Of the three principals, he was the calmest and most assured. "A man of my background and capabilities playing chauffeur. But I did it," he insisted. "And after we got Jean started—"

"—we?" Jean screamed. "You didn't do a—"

"—on the road to fame and fortune, instead of giving my investments and interest the care they deserved I still had to devote the major part of my time to guiding your career and keeping you out of trouble." Now Marino stood and Mama tripped over her mules as she retreated. "Although I couldn't keep you completely out of trouble, because no one would help me, I kept lots of it out of the papers. I didn't pick a figure out of a hat," Marino was solemn. "Fifty thousand is a reasonable, very conservative figure."

"Just what did you keep out of the papers?" she asked.

"Your running away to San Berdoo," Marino replied. "How your dear mother—whom I still love—and I found you in bed with that cabdriver in San Francisco. How you were holed up in cheaper hotels than the one you found me in the other day. But to return to something you really don't like—the Bern affair. Don't you think my helping you put across your fake suicide is worth something?"

"Fake suicide?" Mama raised her head. "What're you talking about, Marino?"

Speech struggled with sounds until Jean beat her temples with both fists. "It was your idea!" she screamed at Marino. "Your idea, you filthy bastard!"

"That should cost you another thousand," Marino said. "And then there's that big secret Landau dared you to tell me. I don't know what it is, but it had something to do with Bern. Right?" He smiled, quite pleased with himself because Jean had poured herself a drink and completely missed the glass. "I've got some ideas and if I told them to people—well, you'd have to deny them, Jean, and tell them what really happened. Either way, the investigation would be opened up again."

Jean held the glass with both hands and brought it to her lips. Finished, she replaced the glass on the commode and crossed slowly to stand behind her mother. She stared at Marino, but his eyes did not waver or blink; defeated, she raised both hands.

"I haven't got fifty thousand," she said. "But I told Mama we were going to give you ten. Ask her."

"It's true," Mama swore quickly. In truth, she had persuaded Jean to give Marino five thousand, but the situation was too explosive to quibble about a mere five thousand more, especially since it was less than Jean earned in two weeks. "We'd agreed to give you ten thousand dollars. We were going to tell you as soon as you came over."

"Which is why you had all the locks changed," Marino agreed with mock solemnity. "I'd like to pack," he said after a glance at his watch. "I'm not going to contest the divorce or say anything about certain things Mama Jean likes and certain things about you, Jean. Not unless I have to. When do I get the fifty thousand?"

"I'll speak to Arthur," Jean said. "Now hurry and get out."

Marino nodded, then cleared his throat. "Of course"—he looked soulfully at his wife—"there could be a smaller payment and a reconciliation."

"Nothing doing." Jean pressed her nails into her mother's shoulder. "Mama Jean and me—we could learn to live with a phony and a free-loading bum who runs around with other women. But a blackmailer's something else again. I'll tell Pops you're going to call him and he should see you."

"Call him while I'm packing," Marino said. He looked around the lovely room, stared at Mama and stepped forward to offer her his hand. "It had to end sometime." His voice was low and strangely sad. "But I wish you didn't have to find me in such a lowdown place."

Arthur threatened, then negotiated, then settled for thirty-two thousand dollars, which Marino took in old fives and tens. On September 9, Mama filed unoriginal charges of cruelty against Marino: that he used violent language, had a harsh temper and delighted in embarrassing her in the presence of friends. The charges were similar to those Jean had filed against Harold Rosson. In her detailing of specifics Mama swore that on numerous occasions Marino had abused and threatened her, the servants and other members of the household; that he had flown into rages whenever she shopped for a dress or two, although he spent prodigally on his own raiment; and that he had frequently caused her anguish and humiliation in public places, particularly restaurants, where he created scenes over food and service.

At September's end Jean accompanied her mother to the courtroom of Judge Elliott Craig, who had recently heard the actress in her own recital of suffering. In this old-home-week setting Mama was divorced from Marino Bello, whom the newspapers described as a "mysterious, mustached man, owner of several mines." Because Mrs. Bello did not petition for a division of property, Marino kept every one of his mines. Mama was packed off to Catalina for a rest.

Jean finished *Riff-Raff* at the end of October and was in such good spirits that she didn't care that George Lewis, a columnist for the Los Angeles *Post-Record*, devoted some of his cinematters column to a spoof of Jean's pretensions to authorship. Lewis wrote that her novel would never be published, because it was hinted about town that Jean's ghost writer had become "nervous." In later years a manuscript novel, bound in needlepoint covers and locked with an ornamental hasp, was purchased by MGM from Mrs. Bello. *Today Is Tonight*, coauthored by Jean Harlow and Carey Wilson, was never produced.

Jean dismissed the matter with a laugh, because she was going to star in *Wife vs. Secretary*, scheduled to begin production on November 25. Myrna Loy would play the other woman, and Jean's platinum sheen would again be set against Gable's dark frame. Coupled with this was really good news: Nat Levine of Republic Studios had agreed to purchase the Beverly Glen house and furnishings for $125,000, giving her a net profit of $15,000, which she pledged to Landau. Free of her major burdens—Marino and the house—Jean intended to sell both cars, pay the household help their salaries and reward them with generous gifts, then camp out in a smaller furnished house which Mama could manage with the minimum staff of a live-in cook, day maid and laundress.

So delighted with events that she just had to use the pool, which she was soon going to be rid of forever, Jean dove in and swam about until she was exhausted. Catching cold promptly, she had to leave the set next day and remain in bed from Wednesday through Monday, which kept her from appearing in the *Examiner's* Christmas Benefit Show for the relief of the local poor.

She was ill and uncomfortable, but happy. As she lay in her bed, a hot water bottle at her feet and an open box of chocolate rumballs at her side, she phoned William Powell and told him she wanted his help in trimming the Christmas tree. The future looked bright indeed. *Wife vs. Secretary* was going to be lots better than *Riff-Raff,* she was holding her own with Myrna Loy, the house had been sold, she was rid of Marino, and she had just told her lawyer to negotiate settlements with the insurance companies, Dorothy Milette's family and Sacramento County.

The next year—1936, when she would begin to earn $4,000 a week—was the first one she had looked forward to with pleasure since her arrival in California. She decided to ask the studio to give her the Christmas present she wanted most: a good picture with Bill Powell.

Wife vs. Secretary was finished in the middle of January, and preview reactions praised Jean's performance in a triangle that was different in design from the standard one. This time she played a sympathetic Miss Typewriter who did not raise her voice above a conversational tone even in scenes of stress, so that for once her voice was rated excellent by important reviewers. Moving from scene to scene with actual ease, neatly garbed in dresses that were not costumes, Jean handled her dialogue naturally, with such bright humor that she excited some consideration at the studio for roles other than that of a scatterbrained, goodhearted chippy. Although the three principals all profited from the intelligent script and direction, Jean enjoyed most of the psychological benefits.

Impressed by her willingness to abide by the financial arrangements she had made with him and by her insistence that she did not want to live extravagantly, no matter how much Mama bleated about position and caste, Arthur helped Jean find a two-story, semi-furnished house, quite suitable for human occupancy and available at a reasonable rent of three hundred dollars a month, on North Palm Drive in Beverly Hills. Vetoing all pleas and suggestions made by Mama that they buy another house, Jean would only agree to keep the Pierce-Arrow and the Cadillac, although she felt it was ridiculous for her to drive the Cadillac limousine. Still, her studio contract provided her with the services of a chauffeur, and a point was stretched to make a uniformed man available to drive Mrs. Bello—at times become strangely stubborn because of the recent *Time* article which had presented her as a forceful personality—to the market, to the hairdresser and to a pier if she wanted to fish.

In the little trips Mama took to the suburbs, she might come upon a what-not or muffin stand, an ironstone vase or Derby teapot, and Jean indulged these minor purchases. By April, when Jean realized that her mother's interest in antiques was sincere, she hired a full-time chauffeur and encouraged her mother to take more and longer trips to search for the china and silver that would be her stock if she ever opened her own antique shop. These trips kept Mama away from the studio, which made them worth the five or six hundred dollars a month she frittered away.

Meanwhile, Jean's lawyer convinced the insurance companies concerned with the Bern policies of the wisdom of inexpensive compromise. The Milette heirs—a sister and a brother-in-law—were encouraged to press their claims, which compelled Sacramento County to withdraw its hand. And when the insurance companies offered to pay $10,000, the heirs agreed to a settlement of two thousand dollars to be divided between them. The remaining eight thousand dollars was given to the attorneys for legal fees.

How much more Jean had to pay her attorneys was something she and Landau would not divulge, but the major objective had been accomplished: Jean had freed herself of all legal involvements and had fought to the finish against strangers whom she had never met and did not want to meet, but who, she believed, had used bigamy to make themselves some money. She did not care whether Bern had ever been married to Dorothy Milette or whether their common-law relationship had validity; what made her angry was the lack of principle that made supposedly Christian men and women willing to shake hands with the devil before they dropped one of his coins into the collection plate.

Although she no longer wished to have any dealings with the law, Jean was advised she now had the opportunity to build a sizable estate, and that it would be wise to petition the courts to make Jean Harlow her legal name. She agreed, and on July 1, 1936, she made a two-minute appearance before Superior Judge Douglas L. Edmonds, answered brief questions briefly and laughed with delight before she replied that she knew of no pending litigation in which she was involved. The actress' screen name was made her legal name, and as she left the courtroom in her blue silk print dress, silver fox fur and chamois accessories, she posed and chatted pleasantly with photographers and her public. The goddess walked upon her earth and found it good.

People close to Jean congratulated her, because the newspapers had devoted little space to the insurance and name change, and not one local paper had made scandalous mention of Paul's suicide. She had prayerfully wished on every occasion during the past holiday season that 1936 would be a happy year, and it appeared that her wishes had been heard. And now another of her wishes was about to come true: the studio had announced that after Jean completed *Suzy,* with Cary Grant and Franchot Tone, she would be rewarded with a six- or seven-week vacation, then cast in *Libeled Lady,* with Spencer Tracy, Myrna Loy and—William Powell.

For about ten days Jean divided her time between the golf courses in and around Los Angeles, where she made her shots and walked from green to green under an umbrella, and the beaches close to Kay Mulvey's house, where she discovered that raw eggs mixed with sand and salt water gave consistency to the batter and made for a better mud pie. Evenings she spent with Powell, usually at the Wilsons, attempting to follow the animated conversations about movies as an art form, wealth as a handicap and how movies could be ever so improved if their control were given to writers and directors.

Although MGM had developed the most highly polished films in the world, the gloss and sheen were too evident, the actors too well scrubbed, the treatment of themes too two-dimensional to assure the audience that what it observed and enjoyed was not raw life with its third but unpleasant dimension of depth. Contrary to the broader policy of some of the other studios—especially Warner Brothers, which led in the production of contemporary, social and controversial films with *Wild Boys of the Road* (1933), *Massacre* (1933), *Black Fury* (1935) and *The Black Legion* (1936)—MGM still aimed its films at the ladies who lunched in Schrafft's and occupied the greatest number of seats in first-run theaters. That women tended increasingly to control family finances was noted by the Lynds in *Middletown in Transition* (1937); thus the tastes of the good, upperclass ladies and young matrons, the dreams and ladylike sexual sublimations they preferred, were of greatest importance to Mayer and his staff.

Yes, Mayer was willing to admit if cornered, the world

and the United States were in trouble; but why should movies be compelled to document and enlarge upon the mistakes of politicians, the protests of malcontents, the obsessive pessimism of men who only saw the world in terms of decay? Films were a business, and forty years of hard profit-and-loss experience proved that people went to the movies to escape, not to be reminded of their troubles. If isolated pockets of masochists enjoyed seeing their problems larger than life, and if there were producers mercenary enough to pander to such an illness, as a man of charity, one who refused to judge his contemporaries, Mayer was willing to leave to venal producers the entertainment of the socially sick. MGM was a studio devoted to entertainment, the average American woman demanded the most entertainment, and it was her support of movies that made it possible to create so much happiness, diversion and escape in the two dimensional perfumed suburb visible on the screen.

Made eloquent by experience and unencumbered by theory which provided employment for brain trusters but wasn't worth a nickel in the marketplace, Mayer bustled about the studio (appearing, it seemed, from secret trapdoors) to make his point again and again: the moving picture filmed a world of dreams, a world of escape, a world where the viewer could take part in the scenes and delights of Arcadia with its country clubs, moonlit terraces, luxurious bathrooms, and gentlemen and ladies always dressed for dinner and love play.

Mayer and his ranking executives (even Thalberg, now out of favor) disliked the popular contemporary authors, their typewriters atop garbage cans, who wrote not about America's greatness but her faults. They were in agreement that Sherwood Anderson, Theodore Dreiser, Upton Sinclair, James T. Farrell, Albert Halper, Erskine Caldwell and John Dos Passos had made disagreeable discoveries about American life which should never have been described or published. Sinclair Lewis had presented a dreadfully awry American portrait for all the foreign world to see and gloat over, and it was incumbent upon

MGM to balance the damning presentations of *Main Street* and *Babbitt* with Andy Hardy, the pessimism of *Arrowsmith* with the passionate optimism of Dr. Kildare. And to confound the charge that American cruelty to minorities could also be practiced against domestic animals, the studio writers barked out warm, kind screenplays for Lassie. A decade later Columbia used Dagwood as the breadwinner of its family films, but most men in the audience preferred to identify with Lewis Stone rather than Arthur Lake, so the Hardy saga was much more popular and profitable.

For understandable reasons Jean loved *My Man Godfrey*, in which William Powell played a man who, ruined by the crash, becomes a clever, irreverent bum. She badgered Landau to persuade Mayer or Thalberg that the writers of the picture be assigned to do a similar story in which she could star with Powell. Perhaps the roles could be reversed! Jean could be the young head of a banking house or ranch wiped out in the depression, or her father could have headed the enterprise and been ruined and reduced to sitting silently in a wheelchair; victims of adversity, they could have been brought down to living in a Hooverville. Powell could be a charming playboy, squiffy at the wheel of his Packard, who swerved in time to avoid hitting a dog, cat, newsboy or old lady, and ran off the road to crash into the side of the tin hut erected by Jean to shelter her poor father—with no one hurt. Any writer could take it from there. The story kernel was suggested to Mayer and rejected by him with oaths, but the theme of the bright young woman dedicated to restoring the inherited fortune dissipated by her foolish father became the economic theme of *Saratoga*.

Even if only for ninety minutes, the movies were an escape, a refreshing dream, and Mayer was determined to keep them always spic and span, glamorous and pleasant. This was a moral judgment that he imposed upon the studio as his conclusion of what was best for the studio's earnings and the national health, and people unable to see the dream world of films in Mayer's focus could go produce elsewhere. *Libeled Lady* was about newspapers, millionaires and good American hotels in foreign lands; all of these were fun and there was nothing wrong with fun. In these dark days of monumental mismanagement and costly governmental blunders, the country needed laughs to enable the pioneer spirit to endure realities, and as long as Mayer held the baton, none of the pop concerts programmed by MGM were going to have discords in their scores.

Jean's interest in subject matter was without social qualification; she wanted no more than to be given roles that would give her status in an industry that discussed her abilities with snorts of derision and sighs of desire. Although Jean was intimidated by the cool assurance of Myrna Loy and her flair for handling gags and bright dialogue with equal aplomb, Jean enjoyed working with Powell; but she did not accept the picture wholeheartedly because in the final reels the romantic arias were whispered in the moonlight by William and Myrna, and once again she was paired with rough-and-ready Spencer Tracy, with whom she conducted a rowdy cinema love affair that identified her as having peeled for the marriage bed without ever having heard the peal of marriage bells.

Although she ended up with Tracy in the picture, once the lights were dimmed at the end of each day of shooting and make-up was washed off, Jean usually had dinner with Powell. A year before Walter Winchell had published in his column notice of a letter from Arthur Landau which denied a marriage between Jean and Powell, although several of Winchell's "keyhole keeks" had told him the knot had been tied on September 18. Privately Jean wished the rumor had been true, but she was grateful that Kay Mulvey helped her get a break with reporters and that items about Powell and her were being written tastefully, or as tastefully as they could be.

To increase her popularity rather than notoriety with reporters, Jean made glamor her business and appeared in

338

high fashion for interviews and photographs. Adrian's creations for Jean were the delight of the fan magazines, which had proliferated during the Thirties. Jean discovered, to her surprise, that not only had her hair style and color retained its popularity, but that her recent preference for silver foxes had had a salutary impact on the retail fur market. Shoe manufacturers blessed her loyal preference for the high spike heel. Powell encouraged Jean to dress her part and to keep informality a private matter.

Her interest in Powell and the full schedule of work and fashion kept Jean out of the sun until an afternoon in August, when she engaged a seaplane, flew to Catalina and sunned herself on the beach. By nightfall, when she was returned to the mainland, she was feverish. Some hours later she began to suffer painfully as second-degree burns blistered her back, legs and arms so that she could neither stand, walk nor lie down. Her lips were so puffed she could not speak.

Over the insipid protests of Mama, in the throes of her religious fervor and prayers, Powell telephoned Dr. Sidney Burnap to treat the star. After the enlarged blisters were lanced and drained, Jean was sprayed with tannic acid and most of the blisters were treated with boric acid soaks to reduce the danger of infection. Elixir of aleurate was prescribed for the pain, and the sheets above Jean were held on a cradle because Dr. Burnap had decided upon the open treatment for burns. In addition to wet soaks and barbiturates, Dr. Burnap advised good sense on Jean's part. The previous summer Jean had also suffered a severe sunburn, and in the opinion of the doctor, in whom Jean had had a worshipful confidence ever since he had removed her appendix, her days of posing in direct sunlight for swim photographs were over. Approving of a lovely shot of Jean in a black tank suit which illustrated the *Examiner's* coverage of her current mishap, Dr. Burnap told the sick actress it would be best to rely on prints of this shot if other such photos of her were required.

In superstitious fear of August, which Jean insisted was one of her two worst months (the worst was September), she swore to be guided by sound medical advice. Kay Mulvey bought several more beach umbrellas, and Arthur planned to speak to Thalberg about having the studio's lighting engineer devise a cold light under which Jean could work. He would also see if the Max Factor chemists could develop invisible cosmetic creams or lotions that Jean could wear without discomfort.

But it was impossible to do away with the tradition of the outdoor photograph; there *were* scenes that had to be shot in the natural sunshine, and a series of stories filtered into the papers to the effect that Jean could not stand strong sunlight because she was an albino, which explained the color of her hair. Because she associated albinism with deformity, Jean told Arthur she wanted some new honeyblonde wigs made up by the studio, and that in future pictures she wanted her hair to be more natural in color.

A week of rest and medication enabled Jean to return to the set for the final scenes of *Libeled Lady,* which were finished on September 1, the very day Irving Thalberg caught his fatal cold. Two weeks later he was dead of pneumonia.

Mourning for Thalberg was industry-wide, but interest quickly shifted to wide speculation about the course MGM would follow now that Thalberg was gone. In recent years Thalberg had been stripped of authority; however, even though his feud with Mayer had occupied much of his creative time, his unit had still been able to complete the studio's quality films, *The Barretts of Wimpole Street* (1934) and *Mutiny on the Bounty* (1935). Thalberg films still to be completed were *The Good Earth,* with Paul Muni and Luise Rainer; *Maytime,* with the voices of Nelson Eddy and Jeanette MacDonald; and *A Day at the Races,* with the Marx Brothers. Executives assigned to these films by Thalberg were summarily removed and replaced by men whose loyalty to Mayer had never been questioned.

Then there was a decision to be made concerning the almost half a million dollars' worth of background costs for *Marie Antoinette,* a project Thalberg had been preparing for his wife. But Norma Shearer insisted she should retire from the screen, and until she had completed formal mourning and her attorneys had confirmed the continuance of her husband's financial interests in certain films he had produced, her appearance on the screen as the ill-fated French queen could not be assured. After Thalberg's financial interests were fortified against pirates and Miss Shearer had a new contract that guaranteed her the brightness of a star of first magnitude, *Marie Antoinette* got under way. This picture, with *The Good Earth,* neither of which bore his name, did more to insure Thalberg's memory than the new MGM building named after him.

Thalberg's death had also brought to a head the problem of what films MGM would continue to make. Despite the payment to Bioff and Browne, government-sanctioned union organization and collective bargaining had become unshakeable facts of life. Production costs were also on the increase, because the national stockpile of manufactures had at last been depleted to force prices upward. Thus the studio's New York offices saw no reason for expensive films when the stars under contract could be used in pictures of modest budget. Most of the public was still willing to accept happy pictures about happy people and their happy problems happily resolved through happy sex, happier love and the afflatus of marriages made in heaven.

Mayer agreed with Nicholas Schenck that economies could be effected and that as long as the studio had the stars it would always be able to sell its product without difficulty. But Mayer, because of pride of ownership, wanted to see big, expensive, spectacular films introduced by the cameoed lion. The death of Thalberg also made it imperative to search the palace for signs of defection, to rid the studio of men mean enough to say that it was a pity Thalberg had died when Mayer was older and more deserving of a state funeral. Things were not serene on the lots of MGM.

Jean discovered that her unlucky September month had stretched itself into October, and that in the autumn of the year Mama was becoming more difficult to control.

Since the divorce, Mama had become increasingly peculiar and had spent more and more of her time walking about with her copy of *Science and Health* and a leather-bound copy of the *Time* issue that had featured Jean on the cover. Too many of her actions and responses bore the unmistakable stamp of neuroses which expressed themselves in illogical, uncontrollable impatience, an inability to assess reasonable values to details of the household routine and utter inability to correlate and face facts.

Jean felt she could cope with moroseness and bad temper, with sudden tears and sudden prayers, but what disturbed her was the growing feeling that her mother now believed every verse of the biographical myth created by imaginative writers. Even worse, she believed that Jean, unmoved by her maternal sacrifices and dedication, was determined to treat her as if she did not exist and had never sacrificed her own talents and ambitions to guide her daughter to international fame.

Mama had her own scrapbooks, and they were thick with articles that lauded her showmanship, her brilliant understanding of publicity, her class and beauty. And they all attested to the love she lavished on her daughter. Why, there were articles that praised her youthful appearance, writers who told their readers how Jean and she looked like sisters rather than mother and daughter. She had nursed her daughter through childhood illness and heartbreak, had endured a separation until Jean had become ill with polio, and then had returned to Kansas City to pray her well. During Jean's adolescence she had been both friend and mother to the girl, sympathetic, understanding and all-forgiving. When Jean had failed to get anywhere in pictures, Mama had thought of buying the limousine and uniform, had been willing to sacrifice her jewelry to buy the fine feathers Jean wore to impress the casting directors; she had brought Jean to the attention of an important agent and persuaded him to represent her unknown daughter.

Even when Landau had lost confidence in Jean, her mother's dedication had never wavered. She had arranged interviews, coached Jean in the social graces and bright sayings, helped stage her personal appearances, taught her how to walk, speak, comb her hair and act. Until Jean had become stubbornly blind about her reputation, Mama's guidance had helped make Jean a great lady. But now her ungrateful daughter refused to take her to Washington next year for another President's Birthday Ball. And what was worse, Jean kept speaking to disreputable people who, after they were arrested, always offered her as a character witness.

"You could have been killed," Mama said as she waved a copy of the *Herald* at Jean. "It's all in here how that man slugged a woman with a whiskey bottle."

"They think he slugged her," Jean hedged. "I read the paper. He was arrested by the cops for drunkenness and vagrancy."

"Paul Anthony Taylor," Mrs. Bello read from the article. "Quite a name. The police found a note in his pocket with your name and our address on it. And he admitted that you were his next victim."

Jean stretched out on a sofa and buried her head under a pillow. "Let me alone."

"No you don't." Mama tossed the pillow across the room. "I deliberately gave the cook some hours off so we could talk. And you're going to listen." She crossed to a window for better light. Glancing several times from the paper to her daughter, she began to read in a moist, ironic style. " 'I'm in love with Jean Harlow,' he was quoted by officers as declaring. 'I want to meet and win her over. She's the most wonderful creature I have ever seen—and I've seen a lot of 'em. Miss Harlow was very kind to me,' he added. 'I talked to her for about twenty minutes about the films, psychology and astrology.' " Mama lowered the paper to accuse her daughter. "Why don't you talk to me about astrology and psychology? Why don't you talk to me about religion, which would be good for the little soul you have left?"

"Let up on me," Jean said. "I don't know how he got on the lot. He said hello, and because he was dressed in work clothes, I said hello. You know I always talk to people. I can't help it if some of them are nuts."

"How do I know you didn't take that bum to your dressing room?"

Jean sighed. "Aren't you being especially nasty today?"

"It's no more than you deserve," Mama sobbed. "I gave up my career and husband to make you famous. I submerged myself, sacrificed myself to guide you through thick and thin and this is how you pay me back! Do you know who really should be before the camera?"

"You, I suppose," Jean replied correctly.

"Yes." Mama opened *Time* to the article which she could recite almost by heart. "But the studios aren't any better than the public. Both want trash."

"My number one fan." Mockingly, Jean blew kisses at her mother. "Thank you very much."

"You're on those beautiful sets and you wear beautiful clothes," Mama wailed, ignoring Jean's sarcasm. "So you have your fill of fine things. But I have to stay in this miserable little house all day with a cook for company."

"It's a nice house," Jean said. "A good address on a good

344

block. And I'm gonna get ahead at the bank. Doesn't that mean anything to you?"

"And you won't take me to Washington and you took Marino away from me. You took him away because you couldn't stand him loving me and not you. You always wanted him but he wanted me. Do you want to know why?"

"What difference does that make? You're going to tell me anyway."

"Because I can love, really love, and you can't. I've known ecstasy and you haven't. You're a fake."

"Damn you—shut up!"

Startled by the vehemence of her daughter's reply, Mama could only stretch a hand as Jean ran from the room. Then she pursed her lips and began to read again the newspaper account of her daughter and the suspected slugger. She heard the slam of a closet door and put the paper aside as Jean returned with a polo coat across her shoulders.

"I'm going out for a drink and a bite," Jean said as she searched her purse for a set of car keys. "I'm willing to take you along."

But Mama had not heard, for she had launched into another monologue. "You've been seduced and corrupted by Jews!" Mama wept. "Landau and Bern. Mayer, even Thalberg when he was alive. You've become a sinful atheist and believe in doctors instead of Christ."

"And you've become a witch!" Jean yelled. "For your own good you oughta be locked up!"

"You'll pay for your sins," the weeping woman continued. Her hair had become undone and movements of her head scattered small pins on her lap and the chair. "You'll pay through eternity."

"An absolute witch!" Jean yelled. Then she calmed herself by breathing deeply before she shrugged wearily. "If you'll shut up, stop crying and try to be normal I'll take you with me to Washington." She paused to laugh bitterly, with wonder that they had come to this. "And maybe just like Cinderella, you'll meet the President at his Birthday Ball. And there might be a genuine prince there. Who knows?"

"Cinderella?" her mother was incredulous. "You're the Cinderella."

"Then you must be my fairy godmother," Jean said. She smiled and tried to make a joke of it.

"More than a fairy godmother. A real mother—which is something you'll never understand because you can't know motherhood."

"You really are a witch."

"A real mother," Mama continued. "So I gave up everything to give everything to you. To make you what I could've been. Cinderella appreciated what her fairy godmother did for her because she had a heart instead of a stone. And she wasn't a tramp."

"Mama!" Jean began to shake the hysterical woman. "Mama!"

"Let go of me. You're a whore in your heart, and that's why you can't be saved!"

It was dreadful, revolting to see her mother's disintegration, to be a witness to a collapse of reason and pride in a woman with a beauty of her own, now trembling and staggering about the room with loose hair and wild eyes as she called with breaking voice for Marino to return, because she missed him, loved him, needed him.

"He wanted a reconciliation." She wept with the heartbreak of a woman whose shadows, taken from her, have been replaced by realities. "He wanted to patch things up, but you said no and you made me listen to you. And now you're thinking of getting married again and I'll be alone."

Gently calling her mother by name, Jean attempted to soothe her as she reassured her that everything would be well and wonderful between them again, and that even if she did marry sometime soon, there would always be a place for Mama Jean. But right now did she want to take a trip, go back to Kansas City or New York? Paris or London for Christmas? Would she like to go to Japan or Hong Kong? Or did she want to stay at home and open her antique shop in time for the Christmas holidays? It would take a lot of work, but it could be done.

"Marino and I were in love until you came between us," Mama sobbed. "We were so happy in Chicago—until you became ill and I had to go to Kansas City to save your life."

"Fix yourself, Mama," Jean coaxed. "We'll drive to the shore for seafood. And I won't talk to strangers anymore. I promise. That guy looked like a nut and I shouldn't've talked to him. I'm sorry. Now let's go out."

"No."

"Why not? Because I'm a sinner?"

"Because you're Cinderella and I hate you for taking everything from me!" Mama screamed as she ran after Jean to catch her at the door. "But when the time comes, I won't have to wave a magic wand to take everything from you!"

Chapter Twenty-three

One subject of film making until 1940 has never been written about or analyzed in depth: the speed with which sophisticated sound films were made. From the day when Jean Harlow's contract was purchased by MGM she never appeared in a film that took more than three months to shoot. *Reckless,* with its large cast of stars, music and production numbers, was shot in twelve weeks, and *China Seas,* with its shipboard spectaculars and hundreds of extras, was completed in eight and a half. *Suzy,* another picture with songs, diversified scenes that ranged between the race track and aerial combat, songs and stellar cast, was begun on April 6, 1936, and completed its shooting schedule on May 29, 1936; *Libeled Lady* was begun on June 13, 1936, and struck its sets on September 1, 1936. *Red Dust,* begun on August 19, 1932, and seriously interrupted by Bern's suicide, was completed on October 8. But a more remarkable achievement is to be found in *Dinner at Eight,* a film with a running time of 110 minutes and a cast that included Marie Dressler, John and Lionel Barrymore, Lee Tracy, Edmund Lowe, Billie Burke, Jean Hersholt, Karen Morley, May Robson and Grant Mitchell. This important film was directed by George Cukor, who began shooting on March 16, 1933, and completed the picture the next month on April 17. *Viva Villa,* with Wallace Beery, shot on location in Mexico with a cast of thousands, was begun on October 30, 1933, and, allowing for the three major seasonal holidays, was completed on January 12, 1934.

The entire production organization at MGM had become so expert in its planning, proficient in its implementation of plans and automated in technique that rarely did a picture take more than three months for its rough cut. And MGM did not pamper its stars with long vacations between pictures; if stars were signed for forty weeks of work a year they averaged at least twenty-five weeks before the cameras and ten more in wardrobe, rehearsals and other preparations to make them ready for shooting. This old-time procedure is even more interesting when it is compared with the production and working schedules of contemporary stars and their films. *Something's Got to Give,* the uncompleted film which was begun under the direction of George Cukor (of *Dinner at Eight*) and which starred and abandoned Marilyn Monroe, closed down after an expenditure of far more than a million and a half dollars and after twelve days of shooting—two weeks and two days of work—during which only seven and a half minutes of useable film had been shot.

In the Thirties there was no confusion on the set, a minimum of pique was permitted while at work and there was no nonsense as to who was in charge of direction and production. A star was permitted, even encouraged to feign temperament after a day's work was completed, but production always demanded an honest day's performance for an honest thousand dollars. John Barrymore, after a night of roistering, would shave his face and tongue and be ready for a long day's work. Since the dismissal of D. W. Griffith and Eric von Stroheim, pictures had entered a period of assembly as automated as any to be found in an automobile plant.

Roosevelt's defeat of Alfred Landon and the *Literary Digest* rankled Mayer. Other executive producers might be pleased to send their stars to Washington for another President's Birthday Ball, but not Louis B. Mayer. If Jean Harlow and Robert Taylor wanted to appear at the event, they would do so *after* they completed their roles in *Personal Property,* a movie based on the stage play *Man in Possession.* Mayer would permit no delay in the start of their picture, nor any interruption of the shooting schedule. Pleased with himself as an absolute ruler, Mayer returned to his major problem of keeping MGM safe from taxes, unions and the U.S.A., and refused to see anyone even remotely connected with *Personal Property.*

With murmurs of defiance led by a mutinous Harlow, *Personal Property* was begun on January 4, 1937. But defiance and mutiny were replaced by long days of shooting. Through the cooperation of crew, cast and director, the picture was completed on January 21, setting some sort of record for an A-production even in an era when movies were pushed through as though on a production line. The director, Woody Van Dyke, had done what he could to speed the stars to Washington, and if *Personal Property* was not the best picture made by the director and its principals, the film was adequate to its purpose. *Variety,* in its trade review, observed "that there is a place for a boudoir story on picture screens provided the proper subtlety and smartness is employed in the telling. . . . 'Personal Property' . . . . [is] aimed for the high school trade and it hits the mark right in senior year. . . . Miss Harlow is hoydenish and coy in her own inimitable style. She wears some striking costumes which cleverly convey the ideas which the designer had in mind. There is more of Miss Harlow on display when she's all dressed up than some girls reveal in their step-ins." *Variety* did not mention that Jean's hair was no longer platinum, but it was evident that whatever shade her stage wig might be, in the public's eye she would always be the great all-American piece in the white halo.

During the last week of work on *Personal Property,* when the crew assigned to the picture had applauded the stamina of the actors, there had been no time for Jean to exercise the usual precautions she had been instructed to take against extended exposure to strong light. The emotional drive, the tension that began afresh each day, made it more difficult to induce sleep at night, even with barbiturates or alcohol. Each morning, still drugged with sleep, she had to be shaken awake, have scalding coffee poured down her throat, be assisted to the bathroom and then be helped to dress before she was driven to the studio. During the daily ride from Beverly Hills to Culver City, which Jean cursed with every turning of the wheels, Mama or a maid would massage Jean's hands and feet, rub them until they were warm, and feed Jean more hot coffee from a thermos.

Mama and Blanche Williams always had two copies of the script of *Personal Property* with them, and they used them in a game designed to raise Jean's spirits. Both copies were full shooting scripts, and Mama and Blanche would tear the pages completed the day before from one of the scripts, to reduce the thickness of the manuscript so that Jean could see how much had been done. Every day the script became thinner by comparison with the full script. Jean would arrive at the studio by seven, for dress, make-up and hair styling took a full hour, and the technicians assigned to get the Blonde Bombshell ready for the camera would be waiting with new dirty jokes Jean had to laugh at before she admitted them to her bungalow.

Surrounded by people who liked and admired her, delighted with the 150-carat star sapphire ring William Powell had given her as a Christmas present—a twenty-thousand-dollar unofficial engagement ring that Jean swore she wore even when she showered—Jean's spirits would visibly rise. Her eyes would begin to sparkle, her hands and body would move with new energy, her voice would gain strength and soon she would look stronger than anyone on the set. She would kid Van Dyke that he was getting old and limp, feel Robert Taylor's biceps and assure him that girls in the audience would squeal when he took a bath in the picture, just as men had whistled when they saw her bathe in *Red Dust*. Good-naturedly she would swear at the crew, threaten to cut their balls off and drop them in Mayer's chicken soup if they didn't do better than the day before. First she would assure them of her protection if Mayer or anyone else bawled them out for being too ambitious, then she would shout at William Daniels, the cameraman, to hurry up because she had another appointment in Washington with the President.

Lunch was ten minutes alone in her bungalow, where she nibbled on crackers and cheese and studied her lines for the afternoon. By the end of the day Jean would be completely drained, as if she had been squeezed through the rollers of a mangle, and on the drive home she would sip hot milk generously laced with rum, totter into the rented house and yell for the cook and Mama to undress her. Nude, she would slip into the bed, whose sheets had been warmed by an antique bed warmer, and an old-fashioned iron heated in the oven would be wrapped in a towel and placed at her feet. Then she would be permitted to weep and curse until she felt herself become warm, comfortable and ready for dinner. Mama and the cook would now help Jean sit erect while she drank a cup of hot bouillon, took her phenobarbital and slowly counted the remaining pages of the script still to be shot. Then she would sigh, close her eyes and nod for the bedroom lights to be dimmed.

"Jean dear, a pillow on your feet?" Mama would whisper.

"A pillow," Jean would reply. "Then you can leave me alone, please."

Mama would fix the pillow, ignore her daughter's request for privacy and sit in a far corner, praying audibly for Strength of Mind.

Two days after the picture was finished, Jean was helped by her mother into their compartment on the Santa Fé Chief. Forehead pressed against the cold glass of the window, Jean asked Mama to call the porter, because she wanted her berth made up and the little she would eat sent in on a tray. Jean seldom left her berth between Los Angeles and Chicago, and only between New York City and Washington did she feel well enough to leave her compartment to lunch in the dining car.

So weary she could only nod at the flowers, candy and trays of hors d'oeuvres in her suite at the Mayflower Hotel, Jean greeted the press, begged to be excused, rested for a full day and saw only an MGM representative from New York and four officials of the March of Dimes. Sleeping every moment that she could, Jean spent most of her waking hours either in the tub or on the telephone to Hollywood and permitted Mama to do what she pleased about her own interviews and her shopping trips to Garfinkle's and the quaint antique shops in Georgetown.

Three days before the ball, on a particularly cold and unpleasant morning, Jean was driven to Annapolis for a visit to the Naval Academy. The following day, January 29, she made twenty-two personal appearances throughout metropolitan Washington, Alexandria and Mount Vernon. She put in brief appearances at other national monuments, including both houses of Congress, where she signed autographs for the solons. Chosen by his peers to welcome the actress was Senator Robert H. Reynolds from the Tar Heel State, who reluctantly agreed to buss the actress for the benefit of the assembled press agents and photographers.

"This gentleman doesn't seem to want to go through with it," Jean said as Reynolds hung back.

A Southerner and gentleman, Reynolds accepted the challenge, kissed Jean smartly without dropping his cigarette—which he considerately removed from his mouth to hold in his right hand—and bowed at the laughter and applause.

"How was it, Miss Harlow?" she was asked by a member of the National Press Club.

Jean plunged herself into deep thought and tightened

her lips, because she had just been skewered by a stab of pain. At last she smiled. "If that's the best a senator can do I'm glad I didn't get to the Cabinet."

The senator, who had some reputation as a wit, bowed gallantly, and then not so gallantly observed that Miss Harlow's kiss "didn't compare with a North Carolina kiss."

The next day, January 30, Jean and Robert Taylor, both of them feeling grippy, met the press and notables at a ten o'clock breakfast in the Mayflower dining room, but the bar had opened at nine, to whet the appetites of the hundred and thirty invited guests. After Jean and Robert made their grand entrances, both played their parts with such fervor that no critic could find fault. Throughout the lengthy, tedious, too noisy breakfast Jean would have given a hundred dollars for a drink. Although her small feet were large blocks of ice, she substituted coffee for stronger stuff, and she managed to control her visits to the ladies' lounge because she was aware that certain invited newspapermen would use anything as the peg for a funny column.

She was forced to turn down many requests for her presence at public buildings, and the Army felt slighted because Jean would not visit Fort Myers, but she pleaded a woman's excuse—that it took her just hours and hours to dress. Finally, she returned to her suite, where she buried herself under a welter of blankets which could not stop her teeth from chattering. The ball demanded that she appear in a sleeveless dress and low decolletage, and as Jean made herself ready for the evening she told Mama that if tradition had not denied her a brassiere, she would have worn one with fur-lined cups.

Everyone who danced with Jean that night remarked at her cold hands, and repeatedly she explained that they were signs of a warm heart. Taylor himself was chilled, and both stars longed for the mildness of Southern California. The Birthday Ball was distributed among seven Washington hotels, and at each of these she had to be bright, gay and cooperative.

At last, after dozens of dances where she was a mechanical partner, after hundreds of pleasantries to which she responded automatically, after a goodly number of feels, pats and pinches, which she endured, after—it seemed—several thousand dance programs she had signed, the ball ended, and Jean could leave. But not before she had shaken hands with and kissed every musician and all the ushers lined up for this little attention.

Dress and all, Mama put Jean into bed and assured her there was no need to call the hotel doctor. The human body was spiritual, not material, and there was no need for a thermometer, a doctor or his medicines as long as the Mind was able to concentrate on Christ and the spiritual truth of man's being.

"Why, do you know what Mrs. Eddy did when she lived in Lynn, Massachusetts?" Mama asked her shivering daughter. "Mrs. Eddy saw a man sitting on the sidewalk, so crippled and misshapen that his knees almost touched his nose. And she walked up to him and, with her lips almost touching those of the poor cripple, whispered 'God loves you.' Do you know what happened, Jean?"

"He got up and walked," Jean said. "Are my lips blue?"

"He did!" Mama exclaimed. "Now that should give you courage. Do you want me to read the eighth chapter of Mark to you? Verses twenty-two to twenty-six?"

"I'm not blind!" Jean wailed. "Just freezing to death! Call room service for a pint of whiskey and all the hot water bottles they've got in the hotel."

"You haven't any fever," Mama replied as she stroked her daughter's head.

"Of course not, you nut." Jean was now in tears. "I'm freezing to death."

By the time Jean, Mama and Robert Taylor transferred to their compartments on the Santa Fé Chief in Chicago, a good part of the United States had been struck by the influenza epidemic. A discerning newsman for the Chicago *Tribune* took it upon himself to tell the stationmaster that the Platinum Blonde looked very pukey, the observation was relayed to the conductor of the Chief, and when the crack train arrived at Albuquerque, Jean and her mother were confined to their berths and ministered to by nurses, despite Mama's continued protests. Robert Taylor had a miserable cold, but he was ambulatory and able to leave the Chief without assistance when it arrived in Los Angeles. Jean and her mother had to be helped into the studio limousine by studio guards in mufti, identified as close friends.

If Jean thought she had discomfited Mayer by completing her picture assignment in three weeks, Mayer now made the most of his turn. Since the election of "that man" to the White House the climate of Washington had changed in every way; the studio stars had made the eastern trip without his blessing, which was, Mayer told everyone, a dangerous way to travel. Vilifying Jean and her mother as idiots deserving of each other, Mayer ordered that neither of them was to appear at the studio until they were well and Jean was ready for work.

Throughout the remainder of February and all of March, Jean remained at home. Finally she felt well enough to go to Palm Springs. There she enjoyed the desert warmth, but only appeared out-of-doors in the lengthening shadows of afternoon, after the sun had begun its descent beyond San Jacinto Mountain. Palm Springs was still a charming little town. Days and nights were always clear, and from Jean's bungalow at the Desert Inn she could see the stark granite mountains to the east. Time and again she exclaimed at the wonder of the sand dunes along Route 99, for the setting sun would reflect ridges, pockets and slopes of pastel color. Once she hiked the mile into Tahquitz Canyon to see the waterfall and scolded her Cahuilla Indian guide for chewing gum stolidly instead of exclaiming with her at the scene's primitive beauty.

Discontented again with Hollywood and her role in films, she began to weigh a marriage that would permit her to retire permanently from the screen. She was solvent now, with almost all debts paid off except the thirty thousand dollars she still owed Pops. But he, as always, would be willing to wait, and if she retired to the desert to think, read and plan her life, she might be able to become a real woman. But why not an actress, she asked herself, and had to smile bitterly. It did not matter, never would, for she would always be starred as a sex symbol.

Still thinking of retirement, Jean drove about in her small touring Ford to admire the oleander bushes, tall as trees, with their slender wax-green leaves and white, pink and red blossoms. A sense of reality compelled her to dismiss all thoughts of retirement. If she married the man everyone said she was going to marry, she could not expect him to give up a grand career to retire with her to Palm Springs. Then, too, she would never be able to go into the sun and in Palm Springs, a town of light, she would become a prisoner of shade and shadows.

It was time to go home; she felt a little better and wanted to return to work. Besides, for more than a week now, whenever she brushed her teeth she had felt pain in both jaws. One morning while Mama was having her hair done, Jean telephoned Landau and told him to make an appointment with her to see a dentist and not to let her mother know of this arrangement.

"It's getting so my mouth hurts even after I brush. And especially when I'm chewing," Jean told her agent. "And if it weren't for my teeth I'd be really bothered, because I've begun to feel so bad down below."

"You're to come right home," Arthur said.

"This morning I could hardly open my mouth wide, Pops," she continued.

"It's nothing," Arthur assured her. "Doctor Buckmiller'll

X-ray your mouth and it'll be nothing at all. Take my word for it. So when're you coming back?"

"Is the studio getting something ready for me?" She felt increasing fear of a dentist and refused to answer his question.

"Another picture with Gable."

Jean groaned so theatrically Arthur had to laugh. "And what kind of whore am I now?"

"You're a rich girl and not a whore," Arthur replied. "And there're some great pictures being set for you. You'll like this one. It's about race horses. Wonderful sets and lots of action. You'll like the part. Gable's all for it. So when're you coming home?"

"In a day or so," Jean said, then sat silently staring at the phone. She heard Landau suggest that she ought to hire a chauffeur. "I'll drive myself," she said. "It'll keep my mind off my teeth. They ache right now."

Another problem to keep Jean's mind off her teeth was the assignment of Bernard Hyman as the producer of *Saratoga,* and just what this meant for her on the barometer of Mayer's favor. It was no secret in the industry that Bernard Hyman had been one of the men closest to Irving Thalberg in friendship and business. It was also no secret that Mayer had embarked on a deliberate program to humiliate members of the Thalberg group by taking them off "class" pictures and putting them to work on the studio's assembly line productions. Therefore, Jean concluded, the assignment of Hyman as the producer of *Saratoga* could only mean that Mayer considered her next picture to be a product and no more. This meant that, as long as Myrna Loy was under contract to the studio, she would never be given the chance to play in a smart comedy with William Powell. It was a bitter conclusion, and at another time she would have rebelled. But now she still felt weak, not at all recovered from her February illness, and, try as she might, she could not rid herself of the pain in her mouth and general physical discomfort.

Within a week of her return home and despite Mama's fervent prayers, the pain in Jean's mouth had become so unbearable she begged Arthur to make an appointment and promised to keep it. Spirited from the studio to the dentist's office to avoid Mama and her Reader of the moment, the actress had her teeth and jaws X-rayed by Dr. Leroy Buckmiller. The developed plates revealed that several of Jean's third molars were impacted, the gums were infected and it was immediately evident that Jean's illness was more than hypochondria, for the infection from her gums had drained into her whole body. Dr. Buckmiller scheduled an appointment with Dr. Berto Olson, one of the foremost oral surgeons in California, and Dr. Olson supervised the administration of a general anesthetic before he removed the impacted teeth and treated the infected gums. All of this was kept secret from Mama until the surgery had been completed.

It was important for Jean to convalesce in a place where she would be given the attentions of medicine unimpeded by the ministrations of religion, so she was moved to a private hospital room where she slept for long hours under sedation and spent waking hours with only the closest friends as visitors. Mama came, though she disapproved more and more vocally of medicine, hospitals and doctors and her visits usually were harangues addressed to the walls and ceiling, for no one with ears would listen to her.

On April 12 Jean wrote Landau a short thank-you note for the plant and flowers he had sent to the hospital:

Pops—how sweet of you to remember me—so beautifully. The plant was like a ball of sunshine—and the red roses and gardenias were a picture—

They brought a great deal of sunshine and happiness to me and added such cheer to the usual hospital room—

After this experience I never want to *hear* of wisdom teeth—I have looked like a "double exposure" of Harlow for so long that when I am normal probably I will feel sorry for the old sunken face—

Love *Jean*

There was an added week of convalescence at home before *Saratoga* began on April 22. Clark Gable was to act as Duke Bradley, Lionel Barrymore as Jean's grandpa, and Frank Morgan, Walter Pidgeon, Una Merkel and Hattie McDaniels were other star members of the cast. In that week Jean began to study her lines as she was fitted by wardrobe for her role.

To dispel the industry-wide rumors that her recovery was not complete, Bernard Hyman and Jack Conway, the director, agreed that Jean should make the most brilliant appearance possible on the screen. True, Jean was increasingly tired and, what was more unusual, snappish with people she liked. She had even been angry with Kay Mulvey and Powell, which certainly was unusual.

A week after *Saratoga* went before the camera, local papers wondered whether Jean had found someone she preferred to Powell, inasmuch as she had been seen night-clubbing for four nights running with Donald Freide, an Eastern publisher. True, Powell resented Jean's telling people that she loved her star sapphire ring even if it was vulgar, but professional prophets refused to believe Jean's dates with Freide were serious enough to photograph them together.

Saratoga had been scheduled as a thirty-day film. But by May 19, when Conway should have been close to completion, the picture was so far behind schedule that Bernard Hyman—already out of favor—no longer dared conceal this from Mayer.

Mayer was preparing for a very important European trip with a selected coterie of friends and executives, a good-will expedition supposedly arranged to see that Robert Taylor got off to a good start in *A Yank at Oxford,* a hands-across-the-sea picture to bring twentieth century American go-getter education to that medieval English university.

Everyone in the industry was aware of the grandeur and scope of this European expedition, which was to capture more talent for the Culver City lot. And in Europe actors and actresses, composers and musicians, and the entire population of Budapest, with its gypsy fiddlers and tambourinists, made themselves ready for purchase by the dynast. Also, as the trip was not to be encumbered by Mrs. Mayer or other dowagers, the little touches of home normally provided by girdled matrons would be arranged for by other persons.

Nevertheless, since Hyman sounded so unhappy and no longer so upstart, and approached Mayer as a prodigal but repentant son in need of a father's help, Mayer agreed to come to the rescue of *Saratoga.* He would spend an evening in heart-to-heart talk with Jean, who probably needed some help in interpreting the part of Carol Clayton.

Even Jean was impressed that Mayer took time to telephone her at home. He was a busy man, he told her, and too tied up at the studio for a friendly, informal talk with a girl he had always liked, despite what anyone said. He hoped she could come that evening to a house he had rented at Malibu, a retreat where he went to get things done he found impossible to accomplish at the studio. She agreed to meet him within an hour.

"Be prompt," Mayer said pleasantly before he hung up. "You know the Malibu colony? It's on the street just at the beach front. I'll be standing outside exactly at eight, so I'll appreciate your not keeping me waiting. And don't bring your mother because this is a business talk."

"Then Pops is going to be there?" she asked.

"Who's under contract to me?" Mayer asked. "You or him?"

At the beach house Mayer was brisk affability and little *gemütlich* jokes as, with many hand pats, he led Jean to a chair before a French window that enabled her to see the moon shining on the waves. Mayer loathed the sight of the sea, and his parting of the draperies at the picture window was a genuine proof of affection. He asked how she felt, told her not to worry about the extracted teeth because, thank God, she didn't even require the smallest dental bridge, which could become the biggest nuisance to the wearer. Jean took the weak drink and smiled at Mayer. Despite his plaid shirt and sweater, his poking at the logs in the fireplace and warm recollections about a hunting lodge he had once visited in the Canadian Rockies, he still looked formal, feral and too freshly barbered.

"But to business," Mayer said cheerily. He seated himself on a polished log stump drawn to the side of the fireplace. "What's the problem?"

"You mean on the picture?"

Mayer nodded rapidly and refused to fill Jean's glass. "You're driving," he said. "And we want you on the set bright and early tomorrow morning."

"I haven't been late yet," she said.

"Who says you have?" Mayer was genial. "Before you go we'll have hot tea or coffee. Meanwhile, Jean, I've been thinking."

"Yes?"

Mayer polished a thumbnail against his sweater. "It's time to put your cute little *Tuches auf der Tisch*. That means to get down to cases with each other. Two years from now we'll be writing another contract for you. So it's time that we become now what we haven't been for five years—friends. Real intimate friends. You get my meaning?"

362

"You're helping me," she replied.

"So if the picture takes a little longer it'll take a little longer." Mayer leaned forward as if to take Jean's hand, but he only offered her a cigarette from a box on the end table. "But I want to know before I leave for Europe that the picture is finished and that we're really friends with no secrets from each other." He paused while Jean lit her cigarette and flipped the match into the fireplace. "So everything is settled? You'll do the best you can on the picture? Good. So I've got a nice present for you."

"You didn't have to, Mr. Mayer," she said. "Working for you is present enough."

"If only everyone felt that way," Mayer said, beaming. "Still, before I go to Europe I'd like to show you that I appreciate your work and hold no grudges against you for going to Washington. Though you did become awfully sick there."

"The flu was all over the country."

"But not so bad in California," Mayer said. "Anyway"— he clapped his hands and smiled—"I've got a present for you. A mink coat," he continued rapidly. "I hear you've been collecting them."

Jean tossed away her cigarette. "From who?"

"Does it matter?" Mayer laughed. "But if you insist, I'd say from rich men. Who else can afford them? Some women collect perfumes and other such foolishness. Mink coats show a business head. And wait until you see this coat."

"I don't think I can take it, Mr. Mayer."

He laughed again. "Take it? I'm giving it. It's in there"— he gestured toward the corridor that led to the bath and bedroom—"so get undressed and try it on."

"I can't," Jean shook her head. "You see, I haven't got a present for you. At least nothing I really want to give you."

Mayer trotted from the room and returned quickly with the dark mink coat. He spread it across the sofa, and in the flicker of the flames the skins gleamed with the sheen of burnished copper. Proudly, he gestured that the coat was Jean's. "And I'll bet my life and the furrier's too that in your collection there isn't a coat like this. Every skin chosen for the skin and body of a queen. Or a goddess. So what else would you like to give me when I've already made clear exactly what I want?"

"Plenty," Jean said as she crossed to stroke the coat. "I'd like to give you the clap. And if I had it you could have it for nothing. Matter of fact I'd pay you."

Shocked, unbelieving, Mayer staggered and placed one hand over his heart, the other over his groin. "Filthy!" he shouted. "Filthy rotten thing! Your mouth should be washed out with lye. No wonder you had rotten teeth! Get out!" He ran screaming toward the front door of the little house. "Out and out of my sight forever! And I'm warning you—if you don't stay on schedule I'll put you on suspension. Ungrateful girl!" He opened the door and pointed dramatically at the darkness. "From now on you're no concern of mine. And I wouldn't give you myself even if you got down right now on your hands and knees and apologized."

Humming as she drove from the beach toward Beverly Hills, Jean enjoyed her memory of the scene. If she had not felt physically so rotten she would have stopped at a bar, picked up the first likely looking man, laid him, then telephoned Mayer to tell him what she was doing and what he could do with his mink coat, skin by skin. But she did not know the telephone number of the Malibu house. And she did feel low and really sick.

Instead of going directly home she drove to the Landaus', found them in and told Arthur they had to speak privately. Closed in Arthur's den, with wild laughter and extravagant hilarity as she acted out both comedy roles, Jean reconstructed her triumph. But Arthur did not congratulate her. Rather, he sat at his desk and stared at his fists.

"You're not to tell anyone," he said at last.

"That's impossible," she said. "I've already told you."

"And I don't believe you."

Jean tilted her head and closed an eye. "Are you calling me a liar?"

"Let's say that for your own good I'm just going to believe you were dreaming."

"Are you saying it didn't happen?"

Arthur shook his head. "No, I'm saying it couldn't have happened. Matter of fact, Jean, right now you're at home."

"But Beatrice—" Jean spluttered and pointed toward the rear of the house. "She saw me come in! She asked me how I felt. Said I looked good. Asked me if I wanted coffee! What're you trying to do?"

"I'm trying to send you home to get some rest," Arthur replied. "If you're tired I'll drive you. I can cab back."

"How can you drive me home if I'm not here?"

"In the movies logic's never been a problem," Arthur said wryly. "Seeing is believing." He stood and moved toward the door. "Let me drive you home."

"Mama's gonna ask what Mr. Mayer wanted," Jean said.

"He wanted to talk about your health, because you don't look well, and about the vacation he promised after you finish the picture," Arthur suggested. "And on the way back you dropped in to see us. Why don't you call her now to make it sound better?"

Jean scowled at the suggestion. "I wonder if Mama would've taken the coat?"

"That's no way to talk," Arthur said angrily.

"Well, you should hear the way she talks about me to me." She sighed. "Okay, I may as well get started for home so she can pray over me for at least an hour."

The next day, disinclined to take any further notice of the star who had so grievously insulted him, Mayer ordered the photograph he had once had taken with Jean removed from his office, and Conway and Hyman were called to stand on his carpet. Waving aside all excuses, Mayer frostily told them the picture had to be completed by June 5 and banished them from his sight until his order was obeyed.

The pace of production was speeded, and Eddie Mannix appeared on the set several times a day to bawl out everyone about getting their backs into things to finish the Goddamn picture. In his early career Eddie Mannix had been employed by Nicholas Schenck as a sergeant-at-arms in his Palisades Amusement Park; now a proven executive of voice and fists, he was the trouble-shooter charged by Mayer with overseeing the physical progress of pictures in production, and his strong voice punctuated by short jabs of his fists made Mannix the sort of a man who could have shortened the construction schedule of any of the pyramids or the Great Wall of China.

As more feet of film were shot daily, Jean began to sleep in her bungalow. Occasionally, to Kay, Powell and Landau, she would admit to feeling rotten. People in the make-up department noted how the usually cheerful actress sat with tight, bloodless lips while she was prepared for the set. And most alarming of all, she no longer demanded a new dirty story for admission to her bungalow.

Chapter Twenty-four

On the morning of Saturday, May 29, the producer and director of *Saratoga* were confident they would complete the picture by Mayer's deadline. Tempers were beginning to fray, but all the people concerned with the film were determined to control themselves. Shooting began and progressed smoothly, although Jean seemed to be unusually lethargic even when she took her place before the camera. This morning the scheduled scene was set in a boudoir, and Conway hoped for an electric quality to be generated between Jean and Gable. True to the formula of films, they were supposed to loathe each other, but as yet they did not realize this was love. As Gable swept Jean from her feet to carry her to a chaise, he noticed that she was in a cold sweat under the lights, that her weight was limp. Instead of dropping her to the chaise—which would have been good for an audience laugh—Gable lowered her gently and waved his arm to break the scene, then called to tell Conway Jean was ill. As she rose from the chaise to protest she could go on, she collapsed.

Smelling salts revived her. As she was helped from the set to her bungalow by Tom Andre, the assistant director on the picture, she apologized for disturbing everyone. But she still felt so weak that walking and holding her head erect required great effort.

After some minutes of recuperation in her bungalow, Jean was advised by Conway and a studio nurse to go home and rest over the weekend. Illness, like storms and earthquakes, were acts of God, and Mayer would have to recognize a more sovereign authority. Before she left for home Jean was driven to the set of *Double Wedding,* where Powell was working with Myrna Loy, to break her lunch date with Powell and assure both stars she would be well and taking telephone calls by evening.

At home Mama was radiant with joy as she helped Jean prepare for bed, for that morning she had felt vibrations of great events to be, of great revelations and conversions to be made through her. Jean's continued poor health proved that doctors, dentists, nurses and their medicines had failed; the truth of Science would now expose them as failures and frauds. The only outside advice Mama would have heeded was to keep Jean quiet, which she intended to do. But she also intended to bar all visitors from the house for the weekend. Two days alone with her daughter was little enough time for even a devout Scientist to separate Jean's pure Mind from gross matter. But in two days Jean would understand the truth of Mind, and through this understanding the health of what ignorant people referred to as the Body would also be restored.

For the exorcising of malicious influences and material poisons, Mama required absolute privacy, so the cook was given the weekend off. Because Jean was too weak to answer the telephone, Mama took all the calls and brightly told everyone that Jean was resting quietly and comfortably, with no fever or other physical symptoms of illness. She didn't bother to explain that Science considered these things to be chimeras and delusions created through ignorance.

Mama's telephone pronouncements were no more radical than the faith inspired by Mary Baker Glover Patterson Eddy, who, along with Joseph Smith, translator of the golden tablets of Moroni, are the founders of the two native American religions that have become important and dignified international churches. Christian Science, as Mormonism, were inspirations of the American scientific mind of the nineteenth century, which had begun to seek mental rather than medicinal cures for illnesses; both faiths were also protests against the new American emphasis on industry rather than agriculture.

Every Scientist is his own practitioner, which gives him license to practice if he can find a willing subject, and Mama now had one of the most famous women in the world as her patient. Although Mrs. Bello had become acquainted with Science through her mother, she had not given serious attention to its practice until her arrival in Los Angeles some ten years before, when she had discovered one of Marino's first infidelities. Her own need for the man compelled her to forgive Marino, but a sense of pride drove her to seek release from what she had begun to think of as a sexual indenture to her husband. In Mary Baker Eddy's chapter on "Marriage" in *Science and Health,* Mama found advice that could, if practiced, give her release from the bondage of sex. Complete celibacy was the key to the purest spiritual state; intercourse, even if it was marital, had its appeal in sensation, physical sensation depended upon matter, and matter was error. Therefore, the elimination of intercourse eliminated matter which eliminated evil error from the Mind. (Such a religious conclusion brought it directly into conflict with Catholic and allied Christian doctrines, which considered sex God-given and good in its origin, but this was of no importance to Mrs. Eddy, a seeress who soberly suggested that parthogenetic conception was possible to virgins—and other ladies, too—if they became sufficiently spiritual.)

Although Malicious Animal Magnetism was being played down in contemporary Christian Science circles, there was no doubt in Mama's mind that Marino was able to exercise an M.A.M. which made her a captive to his body, a slave to the physical sensations he could arouse in her, a creature of error because she surrendered so willingly to the desires of the flesh, which is matter. As penance she devoted herself to other good works in the hope that they would tip the scales of Mind in her favor: she spoke and praised Science to all who would listen, and in whatever city or town she traveled she made it a mission to visit at least one bookstore to search out the malicious slanders against Mrs. Eddy and her religion.

Wherever Mama found any writings listed on the *index expurgatorius* of Science, she bought the offensive books or pamphlets and loudly denounced the bookseller as she destroyed the obnoxious publications in his presence. On one visit to New York City she had had a grand day along lower Fourth Avenue (now Park Avenue South) where most of the city's second-hand bookshops are concentrated. As news was telephoned from shop to shop that another well-heeled Christian Scientist was on a bookburning crusade, the shopkeepers made ready all the muckraking material about Science they had on hand and raised the prices. In two shops Mama had found copies of Mark Twain's attack on Science; she had delighted some browsers and outraged others by ripping the books into tatters. In Los Angeles and San Francisco booksellers knew that Mrs. Bello would always buy any book or pamphlet offensive to Scientists and was one customer who never haggled over price.

Destroying books inimical to Science had not helped Mama liberate her Mind from the lure of Marino's matter, and now she knew why. Jean's illnesses and the remedies applied by doctors were an affront to true religion. Mrs. Eddy had told her so in a dream. Newspapers, magazines, the telegraph and radio—all implied that Jean Harlow, the daughter of a Christian Scientist, did not honor her mother's religion. How then could Mrs. Bello know spiritual peace and clarity of Mind if she permitted her daughter to persist in error?

The sign Mama needed had been given to her, and now she had the opportunity: Jean was ill but alone in the house with her mother. The clear path of religious duty and maternal obligation lay before her. Years before, when Jean had been little and stricken with infantile paralysis, her mother had prayed her well, healed her, enabled her to walk without contraptions of iron and leather. She would do so again.

Sick exhaustion enabled Jean to sleep fitfully Saturday night, but Sunday morning she was too weak to leave her bed and had to be dragged by her mother to the bathroom. By noon the telephones had rung so many times that Jean complained the noise was giving her a headache. Mama obliged by taking the receivers off their hooks.

Lack of callers enabled Mrs. Bello to minister as she saw fit, to sit at Jean's bedside, comb her daughter's lovely blonde hair and assure the feverish young woman that her warm forehead was not really warm because Mama was concentrating on coolness and health and Jean should do likewise. Later Mama sang in the kitchen as she prepared cold lemonade for Jean. She had just given her daughter a sponge bath, put a fresh baby-pink ribbon in her hair and massaged her little feet. Toward evening Jean complained of pains in her stomach and back, had to vomit, and lay for almost an hour with her head pressed against the cold enamel of the commode before she could be helped again to bed.

Jean's failure to appear on the set Monday morning caused some concern, especially since her phone lines were still busy. A studio messenger returned to tell the director that Mrs. Bello had refused to admit him to the house but had promised to telephone later to tell them when Jean would return to work. Shooting continued in a makeshift manner; Conway filled in his time with close-ups of Gable and the other stars in the picture. True to her word, Mrs. Bello telephoned in the late afternoon and cheerfully, with much good nature, told Conway that Jean was feeling wonderfully well and would certainly be at work by Tuesday immediately after lunch. Another long night of rest and the luxury of a late rising would put the actress on her feet. Certainly the studio could not deny Jean an added morning of rest when her record for punctuality and cooperation was so well known by everyone.

When Jean did not appear for work Tuesday afternoon, Clark Gable left the studio to pay a personal visit to Jean. About three o'clock a disturbed Gable returned to draw Frank Morgan aside and tell him that Mrs. Bello had met him at the door but would not let him in the house. She had been cheerful and had not looked or sounded at all concerned about Jean, as a mother might if her daughter were seriously ill. Still, Gable could not understand why Mrs. Bello had refused him permission to see Jean.

"She said Jean was sleeping," Gable told Morgan and Jack Conway, who had joined them. "But if she's sleeping that much it means she's weak and ought to have a doctor."

Conway gagged, threw up his hands and left the set for a conference with the producer. Both men now knew they could not complete the picture by Saturday, and in panic Bernard Hyman telephoned Landau to tell him that Gable had spoken to Mrs. Bello but had not been permitted to see Harlow. Landau knew that under ordinary circumstances they would have brought this to the attention of Eddie Mannix or Mayer himself, but he also knew of Mayer's edict that Hyman and Conway were not to speak to him until *Saratoga* was completed. Gable was asked to join Conway in Hyman's office, and Frank Morgan came with him. Again Gable told the story of Jean's cold sweat when he had lifted her in his arms, and when Landau arrived he had to repeat in detail that afternoon's conversation with Mrs. Bello.

"She said she was thrilled that I'd come to the house," Gable told the assembled men. "But why wouldn't she let me in?"

"Did you ask to see Jean?" Landau asked.

"I did." Gable was irritated. "I even asked if a doctor'd seen Jean. She just laughed and told me that very soon she'd have to introduce me to Science."

"What kind of science?" Hyman asked. "Medical science? Since when is she a doctor?"

"Christian Science," Landau explained. "And don't ask me anything about it."

"Me neither," Hyman said quickly. "All right." He looked at the telephone, "I guess it's up to me to call Mannix."

"I'd say so," Conway agreed.

"Or we might go out to the house," Hyman hedged. "I don't want to ask for help if we can handle this alone. I'm going to see Mrs. Bello. Anyone who wants to come along is welcome."

As Arthur turned left from Santa Monica Boulevard into North Palm Drive, the men with him agreed that his plan made sense. If the neighbors should see five men approach Jean's house, and two of them were Gable and Morgan, they might suspect some crisis and telephone the newspapers. Instead, Arthur would ring the bell by himself, gain admission to the house, and then signal for the others to enter quickly behind him.

Normally he would have been polite to Mrs. Bello, engaged her in small talk, asked what was new at the beauty parlor. But this was not a time for niceties, and when Mama Jean answered the bell Arthur stuck his foot inside to prevent her closing the door. But he could not push the door open because it was on the safety chain. At the maximum, with the chain in place, the door could not be opened more than seven inches.

"So many visitors," Mrs. Bello said sweetly. "But you can't come in. I'm sorry."

"So am I," Arthur replied. "I have to see Jean."

"She's under treatment and resting."

"Whose treatment?"

"Mine," Mama said. "And she's being relieved of most of

the evil in her. I'm doing wonders." She nudged Arthur's shoe with her toe. "You're keeping me from my patient."

Arthur pushed his foot forward so that Mrs. Bello would have had to slam the door on his calf. "See the car out there?" He pointed to the driveway. "Jack Conway, Bernie Hyman and a couple of other people are in it who'll make awfully good witnesses."

"Get your foot out of my door or I won't be responsible if I break your leg! Why are you making me think evil? There's an aura of evil around you, Mr. Landau! The air is filled with evil vibrations. Do you know that I received an emanation that you were driving here? I never should've opened the door!"

"Take off the chain," Arthur said. "Otherwise I'm going to yell for help and have Conway get the police. Jean'll be furious with you for the publicity." He lowered his voice and reached out to touch her hand, which rested on the chain. "Mama Jean, everyone at the studio is worried. No one wants to hurt Jean. But you've got to let Conway and Hyman in to see her. They're in trouble now with Mayer."

"He's an evil influence," Mama said. "It's all I can do to combat his emanations."

"So let us in the house," Arthur insisted. "You'll tell us what to do and we'll help."

"Mr. Gable was here a little while ago. Didn't he tell you Jean was all right?"

"He did," Arthur nodded. "And he's back here with us. Frank Morgan, too. It's impolite to keep them sitting in the car, especially a fine gentleman like Mr. Morgan. And everyone knows you're a real lady."

Mama tightened her grip on the chain and sniffed noisily. "Is there anyone who dares say I'm not? All right, come in and see that Jean's all right. And then I'll thank all of you to leave."

"A minute, no more," Arthur promised.

In the bedroom, Mama pointed triumphantly to Jean and asked them if her daughter did not look better now than when she had left the set on Saturday. The assembled men were too appalled to reply, for Jean lay semi-conscious, belching noisily and moaning that she was racked with a pain that started in her stomach, radiated throughout her entire chest and tortured her back and shoulders. She was nauseated and had vomited just before they arrived. Her cheeks glowed with fever, and through dry parted lips she continued to plead brokenly for help, for Powell, Kay Mulvey and Pops.

Frank Morgan took Jean's pulse and found it dangerously erratic. This was not the time to count on miracles, he told Hyman. He advised him to call a doctor, because Jean looked very ill and extended fever was dangerous to any adult. Laughing, Mrs. Bello told them that they were two Jews and three ignorant amateurs, all of them needlessly alarmed. Then she ordered them to go and take their evil thoughts with them. When they refused to leave she began to weep, cry that Jean was her daughter and only child, her responsibility, and they had no right to force their way into her house where they were unwelcome guests. When they still refused to go she begged them to join her in reading from *Science and Health*. She had three or four more copies in the house, and just an hour's reading would convince them how sadly they had erred in their assessment of Jean's condition.

"Evil is strong and stubborn," Mama told them. "It doesn't give up without a struggle. Right now evil is struggling to stay inside Jean, but she's strong, I'm strong, and together we're concentrating on good. Together we'll know a glorious triumph. I did it once when she had infantile paralysis—"

"Jean never had infantile paralysis!" Arthur shouted. "Bernie, you've gotta call Mannix! If you don't I will!"

It was important for the studio to keep the papers from discovering how Mama had endangered her daughter's life by playing faith healer. It was equally important to see that Jean received the best of orthodox medical attention. Trying to do both at once turned out to be difficult, even dangerous. If Mama were pressed too hard, she might call in members of her faith to have them tell the world the story of her gallant fight to save her daughter. If she weren't pressed hard enough, she might pray Jean to death.

Dr. E. C. Fishbaugh, a well-known internist, examined Jean, diagnosed her ailment as cholecystitis—inflammation of the gall bladder—and recommended immediate hospitalization and preparation for surgery. By this time Jean was so weak with illness and pain she could not speak coherently, and Mrs. Bello refused to allow Jean to be moved to any building where she would not have jurisdiction. In compromise, because *Science and Health* did permit a surgeon to give a hypodermic to relieve unusual pain, she allowed this ministration.

As soon as Jean was asleep, Mama wanted to continue with her mental healing. Another compromise was effected: if Mrs. Bello would permit the introduction of nurses, the doctor and Jean's friends would agree to Mama's mental therapy and even assist if they could.

After more argument and respectful pleading by Hyman, Conway, Gable, Morgan and Landau, Mama agreed to share the care of her unconscious daughter with professional nurses. Again the doctor asked for permission to remove Jean to a hospital, where she could be given an intravenous lipiodal injection to prepare her for X-rays that would facilitate a search for gallstones, but Mama refused to relinquish her authority and threatened to change her mind about the nurses if there was any more discussion.

Nurses arrived on the scene to do what they could. It was time-consuming to send blood and urine samples to an outside laboratory, but everyone hoped that when and if Mama became more rational, she would see the wisdom of moving Jean to a hospital. Meanwhile Jean was fed intravenously because her strength was at low ebb and she was unable to take food in any form. But food was unnecessary, Mama screamed at the nurses as she began to exercise the first of her major and disastrous tyrannies. Worked into a righteous rage, shrieking that she had agreed to a hypodermic only for the relief of Jean's pain, she threatened to destroy the medical equipment brought into the sickroom. Only after Arthur agreed to read with her in *Science and Health,* a book he really wanted to see, would Mama agree to leave Jean alone with the nurses.

"But they'll fail," Mama told Arthur. "Then they'll have to call on me. And as a good Scientist I'll forgive them."

"That's wonderful," Arthur said as he opened his copy of *Science and Health.* "Where do we begin?"

A patient in Jean's condition certainly belonged in a hospital, but next morning Mama still refused to consider such a move. Reporters had begun to gather around the house, and a studio spokesman who had arrived during the night told the assembled newsmen that Jean's illness was exaggerated, at worst no more than some kind of small stomach ache.

"Thank God, she's resting quietly," was the devout statement Mrs. Bello gave to the press on June 3, 1937. The *Hollywood Citizen* also quoted Dr. Fishbaugh as saying that "Miss Harlow just had a cold," and everyone agreed that someone with a cold could certainly be treated at home. There the matter rested, because on this day Edward VIII, who had abdicated his throne on December 11, 1936, had married Wallis Warfield Simpson, and accounts of this wedding and recapitulations of the most famous romance of the century were much more newsworthy.

Dr. Fishbaugh called in a colleague, Dr. Chapman, for consultation. In sanctimonious, suspicious, but always maternal tones, Mama questioned every therapy and demanded to know what specific medicines and drugs were supposed to do and whether either of the two doctors now on the case, the nurses, laboratory technicians or pharmacists set themselves up as greater healers than Christ, who had not healed by miracles but through the fullest use of his Mind and Wisdom, which had been recognized and understood by no one except Reverend Leader Eddy, who in her goodness had made His knowledge available to everyone willing to see and acknowledge the Truth? The medical regimen continued to function with a limp because it could not overcome Mama's pernicious presence. She insisted upon sleeping in a chair in Jean's room and, awakening at the slightest movement, was able to frustrate the nurses by interfering with the orders of both doctors. Eyes shut, hands pressed to her ears, Mama refused to consider Jean's transfer to a hospital, and Jean was never sufficiently conscious to override her mother.

Newspapers and radio newscasts, still concerned with Edward and Wallis, were unaware of the contest over the actress. Accordingly they reduced their coverage of Jean's illness to casual reports of improvement that would soon permit her to resume work on *Saratoga*. But Jean's prolonged illness did not square with the triviality assigned to it by the press, and Mannix telephoned to ask anyone who answered the phone what was going on. If Jean was faking illness that could only be overcome by another raise in salary she would find herself out on her ear. Conway and Hyman swore by their careers that Jean was seriously ill and pleaded with Mannix to beg Mayer to visit Jean and see for himself how sick she was. Only Mayer could order Mrs. Bello away from Jean's bedside. Reluctantly, because Mayer had been explicit in his orders concerning *Saratoga,* Mannix bore the request of the producer and director to his boss. Mayer shrugged and turned away.

Friday morning Dr. Fishbaugh warned everyone that Jean belonged in a hospital. Shortly before dawn one of the nurses had reported that Jean was scratching, and as the nurse had bent over the bed to restrain the semi-conscious woman she had also noted the unusual pallor of Jean's skin. This might have been due to her illness and an anemia produced by a lack of food, but what concerned the nurse was the distinct ammoniac odor in the mouth of the actress, an odor like that of urine. The nurse had telephoned Dr. Fishbaugh, who had examined Jean's mouth, discovered an erythema of the mucous membranes, and noted that Jean's tongue, gums and lips were quite swollen—all symptoms of secondary mouth infections and indicative of nephritic degeneration. When Jean had awakened she had begun to cry incoherently because of a frightful headache; massive sedation had been required.

An acute infection from the gall bladder was coursing through Jean's bloodstream, because her kidneys were damaged and no longer capable of acting as filters for body waste. This condition was piling up an accumulation of wastes and a uremia that would have created a critical condition for anyone in good health. And Jean had had a record of aggravated ill health for an entire year previous to this illness. The damaged kidneys were failing, and the acute infection developed by the diseased gall bladder was further attacking the damaged kidneys, literally tearing them to pieces.

Whether the people around Jean understood what was happening or not was unimportant, the doctors warned Mrs. Bello and the other people assembled in the living room. What was important was Jean's immediate removal to a hospital where she could be operated upon without delay. The gall bladder would be drained, the infections drained off; this would give the actress at least a fair chance of recovery. What neither doctor could understand was why Jean's medical history had not mentioned a kidney ailment that must have troubled her for years.

Arthur felt faint. If Mama was praying to keep Jean out of the grave it seemed that another hand, ghostly and more powerful, was dragging Jean into death. It was too macabre and gruesome to be given serious thought, but the knowledge of what had happened almost five years before, on July 2, 1932, could not be dismissed. Paul Bern had beaten Jean with a cane across the back, had struck her over the kidneys. Medical examination had revealed bruises and possible damage. Dr. Sugarman had advised treatment, Jean had refused to heed the doctor, and for the next five years had complained intermittently, sometimes in pain, that she was being bothered by her kidneys. And all the while she had refused medical treatment and permitted her kidneys to deteriorate. Bern's blows had damaged Jean's kidneys, made them weak, and subsequent infections had been predisposed to settle in the kidneys, to make for increasing and progressive damage until this day had come.

If Jean died, a dead man might have succeeded in murdering her years after his own suicide.

Whatever Arthur knew of the beating Bern had given Harlow could wait for another time, when he could speak to Dr. Fishbaugh privately. Now it was important to get Jean into surgery. After Fishbaugh and Chapman returned to the sickroom to wait for a decision that would allow them to act, Arthur tried to reason with Mrs. Bello.

"They're wrong," she insisted, dabbing at her eyes in gentle melancholy. "If all of you'd just let me alone with her she'd be well. I ought to have you arrested for interfering with my patient."

Arthur stretched his hands toward her, pleading. "For what? For trying to reason with you? Mama Jean, your Baby's sick."

"She's not! She's just pretending, to make a fool of me. I hate her!" Mama began to cry and beat her hands together. "She just won't admit what I've done for her. Won't give me credit for anything. You know what *Time* said about me! Why won't she admit it?"

380

"I'll speak to her after she gets well," Arthur promised. "Things'll be different. She told me you want Marino back."

"I don't!" Mama began to sob into the light silk scarf around her throat. "I want to break the power he has over me. A Scientist knows that sex is only the most inferior form and perversion of love. But she shouldn't have taken him away until I was ready to give him up!"

"Let's get her well," Arthur continued to plead. "Let's move her to a hospital and have her operated on."

"That's what she wants. To prove to everyone that I'm a failure."

A cold chill coursed down Arthur's back at what he had to say. "She'll die. Your Baby'll die."

"There is no death," Mrs. Bello replied. "You're asking me to sin against my faith. You've no right!"

"Your faith doesn't demand that she die."

"She won't die. If all of you left this house she'd start getting well. Doctors and nurses indulge in mental malpractice and this place is filled with evil mental influences. Look!" She pointed at the windows. "They're so strong they've set the curtains to moving! I can feel their evil wings around my head!"

"Then let's get Jean out of here," Arthur said quickly. "We'll put her in a private hospital room and no one'll be able to find her."

Mama dried her eyes. "You don't credit me with much intelligence. Don't argue," she snapped before he could answer. "I want all of you—and that includes the doctors and nurses—out of my house."

"You'll have to put us out," Arthur said over his shoulder as he hurried toward the sickroom.

There were several courses he could follow. Bernard Hyman cooperated by going to the studio research department, where he asked that two or more researchers be put on an emergency assignment to find out if anything in Christian Science permitted the use of orthodox physicians or surgery on Scientists. At the same time it was imperative to get in touch with Dr. Carpentier and Marino and have both men appeal to Mama Jean. And last, because through him lay the quickest resolution of this emergency, Arthur knew he had to see Mayer and persuade the stubborn, angry executive to intervene and save the life of a woman who had humiliated him.

Dr. Carpentier had gone to Detroit to buy a new automobile and was not expected to return to Kansas City until Sunday night. Marino was not expected to return from Nogales until Sunday night. Mayer still refused to relax his decision about anyone connected with what he now swore was an ill-fated picture.

Until some way could be found to break the impasse, the doctors attempted to rouse Jean from her comatose state long enough to explain to her the serious nature of her illness and get her permission for removal to a hospital for surgery. But Jean became weaker by the hour and the frustrated doctors could only continue their acidosis tests and make another urinalysis to determine how much longer they dared wait before corrective surgery would be useless. Saturday was a continuing nightmare of frustrated attempts to reason with Mrs. Bello. On Sunday morning Bernard Hyman had the researchers move to his office with all the books, pamphlets and other writings on Christian Science they had assembled. Hyman himself had telephoned several Christian Science Readers for advice on how to proceed, but the Readers would only suggest that some Readers were more competent than others; each one felt confident that if he could see the patient and study her illness, she would be restored to health. Not one of the Readers to whom Hyman spoke would tell him if Science made any provision for doctors. The two researchers admitted they could not understand *Science and Health* or anything else written by Mrs. Eddy, because almost every sentence written by the seeress was for them—simple Christians—a tautological mist.

At last one of the researchers thought of looking through Dakin's unfriendly biography, *Mrs. Eddy* (1929), which had a fairly complete index. In this book the researchers found several valuable leads, for Dakin stated that in her last years Mrs. Eddy had utilized the services of dentists and "had also condoned the use of physicians by others, despite the fierce assertions in her earlier writings that doctors could avail nothing." But of even greater help to the desperate producer was Dakin's citation from *Science and Health* of a paragraph that gave them hope that they could reason with Mrs. Bello:

> If Christian Scientists ever fail to receive aid from other Scientists—their brethren upon whom they may call—God will still guide them into the right use of temporary and eternal means.

Perhaps the "use of temporary and eternal means" could be construed as permission to call upon doctors for aid. But still more rewarding was Dakin's citation from Mrs. Eddy's *Manual of the Mother Church, The First Church of Christ, Scientist, in Boston, Massachusetts* (1895):

> If a member of this Church has a patient whom he does not heal, and whose case he cannot fully diagnose, he may consult with an M.D. on the anatomy involved. And it shall be the privilege of a Christian Scientist to confer with an M.D. on Ontology, or the Science of being.

At least Mrs. Eddy had admitted some use of medical science. Hyman skipped along quickly, then came upon another citation from the *Manual* which suggested that Mrs. Eddy's "early ecstasy [had] succumbed to reality":

> Until the advancing age admits the efficacy
> and supremacy of Mind, it is better for Christian
> Scientists to leave surgery and the adjustment of
> broken bones and dislocations to the fingers of a
> surgeon, while the mental healer confines him-
> self to mental reconstruction and the prevention
> of inflammation.

Here, at last, was textual chapter and verse. They rushed back to North Palm Drive.

Mama Jean shook her head in impatient denial as the quotations were pointed out to her in *Science and Health* and the *Manual*. Pressed for a reply she insisted tearfully that no matter how she was persecuted, no one could compel her to make a hasty decision; what was right and good could only be established by long prayer and rigorous self-examination. No—she would not admit failure in her treatment of Jean. Furthermore, she had not received aid from other Scientists because she had not thought the emergency great enough to call upon any of the Readers whom she knew. Until she had called in at least three or four Readers and until they, with their superior knowledge, agreed it would be best to use a surgeon, it was blasphemous to say that the powers of Science had been exhausted. But Mama was willing to compromise: the physicians and nurses would withdraw and permit a group of Readers to take over for three full days and nights of prayer and mental healing; if the Readers alone could not help Jean, the doctors would be permitted to return to the case.

"And if the doctors advise hospitalization and surgery?" Arthur asked.

"They'll have to get the approval of the Readers," Mama said. "I think that's only fair."

To Mama, living so deep in a glade of delusion where the sunlight of reality could never penetrate, there was nothing inconsistent in her position. For more than ten years she had dwelt in secret places and built her towers of fantasy on and with sand; the towers had stood to defy the logic of normal achievements and rewards, and with time she had lost the need and empirical ability, as had so many around her, to distinguish between healthy and unhealthy architectures of the mind. Convinced of the debt Jean owed her, convinced that through motherhood she had sacrificed her own beauty, intelligence and ability for a daughter less worthy than she, convinced that she alone was responsible for the monument that was her daughter, she felt no need, as would a woman of normal mind, to be objective in her assessment of the truth, at least some of the time. Convinced that she had done what she imagined she had done, Mama Jean's fantasy had become true history. And in her own way she had become as much a victim of fantasy and banal publicity as had Paul Bern. Disturbed, highly emotional, torn by conflicts of love and hate, desire and frustration, she had become increasingly unwilling—then incapable—of reflecting upon the past in any perspective unrelated to hysteria or glossy falsehood. Intellectually she had become a bankrupt; emotionally she was rich in self pity, therefore, she could be prodigal and cruel with the welfare of anyone who had crossed her, or worse—denied the truth of her fantasy. Pathologically, Mama Jean was deserving of comfort, pity and understanding; practically, because her emotional disorientation had brought her daughter so dangerously close to death, there was no time to provide therapy for the mother.

It was imperative that Mrs. Bello be got out of the way. Hyman telephoned William Powell to tell him the truth of Jean's illness, then drove directly to Louis Mayer's home in Santa Monica and refused to leave unless he was granted an audience. (Five years later Hyman was to die suddenly of a heart attack while a guest in Mayer's home.) Ushered toward the presence, Hyman grasped the initiative and entered shouting—that Harlow was dying because her crazy mother would permit neither hospitalization nor emergency surgery, and that Mayer alone could save the life of the actress.

Mayer was stunned into silence at the vehemence of Hyman's outburst. But before Mayer could scream Hyman's head off, the distraught producer was on the phone and speaking to one of the nurses.

"She's worse off than just out of her head," Hyman turned to tell Mayer. "Jean's unconscious. Don't you believe me that she's dying?"

"Idiot, give me that," Mayer snapped his fingers for the phone. "Why didn't you come to me right away instead of fooling around?"

The ambulance that carried Jean from Beverly Hills to the Good Samaritan Hospital in Los Angeles did not use its bell, and Jean's admission as a patient was not publicized. A quick but thorough examination of the unconscious actress convinced the doctors in attendance that she was now too weak for surgery.

Throughout the night two emergency blood transfusions were given Jean, but by nine o'clock next morning the doctors and nurses noticed the onset of Cheyne-Stokes respiration—the heavy breathing and weak, shallow exhalation which is a harbinger of death. This syndrome was accompanied by convulsive spasms that signaled an advancing cerebral edema. An intravenous injection of adrenalin was administered to help Jean's breathing, but she could not be roused from her coma for more than moments at a time.

In a last-ditch attempt to save the actress, a rescue team of the Los Angeles Fire Department was rushed to the hospital. Under the direction of Fire Captain Warren H. Blake two firemen set up an oxygen tent and adjusted a mask over her face.

"We knew Jean Harlow and we did everything that years

of training, experience in hundreds of cases and daily life-saving drills have taught us," Captain Blake later told the press. "We made the trip to the hospital in record time. From the first it appeared a hopeless task to resuscitate her. We went into the hospital on the run. Miss Harlow was semi-conscious. We set up four oxygen tanks and connected them with a mask over her face and began to pump oxygen into her lungs. Her mother was talking and shaking her lightly, trying to rouse her. Miss Harlow was talking, incoherently. William Powell stepped up to say something to her, but couldn't. He broke down and stepped back. We've faced a lot of tragic scenes in our work, but nothing so tragic as that. Miss Harlow was pronounced dead at 11:37 A.M. We kept pumping oxygen until 11:40."

At Jean's bedside when she died were her mother, William Powell and Dr. Fishbaugh. Marino Bello and several other people were across the hall. As Fishbaugh nodded that Jean was dead, Powell sobbed and rushed from the room. Mrs. Bello succumbed to hysteria and had to be given sedation. Blanche Williams and Herbert Lewis, whom Jean had used as a chauffeur, pressed their faces to the corridor wall and wept. Landau and Hyman helped each other downstairs and were led into a small office by a nurse who lost her professional calm and joined them in tears.

Chapter Twenty-five

On June 7, 1937, death came to the Platinum Blonde at the age of twenty-six. The thunderclap stunned Hollywood and every movie fan. When the shocking news could be accepted, the immediate response was that no one had even hinted she was so ill; and if she had been so ill why hadn't she been taken to a hospital immediately? The *Hollywood Citizen* of June 7 reported that "The hospital for a time presented a scene of confusion. All departments refused to discuss or to call Dr. E. C. Fishbaugh, Miss Harlow's physician. Fifteen newspapermen were refused admittance." Then, because business does not step aside for death, the newspapers wondered what would be done with *Saratoga*. The picture had not been completed; would a half-million dollars be wasted?

Rudolph Valentino had died in 1926. In the following decade, although other notables of the screen had passed from the scene, none of them had been newsworthy enough to merit a Hollywood funeral bigger than a Hollywood première.

When she recovered enough to talk, Mama Jean wailed that Jean would not lie in state, that she wanted her beautiful martyred daughter to be remembered as she was in life. Her wishes were noted but given little attention, because all efforts were now concentrated on keeping the full facts about the fatal illness from the papers. Facts had to be amended and events altered to make it appear as if Jean, rather than her mother, had refused the hospitalization and rejected the surgery that might have saved her life.

If a small, private funeral were held, too much space might be devoted to an analysis of whether Jean's purported refusal of surgery should have been honored. In such an analytical discussion someone was bound to observe that an unconscious woman would at all times be unable to discuss her illness, and a delirious woman would not have been able to make a rational decision. The decision, then, would have to have been made by Mrs. Bello, and what had kept her from doing her obvious logical duty? Religion? This would have meant unconstructive criticism and an attack on a strong and organized faith; no studio dared have itself linked to an attack on any religion observed by contemporary, civilized men.

Mama and Marino, now consoling each other, could say that a small, private funeral would have been Jean's wish, but Marino knew that his former wife had to be protected. As releases were fed to the press about the love of mother for daughter, how the two Jeans had been as sisters, most devoted, ever-loyal, plans were made in private for a funeral that would not only fill many, many newspaper columns, but would also give Hollywood a chance to mourn in the grand manner demanded of it by motion picture fans. There had been eleven years of emotional drought between Valentino and Harlow. Big plans and full coverage were the order of the day.

The telephone switchboard at MGM was so jammed with calls from all over the world that communication broke down. When callers could not reach Jean's studio, they instructed the operators to transfer them to any one of the other major studios or even to major theaters, department stores and hotels in Los Angeles, to demand information about the goddess from bewildered clerks. Solemn attendants at Pierce Brothers mortuary informed thousands of people who telephoned or came in person that there would be no display at the funeral. The body would not lie in state, and the coffin would remain closed except to those who had been closest to the actress.

This news added strength to rumors that now swept the

civilized world about the *true* cause of Jean Harlow's death. People of little imagination solemnly told each other the actress had been the victim of an inept abortion. Who was the guilty man—or men? Was he—or they—going to be punished? Were the studios going to cover up this scandal as they had so many others? Police headquarters in Los Angeles and Beverly Hills could not cope with the tipsters, clairvoyants, and just plain amateur sleuths who demanded an investigation or offered information to crack the vice and abortion ring responsible for Harlow's death.

Then there were the hallucinated and more imaginative, who spoke knowingly (they had been in Hollywood or had once received a postcard mailed from some point west of the Rockies) of more sinister reasons. Jean had been the victim of kidnaping or pagan sexual rites. This demanded national investigation. Respectable degenerates concluded she had had intercourse with a gorilla and been ruptured by the coupling; attic literati reread Robinson Jeffers' *Roan Stallion*. Drink and narcotics also were suggested as the agents of death.

Many women swore that Jean had died because she had dieted too strenuously—as suggested by Earle E. Liederman, a "noted physical culturist" recently arrived in Hollywood from New York. Others announced that she had contracted cancer because of the fluid, wax or cotton batting that had been injected into her breasts to make them large and voluptuous. European sophisticates told each other that Harlow had died of syphilis and told the commoners that Jean had died because the American bleaches she had used to lighten her hair had finally penetrated the scalp and poisoned her brain.

Another strong rumor circulated as to why the body of the actress would not lie in state and why her coffin would be sealed before final services: Jean's illness had turned her beautiful face and pink body black, and she had become ugly to look upon.

Long newspaper biographies of Jean's life appeared in all the papers, and each version had new legends added to it. But no newspaper failed to include a full account of the Bern and Milette suicides or to reprint Bern's farewell note. In fact, one edition of the *Examiner* had two reproductions of the suicide note on the same page.

MGM halted all work at the studio the day after Jean died, and all other studios observed a minute of silent prayer at 9 A.M. Landau locked himself in his office, destroyed the records of Jean's debt and refused to answer his telephone. He had to remain silent. It was all over; best just to bury the girl and all her secrets. She was only twenty-six, but she had lived full dream lives with millions of men, had been the ideal of millions of women. Her immortality would continue—even though Bern and Mama Jean had murdered her.

Because Mrs. Bello was still in deepest shock and incapable of any coherent statement, MGM had taken over the funeral arrangements. And to compensate for the spare sincerity of Clark Gable, who had said that he was "too overcome by grief to make any comment," Louis B. Mayer composed a beautiful release:

> This is the end of a rich personal friendship. This girl whom so many millions adored was one of the sweetest persons I have known in thirty years of the theatrical business. I have lost a friend. The world has lost a ray of sunshine. She was a delight to handle as a star. She was one of the most charming, thoughtful and reasonable players with whom I have been associated. She made all who had anything to do with her in an executive capacity ever anxious to please her, to contribute to her happiness.

From the company's New York offices, Nicholas M. Schenck contributed his brief, more conservative eulogy:

> She was a marvelous girl and a great actress. I feel terribly sorry and sympathize with all of her friends, of which there were many.

Edward Mannix, in Hollywood, was far less restrained than the New York official:

> A sweet child has passed from us. It will seem strange not to see that lovely face and bright smile in the doorway of my office. It was a rare delight to work with her always. She was not only a great artist, she was a wonderfully sincere, honest human being.

These attended to, the telephones between the Hollywood studio and its New York offices were used to discuss the wisdom of Mayer's second statement, which had been published by the press.

> "[I have] been asked several times what would become of the incomplete picture *Saratoga* in which Miss Harlow was co-starring with Clark Gable before she was taken ill. The story *Saratoga* in the form it was photographed up to this time is no more. In accordance with our policy it was written for two distinct, strong personalities, Clark Gable and Jean Harlow. Jean Harlow has passed on. Therefore production on the picture will be indefinitely delayed until we can rewrite the story to fit some other feminine personality. All that has been photo-

graphed to date, and we were within a week of the picture's completion, will be discarded."

To prove the abandonment of *Saratoga* was not a capricious decision, Mayer also announced that the final, polished script of *The Best Dressed Woman in Paris,* which Edgar Selwyn was to have produced for the studio, would also have to undergo changes to fit another star. *Tell it to the Marines,* in which Jean would have co-starred with Robert Taylor and Spencer Tracy, and Hunt Stromberg's films *Maiden Voyage* and *Spring Tide* would also have to be rewritten. Two other original properties bought for Jean Harlow, *The Four Marys* and *U.S. Smith,* were being shelved.

In addition to these films, arrangements had been made for Jean's loan to Twentieth Century-Fox, for whom she would have made *In Old Chicago,* with Don Ameche and Tyrone Power. Darryl F. Zanuck had planned this feature to be one of his studio's most important pictures for 1937-38, but now the actress who had for years been among the first ten stars at the box office was beyond all loan-outs or business arrangements. Alice Faye—also blonde and curvacious—replaced Harlow.

Preparations for the final rites continued, and each new step was reported by the national and international press.

Throngs milled around the mortuary and chanted for permission to see the dead star. Acting Chief of Police Harry Seager of the Los Angeles department pleaded without success for the public to disperse and respect the grief of family and close friends: "The family of Miss Harlow has announced that private services will be held for her. There will be nothing for the public to see, and all peace officers join in requesting that they do not attempt to visit either funeral parlor or the cemetery." The mob was not moved, and plans were completed to have MGM's private police force patrol Forest Lawn

Cemetery. They would be reinforced by cemetery attendants, the police of Glendale and state troopers.

"The world didn't understand my baby," Mrs. Bello sobbed as she was helped from the funeral parlor. She had insisted upon choosing and delivering the garments Jean would wear at burial, and she had given instructions that her daughter's hair was to be brushed back from the forehead and puffed over the ears in the style most familiar to her millions of fans throughout the world. "Our friends knew she was not the type portrayed on the screen. She has never said an unkind word about anyone. She was always cheerful, always looked for the best in everyone." From the mortuary came a pronouncement that "Miss Harlow is as beautiful in death as she was in life."

Behind the barred door of the mortuary's Tennyson Room, which was guarded by MGM police, Jean Harlow lay in her bronze and silver casket lined with pale translucent silk. Mortuary officials described it as "very beautiful but not overly expensive," for at five thousand dollars the casket was a steal. Professional embalmers had worked with studio beauticians to restore Jean's famous features, marred by illness and death. In their loving restoration the embalmers were assisted by Violet Denoyer, Jean's personal make-up artist at the studio.

At first Mrs. Bello, who, the newspapers reported, would inherit close to a million dollars from the estate, had chosen a dress of white for her daughter, but at the last minute she had ordered it exchanged for a gown of pink *mousseline de soie*, trimmed in hand-painted roses, daisies and bluebirds. The gown was one the actress had worn in *Libeled Lady*. Silver and white sandals were on her feet. She did not wear jewelry. In death the star's hair was not platinum blonde but honey brown. The coffin was placed beneath a portrait of Alfred Lord Tennyson, and upon a small table a volume of the laureate's poetry was opened at "Crossing the Bar."

394

Sunset and evening star,
    And one clear call for me!
  And may there be no moaning of the bar
    When I put out to sea.

The next day the Los Angeles *Examiner* was unkind enough to note that "It was learned yesterday that the uremic poison from complications of which Miss Harlow died may have been developing over a long period; for, those close to her said, her health had been a matter of concern for many years."

Arthur Landau shuddered.

On North Palm Drive an endless stream of cars and pedestrians moved slowly along the pleasant street to catch glimpses of screen figures as they entered Jean's house. Applause and cries of sympathetic encouragement greeted William Powell when he came to call on Mrs. Bello. Disgusted police officers routed amateur photographers and autograph hounds as they invaded the grounds. A well-dressed lady from Pennsylvania told reporters that she had just come from the mortuary where "the women folks are just dying to have a last look at our favorite star."

To foil the "just dying" fans, services were advanced from eleven in the morning to nine in the hope that many of the curious necrophiles would not make it to the cemetery at so early an hour. But June 9 was a temperate day with only slight cloudiness and moderate southerly winds. By seven that morning, an hour before gates of the park were opened to admit a caravan of vans loaded with floral tributes, Forest Lawn Memorial Park saw the gathering of thousands of pilgrims. They brought along their lunch hampers, cameras and autograph books.

At the Wee Kirk o' the Heather, two hundred and fifty notables would have their admission cards carefully scrutinized for forgeries before they would be admitted to the small Gothic chapel covered with ivy. Newspapers valued the flowers that filled the chapel at more than $15,000, and the Los Angeles *Evening News* devoted almost two full columns, printed in 5½ point agate type, to a list of only the more important floral tributes. On the bronze casket lay a blanket of 1,500 lilies of the valley and 500 gardenias, a joint tribute from Jean's mother and Powell, but the floral offering that excited the greatest comment and created the most delicious mystery was the single white gardenia that Jean held in her half-closed hand. Attached to the stem was an unsigned note that read: "Good night, my dearest darling."

Up the winding hill along the path bordered by colorful flowers walked the first of the mourners—Mrs. Bello. She was assisted to her place in the kirk by Carey Wilson and Police Chief Charles Blair of Beverly Hills. Behind them, eyes shielded by dark glasses, came William Powell and his mother, Mrs. Nettie Powell. Dr. Montclair Carpentier and Marino Bello stopped to console each other before they entered the church.

Muted chords from a hidden organ were a signal for the guards to lock the bronze doors, then the casket was opened briefly so that Jean's parents, stepfather and Powell might see the star for the last time. Someone present inside the chapel told a reporter for the *Hollywood Citizen* that Miss Harlow's body was "the most natural looking I ever saw. She looked as though she were asleep, needing but a tap on the shoulder to sit up and greet her friends. She looked so natural it was frightening." After the lid was replaced and the principal mourners had been seated in the family room, the church doors were again opened and the invited mourners, cinemaland's first aristocracy and reigning nobles, filed solemnly into the pews to sit with bowed heads. Before services could begin, Barbara Brown, one of Miss Harlow's stand-ins, became hysterical and had to be helped from the church.

Now the organ swelled out "None But the Lonely Heart,"

then muted its solemn tones as the clear mezzo voice of Jeanette MacDonald filled the church with the "Indian Love Call," reputed to be one of Jean's favorite songs. The singer did not falter, her voice was rich and true, and a caged bird trilled an accompaniment during several of the glissandi. After Miss MacDonald returned to her pew, the Christian Science service was begun by Mrs. Genevieve Smith, later identified by the Los Angeles *Times* and several other local newspapers as the Reader who had officiated at the burial services for Paul Bern, which was quite all right, because after five years who would remember that the producer had been Jewish, and that the presiding rabbi at his funeral had been Edward F. Magnin?

Mrs. Smith read selections from the Psalms, the Gospel of St. John and Revelations. Then the Lord's Prayer was recited in chorus by the mourners and Mrs. Smith read the Scientific Statement of Being from *Science and Health*:

> There is no life, truth, intelligence nor substance in matter. All is infinite Mind and its infinite manifestation, for God is All-in-all. Spirit is immortal Truth; matter is mortal error. Spirit is the real and eternal; matter is the unreal and temporal. Spirit is God and man is His image and likeness. Therefore, man is not material; he is spiritual.

Finally, Mrs. Smith recited "Christus Consolator" and Nelson Eddy rose to sing "Ah, Sweet Mystery of Life," whose ringing lyrics conclude that "It is love and love alone that rules the world."

A Forest Lawn attaché announced the conclusion of the ceremonies, and a signal relieved the guards who had patrolled the knolls and protected all entrances to the kirk, the crypt and the lawn.

The Los Angeles *Times* noted that the rites were "without

theatricalism. Hollywood, which is famous for putting on shows, put on none yesterday morning, or else achieved so subtly that one was not aware of it."

The show provided by the uninvited was described in controlled prose by the city's *Examiner*:

> And then when those of prominence had come and gone and the sorrowful relatives had driven away, the fans rushed through the unlocked gates and trudged half-a-mile up the hill to the vault where the body of their favorite film star lay in a beautiful casket.
>
> There they scrambled madly for bits of flowers, ferns, that lay scattered on the lawn where a few moments before a lavish blanket of color had hidden the green grassway.
>
> Young girls and boys, women carrying babies, elderly women who found the climb a test of strength, came on to gather at the doorway of the church where the great had gathered an hour previously to pay their last respects to their friend and fellow worker.
>
> The doors of the little church then were swung open and with hushed lips and careful tread Jean Harlow's fans filed down the aisle to stand for a fleeting moment at the spot which a few minutes before had been the garlanded bier of the film star.

The body of the star was sheltered in a mausoleum not far from the Wee Kirk until a decision was reached about the remains: would they be placed in a permanent crypt or cremated?

At a somber family conference, where Marino sat with Dr. Carpentier rather than with Jean's mother, they discussed letters, telegrams and telephone calls from the public demanding interment of their goddess. Not one communication in the lot favored cremation, which was associated with a defiant atheism. At last it was announced that Jean would lie in a private crypt lined with marble in Forest Lawn's "Sanctuary of Benediction," the most honored place of rest in the park's "Memorial Court of Honor." The massive casket, with its silver nameplate that reproduced Jean's own signature and gave the years of her birth and death, would be entombed in the marble and bronze Sanctuary that sheltered the remains of Irving Thalberg, Marie Dressler and Alexander Pantages. Jean's body would lie in a crypt to be named the "Jean Harlow Room."

A marble statue of a pensive child stood before the bronze gates of the room, which was ten feet long and nine feet wide, with walls lined with multicolored marble from France, Italy and Spain. Memorial light would be supplied by candles that would burn eternally in two mosaic candelabra that had once graced the altar of the church of Santa Sabina, on one of Rome's seven hills. Natural light would be filtered through an authentic reproduction of a medieval stained glass window. Fresh flowers would be placed daily in a marble vase atop a wrought iron pedestal. Several bronze chairs would be placed in the room for the comfort of selected visitors when they came to meditate in silence. Jean's body would occupy the middle receptacle in her crypt; one of the other two would some day shelter the body of her mother. Whose body would rest in the third receptacle remained a mystery.

Mrs. Bello disclosed that the room had been purchased at a cost of $25,000 by William Powell, then went on to say: "We appreciate Mr. Powell's gesture of love, and we believe that it is only fair to him to disclose that, as a shrine for Jean, he bought the room where she will lie forever, and with us, he will be enabled to visit it, knowing that in spirit, she is not far away."

The local *Daily News* informed its readers:

> In the Memorial court adjoining [the Sanctuary] are Lon Chaney, Will Rogers, Wallace Reid, Earle Williams, Ernest Torrance, Mitchell Lewis, Jack and Lottie Pickford, Charles Mack, Lowell Sherman, Russ Columbo, Frank Joyce and others.
>
> Buried in the ground outside are Ross Alexander, Fred Thompson and other celebrities.
>
> The ashes of Chic Sale, noted comic, are in the mausoleum.

Dr. Carpentier studiously avoided his former wife. It was quite obvious to him that their daughter's death had been a vain sacrifice to a religious obsession which could not be excused by any reference to faith. Before he left for Kansas City, the sorrowing dentist was taken to Jean's studio bungalow by Kay Mulvey. In silence he examined the appointments, opened a closet and picked up a pair of Jean's small shoes. He held the shoes in one hand, moved to the dressing table and played with a rabbit's foot, then asked Kay if he might take the shoes and rabbit's foot. Kay nodded. The dentist thanked her and returned to Kansas City.

Distributors' reports informed the studio that *Personal Property* was in its third and fourth runs and still doing good business. An impressive mountain of mail demanded that the studio complete *Saratoga*, even if it had to employ a double for Jean. Let the picture be her real monument, they begged.

Hearst's Los Angeles *Examiner* carried an editorial plea:

> Thousands of devoted admirers of Jean Harlow are demanding that they be given the consolation of seeing their beloved film actress in "Saratoga," her unfinished motion picture.

They protest Louis B. Mayer's announced plan of remaking "Saratoga" with a new personality and refuse to accept a substitute for their beloved Jean. . . .

Great pieces of art, unfinished novels, and paintings interrupted by death, have been in the past handed over to other artists to complete.

Jean Harlow was an artist and did her work up to the time she was called . . . that work should not be disregarded.

May it be suggested, Mr. Mayer, that Jean's friends in Hollywood, those who loved her best, the stars in the motion picture colony, and the thousands of men and women who discovered her and created her a star be consulted?

Let the public be the judge.

May it also be suggested, Mr. Mayer, that in Hollywood there is some young actress who would be glad, as a tribute to Jean Harlow, to play those few remaining scenes?

It would indeed be a gracious gesture for some actress to step forward and finish the picture in memory of the great little trouper who has been called upon to play another and greater role.

Who could resist such an appeal? Not Louis Mayer, who wept at the sight of old oaken buckets and the sounds of sentimental music, and who found the pressures from the New York office hard to resist. Replacements were signed to finish *Saratoga*. Scenes were rewritten to eliminate the need for them to speak, and Geraldine Dvorak was photographed at a distance, under a broad-brimmed hat or with her back to the camera, when the shot called for motion; Mary Dees doubled in the long full-face shots. The completed film was previewed on July 13 in Glendale, the city where Jean Harlow lay in the "Sanctuary of Benediction." *Variety* observed that "Miss Harlow's performance is among her best in years," and that scenes shot with a double had been edited so skillfully that audiences would "not easily distinguish the substitution."

The *Examiner* had earlier informed its readers that Walter Winchell, famous Broadway and Hollywood columnist, had solved the mystery of the lone gardenia in Jean's cold hand. The flower, which had excited speculation and heated debate throughout the country, had been sent by Donald Friede, the New York publisher who had become friendly with Jean when he had visited her to negotiate for the publication of her novel.

But most newspaper readers were more concerned with the rapid shrinkage of the star's estimated fortune. On the day she had died, and for several days thereafter, bold banner headlines had proclaimed Jean's fortune to be in excess of a million dollars. Not only had she inherited a huge fortune from Paul Bern, but her attorney, Mr. Silberberg, was reported to have acknowledged that Jean had taken out an important insurance policy with Lloyd's of London and had invested a greater part of her weekly salary in endowments, annuities and other solid securities.

Mr. Silberberg quickly denied that he had ever mentioned a Lloyd's policy to reporters. He had heard of this policy, and of endowments and annuities—probably from the papers—but Lloyd's, other institutions and he were unaware of the existence of big investments. Jean had carried some minor insurance policies with American companies, but Mr. Silberberg doubted if their total value was anywhere near $50,000.

Close calculations revealed that Jean had earned almost a million dollars under the Metro banner, and stars in the industry were as shocked by the revelation that Jean had left so little as they were by the actress' untimely death. There was something wrong with an environment where fabulous sums were earned, where help could be employed for very little, where taxes were not confiscatory, but where thousands of dollars were spent in a way that could not be accounted for.

On June 17, 1937, Mendel Silberberg filed Jean's will for probate. The key provision read: "I, Harlean Rosson, also known as Jean Harlow, do give, devise and bequeath to said Jean Harlow Bello all my property of whatever kind of which I shall die possessed." The formal language of the will also provided that anyone who contested the will or made any claim to the estate should be paid only one dollar, and that if Mrs. Bello died first, the estate should go to Jean's maternal grandparents, Sam and Ella Harlow.

The probate petition stated that Miss Harlow had left "cash and personal property estimated in excess of $10,000 and having no probable income." There were no annuities or endowments, no insurance policy with Lloyd's.

Mendel Silberberg and W. A. Bullis, who had been named in the will as executor and alternate executor, filed a joint petition of renunciation and requested the appointment of Mrs. Bello as administratrix. On August 27 Superior Court Judge Clarence L. Kincaid admitted the will to probate and approved Mrs. Bello's appointment. Mrs. Bello told the press that of the fortune Jean had earned in the movies, only about $41,000 was left. Court-hardened reporters were astonished when Mrs. Bello admitted the mysterious dissipation of her daughter's estate. "There was very little cash, three automobiles, some furs, jewelry, some clothing—not even as much as I have—no furniture, just some old heirlooms."

But even the $41,000 was not firm because of two major and several minor assaults made against the estate. The first major assault was filed by Mrs. Harriet A. Breese, the landlady of the house on North Palm Drive, who demanded a $50,000 bond to cover damages to the house which she believed would amount to $10,000; also, there was a matter of $820 in rent which had not been paid from early June through September 27, when Mrs. Bello had vacated the house.

The second assault was made by Nat Rogan, the Los Angeles Collector of Internal Revenue, who filed an income tax lien against the estate for $10,244 to cover taxes due the federal government for 1935 and 1936.

Mrs. Breese later reduced her estimate of damages to $618, and this and the rent due were paid. The federal government received its $10,244. After all claims were settled, Mama Jean had about $28,000, still a tidy sum for ordinary people. But Mrs. Bello was not an ordinary person. In recognition of this, MGM purchased Jean's novel for $5,000, and until Mrs. Bello died in 1958, the studio paid her a pension of $500 a month.

Although Mama Jean attempted to take some interest in the erection of a statue to Jean in Rockefeller Center, she did not have the heart to maintain a sustained enthusiasm. She approved of the Jean Harlow Memorial Fund sponsored by Miss Mona Merle, chairman of the honorary committee in charge of the project. Miss Merle explained that a drive for funds would be undertaken by beauty shops across the nation as the "beauty world's way of saluting one of the loveliest women in Hollywood." The project committee had in mind a statue of the deceased star, slightly less than life size, to be mounted on a pedestal of bronze or contrasting stone, and several sculptors had been asked to submit designs for a statue to be called the "Goddess of Beauty." Shops in New York and other cities began to solicit funds, but Metro-Goldwyn-Mayer refused to sponsor the memorial, the officials of Rockefeller Center politely withheld comment, Mrs. Bello was still too deep in grief, and the campaign collapsed.

Mrs. Bello's new apartment could not accommodate Jean's wardrobe, so she arranged to store the star's dresses, gowns and furs in the Bekin warehouse in Hollywood. For many years thereafter she would visit the warehouse, smooth and arrange the pleats of gowns, the hems of dresses and the fullness of sleeves, and speak to the garments as if they were alive. Kay Mulvey continued to care for the aging woman and catered to her by repeating over and over again stories of her friendship with The Baby—how Jean had played with Dick on the beach and had ridden his little three-wheeled bicycle. Then there were the stories Mama loved to hear about Jean's warmth and goodness of heart, how she had been loved, adored and worshiped by the little people on the lot with whom she had lunched and shot craps.

For more than twenty years Kay patiently repeated the stories while Mama Jean played with Jean's jewelry. Often, very often, Mama spoke of suicide, because life was meaningless without Jean; but suicide was sinful, and if she killed herself she would not meet Jean in paradise. So she was willing to live out her life, but was impatient for the day she and the jewelry would be buried in the crypt. Jean would be waiting for her, Mama was certain, an angel of coral and silver; and in paradise the mother would help dress the daughter in jewels she had never parted with despite her desperate need of money. The jewels were the sacred gift Mama would bring to her Baby in Heaven, and Jean would count them and say that all of them were there.

When Marino died in 1953, Mrs. Bello attended his funeral in Forest Lawn and seemed pleased that the newspapers had given his occupation as public relations counselor. Five years later Mama Jean died of a heart condition at the Good Samaritan Hospital, but not in the same room Jean had occupied.

What made Harlow so ideally suited for the all-American dream was her all-American appeal: A man didn't have to think of money when he dreamed of Harlow, so desirable, so willing, so available; she might be found in commonplace settings, perhaps behind the counter of a cigar stand, or at the coffee urn of a luncheonette, or offering to wait on him in a dime store, or standing next to him in an elevator, or taking the seat next to him in a bus. Not that she was ordinary—all men were immediately aware of her unnaturally blonde hair, and were compelled to wonder if . . . They were aware of the full, slightly moist lips, the softness of feature strengthened by the good chin; they were also aware that here was a woman who said the brassiere was an unnecessary garment, actually unhealthy, and was so quoted by reputable international journalists assigned to report top international news.

And for the first time in modern occidental history it appeared as if women were willing to accept another woman whose sexuality captivated their men. Just looking at Harlow made every woman feel secure, for it was most obvious that the Nordic temptress had a frontier heart of gold, and a woman with so rare a heart would never assault an American home.

Yes, she might go to bed with a married man, not in some foreign decadent desire to break up his marriage and home, but to strengthen his ego, to make him feel good and important. She might be an easy woman with the heart and loins of gold, but love, obligation and marriage were sacred institutions that she revered. She was the perfect, trustworthy harlot, who would entertain a man with a good cup of coffee before taking him to bed, then would send him home with a generous cut of pie for his wife and kiddies, and the recipe, too, if he cared to have it.

Without embarrassment Jean had often admitted to being the worst actress in Hollywood, but what did this matter as long as she was a draw at the box office? In theaters throughout the world audiences stirred and whistled a welcome when her name appeared on the screen. And everyone loved Jean for creating a type they could understand and know—a friendly, regular, democratic woman of experience with a heart of gold, who could be had by the right man for the price of a beer. If, in her pictures, she was lucky enough to wind up as mistress of a millionaire, she was still willing to be kind and regular to a delivery boy.

On the screen and off she was aware of her beauty and

took pride in her appearance and the line of her body, but haughtiness, allure and any kind of phoniness made her laugh. Self-conscious, awkward, she was aware that her pronunciation of the General American Dialect, with its flat *a* and unrounded vowels, was not the best of dictions. She knew that her voice was something no fishwife would have, that she could not be graceful in entrances or exits. But all of these were compensated for by human warmth, and the incandescent good humor Jean radiated from the screen made her the choice of all men. Women reproved her for behaving wickedly with her body, but loved her for not being wicked in mind. As she flounced through a scene and strode wildly about to indicate anger, despair, disgust, there wasn't a woman in the audience who could not have acted as well, and this made them love the star even more.

She gave fully, tried to measure up to the more polished performers about her, and cooperated as willingly with people she disliked as she did with those whom she considered her friends. She made no secret that, once she accepted the stereotypes of the continuing role, the hilarious situations in which she was cast gave her genuine pleasure; and her infectious gaiety throughout production imparted a joyous sparkle to the work of the people cast with her and made them shine all the more. The sincerity of her awkward performances had to be admired, and at last it even endeared her to critics. For in objective evaluation Jean Harlow best portrayed the modern American woman of the Depression Thirties: an unabashed gold-digger but also, when the chips were down, the best little cook, lay and sweetheart in the world.

In an industry where all superlatives are commonplace, it is doubtful whether any professional actress lived with more tragedy than Jean Harlow, who only portrayed gay, carefree, easy-come-easy-go women on the screen. With success, fame and adulation achieved, she could not rid herself of people who kept her from personal happiness. In both her Hollywood marriages she further endeared herself to her public by choosing men of unromantic appearance, men who could have been anyone's next door neighbor.

That Bern, who seemed such a simple man, should have been so complicated a personality was another tragedy for Jean. And his suicide was a wound the newspapers never allowed to heal. Thirty years later it is still good for a Sunday column. But even as the newspapers republished Bern's suicide note again and again and again, the reaction of the public was ambivalent: it was hungry for private scandal, yet it seemed to love Harlow the more for her personal tragedy.

And when Jean Harlow smiled from the screen, her eyes seemed strangely flecked with bewilderment, and in her voice there was always a little wince of pain.

KTTV in Los Angeles shows Harlow films either at one o'clock in the afternoon or on their late, late show, which begins at two or three in the morning. Occasionally youngsters tune in to films scheduled in the afternoon, and not only do they laugh at Jean's shaved eyebrows and the funny clinging gowns she wore, but her voice and gestures break them up. Really, she is just too much. If this is the sex their parents went for, no wonder the world has gone to pot. But since Harlow there has been no star whose surname has become an international synonym for sex. And if there is a human future, and later anthropologists study the Western World of the third decade of the twentieth century, they will agree that Jean Harlow was the woman who first typified the distinctive, unique American type of beauty, which has since been imitated throughout the world. Succeeding decades have modified that beauty, but basically it is gay and carefree, healthy and athletic, wholesomely sexual without being furtive or dirty.

And always, it is blonde.